SOMETHING ABOUT THE AUTHOR

SOMETHING ABOUT THE AUTHOR

Facts and Pictures about Contemporary Authors
and Illustrators of Books for Young People

Anne Commire

VOLUME 10

GALE RESEARCH
BOOK TOWER
DETROIT, MICHIGAN
48226

Also Published by Gale

CONTEMPORARY AUTHORS:
A Bio-Bibliographical Guide to
Current Authors and Their Works

(Now Covers About 46,000 Authors)

Special acknowledgment is due to the members of the
Contemporary Authors staff who assisted in the prep-
aration of this volume, and to Gale's art director,
Chester Gawronski.

Associate Editor: Agnes Garrett

Assistant Editors: Linda Shedd, Rosemary DeAngelis Bridges

Library of Congress Catalog Card Number 72-27107
ISBN 0-8103-0068-0

GRATEFUL ACKNOWLEDGMENT

is made to the following publishers, authors, and artists, for their kind permission to reproduce copyrighted material. ■ **ABINGDON PRESS.** Illustration by Lee J. Ames from *The Great Green Apple War* by Barbara Klimowicz. Copyright © 1973 by Abingdon Press. /Illustration by Steele Savage from *Bless Your Bones, Sammy* by Frances Fitzpatrick Wright. Copyright © 1968 by Abingdon Press. Both reprinted by permission of Abingdon Press. ■ **ADDISON-WESLEY.** Illustration by Sandy Huffaker from *H. Philip Birdsong's ESP* by Harriet Lawrence. Text © 1969 by Shirley Harriet Lawrence. Drawings © 1969 by S. Sanford Huffaker. /Illustration by Walter Einsel from *did you ever see?* by Walter Einsel. Copyright © MCMLXII by Walter Einsel. /Illustration by Marc Tolon Brown from *Science Games* by Laurence B. White, Jr. Copyright © 1975 by Marc Tolon Brown. All reprinted by permission of Addison-Wesley Publishing Co. (Young Scott Books). ■ **ASTOR-HONOR, INC.** Illustration by Margery Brown from *Dori the Mallard* by Gordon Allred. Copyright © 1968 by Astor-Honor, Inc. Reprinted by permission of Astor-Honor, Inc. ■ **ATHENEUM PUBLISHERS.** Illustration by Nancy Winslow Parker from *Oh, A-Hunting We Will Go* by John Langstaff. Illustration copyright © 1974 by Nancy Winslow Parker. /Illustration by Gail Owens from *A Home With Aunt Florry* by Charlene Joy Talbot. Copyright © 1974 by Charlene Joy Talbot. Reprinted by permission of Atheneum Publishers. ■ **ATLANTIC, LITTLE-BROWN, CO.** Illustration by Marc Brown from *I Found Them in the Yellow Pages* by Norma Farber. Illustration copyright © 1973 by Marc Brown. Reprinted by permission of Atlantic, Little-Brown, Co. ■ **THE BETHANY PRESS.** Jacket illustration by Darrell Wiskur from *Summerhill Summer* by Joan Gilbert © 1967 by The Bethany Press. Reprinted by permission of The Bethany Press. ■ **THE BOBBS-MERRILL CO.** Illustration by Vic Dowd from *Dorothea Dix* by Grace Hathaway Melin. Copyright © 1963 by The Bobbs-Merrill Co. /Illustration by Gray Morrow from *Carl Ben Eielson* by Hortense Myers and Ruth Burnett. Copyright © 1960 by The Bobbs-Merrill Co. /Illustration by Leslie Goldstein from *Liliuokalani* by Shirlee Petkin Newman. Copyright © 1960 by The Bobbs-Merrill Co. /Illustration by Gray Morrow from *Teddy Roosevelt* by Edd Winfield Parks. Copyright © 1953, 1961 by The Bobbs-Merrill Co. All reprinted by permission of the Bobbs-Merrill Co., Inc. ■ **BRIGHAM YOUNG UNIVERSITY PUBLICATIONS.** Illustration by Dee R. Taylor from *I Can Do* by Barbara J. Taylor. © 1972 by Brigham Young University Publications. Reprinted by permission of Brigham Young University Publications. ■ **CHATTO & WINDUS, LTD.** Illustration by Heather Corlass from *The Young Visitors* by Daisy Ashford. © Daisy Ashford 1919. Reprinted by permission of Chatto & Windus, Ltd. and Doubleday & Co., Inc. ■ **CHILDRENS PRESS.** Illustration by Jim Lamb from *Archelon and the Sea Dragon* by Frances K. Pavel. Copyright © 1975 by Regensteiner Publishing Enterprises, Inc. Reprinted by permission of Childrens Press. ■ **COWARD, McCANN & GEOGHEGAN, INC.** Illustration by Raymond Briggs from *First Up Everest* by Showell Styles. Illustration © 1969 by Raymond Briggs. /Illustration from Sarasota Chamber of Commerce. Copyright © 1970 by Mary Ellen Smith. Both reprinted by permission of Coward, McCann & Geoghegan, Inc. ■ **THOMAS Y. CROWELL CO.** Illustration by Lisl Weil from *Upstairs and Downstairs* by Ryerson Johnson. Illustration copyright © 1962 by Lisl Weil. /Illustration by Anne Marie Jauss from *Dragonflies and Damselflies* by Mary Geisler Phillips. Copyright © 1960 by Mary Geisler Phillips. /Illustration by Lucienne Bloch from *Sandpipers* by Edith Thacher Hurd. Illustration copyright © 1961 by Lucienne Bloch. /Illustration by Kazue Mizumura from *The Prince Who Gave Up a Throne* by Nancy Serage. Copyright © 1966 by Kazue Mizumura. All reprinted by permission of Thomas Y. Crowell Co. ■ **DAVID & CHARLES, LTD.** Illustration by Mary Dinsdale from *Joanna All Alone* by Geraldine Kaye. © illustration by David & Charles, Ltd. Reprinted by permission of David & Charles, Ltd. ■ **ANDRE DEUTSCH, LTD.** Illustration by Quentin Blake from *Agaton Sax and the Scotland Yard Mystery* by Nils-Olof Franzen. Copyright © 1967, 1969 by Nils-Olof Franzen. Reprinted by permission of Andre Deutsch, Ltd. ■ **T. S. DENISON & CO., INC.** Illustration by Howard Lindberg from *The Gold Seekers* by Margaret L. Posten. Copyright © 1967 by T. S. Denison & Co., Inc. Reprinted by permission of T. S. Denison & Co., Inc. ■ **THE DIAL PRESS.** Illustration by Leigh Grant from *Naomi in the Middle* by Norma Klein. Text copyright © 1974 by Norma Klein. Pic-

II

PHOTOGRAPH CREDITS

Something about the Author

EUGENE ACKERMAN

ADAIR, Margaret Weeks   ?-1971

PERSONAL: Born in Portland, Ore.; daughter of William Stone (a purchasing agent for Great Northern Railroad) and Kate L. (McPherson) Weeks; married Wistar Morris Adair (a retired banker); children: Henry Rodney, Wistar Morris, Jr. *Education:* Oregon State University, student, four years; San Jose State Teachers College, diploma. *Home:* Tigard, Ore.

CAREER: Former teacher in public and private schools, playground supervisor in athletics and crafts, and director of children's theater, all in Oregon. Owner and director of private pre-school. Organizer of public library board and its first voluntary librarian. *Member:* Puppeteers of America, Oregon Society of Artists, Tualatin Valley Writers' League, Portland Arts and Crafts Association. *Awards, honors:* First runner-up in *Boys' Life* book competition.

WRITINGS: Do-It-In-A-Day Puppets, John Day, 1964; *A Far Voice Calling,* Doubleday, 1964. Contributor to teachers' magazines and other periodicals.

WORK IN PROGRESS: A novel for boys and girls to age sixteen about a journey from New York to Oregon by way of Panama in the Gold Rush days; three other books.

HOBBIES AND OTHER INTERESTS: Camping, oil painting, clay modeling, the theater, puppets, and children and their pets.

(Died December 19, 1971)

ACKERMAN, Eugene (Francis)   1888-1974

PERSONAL: Born January 1, 1888, in Huntingdon, Ind.; son of Francis and Margaret (Brady) Ackerman; married Juliana Buck, November 15, 1916. *Education:* Attended Marquette University. *Religion:* Roman Catholic. *Home:* Chestnut Drive, Blowing Rock, N.C. 28605.

CAREER: New York Herald, New York, N.Y., reporter, 1910-16; Government of Poland, director of public relations, 1918-19; Forstmann Woolen Company, New York, N.Y., vice-president, 1923-39; American Wool Growers Association, New York, N.Y., director, 1939-47; International Wool Bureau, London, Eng., director, president, 1950-53. *Military service:* U.S. Navy, lieutenant, 1916-18. *Member:* Knights of Columbus, Metropolitan Club, Wee Burn Country Club, Naples Beach and Golf Club, Blowing Rock Country Club. *Awards, honors:* University of Indiana Writers' Conference, award for most distinguished work in childrens literature by an Indiana author, 1960.

WRITINGS: Jeb and the Bank Robbers, Bobbs, 1958; *Tonk and Tonka,* Dutton, 1962.

SIDELIGHTS: Juliana Ackerman wrote SATA: "Mr. Ackerman, with a lifelong interest in literature and writing, felt that childrens' books should be accurate historically and, in the case of animals and birds, accurate from a natural history viewpoint. At the time of his death he was working on a black bear story laid in the Everglades."

(Died May 2, 1974)

ADORJAN, Carol (Madden)   1934-

PERSONAL: Surname is pronounced A-*dor*-ian; born August 17, 1934, in Chicago, Ill.; daughter of Roland Aloysius and Marie (Toomey) Madden; married William W. Adorjan (an industrial representative), August 17, 1957; children: Elizabeth Marie, John Martin and Katherine Therese (twins), Matthew Christian. *Education:* Mundelein College, B.A. (magna cum laude), 1956. *Home:* 812 Rosewood Ave., Winnetka, Ill. 60093.

CAREER: High school English teacher in Chicago, Ill., 1956-59. Off-Campus Writers' Workshop, corresponding secretary, 1967-69. *Awards, honors:* Josephine Lusk Prize from Mundelein College, 1956, for short story, "Coin of Decision"; first prize from *Earplay 1972* at University of Wisconsin, for "The Telephone."

WRITINGS—For children: *Someone I Know,* Random House, 1968; *Jonathan Bloom's Room,* J. Philip O'Hara, 1972; (contributor) N. Gretchen Greiner, editor, *Like It Is,* Whitman Books, 1972; *The Cat Sitter Mystery,* J. Philip O'Hara, 1973. Author of "The Telephone," a radio play. Contributor of short stories and articles to national magazines, including *Today, American Girl, Ingenue, Four Quarters,* and *Redbook,* and to newspapers.

WORK IN PROGRESS: A children's book, a radio play, short stories.

SIDELIGHTS: "For as long as I can remember, I have been interested in writing. I loved books and spent many an

CAROL ADORJAN

hour during my earliest summers trotting back and forth to the library with armloads. I loved the look, the feel, and, most of all, the smell of books, but, until I was a senior in high school, I seldom read. There were too many other things to do—among them, writing! The first story I can remember clearly was written when I was seven or eight. It ended with a little dog 'barking and barking and barking.' When someone asked me why I had ended the story that way, I told him, 'Because I didn't know how else to end.' As an eighth grader I wrote a mystery novel, chapters of which I read to my classmates when the weather prohibited outdoor recesses.

"As a teenager, I was interested in everything, and, more important, everybody. My primary interest was school—or at least that part of it that began with the three o'clock bell: the school newspaper, student council, and various other meetings. I wanted to change the world—be a great actress, a great teacher, a great social worker, but I always knew that whatever else I did, I would write too.

"Today nearly everything I do is somehow related to my writing. I belong to a writer's workshop and also took up photography as an adjunct to the writing. Most of my ideas are 'home-grown.' All three children's books and several of my teen-magazine stories were inspired by experiences of my oldest daughter at various stages of her life. My first *Redbook* story was inspired by my twins.

"My life has been quite ordinary and I have seen very little of the world. But a writer need not travel (most days I feel lucky to get around the block) to have experiences worth writing about. Each of us is unique and, therefore, each has his own special vision. It is that vision which transforms the ordinary into the extraordinary. The most important journey a writer or anyone can take, it seems to me, is into himself. It is there—on the inside—that he finds the child who never tires of asking questions and exploring possibilities.

"Someone asked me recently if I was still writing. For some reason I thought of that little dog in my first story. 'Oh, yes,' I answered. 'I expect to go on writing and writing and writing because I don't know how else to end.'"

HOBBIES AND OTHER INTERESTS: Photography.

AHERN, Margaret McCrohan 1921-
(Peg O'Connell)

PERSONAL: Born February 16, 1921, in New York, N.Y.; daughter of John and Margaret (O'Connell) McCrohan; married Edward Ahern (a postal superintendent), July 16, 1947; children: Michael, Maripat, James, Joanne, Edward, Jr. *Education:* Attended Harrison Art School, 1939-40, American Academy of Art, 1941-43, Chicago Academy of Fine Arts, 1943, and Chicago Art Institute. *Religion:* Catholic. *Home:* 1901 South 18th Ave., Maywood, Ill. 60153.

CAREER: New World, editorial cartoonist, 1943-45; free-lance cartoonist and illustrator, 1950—; National Catholic Welfare Conference Features, cartoonist, 1958—. Cartoonist for television panel, "Cartuno," 1950-51, for monthly strips, "Beano" and "Angelo," for syndicated panel, "Speck the Altar Boy," 1954—, and for syndicated panel, "Our Parish," the last under pseudonym Peg O'Connell. *Member:* West Suburban Art Guild.

WRITINGS: Speck the Altar Boy, Doubleday, 1958; *Presenting Speck the Altar Boy,* Doubleday, 1960; *A Speck of Trouble,* Doubleday, 1964; (under pseudonym Peg O'Connell) *Our Parish* (cartoons), John Knox, 1968.

Illustrator: Velma Neiberding, *Sugar and Spice,* Catholic Home Journal Press, 1949; William Gillooly, *Mickey the Angel,* Newman, 1953; V. Neiberding, *Nice Guy,* Catholic Home Journal Press, 1954.

AITKEN, Dorothy 1916-

PERSONAL: Born July 19, 1916, in Colorado; daughter of Dudley Acey (a farmer) and Myrtle (Agler) Lockwood; married James Julius Aitken (a clergyman), May 27, 1939; children: Jerrold James, John Dudley, Judith Maydell Aitken Stoehr. *Education:* Student at Union College, Lincoln, Neb., 1938-40, Seventh-Day Adventists Theological Seminary, Washington, D.C., 1943-45, and Alliance Francaise, 1950. *Religion:* Seventh-Day Adventist. *Home:* 7410 Aspen Ave., Takoma Park, Md. 20012. *Office:* General Conference of Seventh-Day Adventists, 6840 Eastern Ave., Washington, D.C. 20012.

CAREER: Teacher of English and librarian in Redfield, S.D., public school, 1962-63; dental assistant in Washington, D.C., 1968-71; General Conference of Seventh-Day Adventists, Washington, D.C., editor of children's lessons, 1971-73. Free-lance writer, 1960—. Teacher of German and Spanish in Takoma Park, Md., 1969-70.

WRITINGS—All for young people: (Editor) James Julius Aitken, *In Step with Christ,* Pacific Press Publishing, 1963; *Bride in the Parsonage,* Southern Publishing, 1966; *White*

DOROTHY AITKEN

Wings Green Jungle, Pacific Press Publishing, 1966; *My Love the Amazon,* Southern Publishing, 1968; *The Hard Way,* Southern Publishing, 1969; *Cherry on Top,* Review & Herald, 1973. Contributor to *Guide* and *Signs of the Times,* and other religious journals, sometimes in German, Spanish, or French.

WORK IN PROGRESS: Of Course I'm Scared, and a devotional for teen-agers.

SIDELIGHTS: "I come from a family of storytellers. My old auntie who came to Nebraska in a covered wagon was full of stories of the old days. I used to brush her long gray hair and listen hours on end to her stories. My father also, was a great storyteller. So I guess I just inherited a love for good stories.

"I wrote my first prize-winning article when I was in the fourth grade. The subject was 'Temperance,' and I was very embarrassed to have it read aloud before the whole school. I wrote a lot when I was a child, but always hid my works, for my mother did not appreciate my 'genius' inasmuch as it took time away from my chores. In my teen-age years, I destroyed all my writings for fear of having them fall into hands of 'unbelievers' who would taunt me."

The Aitkens lived in South America for eight years, and in Berne, Switzerland, for eight years. Dorothy Aitken has travelled most of the world gathering material and assisting her husband in his work.

ALLRED, Gordon T. 1930-

PERSONAL: Born December 27, 1930, in Iowa City, Iowa; son of M. Thatcher (professor emeritus, Weber State College) and Pearl (Oberhansley) Allred; married Sharon Wallace, October 26, 1956; children: Mark, Anthony, Kathryn, Amy, John, Robert, Christopher, Aaron, Shannon. *Education:* University of Utah, B.S., 1957, M.S., 1958; Northwestern University, postgraduate study; University of Utah, Ph.D., 1972. *Religion:* Mormon. *Home:* 2006 Polk Ave., Ogden, Utah 84401.

CAREER: Associate editor, *Improvement Era,* 1956-58; writer for U.S. Forest Service Intermountain Region, 1959-62; Weber State College, Ogden, Utah, professor of English, teaching fiction writing and modern literature, 1963—. Free-lance writer. *Military service:* U.S. Army, 1954-56; served in Japan.

WRITINGS: Kamikaze, Ballantine, 1957; *If a Man Die,* Bookcraft, 1964; *The Valley of Tomorrow* (novel), Bookcraft, 1965; *Old Crackfoot* (young adult novel), Oblensky, 1965; *Dori the Mallard* (young adult novel), Astor-Honor, 1968; *Lonesome Coyote* (young adult novel), Lantern, 1969; *The Hungry Journey* (non-fiction), Hawkes Publish-

He bounded exuberantly, thrusting his way through reddening tumbleweeds and picking up a marvelous quantity of cockleburrs. Then suddenly he stopped, tail stiff, ears lifting. ■ (From *Dori the Mallard* by Gordon Allred. Illustrated by Margery Brown.)

ing, 1973; (edited and compiled) *Immortality,* Hawkes Publishing, 1974. Author of articles and stories for magazines, including: *True, Argosy,* and *Cavalier.* Co-author with Dr. Lindsay R. Curtis of "For Women Only," nationally syndicated medical column.

WORK IN PROGRESS: The Nederlander, novel on the life of a Dutch resistance leader; *The Breath of Life: Characterization in Modern Fiction,* for fiction writers and students of modern literature.

ANDERSON, Lucia (Lewis) 1922-
(Lucia Z. Lewis)

PERSONAL: Born August 9, 1922, in Pittsburgh, Pa.; daughter of Constanty and Maryanna (Kulwicki) Zylak; married second husband, Allan G. Anderson (a professor of mathematics), April 30, 1955; children: (first marriage) Jeff, Kristina; (second marriage) Patricia Lynn. *Education:* University of Pittsburgh, B.S., 1943, M.S., 1944, Ph.D., 1946, additional study at Graduate School of Public Health, 1950; also studied at University of Pennsylvania Medical School, 1945. *Home:* 41 Bourndale Rd. N., Manhasset, N.Y. 11030. *Office:* Queensborough Community College of the City University of New York, Bayside, N.Y. 11364.

CAREER: University of Pittsburgh, Pittsburgh, Pa., started as instructor and became assistant professor, 1948-53; Duquesne University, Pittsburgh, Pa., assistant professor of biology, 1953-55; Western Kentucky State University, Bowling Green, 1958-65, began as associate professor, became professor of biology; E. R. Squibb, New Brunswick, N.J., 1965-66, senior research scientist; Parsons College, Fairfield, Iowa, associate professor of biology, 1966-68; Queensborough Community College of the City University of New York, Bayside, N.Y., associate professor, 1968-70, professor of microbiology, 1970—. *Member:* American Society for Microbiology, American Association for the Advancement of Science, New York Academy of Science, American Academy for Microbiology, Kentucky Academy of Science.

WRITINGS—Under name Lucia Z. Lewis: (With Anna M. Fisher) *Laboratory Exercises and Outlines in Microbiology for Nurses,* Lippincott, 1951; *The First Book of Microbes,* Watts, 1955, 2nd edition, 1972,; *Microbiology for Nurses,* Kendall/Hunt, 1974. Contributor of scientific articles to *Antibiotic Annual, American Biology Teacher* and *A.S.M. News.*

WORK IN PROGRESS: Audio-visual material for microbiology; experiments for young people in microbiology.

SIDELIGHTS: "I first became interested in writing about microbiology for young people because there was so very little material published on this topic geared specifically for the younger reader. My own children would question me about this topic and I thought it would be interesting to try to explain a rather complex scientific field in such a way that a young person could understand and even learn.

"For many years, I have been active in the American Society for microbiology. I was on their education committee for ten years and served as chairman of the newly formed committee on Elementary and Secondary Microbiology of the Board of Education and Training. I have conducted workshops and National Science Foundation institutes for elementary and secondary science teachers to explain microbiology in a way they could use in their own classroom situations.

"My husband and I have recently returned from a sabbatical leave which was spent travelling around the world, seeing and meeting colleagues in our fields, visiting universities and enjoying the sights."

HOBBIES AND OTHER INTERESTS: Collecting and reviewing children's books dealing with any aspect of microbiology; preparing annotated bibliographies for the American Society for Microbiology.

APSLER, Alfred 1907—

PERSONAL: Born November 13, 1907, in Vienna, Austria; son of Herman and Helene Apsler; married Ernestine Gerson (now a college teacher), December 26, 1936; children: Robert G., Ruby Mae. *Education:* University of Vienna, Ph.D. 1930. *Home:* 5565 East Evergreen Blvd., Vancouver, Wash. *Office:* Clark College, Vancouver, Wash.

CAREER: Clark College, Vancouver, Wash., chairman of social science division, and teacher of history, 1956—. Public speaker; television lecturer; conductor of educational tours, 1961, 1963, 1968; Vienna Teacher's College, Vienna, Austria, coordinator of gerontological programs, 1973—, lecturer, 1975. *Member:* American Association for United Nations (president, Vancouver chapter, 1957-58), American Association of University Professors (president, Clark College chapter, 1957-58), National Education Association, Northwest Political Science Association, Oregon Historical Association, Oregon Freelance Club, Vancouver Optimist Club (president, 1958-59), Portland City Club. *Awards, honors:* Certificate of Recognition from Freedoms Foundation for editorial writing. 1952.

WRITINGS: Northwest Pioneer: The Story of Louis Fleischner, Farrar, Straus, 1960; *Sie Kamen Aus Deutschen Landen* (a German reader), Appleton, 1962; *Fighter for Independence: Jawaharlal Nehru,* Messner, 1963; *The Court Factor,* Jewish Publication Society, 1964; *Sun King: Louis XIV of France,* Messner, 1965; *Prophet of Revolution: Karl Marx,* Messner, 1967; *Iron Chancellor: Otto Von Bismarck* (Junior Literary Guild selection) Messner, 1968; *Ivan the Terrible,* Messner, 1971; *Introduction to Social Science,* Random House, 1971, 2nd edition, 1975; *Vive de Gaulle: The Story of Charles de Gaulle,* Messner, 1973; *Communes through the Ages,* Messner, 1974. Contributor to newspapers and to national youth magazines.

SIDELIGHTS: "My main interest has always been people. As a high school student in Vienna I became a student leader. We were then very idealistic and thought we had the answers to all the world's problems. If only everybody would follow our lead we could certainly transform this globe of ours into a paradise.

"Travel was also one of my passions. We wandered through the alpine countries, from town to town, with packs on our backs, and prided ourselves on how far we could travel with little or no money.

4

ALFRED APSLER

"I was a teacher and a journalist when Austria was swallowed up by the Nazi onslaught. I barely made it across the mountains into Switzerland, and so was saved from almost certain annihilation. Coming to America, I had not only to start a new life, but also do it by using a new language. So it took several years, but eventually I made the way back to my original tasks: teaching and writing."

"I taught history and human relations for many years. So my writing is just an extension of what I do in the classroom, namely: making people and events come to life; trying to convince listeners and readers that the story of man is exciting, colorful, and, also, entertaining."

ARMSTRONG, George D. 1927-

PERSONAL: Born May 26, 1927, in Chicago, Ill.; son of George Douglas (a businessman) and Gladys (Sine) Armstrong; married Gerry Breen (a writer; singer), April 24, 1954; children: Rebecca Lee (Mrs. Scott Shepherd), Jennifer Ann. *Education:* University of Chicago, B.A., 1948; attended Chicago Academy of Fine Arts, 1948-50. *Home:* 1535 Lake Avenue, Wilmette, Ill. 60091.

CAREER: Illustrator; folk music performer. Records include *Simple Gifts,* Folkways Records; *Golden Ring,* Folk-Legacy; *Five Days Singing* (Vol. 1 & 2) Folk-Legacy; *Discovering Music Together,* Follett Education Corporation; *Language Experience,* Encyclopedia Britannica. WFMT (98.7 FM), Chicago, Illinois, host of weekly radio program, "The Wandering Folksong," 1974—. *Military service:* United States Army, 1945-46. *Member:* Hugo's Companions, Analytical Psychology Club of Chicago. *Awards, honors:* Printing Industry of America award, 1964, for *Magic Bagpipe;* Chicago Book Clinic Design award, 1967, for *Boat on the Hill.*

ILLUSTRATOR: Gerry Armstrong, *The Magic Bagpipe,* A. Whitman, 1964; Gerry Armstrong, *The Boat on the Hill,* A. Whitman, 1967; Gerry Armstrong, *The Fairy Thorn,* A. Whitman, 1969; Arthur Parker, *Skunny Wundy: Seneca Indian Tales,* A. Whitman, 1970; Lillian Budd, *Full Moons: Indian Legends of the Seasons,* Rand McNally, 1970; Yuri Korinetz, *There Far Beyond the River,* O'Hara, 1973; Betty Biesterveld, *Six Days from Sunday,* Rand McNally, 1973; Phyllis R. Naylor, *An Amish Family,* O'Hara, 1974. Has also illustrated numerous books in the fields of folklore, history, anthropology and fiction.

WORK IN PROGRESS: Illustrations and cover art for *In the Middle of the World;* plus story illustrations for several textbook publishers in the Chicago area.

SIDELIGHTS: "I began my career as an artist in an ad agency. After a year I quit. I didn't want my artwork to be judged on whether or not it could sell beer! So for twenty-six years I have been painting pictures for story books, school books, encyclopedias and museum exhibits. I specialize in anthropology, history, American Indians and folklore.

"My career as a musician began when I took up the bagpipes at the age of eleven. I piped in the 'Stockyards Kilty Band' for a number of years and then joined the 'Chicago Highlanders' for quite a while. I now play pipes in the family's folkmusic concerts. My wife, daughters and I often perform folkmusic concerts for festivals, schools, clubs and organizations. I sing and play the guitar and mountain dulcimer."

HOBBIES AND OTHER INTERESTS: Sherlock Holmes, psychology, mythology, reading and bicycling.

GERRY AND GEORGE ARMSTRONG

There was much laughter among the leprechauns and they gathered around with mischievous smiles. ■ (From *The Fairy Thorn* by Gerry Armstrong. Illustrated by George Armstrong.)

ARMSTRONG, Gerry (Breen) 1929-

PERSONAL: Born October 28, 1929, in Detroit, Mich.; daughter of Edward Patrick (a realtor) and Leona (Griese) Breen; married George D. Armstrong, Jr. (an illustrator), April 24, 1954; children: Rebecca Lee, Jennifer Ann. *Religion:* Roman Catholic. *Home:* 1535 Lake Ave., Wilmette, Ill. 60091.

CAREER: Folk singer and folk song collector. Performer with husband, George D. Armstrong, Jr., at folk festivals, including English Folk Song and Dance Society Festival, Stratford-on-Avon, England, 1954, at concerts, and on radio and television. Recording artist with husband on long-play albums for Folkways and Folk-Legacy labels. *Awards, honors:* Printing Industries of America, Graphic Art Award, 1965, for *The Magic Bagpipe;* Chicago Book Clinic Award, 1967, for *The Boat on the Hill.*

WRITINGS–All illustrated by husband, George D. Armstrong Jr.: *The Magic Bagpipe,* Whitman, 1964; *The Boat on the Hill,* Whitman, 1967; *The Fairy Thorn,* Whitman, 1969.

WORK IN PROGRESS: Children's book on the new archeology, illustrated by husband.

SIDELIGHTS: "When I was eleven years old, our sixth-grade teacher asked what we planned to be when we grew up. I was going to say, 'A wife and mother,' but nobody else was saying that, so I decided it wasn't a good answer. I loved to sing, but it seemed show-offy to claim to be a singer, so I couldn't say that. I loved stories. I often made up fairy tales for my younger sisters and brother; and I'd had a poem published on the children's page in the paper. So, when it was my turn, I said, 'I'll be a writer when I grow up.' And whaddaya know—I AM!

"Actually, I'm not sure if I'm a singer who also writes or a storyteller who also sings. I could never give up either interest. I also enjoy being a wife and mother, as I knew I would. And I'm looking forward to being a grandmother some year.

"In addition to the three books that I did with my husband, I've written numerous short stories for textbook publishers; an article on folklore for an encyclopedia; and some poems."

Her work is in the Kerlan Collection at the University of Minnesota.

HOBBIES AND OTHER INTERESTS: Making corn-husk dolls, patchwork quilts, macramé, sewing, bicycling, baby-sitting, photography; "our interest in folklore has led us to witchcraft, mythology, and Jungian psychology."

ASHFORD, Margaret Mary 1881-1972 (Daisy Ashford)

PERSONAL: Born in 1881 in Petersham, Surrey, England; married James Patrick Devlin; children: two sons, two daughters. *Education:* The Priory, Haywards Heath, Sussex, England.

MARGARET MARY ASHFORD

her father when she was eight), "The True History of Leslie Woodcock" (written at the age of eleven), "Where Love Lies Deepest" (written at twelve), and "The Hangman's Daughter" (written at about thirteen). Her very first story "Mr. Chapmer's Bride" was lost and has never been recovered.

In a preface to *Daisy Ashford: Her Book*, the authoress wrote: "Since the publication of *The Young Visiters*, I have often been asked if I don't myself think it funny. When I first discovered it—not having seen it since it was written—I certainly did. That is one of the most curious things about it—to be able to laugh at what one wrote in such solemn seriousness—and that is why I can never feel that all the nice things that have been said about it, are really due to me at all, but to a Daisy Ashford of so long ago that she seems almost another person. It has all been like a fairy tale, from the accidental finding of the original note book . . ."

It was a fairy tale with a happy ending, for Daisy married the man she loved, and although she wrote no more stories, the couple lived happily ever after until her death at the age of ninety years.

CAREER: Wrote her first book at age nine; gave up writing at age fifteen.

WRITINGS: The Young Visiters; or Mr. Salteena's Plan, Chatto & Windus, London, 1919; *Daisy Ashford: Her Book* (a collection of her remaining novels together with "The Jealous Governess" by her sister, Angela Ashford), Chatto & Windus, 1920, excerpts published under the titles: *Love and Marriage,* Chatto and Windus, 1965, and *Where Love Lies Deepest,* Hart-Davis, 1966.

SIDELIGHTS: Many children write stories when they are young. Daisy Ashford's *The Young Visiters,* written at the age of nine, is unique insofar as this quaint precocious work was published and became a bestseller.

It was author Frank Swinnerton, then acting as a reader for the British publishers Chatto & Windus, who was first captivated by the charming naiveté of a child's view of high society, and persuaded Sir James M. Barrie to write a preface for the book. It sold 500,000 copies in a year, and thereafter was constantly reprinted both in Britain and the United States. There is even a German translation.

In 1920 Ashford's remaining childhood novels and a similar piece by her sister Angela were published under the title *Daisy Ashford: Her Book.* The other pieces by Daisy comprised "A Short Story of Love and Marriage" (dictated to

Ethel and Bernard returned from their Honymoon with a son and hair, a nice fat baby called Ignatius Bernard. They soon had six more children four boys and three girls and some of them were twins which was very exciting. ■ (From *The Young Visiters* by Daisy Ashford. Illustrated by Heather Corlass.)

A play adapted by Mrs. George Norman and Margaret Mackenzie based on *The Young Visiters* was produced on Broadway in 1920. It was published by Samuel French, Inc..in 1936.

FOR MORE INFORMATION SEE: Roger Lancelyn Green, *Tellers of Tales,* Watts, 1965; Brian Doyle, *The Who's Who of Children's Literature,* Schocken Books, 1968; *Sunday Times* (London), January 16, 1972; *New York Times,* January 18, 1972; *Washington Post,* January 21, 1972; *Publishers' Weekly,* February 28, 1972; *New York Times Book Review,* April 15, 1973.

(Died January 15, 1972)

BANER, Skulda V(anadis) 1897-1964

PERSONAL: Born November 23, 1897, in Ironwood, Mich.; daughter of Johan G. R. (a newspaper publisher and poet under the name Asabard) and Mathilda (Bergman) Baner. *Education:* High school graduate; extension courses from University of Wisconsin.

CAREER: Was a prairie teacher in rural North Dakota, a personnel director, a photographer, a dressmaker, a secretary and lecturer on utility subjects for a power company in Ironwood, Mich., worked in radio (as copywriter and announcer) and in advertising in Milwaukee, Wis., and edited a house organ for a milk company.

WRITINGS: Latchstring Out, Houghton, 1944; *Voice of the Lute,* McKay, 1959; *First Parting,* McKay, 1960; *Pims: Adventures of a Dala Horse,* McKay, 1964. Contributor to *Ladies' Home Journal, American Swedish Monthly,* and *American Girl.*

SIDELIGHTS: Blinded by glaucoma, Skulda Baner was an insatiable reader in Braille in both Swedish and English, and corresponded with the blind in Sweden.

(Died January 31, 1964)

BARKER, S. Omar 1894—
(Jose Canusi, Phil Squires; Dan Scott, a house pseudonym)

PERSONAL: Born June 16, 1894, in Beulah, N.M.; son of Squire Leander (a rancher) and Priscilla Jane (McGuire) Barker; married Elsa McCormick (a writer under the names E. M. Barker, Elsa Barker; and a teacher of English), July 1, 1927. *Education:* New Mexico Highlands University, B.A., 1924. *Politics:* Conservative Republican. *Religion:* Protestant. *Home:* 1118 Ninth St., Las Vegas, N.M. 87701.

CAREER: High school teacher of English and Spanish, Tularosa, N.M., 1913-14; high school teacher and principal, Santa Rosa, N.M. 1914-16; instructor in English, New Mexico Highlands University, Las Vegas, 1921-22; member of New Mexico Legislature, 1925-26; professional writer, 1926—, also operating small ranch in New Mexico Rockies, 1929-56. Sometime U.S. forest ranger in earlier days; also Secretary of Las Vegas Cowboys' reunion Rodeo and trombonist in Doc Patterson's Cowboy Band. Chairman of Las Vegas Heart Fund Drive, 1962; member

S. OMAR BARKER

of Las Vegas Hospital board, 1962—. *Military service:* U.S. Army, Engineers, 1917-19; served with American Expeditionary Forces in France; became sergeant. *Member:* Western Writers of America (president, 1958-59), American Poetry League, Wildlife Conservation Association, American Legion, Veterans of Foreign Wars, Disabled American Veterans. *Awards, honors:* Spur Award, Western Writers of America for best western short story of 1955, "Bad Company," published in *Saturday Evening Post;* co-winner of Spur Award for best western nonfiction of 1958, for contribution to *This Is the West,* edited by Robert West Howard; honorary chief of Kiowa tribe, Anadarko, Okla., 1959; honorary Litt.D., New Mexico Highlands University, 1960; Justin Golden Boot Award, Western Writers of America, 1961, for distinguished writing in western field, 1954-61; Spur Award for best western poem, "Empty Saddles at Christmas," published in *Western Horseman Magazine,* 1967; Levi Strauss Golden Saddleman Award, for bringing dignity and honor to the western legend, 1967; lifetime honorary president, Western Writers of America, 1975.

WRITINGS: Winds of the Mountains (poetry), Santa Fe New Mexican Press, 1922; *Buckaroo Ballads* (poetry), Santa Fe New Mexican Press, 1928; *Born to Battle* (story collection), University of New Mexico Press, 1951; *Songs of the Saddlemen* (poetry), Sage Books, 1954; *Sunlight Through the Trees* (poetry), New Mexico Highlands University Press, 1954; (editor and contributor) *Legends and Tales of the Old West,* Doubleday, 1962; *Little World Apart* (novel), Doubleday, 1966; (with Carol Truax) *The Cattleman's Steak Book,* Grosset, 1967; *Rawhide Rhymes,* Doubleday, 1968. *A Cowboy's Christmas Prayer* (poetry), reprinted in about one-hundred periodicals and broadcast on nationwide TV by Jimmy Dean and Tennesee Ernie Ford. Also edited two Western Writers of America anthologies, *Frontiers West* and *Spurs West.*

"Bret King of Rimrock Ranch" series for boys, under house pseudonym (property of Grosset & Dunlap) Dan Scott: *The Mystery of Ghost Canyon*, 1960, *The Secret of Hermit's Peak*, 1960, *The Range Rodeo Mystery*, 1960, *The Mystery of Rawhide Gap*, 1960, *The Secret of Fort Pioneer*, 1961, *The Mystery at Blizzard Mesa*, 1961, *The Mystery of the Comanche Caves*, 1963, *The Phantom of Wolf Creek*, 1963, *The Mystery of Bandit Gulch*, 1964 (all published by Grosset).

Stories, poems, articles, and anecdotes have appeared in about seventy anthologies and in some twenty texts on American literature. Stories and poems anthologized in: John Gunther, *Inside U.S.A.*, Harper, 1947, revised edition, 1951; Harriet M. Lucas and Herman M. Ward, editors, *Prose and Poetry for Enjoyment*, 4th edition, Dent, 1950; Noel M. Loomis, editor, *Holsters and Heroes*, Macmillan, 1954; Harry E. Maule, editor, *The Fall Roundup*, Random House, 1955; Don Ward, editor, *Branded West*, Houghton, 1956; Mark A. Neville, editor, *Interesting Friends*, Rand McNally, 1958; Jim Kjelgaard, editor, *Wild Horse Roundup*, Dodd, 1958; Fairfax D. Downey, compiler, *My Kingdom for a Horse*, Doubleday, 1960; E. N. Brandt, editor, *Saturday Evening Post Reader of Western Stories*, Doubleday, 1960; F. D. Downey, compiler, *Great Dog Stories of All Time*, Doubleday, 1962; E. D. Mygatt, editor, *Search for the Hidden Places*, McKay, 1963; Kenneth Fowler, editor, *Rawhide Men*, Doubleday, 1965; W. R. Cox, editor, *Rivers to Cross*, Dodd, 1966. Approximately 1,500 short stories, 1,000 pieces of nonfiction, and 2,500 poems have been published in more than 100 periodicals in America, England, and Canada; they have appeared in *Saturday Evening Post*, *Reader's Digest*, *Country Gentlemen*, *Farm Journal*, *Argosy*, *Adventure*, *Field and Stream*, *Ranch Romances* (now defunct), *Western Story* (now defunct), and *Maclean's Magazine*, among others. Author of a series of cowboy humor stories in *Wild West Weekly* (now defunct) under pseudonym Phil Squires.

WORK IN PROGRESS: Humor of the Real Cowboy, for Red River Valley Historical Association to be published by University of Oklahoma Press; western greeting card verses for Leanin' Tree Pub. Co., Boulder, Colo.

SIDELIGHTS: "I was born in a log cabin and raised on a mountain ranch far up in the New Mexico Rockies; youngest of eleven. We were a hardworking family who might today be called 'disadvantaged,' but we didn't know it. In my growing-up days, I was about equally familiar with horse and saddle, plough, mowing machine, hoe, crosscut saw, axe, pitchfork, rifle and willow fishing pole. To my strict but kindly Christian raising, I attribute the fact that I have always preferred to write clean stories and poems, chiefly featuring good people rather than bad. I found plenty to write about in the life and times of the American West, both old and modern. They were usually 'ranchfolks.'

"I have always been very much an outdoorsman, a hunter and fisherman, but also very much a conservationist, long before 'ecology' and 'environment' became popular. I'm moderately involved in politics, but not for any office."

"*Little World Apart*, is the partly autobiographical story of a pioneer New Mexico family—called a novel because the publishers couldn't find any other way to classify it." Be-

tween 1929-56, Barker and his wife Elsa did their writing on a ranch in a timbered cove named Rincon Montoso, about eight thousand feet up in the Rockies.

"My wife has been of incomparable help in my writing, both with suggestions and encouragement as well as typing final copies of manuscripts."

BAUMANN, Amy (Brown) 1922— (Alexis Brown; James Barbary, a joint pseudonym)

PERSONAL: Born May 14, 1922, in Shropshire, England; daughter of George Alexis and Lily (Cartwright) Brown; married Jack Beeching (a poet and novelist), 1950 (divorced, 1970); married Heinrich Baumann, 1971; children: John Rutland, Laura Caroline. *Education:* Exhall College, Coventry, England, teaching certificate, 1946. *Home:* 5 Falcon Square, Castle Hedingham, Essex, England. *Agent:* Hope Leresche & Steele, 11 Jubilee Pl., Chelsea, London S.W.3, England.

CAREER: Teacher, writer, and translator; has lived abroad for some seven years—in the Balearics, Morocco, and Canary Islands.

WRITINGS–Under pseudonym Alexis Brown: *Treasure at Devil's Bay*, Blackie & Son, 1961 (published in America as *Treasure in Devil's Bay*, McGraw, 1965); *Schooner on the Rocks*, Dobson, 1966.

Juveniles with Jack Beeching, under joint pseudonym James Barbary: *The Fort in the Forest*, Parrish, 1962(published in America as *The Fort in the Wilderness*, Norton, 1965); *The Engine and the Gun*, Parrish, 1963; *Ten Thousand Heroes*, Parrish, 1963, Roy Publishers, 1964; *The Student Buccaneer*, Roy Publishers, 1963; *The Pike and the Sword*, Parrish, 1963; *The Young Cicero*, Roy Publishers, 1964; *Lawrence and His Desert Raider*, Parrish, 1965; *The Young Lord Byron*, Roy Publishers, 1965; *The Young Mutineer*, Parrish, 1966; *1066*, Parrish, 1966.

Translations from the Dutch under pseudonym Alexis Brown: W. Sevensma, *Tapestries*, Merlin Press, 1965; *Enamelling*, Merlin Press, 1965; *Playing Cards*, Merlin Press, 1966; Ben Minoti, "Little King, Big King," a children's play performed by Unicorn Theatre Co. at Arts Theatre, London, February, 1967; A. Koolhaas, *A Flower for Tomorrow* (short story anthology), Jonathan Cape, 1967; *The Buccaneers of the West Indies*, Penguin, 1968; Carel J. du Ry, *Art of the Ancient Near and Middle East*, Harry N. Abrams, 1970; Carel J. du Ry, *Art of Islam*, Harry N. Abrams, 1971; (from the Spanish) Ortega y Gasset, *Velazquez, Goya and the Dehumanization of Art*, Studio Vista, 1972; (from the German in collaboration with Heinrich Baumann) Werner Haftmann, *Chagall*, Harry N. Abrams, 1973.

WORK IN PROGRESS: Three Long Years, an autobiographical account of life in the Balearic Islands; a play for young people, *The House from Inner Space*.

SIDELIGHTS: Competent in French, Spanish, Dutch, and German. Is now mainly engaged in remedial teaching.

BARBARA BENEZRA

BENEZRA, Barbara (Beardsley) 1921-

PERSONAL: Born April 2, 1921, in Woodman, Colo.; daughter of Earl (a dentist) and Alice (a teacher; maiden name, Smith) Beardsley; married Leo L. Benezra (a chemist); children: Heather Lee DeMare, Paul Louis, Judith Ann, David Allen. *Education:* San Francisco State College, student, 1939-40; University of California, Berkeley, student, 1940-41, General Secondary Certificate, 1944; College of the Pacific, A.B., 1942; University of California, General Secondary, 1943; San Jose State Teacher's College, Librarian Degree, 1960. *Home:* 7170 Hawthorn Dr., Mentor, Ohio 44060.

CAREER: Elementary school librarian in Sunnyvale, Calif., 1960-68; Kennedy Junior High School, East Lake, Ohio, librarian, 1968; professional Dianetic auditor, 1975. *Member:* American Library Association, National Education Association, Church of Scientology, Delta Kappa Gamma.

WRITINGS: Gold Dust and Petticoats, Bobbs, 1964; *Nuggets in My Pocket,* Bobbs, 1966; *Fire Dragon,* Abelard, 1970. Contributor to professional journals.

WORK IN PROGRESS: Peggy Morgan, sequel to the first two books.

SIDELIGHTS: "Like many other authors, I spent a lonely childhood, because my father died when I was three and my mother returned to teaching to support me and my two brothers. This wasn't really bad, however, because it gave me time to read and read, absorbing the styles of writers like a sponge, and to make up plays for little dolls I owned. When I was nine years old, I spent some time with my aunt who had a cabin overlooking the Pacific Ocean. Since I was alone, I spent time writing poetry, the only poetry I ever attempted to write. I also started my autobiography, but concluded I hadn't lived long enough to have adventures I could write about, so I postponed that work.

"While I was growing up I kept a journal and tried to write something every day. In college, I managed to take a writing course each year, and learned a great deal from the teachers. Still, the time comes when you have to stop taking courses and just write, so in 1958 I started writing my first book.

"I have always been fascinated by history, and feel since history is about people, that is how it should be studied. I wanted my readers to realize that people of a hundred years ago had many of the same problems and all of the emotions we experience today. In order to write my books, all historical novels, I read many books about the colorful, exciting times of the California gold rush. I haunted museums and even took a trip into the Mother Lode country of the Sierras to try and recapture the flavor of the times of 1853. By the time I sat down to write my books I felt as though I had walked through the mud that paved the streets of San Francisco then, or walked behind a mule into the Sierras, carrying my pick on my back.

"In order to write *Fire Dragon,* a book about the San Francisco earthquake and fire of 1906, I not only read books and newspapers, but I interviewed nineteen people who had survived that historic event.

"When young people ask me how to learn to write, I usually tell them to sharpen their wits, learn their basic skills from school, but above all, *to write.* Although it is a demanding occupation and very few books are published from all of the manuscripts sent in by hopeful authors, there is always room for a good book.

"People ask me how it feels to be rich and famous. I have to reply that I don't know, since I am neither. However, it is a great source of satisfaction to have a book published with my name on the title page. I enjoy reading letters sent by young readers, and being invited to speak to groups of people about my writing. So I can say, in these experiences, I am rich indeed."

HOBBIES AND OTHER INTERESTS: Singing, painting, traveling, and entertaining friends.

BETZ, Eva Kelly 1897-1968
(Caroline Peters)

PERSONAL: Born March 11, 1897, in Fall River, Mass.; daughter of Michael Forestal (a medical doctor) and Caroline (Cantwell) Kelly; married Joseph P. Betz; children: Joseph P., Jr. (deceased). *Home:* 353 Van Houten Ave., Passaic, N.J. 07055.

CAREER: Former elementary teacher in Rhode Island and Massachusetts; later employed in sales promotion in Paterson, N.J.; free-lance writer. *Member:* Authors Guild, New Jersey Historical Society (honorary life member).

WRITINGS: Young Eagles, D. X. McMullen Co., 1947; *Freedom Drums,* Abelard, 1950, 2nd edition, St. Anthony Guild Press, 1953; *Desperate Drums,* St. Anthony Guild Press, 1951; *Victory Drums,* St. Anthony Guild Press, 1955; *Knight of Molokai,* St. Anthony Guild Press, 1956; *My Little Counting Books,* Bruce, 1957; *The Amazing John Tabb,* Bruce, 1958; *The Man Who Fought the Devil: The Cure of Ars,* St. Anthony Guild Press, 1958; *Priest on Horseback: Father Farmer, 1720-1786,* Sheed, 1958, 2nd edition, St. Anthony Guild Press, 1965.

David, Sheed, 1960; *Priest, Patriot, and Leader: The Story of Archbishop Carroll,* Benziger, 1960; *Yankee at Molokai,* St. Anthony Guild Press, 1960; *The Web Begun,* Bruce, 1961; *Saint Colum and the Crane,* St. Anthony Guild Press, 1961; *Blessed Sebastian and the Oxen,* St. Anthony Guild Press, 1961; *Saint Germaine and the Sheep,* St. Anthony Guild Press, 1961; *Fanny Allen, Green Mountain Rebel,* Kenedy, 1962; *To Far Places: The Story of Francis X. Ford,* Hawthorn, 1962; (under pseudonym Caroline Peters) *The Story of St. Kevin,* St. Anthony Guild Press, 1962; (under pseudonym Caroline Peters) *The Black Madonna: Our Lady of Czestochowa,* St. Anthony Guild Press, 1962; *The Quiet Flame: Mother Marianne of Molokai,* Bruce, 1963; *Virgil Barber, New England Pied Piper,* Kenedy, 1963; *Saint Martin de Porres and the Mice,* St. Anthony Guild Press, 1963; (under pseudonym Caroline Peters) *St. Michael, God's Warrier Angel,* St. Anthony Guild Press, 1963; *William Gaston, Fighter for Justice,* Kenedy, 1964; *Saint Brigid and the Cows,* St. Anthony Guild Press, 1964; *Story of the Rosary,* St. Anthony Guild Press, 1964; *Apostle of the Ice and Snow: A Life of Bishop Charles Seghers,* Holy Cross Press, 1964; *Stout Hearts and Holy Hands: The Life of Mother Angela, of the Sisters of the Holy Cross,* Holy Cross Press, 1964; (under pseudonym Caroline Peters) *The Story of Saint Clare,* St. Anthony Guild Press, 1965; (under pseudonym Caroline Peters) *Lives of the Saints for Boys and Girls,* St. Anthony Guild Press, 1965.

(Died April 7, 1968)

BILLOUT, Guy René   1941-

PERSONAL: Surname sounds like "be-you"; born July 7, 1941, in Decize, France; son of René George (a journalist) and Christiane (Vichard) Billout. *Education:* Attended Ecole Des Arts Appliques De Beaune, France, 1956-1960. *Home and Office:* 222 West 15th St., New York, N.Y. 10011.

CAREER: Free-lance illustrator. Worked six years as a designer in advertising in Paris. *Awards, honors:* Society of Illustrators, two gold medals, 1974; *Number 24,* one of the ten best in the *New York Times,* 1973.

WRITINGS: (Self-illustrated) *Number 24,* Quist, 1973.

SIDELIGHTS: "I work with watercolors and brush, occasionally airbrush. To the best of my knowledge I have been

GUY RENÉ BILLOUT

influenced by Folon, Steinberg, Hergé, Glaser and Japanese art.''

FOR MORE INFORMATION SEE: New York Times Book Review, November 4, 1973; *New York Magazine,* December 17, 1973; *Zoom Magazine* (France), Number 29, March-April, 1975.

BLOCH, Lucienne   1909-

PERSONAL: Born January 5, 1909, in Geneva, Switzerland; daughter of Ernest (a composer) and Marguerite (a pianist) Bloch; married Stephen Pope Dimitroff (an artist), September, 1936; children: George Ernest, Pencho, Sita (Mrs. Boyan Milcev). *Education:* Attended Cleveland School of Art and Ecole Nationale Des Beaux Arts, Paris, France. *Office:* 34844 Old Stage Road, Gualala, Calif. 95445.

CAREER: Free-lance illustrator; artist. University of California Extension, San Francisco, Calif., lecturer, 1950; Architectural Advisory Committee, Mill Valley, Calif., board member, 1959-64; Marin Society of Artists, Ross, Calif., lecturer, 1965-67; California Roadside Council, Gualala, Calif., chairman, beautification committee, 1966-73; Mendocino Art Center, Mendocino, Calif., instructor in egg tempera, 1969-75; Gualala Arts, Gualala, Calif., instructor in mosaics, 1973-74; Evergreen State College, Olympia, Wash., visiting professor, 1976. Has painted many murals and has done album covers. Among the murals (created with husband): a fresco in the San Rafael Presbyterian Church, Calif.; all the mosaics in the Greek Orthodox church, Oakland, Calif.; outdoor tile mosaic, Redwood High School, Marin County, Calif.; casein, YMCA gymnasium, Flint, Mich.; oil on wood, Swiss Pavillion, New York Worlds Fair, 1939; copper and wood, map of Marin County, Marin Savings and Loan, Marin, Calif.; acrylic, Marine Fireman's Union Hall, San Francisco, Calif.; acrylic, children's ward, Marin General Hospital, Marin, Calif. *Exhibitions:* San Francisco, Calif.,

Marin County, Calif., Mendocino County, Calif., and many more throughout the United States.

MEMBER: San Francisco Art Association, Artists Equity Association, Marin Society of Artists, Mendocino Art Center. *Awards, honors:* Ivory Soap Sculpture contest, second prize in the professional category, 1936; Paris Expositions des Arts Decorative, Paris, France, gold medal for lithography, 1937; *Sandpipers,* second of the "10 Best Illustrated Children's Books of 1961" by the *New York Times;* Citizens Participation Roadside award, second prize, 1972. Many more in drawing, acrylic and various other media.

ILLUSTRATOR: Anita Brenner, *I Want to Fly,* Young Scott, 1943, re-issued 1950; Mary McBurney Green, *Is It Hard Is It Easy?,* Young Scott, 1943; Margaret W. Brown, *Willie's Walk to Grandma,* Young Scott, 1944; Margaret Bradford and Barbara Woodruff, *Keep Humming Keep Singing,* Young Scott, 1945; Anita Brenner, *Y O Quiero Volar!,* Editorial Albatros, 1945; Dorothy Baruch, *Christmas Stocking,* Young Scott, 1946; Louise Woodcock, *The Smart Little Boy and His Smart Kitty,* Young Scott, 1947; re-issued, 1970; Mary McBurney Green, *Everybody Eats,* Young Scott, 1949; Jean Monrad, *How Many Kisses Goodnight,* Young Scott, 1949; Mary L. Downer, *The Flower,* Young Scott, 1955; Edith Thatcher Hurd, *Sandpipers,* Crowell, 1961, re-issued, 1970; Edith Thatcher Hurd, *Starfish,* Crowell, 1962, re-issued, 1970.

WORK IN PROGRESS: New book for children.

SIDELIGHTS: When Frank Lloyd Wright saw Lucienne Bloch's glass work he invited her to teach sculpture at his architectural school in Taliesin East. Her interests, however, were shifted to mural painting when she became an apprentice to Diego Rivera, the Mexican painter. Lucienne Bloch met her husband while they were both assistants to Rivera. They have worked on mural projects ever since; he doing the technical fresco work and she, the painting.

The Dimitroffs taught art at the Flint Art Institute in Michigan during World War II. They moved to California with their three small children in 1948 and settled in Mill Valley. They moved to Gualala, in Northern California in 1965, where they have a ranch and studios.

There is a crack in one egg. The wet head of a little sandpiper pokes through the crack. ■
(From *Sandpipers* by Edith Thacher Hurd. Illustrated by Lucienne Bloch.)

LUCIENNE BLOCH

FOR MORE INFORMATION SEE: Illustrators of Children's Books: 1744-1945, Horn Book, 1947; Illustrators of Children's Books: 1946-1956, Horn Book, 1958.

BOCK, Harold I.   1939-
(Hal Bock)

PERSONAL: Born May 11, 1939, in New York, N.Y.; son of Milton and Sarah (Nieman) Bock; married Frances Elkin (an assistant professor), November 4, 1961; children: Richard Allan. Education: New York University, B.S., 1961. Home: 396 Jackson Ave., Mineola, N.Y. 11501.

CAREER: New York Rangers, Hockey Club, New York, N.Y., publicity writer, 1961-63; Associated Press, New York, N.Y., sports writer specializing in baseball, football, and hockey, 1963—. Military service: U.S. Army Reserve, 1961-67. Member: Professional Hockey Writers Association, Baseball Writers Association of America, Professional Football Writers Association of America, New York Hockey Writers Association.

WRITINGS—Under name Hal Bock: (With Rod Gilbert and Stan Fischler) Goal: My Life on Ice (youth book), Hawthorn, 1968; (editor with Zander Hollander) The Complete Encyclopedia of Ice Hockey, Prentice-Hall, 1970, Dynamite on Ice, Scholastic, 1972; Save! Hockey's Brave Goalies, Avon, 1974; (with Bill Chadwick) The Big Whis-

tle, Hawthorn, 1974. Contributor to Encyclopedia Americana and to sports magazines.

FOR MORE INFORMATION SEE: Saturday Review, April 19, 1969.

BOSHINSKI, Blanche   1922-

PERSONAL: Born November 28, 1922, in Fort Morgan, Colo.; daughter of Joseph B. (a farmer) and Gertrude (Stroebel) Tarr; married Edward J. Boshinski, March 16, 1945; children: Laura (Mrs. Luther A. Shipley, Jr.), Sharon. Education: University of Denver, A.B., 1944, Teacher's Certification, 1966. Home: 2174 South Clarkson St., Denver, Colo. 80210.

CAREER: Rocky Mountain News, Denver, Colo., club editor, 1944-45; held office jobs in Tacoma, Wash., 1945; teacher of adult basic education in Denver (Colo.) public schools, 1966-1972. Member: Denver Women's Press Club; Colorado Author's League.

WRITINGS: The Luck of the Blue Stallion, Meredith, 1967; Aha and the Jewel of Mystery, Parent's Magazine Press, 1968. Contributor of short stories to children's magazines, including Humpty Dumpty, Calling All Girls, and Child Life.

BOYLE, Ann (Peters)   1916-

PERSONAL: Born January 21, 1916, in Independence, Mo.; daughter of Robert Mize (a pharmacist) and Lucy (Conway) Peters; married James Hancock Boyle (a lawyer), December 26, 1938; children: Eleanor Ann (Mrs. Richard Riley), Lucy Charlotte (Mrs. Robert E. Buschmann), Jean Boyle Dannenberg. Education: Chevy Chase Junior College, graduate, 1936; University of Kansas City (now University of Missouri at Kansas City), B.A., 1938. Religion: Protestant. Home: 15991 Bliss Lane, Apt. A., Tustin, Calif. 92680.

CAREER: Model for various women's clothing shops, Kansas City, Mo., 1936-38; Barstow School, Kansas City, Mo., teacher in primary grades, 1938-39. Member: Association of Junior Leagues of America, Long Beach Writers Workshop, Quill Pen (vice-president, 1971; president, 1972), Newport Writers, Lambda Beta Writers Workshop, California Writers Guild. Awards, honors: Prize in Writer's Digest Short Short Story Contest, 1962, for "The Christmas Eve Surprise"; first and second prizes for short stories in Long Beach Writers Club annual contests.

WRITINGS: Stormy Slopes (young adult novel), Bouregy, 1971; Sundown Girl, Bouregy, 1971; The Well of Three Echoes, Bouregy/Avalon, 1972; Rim of Forever, Avalon, 1973; One Golden Earring, Avalon, 1974; Dark Mountain, Avalon, 1975; Beyond the Wall, Avalon, 1976. Contributor of short stories and serials to Jack and Jill, Wee Wisdom, Children's Activities, Highlights for Children, and other juvenile magazines.

WORK IN PROGRESS: Untitled young adult novel; an untitled adult novel.

ANN BOYLE

SIDELIGHTS: "Although I have wanted to write fiction for as long as I can remember, I did not begin to write professionally until I had a storehouse full of experience to use. For me, writing is personal, a way to share and interpret my experiences.

"With our three daughters, my husband and I have had wonderful times in the outdoors as well as sightseeing in the various places we lived. Together we camped, hiked, skied on snow and water, swam and rode horseback. In Europe we participated in many of the unusual native ceremonies and customs. Now that our daughters have their own homes, we still cross-country ski, hike and backpack, either my husband and I alone or with members of our family.

"Our experiences, adapted, combined, or altered with imagination are woven in as background for my stories, to help shape the plot or influence the characters. The cat in *Dark Mountain* is a composite of the many cats who have owned us and a cat we met recently with his people on a hike to the bleak, lonely, and boulder-strewn 11,000-foot summit of Southern California's Mt. San Gorgonio.

"In addition to personal experiences, much reading is necessary to check facts like: Do bighorn sheep live in Death Valley as well as in the Joshua Tree National Monument where we have seen them? or, What evergreens grow at 8,000 feet in the San Gorgonio area? A sizeable collection of pamphlets from ranger stations bulges my files, but I still depend on libraries.

"*Sundown Girl* required special research. We hiked up to a number of lookout towers where the lookouts demonstrated their instruments and told of experiences. Once, while we were in a tower, the girl lookout spotted and reported a beginning forest fire. We have been almost too close to such fires, have smelled and seen the smoke, but I added hours of library reading about weather conditions, firefighting, and the habits of forest fires, to make my fire real.

"My husband has always encouraged my writing. He shows infinite patience when I interrupt a hike to jot down notes in my small notebook. We plan all our outings with story possibilities in mind, and sometimes he even gives me an idea that starts me off on another book.

"While my personal life has enriched my writing, writing has enriched my life. My husband tells me that when circumstances prevent me from writing, my disposition suffers. Watching a story grow is a great pleasure, and knowing that people enjoy reading it is a great reward for the work involved."

BRICK, John 1922-1973

PERSONAL: Born January 1, 1922, in Newburgh, N.Y.; son of John T. and Elizabeth (Connell) Brick; married Mary Yakim, December 4, 1943; children: John W., Martha E., Janice A. (Mrs. Dennis Schreckengast). *Education:* Attended New York University and Columbia University. *Home:* 3604 Albee Lane, Alexandria, Va. *Agent:* Mavis McIntosh, McIntosh, McKee & Dodds, 30 East 60th St., New York, N.Y. 10022.

CAREER: Export Trade, New York, N.Y., managing editor, 1945-49; full-time writer, 1950-60; *Life,* Book Division, New York, N.Y., staff writer, 1960-61; University of Toledo, Toledo, Ohio, assistant to the president, 1962-63; U.S. Senate Permanent Investigating Subcommittee, Washington, D.C., professional staff member, 1963-73. *Military service:* U.S. Army Air Forces, World War II. *Member:* Authors Guild (vice-president). *Awards, honors:* Farrar, Straus regional fellowship, 1950, for *Troubled Spring.*

WRITINGS: Troubled Spring, Farrar, Straus, 1950; *The Raid,* Farrar, Straus, 1951; *Homer Crist,* Farrar, Straus, 1952; *The Rifleman,* Doubleday, 1953; *The King's Rangers,* Doubleday, 1954; *They Ran for Their Lives,* Doubleday, 1954; *Eagle of Niagara* (juvenile), Doubleday, 1955; *Jubilee,* Doubleday, 1956; *Panther Mountain,* Doubleday, 1958; *The Strong Men,* Doubleday, 1959.

Gettysburg, Popular Library, 1960; *The Raid* (juvenile), Duell, Sloan & Pearce, 1960; *Yankees on the Run* (juvenile), Duell, Sloan & Pearce, 1961; *Tomahawk Trail* (juvenile), Duell, Sloan & Pearce, 1962; *Captives of the Senecas* (juvenile), Duell, Sloan & Pearce, 1963; *The Richmond Raid,* Doubleday, 1963; *Ben Bryan, Morgan Rifleman,* Duell, Sloan & Pearce, 1963; *Rogues' Kingdom,* Doubleday, 1965; *They Fought for New York* (juvenile), Putnam, 1965; *On the Old Frontier,* Putnam, 1966. Staff writer on *Life Picture Atlas* and "Life Nature Library." Contributor of short stories to magazines.

WORK IN PROGRESS: Several novels.

SIDELIGHTS: The screen rights to Brick's first novel, *Troubled Spring,* were purchased by Metro-Goldwyn-Mayer.

HOBBIES AND OTHER INTERESTS: Reading and fishing.

(Died October 15, 1973)

Tim reversed his rifle and leaped at the Seneca, who parried the first blow with his own weapon. Tim struck again and again with agility and speed, but suddenly the stock of the long rifle splintered and then snapped. ■ (From *On the Old Frontier* by John Brick. Illustrated by the author.)

BROCKETT, Eleanor Hall 1913-1967

PERSONAL: Born April 16, 1913, in London, England; daughter of George Benjamin and Amelia (Waller) Hall; married Charles F. Brockett (a local government official, Westminster City), October 5, 1935; children: Barbara Jane. *Education:* Attended school in London, England, and Ursuline Convent, Konigstein im Taunus, Germany. *Politics:* Socialist. *Religion:* Anglican. *Home:* 39 Sylvan Way, West Wickham, Kent, England. *Agent:* Curtis Brown Ltd., 1 Craven Hill, London W2 3EW, England.

CAREER: Times Book Club, London, England, employee, 1932; Ivor Nicholson & Watson Ltd. (publishers), London, England, editorial secretary, 1933-40; Robert Hale Ltd. (publishers), London, England, editorial secretary and reader, 1940-45; Curtis Brown Ltd. (literary agent), London, England, executive, 1952-53, advisory reader, 1960-62. Free-lance reader, editor, translator, and indexer for publishers, authors. *Member:* National Book League.

WRITINGS: How to Retire and Start Living, Staples, 1955, revised edition, New English Library, 1963; *Choosing a Career,* Staples, 1959, 2nd revised edition,

MacGibbon & Kee, 1966; *Persian Fairy Tales* (retold), Muller, 1962; *Turkish Fairy Tales* (retold), Muller, 1963; *Look at Germany,* Hamish Hamilton, 1964; *Burmese and Thai Fairy Tales* (retold), Muller, 1965.

Translator: (And part author, with Anton Ehrenzweig and Karl Herrligkoffer) *Nanga Parbat,* Elek Books, 1954; Gianni Roghi and Francesco Baschieri Salvadori, *Dahlak,* Nicholas Kaye, 1956; Bruno Traven, *The Cotton Pickers,* R. Hale, 1956; (with Ehrenzweig) Fritz Otto Busch, *The Drama of the Scharnhorst,* R. Hale, 1956; Helen Fischer, *Peril is My Companion,* R. Hale, 1957; Karl Nork, *Hell in Siberia,* R. Hale, 1957; Erich Gimpel, *Spy for Germany,* Hamish Hamilton, 1957; Gabrielle Bertrand, *The Jungle People: Men, Beasts and Legends of the Moi Country,* R. Hale, 1959; Fritz Otto Busch, *The Story of the Prince Eugen,* R. Hale, 1960; Gaston Rebuffat, *On Snow and Rock,* Nicholas Kaye, 1963; Gaston Rebuffat, *Between Heaven and Earth,* Oxford University Press, 1965; Gaston Rebuffat, *Men and the Matterhorn,* Oxford University Press, 1967.

WORK IN PROGRESS: Research on the effect on doctor-patient relationships of the National Health Service in Great Britain.

SIDELIGHTS: "The only remarkable thing about my literary output is its variety. I have a natural curiosity about practically everything, and enjoy inquiring into the mysteries of old age, oriental folklore, Himalayan expeditions, and so on."

HOBBIES AND OTHER INTERESTS: Playing piano, looking at abstract paintings.

(Died June 21, 1967)

BROKAMP, Marilyn 1920-
(Mary Lynn)

PERSONAL: Born September 9, 1920, in Covington, Ky.; daughter of Lawrence Henry (a manager) and Elizabeth (Neuhaus) Brokamp. *Education:* Marian College, Indianapolis, Ind., B.S. in Ed., 1953; Ball State University, M.Ed., 1972. *Home:* 220 West Siebenthaler, Dayton, Ohio 45405. *Office:* Lady of Mercy School, 545 Odlin Dr., Dayton, Ohio 45405.

CAREER: Roman Catholic nun of the Sisters of Saint Francis (Franciscan; O.S.F.); primary school teacher in Indiana, Illinois, and Ohio, 1940—. Consultant to Society for Visual Education. *Member:* National Education Association, National Catholic Educational Association, Indiana Council of Teachers of English, American Association of Elementary, Kindergarten, Nursery Educators.

WRITINGS: (With Sister Marie Padua Holohan and Sister Fidelia Martini) *Primarily Yours,* Sisters of St. Francis (Oldenberg, Ind.), 1966; *Tippy-Toe and Taffy* (juvenile), McKnight, 1966; *Halfway* (juvenile), Vantage, 1970; *Skelly the Sea Horse* (juvenile), Orbis Books, 1973. Also author of *A Friend Always,* published by Standard Publishing Co., three children's plays, and a television script, "Onomatopoeia," produced by WFBM-TV, Indianapolis, Ind., 1970. Contributor to education journals (occasionally under pseudonym, Mary Lynn).

"What is the matter with me? . . . Why am I so different from everybody else?" ■ (From *Skelly the Sea Horse* by Sister Marilyn Brokamp. Illustrated by pupils of St. Mary School, Bloomington, Illinois.)

WORK IN PROGRESS: Two books, *Song of the Psalms* and *More Ways Than One to Somewhere; The Cherryridge Gang,* "written for the middle-grade child, it is typically about a gang and their clubhouse. It contains activities in the language arts area at the end of each chapter. This story is really my own childhood. We had such a gang with jalopy races and a garage clubhouse. I had the second-hand type-writer and wanted a newspaper. In real life I didn't type a newspaper until I taught at a jail. The inmates and I rigged up a little newspaper then."

SIDELIGHTS: "How did I come to write my books and plays? First, I wanted to make teaching and learning more interesting for children. For instance, *Tippy-Toe and Taffy,* emphasizes consonant and vowel substitution. Instead of reading long lists of words, wouldn't you rather read about

a big, fat elephant who's trying to walk without going stamp, stamp or tramp, tramp? Wouldn't you rather read about a giraffe who goes to the doctor to have a voice box put into his throat and must decide whether he wants to say, 'fisbee, fusbee' or 'hippity, hoppity?'

"After teaching many years I realized that children retain only about 50% of what they see and hear but 90% of what they do. Plays, of course involve the children. *Halfway, Skelly the Sea Horse* and *Once Upon a Cereal Box* involve the children in the learning process.

"*Skelly the Sea Horse* involved the students in this way: Together my third and fourth graders looked up information about marine life. I wrote it into a make-believe story and the children drew the pictures for the story.

MARILYN BROKAMP

"*Once upon a Cereal Box* is for the pre-school child. A four-line verse on each page strives to oil the wheels of the reader's or the listener's imagination in showing the many ways of using an old cereal box. It simultaneously strengthens muscular coordination, for each activity is a little more difficult to cut.

"Writing is my hobby. It springs from my profession of teaching. I enjoy the writing, I enjoy seeing my books in print but best of all, I enjoy hearing from children and parents about how much they enjoy the books."

FOR MORE INFORMATION SEE: Criterion, April 11, 1969; *Indianapolis Star,* July 16, 1970.

BROWN, Marc Tolon 1946-

PERSONAL: Born November 25, 1946, in Erie, Pa.; son of LeRoy Edward and Renita (Toulon) Brown; married Stephanie Marini (a ballet dancer and college teacher), September 1, 1968; children: Tolon Adam, Tucker Eliot. *Education:* Cleveland Institute of Art, B.F.A., 1969. *Home and Studio:* 298 Washington St., Hanover, Mass. 02339.

CAREER: WICU-TV (NBC affiliate), Erie, Pa., television art director, 1968-69; Garland Junior College, Boston, Mass., assistant professor, 1969—. *Exhibitions:* Society of Illustrators, New York, N.Y.; numerous one-man shows throughout New England, Pennsylvania, and Ohio.

(From *I Found Them in the Yellow Pages* by Norma Farber. Illustrated by Marc Brown.)

MARC TOLON BROWN

WRITINGS—Self-illustrated: *Arthur's Nose*, Little, Brown, 1976.

ILLUSTRATOR: Isaac Asimov, *What Makes the Sun Shine*, Little, Brown, 1970; Norma Farber, *I Found Them in the Yellow Pages*, Little, Brown, 1972; Peter Dickinson, *The Iron Lion*, Allen & Unwin, 1972; Ted Clymer, *The Four Corners of the Sky*, Little, Brown, 1975; Lawrence White, *Science Games/Puzzles/Tricks/Toys* (4 books), Addison, 1975; Patty Wolcott, *Super Sam and the Salad Garden*, Addison, 1975.

BUCHWALD, Art(hur)   1925-

PERSONAL: Born October 20, 1925, in Mount Vernon, N.Y.; son of Joseph (a curtain manufacturer) and Helen (Kleinberger) Buchwald; married Ann McGarry (one-time fashion coordinator for Neiman-Marcus), October 11, 1952; children: Joel, Conchita, Jennifer. *Education:* University of Southern California, student, 1945-48. *Religion:* Jewish. *Residence:* Washington, D.C.

CAREER: Left high school without diploma to join Marines; left college without degree to live in Paris, with first job there as correspondent for *Variety*, 1948; hired as columnist, "Paris After Dark," on editorial staff of Paris edition of *New York Herald Tribune*, 1949; added second column, "Mostly About People," 1951; two columns combined for American readers in 1952 as "Europe's Lighter Side," later published most often as "Art Buchwald in Paris"; after writing from Paris (and other European points) for fourteen years, Buchwald switched to Washington, D.C., in 1962, and his column, now usually published just as "Art Buchwald," currently is syndicated to 380 newspapers. International Social Service, advisory director. *Military service:* U.S. Marine Corps, 1942-45, with Fourth Marine Air Wing in Pacific; became sergeant. *Member:* Overseas Press Club. *Awards, honors:* Grand Prix de La Humor, France, 1959.

WRITINGS: Art Buchwald's Paris, Little, Brown, 1953; *The Brave Coward*, Harper, 1955; *More Caviar*, Harper, 1957; *A Gift from the Boys*, Harper, 1958; *Don't Forget to Write*, World Publishing, 1960; *How Much Is That in Dollars?*, World Publishing, 1961; *Is It Safe to Drink the Water?*, World Publishing, 1962; *I Chose Capitol Punishment*, World Publishing, 1963; *And Then I Told The President*, Putnam, 1965; *Son of the Great Society*, Putnam, 1966; *Have I Ever Lied to You?*, Putnam, 1968; *The Establishment is Alive and Well in Washington*, Putnam, 1969; *Counting Sheep*, Putnam, 1970; *Getting High in Government Circles*, Putnam, 1971; *I Never Danced at the White House*, Putnam, 1973; *The Bollo Caper*, Doubleday, 1974; *I Am Not a Crook*, Putnam, 1974; *Irving's Delight*, McKay, 1975.

WORK IN PROGRESS: A new book on President Ford.

SIDELIGHTS: One of the most successful humorous columnists in the U.S., Buchwald has invented a new Washington, D.C. where accidental peace is a constant threat. He was once concerned with the growing shortage of Communists in the U.S. and sympathized with party members whose ranks had been increasingly enlarged by the infiltration of FBI agents: "It isn't too farfetched to assume that in a couple of years the entire Communist Party will be made up of FBI informants." The informants would pay their dues, contrary to the regular members who do not. "In no time at all the Communists could become the leading political party in the country."

ART BUCHWALD

"The Art of Living," a play based on his observations but not written by him, ran six months in London.

FOR MORE INFORMATION SEE: Newsweek, February 13, 1956, December 4, 1961; *Editor and Publisher,* August 17, 1957; *Time,* October 3, 1960, June 22, 1962, September 20, 1963; *Look,* March 13, 1962; *New York Times,* May 14, 1967.

CASON, Mabel Earp   1892-1965
(Emily Mary Bell)

PERSONAL: Born March 7, 1892, in Corpus Christi, Tex.; daughter of William Harrison and Elizabeth (Fowler) Earp; married Ernest A. Cason, December 25, 1913; children: V. Rae (Mrs. C. W. Lindsay), Leonard E., Elizabeth Jeanne (Mrs. Bruce Laing), Walter D. *Education:* Attended San Fernando Academy. *Religion:* Seventh-Day Adventist. *Home:* Springmeadow Ranch, Whitmore, Calif. 96096.

CAREER: School teacher, Mohawk, Ariz., 1912-14; advertising artist, Phoenix, Ariz., 1929-34; high school art teacher, Los Angeles, Calif., 1934-44. Author and illustrator.

WRITINGS: Mary Had Ten Little Lambs, Southern Publishing, 1938; (with E. Oren Arnold) *Desert Plants and Animals,* Arizona Printers, 1940; (under pseudonym Emily Mary Bell) *Wolf at Our Door,* Pacific Press, 1948; (self-illustrated) *Ruggy the Mountain Buck,* Pacific Press, 1949; *Song of the Trail,* Pacific Press, 1953; *Desert Enchantment,* Review & Herald, 1963; *Spotted Boy and the Comanches,* Pacific Press, 1963.

Wrote "Key to the Treasure House," for "Voice of Prophecy" radio program, and five scripts for "Faith for Today" television program. Collaborated with E. O. Arnold on an illustrated weekly feature, "Some Wild Westerners You Should Know," for Los Angeles Times Syndicate, 1928-34. Contributor of juvenile and desert wildlife stories, many self-illustrated, to *Children's Friend, Youth's Instructor, Junior Guide,* and other periodicals.

WORK IN PROGRESS: South to the Californias, a book for youth; *By Sun and Star,* a biography of Edward J. Urquhart, missionary in the Orient and World War II prisoner in the Philippines; an illustrated feature series on wildlife; a biography of a missionary raised in the Congo; material on life of a Russian woman, a captive worker in Germany during World War II.

SIDELIGHTS: Competent in Spanish.

(Died April 25, 1965)

CEBULASH, Mel   1937-
(Ben Farrell, Glen Harlan, Jared Jansen, Jeanette Mara)

PERSONAL: Surname is pronounced *Seb*-yu-lash; born August 24, 1937, in Jersey City, N.J.; son of Jack (a mailman) and Jeanette (Duthie) Cebulash; married Deanna Penn, August 19, 1962 (divorced); children: Glen, Benja-min, Jeanette. *Education:* Jersey City State College, B.A., 1962, M.A., 1964; University of South Carolina, further graduate study, 1964-65. *Religion:* Jewish. *Home:* 51 West 90th St., New York, N.Y. 10024. *Office:* Scholastic Magazines, Inc., 50 West 44th St., New York, N.Y. 10036.

CAREER: Junior high school teacher of reading in Teaneck, N.J., 1962-64; Fairleigh Dickinson University, Rutherford, N.J., instructor in reading clinic, 1965-67; Scholastic Magazines, Inc., New York, N.Y., editor for language arts, 1966-72, editorial director, 1972-74, associate editor-in-chief, 1975—. *Military service:* U.S. Army, 1955-58. U.S. Army Reserve, 1958-61. *Member:* International Reading Association, Authors Guild, Mystery Writers of America. *Awards, honors:* Author Award of New Jersey Association of Teachers of English, 1969, for *Through Basic Training with Walter Young,* 1969; Author Award of Newark (N.J.) College of Engineering, 1972, for *The Ball That Wouldn't Bounce,* 1973, for *Baseball Players Do Amazing Things.*

WRITINGS: Monkeys, Go Home (adaptation of Walt Disney film script), Scholastic Book Services, 1967; *Through Basic Training with Walter Young,* Scholastic Book Services, 1968; *The Love Bug* (adaptation of Walt Disney film script), Scholastic Book Services, 1969; *Man in a Green Beret and Other Medal of Honor Winners,* Scholastic Book Services, 1969; *The Boatniks* (adaptation of Walt Disney film script), Scholastic Book Services, 1970; *The Ball That Wouldn't Bounce,* Scholastic Book Services, 1972; *Benny's Nose,* Scholastic Book Services, 1972; *The See-Saw,* Scholastic Book Services, 1972; *Willie's Pet,*

MEL CEBULASH

Benny hid behind a tree. He didn't want anyone to see him crying. ■ (From *Benny's Nose* by Mel Cebulash. Illustrated by Ib Ohlsson.)

Scholastic Book Services, 1972; (under pseudonym Glen Harlan) *Petey the Pup,* Scholastic Book Services, 1972; (under pseudonym Ben Farrell) *Nancy and Jeff,* Scholastic Book Services, 1972; (under pseudonym Jared Jansen) *Penny the Poodle,* Scholastic Book Services, 1972; *Baseball Players Do Amazing Things,* Random House, 1973; *dic-tion-ar-y skilz,* Scholastic Book Services, 1974; *Herby Rides Again* (adaptation of Walt Disney film script), Scholastic Book Services, 1974; *The Strongest Man in the World* (adaptation of Walt Disney film script), Scholastic Book Services, 1975; *Football Players Do Amazing Things,* Random House, 1975; *Basketball Players Do Amazing Things,* Random House, in press. Editor and author of much of the material in Scholastic Book Services "ACTION Reading Kit", 1970. Contributor of short stories to university literary journals. Contributing editor, *Scholastic Scope* (magazine). Contributor of short stories and plays to juvenile texts and magazines.

WORK IN PROGRESS: Coming Close, a novel.

SIDELIGHTS: "Writing was not a dream of my childhood. I was raised in a grim city in New Jersey, and I suppose my early childhood could be described as usual. Fortunately, my mother's deep respect for books led me to a library at a very early age, and reading allowed me to entertain all sorts of dreams and to become all sorts of people. I still believe that reading is the most important subject taught in school.

"In high school, I was a very poor and troublesome student, but more through choice than inability. I regarded the school library as the true place for learning and spent most of my free time there. After school, I worked, played ball and shared many adventures and misadventures with my brother and others. I followed high school with three years in the U.S. Army. The army proved to be an invaluable experience, as I was able to see much of the country and to develop a sense of discipline which later helped carry me through college and through some important writing deadlines.

"The idea of writing entered my mind when I was a senior in college. The first short story I tried was published, and although the stories that followed didn't meet with the same approval, my small measure of success was enough to sustain a continuing effort.

"Just before my first child was born, I left teaching and moved into writing and editing as a full-time activity. My parents and friends looked upon the move as the foolish pursuit of a far-fetched dream. Fortunately, years of reading had led me to believe in the possibility of dreams. My writing has ranged from picture book stories for children to books for adults. I have been especially interested in stories and books for young people who have difficulty in reading, and I suppose these efforts have been most rewarding to me.

Most of my fiction stems either directly or indirectly from experience. I use experience for ideas, but I allow the writing to shape the experience into something new—something that hasn't happened to me or anyone else.

"I've been pleased by the sales of my books, but my real joy in writing has come from the letters I've received from young people. When I think I'm all alone with a typewriter, I remind myself of the many friends I've made through writing."

HOBBIES AND OTHER INTERESTS: The literature and popular music of the 1930's, the works of James T. Farrell ("a friend and inspiration").

CEDER, Georgiana Dorcas (Ana Dor)

PERSONAL: Born in Chicago, Ill.; daughter of Robert and Karen Marie (Holtz) Ceder. *Education:* Columbia Business College, Chicago, Ill., student; special courses at North-

Like a flash she turned and straddled the pig, gripping the heaving sides with her knees. ■ (From *Reluctant Jane* by Georgiana Dorcas Ceder. Illustrated by Mimi Korach.)

western University; private music and language courses. *Religion:* Protestant. *Residence:* Chicago, Ill.

CAREER: Served in Turkey with Near East Relief; did secretarial work for a number of years. *Member:* Women's Overseas Service League, Women's National Book Association, Children's Reading Round Table, Archaeological Institute of America, Society of Midland Authors.

WRITINGS—Juveniles under pseudonym Ana Dor: *Ya-Ya,* Abingdon, 1947; *Ethan the Shepherd Boy,* Abingdon, 1948; *Ann of Bethany,* Abingdon, 1951; *Joel, the Potter's Son,* Abingdon, 1953; *Winter without Salt,* Morrow, 1962; *Reluctant Jane,* Funk, 1966; *Little Thunder,* Abingdon, 1966. Author of short stories for Science Research Associates; contributor of short stories and verse to youth magazines.

HOBBIES AND OTHER INTERESTS: Music, archaeology, the Middle East.

CHAPMAN, (Constance) Elizabeth (Mann) 1919-

PERSONAL: Born January 5, 1919, in Barnsley, Yorkshire, England; daughter of Hubert (a timber merchant) and Beatrice (Ward) Mann; married Frank Chapman (now a research director), November 22, 1941; children: Stephen Godfrey, Nicholas John, Simon Francis Mann. *Education:*

GEORGIANA DORCAS CEDER

ELIZABETH CHAPMAN

Barnsley Technical College, student, 1935-36. *Religion:* Church of England. *Home:* 88 Grange Gardens, Pinner, Middlesex, England.

CAREER: Secretary, 1936-40. Writer for children.

WRITINGS: Marmaduke the Lorry, 1954, *Marmaduke and Joe,* 1955, *Riding with Marmaduke,* 1956, *Merry Marmaduke,* 1957, *Adventures with Marmaduke,* 1958, *Marmaduke and His Friends,* 1959, *Marmaduke and the Elephant,* 1960, *Marmaduke and the Lambs,* 1961, *Marmaduke Goes to France,* 1962, *Marmaduke Goes to Holland,* 1963, *Marmaduke Goes to America,* 1965, *Marmaduke Goes to Italy,* 1970, *Marmaduke Goes to Switzerland,* in press (all published by Brockhampton Press). Writer of story series for *Sunny Stories* (children's magazine), and stories for British Broadcasting Corp. program, "Listen with Mother."

SIDELIGHTS: "As far back as I can remember, I have always been writing something. When I was a young girl, I wrote poetry and also, with a friend who later became a journalist, produced a small, monthly magazine, containing stories, articles, competitions, etc., typed by my friend's father, and distributed to friends and relations.

"Then there was the war, marriage and babies, and there didn't seem to be any time, but in the end, writing for children began because of illness. With two young sons going through measles and chicken-pox, one after the other, there came the awful day of complete boredom, when every book in the nursery was known almost by heart, and there was no-one to go to the library in the town. So I sat by their sides, and made up a story about an old red lorry, called Marmaduke, who lived in a small town in the county of Yorkshire, and travelled across the moors to a big town called Manchester. I had spent my childhood in a similar town in that county, and had known and loved the desolate moors, which were practically on my doorstep, in all weathers. This had been my world when I was young, and so this was where the old red lorry went on his first journey.

"Since then, Marmaduke's world has grown bigger, as mine did, and he has had many adventures in foreign countries. I never write about a country I have not myself visited, as all my stories stem from personal experiences and observations, so I am lucky in that I have had the opportunity to visit these places.

"Many people think that writing for children is easy, but in my experience this is not so. Before starting a story, one has to spend some time getting oneself on to the same fantasy level as children, and one has to make things *happen* all the time. I work in two different ways. Sometimes, I think of a story when I am doing housework or gardening. I mull over it perhaps for several days, and then, when it is clear in my mind, sit down and write it straight down.

"Other days, especially when I have to meet a deadline, I have to sit down at my desk and *think,* and make a start on a story, not really knowing how it is going to turn out. Sometimes, after much labouring, it works out there and then, but other times, I get really stuck in the middle of some situation, and cannot immediately see a way through. I go about my other tasks, turning it over and over in my mind, and always, at last, some solution occurs to me, and the story is finished.

"I still like writing better than anything else. I paint, and I garden, and I cook, and I still love walking over the moors when I get a chance, although this is not easy now that I live in London. However, these are secondary things, and there is nothing so satisfying as typing the last page of a new book, and then later, seeing it in print."

HOBBIES AND OTHER INTERESTS: Walking in Pennine Hills, good food and wine, gardening, painting in oils.

CHASE, Mary Ellen 1887-1973

PERSONAL: Born February 24, 1887, in Blue Hill, Me.; daughter of Edward Everett (a lawyer) and Edith (Lord) Chase. *Education:* University of Maine, B.A., 1909; University of Minnesota, M.A., 1918, Ph.D., 1922; graduate study in Germany, 1913, and postdoctoral study in England, 1923-26. *Religion:* Episcopalian. *Home:* 16 Paradise Rd., Northampton, Mass.

CAREER: University of Minnesota, Minneapolis, instructor, 1918-22, assistant professor of English, 1922-26; Smith College, Northampton, Mass., associate professor, 1926-29, professor of English literature, 1929-55, professor emeritus, 1955-73. *Member:* Phi Beta Kappa. *Awards, honors:* Litt.D. from University of Maine, 1929, Bowdoin College, 1933, Northeastern University, 1948, Smith College, 1949, Wilson College, 1957; L.H.D. from Colby College, 1937; Constance Lindsay Skinner Award, Women's National Book Association, 1956; LL.D. from Goucher College, 1960.

WRITINGS: The Girl from the Big Horn Country (juvenile), Page Co., 1916; *Virginia of Elk Creek Valley* (juvenile), Page Co., 1917; (with Frances K. Del Plaine) *The Art of Narration,* Crofts, 1926; *Mary Christmas* (juvenile), Little, Brown, 1926; *Uplands* (novel), Little, Brown, 1927; (editor with Margaret E. MacGregor) *The Writing of Informal Essays,* Holt, 1928; *The Golden Ass and Other Essays,* Holt, 1929; *Constructive Theme Writing for College Freshmen,* Henry Holt, 1929, 3rd edition, with Henry W. Sams, published as *Constructive Theme Writing,* Holt, 1957.

The Silver Shell (juvenile), Holt, 1930; *A Goodly Heritage* (autobiography), Holt, 1932; *Mary Peters* (novel), Macmillan, 1934; *Silas Crockett* (novel), Macmillan, 1935; *This England,* Macmillan, 1936 (published in England as *In England Now,* Collins, 1937); *Dawn in Lyonesse* (novel), Macmillan, 1938; *A Goodly Fellowship* (autobiography), Macmillan, 1939; *Windswept* (novel), Macmillan, 1941; *The Bible and the Common Reader,* Macmillan, 1944, revised edition, 1952; *Jonathan Fisher, Maine Parson, 1768-1847* (biography), Macmillan, 1948; *The Plum Tree* (novel), Macmillan, 1949.

Abby Aldrich Rockefeller, Macmillan, 1950; (editor) *Readings from the Bible,* Macmillan, 1952; *The White Gate,* Norton, 1954; (contributor of regional introduction) *Look at the U.S.A.,* Houghton, 1955; *Life and Language in the Old Testament,* Norton, 1955; *The Edge of Darkness,* Norton, 1957; *Sailing the Seven Seas* (juvenile), Houghton, 1958; *Donald McKay and the Clipper Ships* (juvenile biography), Houghton, 1959; *The Lovely Ambition* (novel), Norton, 1960; *The Fishing Fleets of New England* (juvenile), Houghton, 1961; *The Psalms for the Common Reader,* Norton, 1962; *The Prophets for the Common Reader,* Norton, 1963; *Victoria,* Norton, 1963; *Dolly Moses,* Norton, 1963; *Richard Mansfield, the Prince of Donkeys,* Norton, 1964; *Thomas Hardy from Serial to Novel,* Russell, 1964; (editor with others) *Values in Literature,* Houghton, 1965; *A Journey to Boston,* Norton, 1965; *The Story of Lighthouses,* Norton, 1965; *A Walk on an Iceberg,* Norton, 1966; (compiler) Sarah Orne Jewett, *The Country of the Painted Firs,* F. Watts, 1968; (editor with M. E. MacGregor) *The Writing of Informal Essays,* Books for Libraries, 1970.

Contributor of stories and reviews to newspapers and periodicals, including *New York Times, New York Herald Tribune, Atlantic Monthly, Yale Review.*

WORK IN PROGRESS: Books on the Old Testament.

SIDELIGHTS: Mary Ellen Chase began writing while in college. The author of over forty titles, she was constantly praised for her wit, human understanding, and scholarship.

Dawn in Lyonesse was adapted by Thomas Job for a three-act play.

... for perfection of design, amazing powers of endurance, and consistent speed under all conditions, in fair winds and foul, neither he nor any other builder ever surpassed the *Flying Cloud.* ■ (From *Donald McKay and the Clipper Ships* by Mary Ellen Chase. Illustration from the Peabody Museum.)

HOBBIES AND OTHER INTERESTS: Gardening and bird study.

FOR MORE INFORMATION SEE: Chicago Sunday Tribune, June 19, 1960; *New York Herald Tribune Book Review,* June 19, 1960; *San Francisco Chronicle,* July 1, 1960; *Christian Science Monitor,* October 9, 1963; Perry Dickie Westbrook, *Mary Ellen Chase,* Twayne, 1965; Carolyn Riley, editor, *Contemporary Literary Criticism,* Volume II, Gale, 1974.

(Died July 28, 1973)

CHERNOFF, Goldie Taub 1909-

PERSONAL: Born May 8, 1909, in Austria; daughter of Morris and Pauline (Mahler) Taub; married David Chernoff, November 25, 1959; children: Richard. *Education:* Attended Pratt Institute, Cooper Union College, and Columbia University. *Politics:* "Humane." *Residence:* Charlotte, N.C.

CAREER: Montefiore Hospital, Brooklyn, N.Y., occupational therapist, 1931-42; Jewish Sanitarium and Hospital, Brooklyn, N.Y., director of occupational therapy and recreation, 1946-50; Sephardic Home for the Aged, Brooklyn, N.Y., director of occupational therapy and recreation, 1951-56; Camp Fire Girls, Inc., New York, N.Y., arts and crafts specialist, 1956-71. Arts and crafts counselor at summer camps, 1929-33, 1955. Director, Children's Camp Program, Pine Park Hotel and Camp, 1946. *Member:* National Council of Jewish Women (group leader in recreation—Brooklyn section).

WRITINGS: Just a Box?, Scholastic Book Services, 1971; *Puppet Party,* Scholastic Book Services, 1971; *Pebbles and Pods: A Book of Nature Crafts* (*Horn Book* Honor List), Scholastic Book Services, 1973; *Clay-Dough Play-Dough,* Scholastic Book Services, 1974; *Easy Costumes You Don't Have to Sew,* Scholastic Book Services, 1975. Member of editorial staff, *Sephardic News, Camp Fire Girl,* and *Program Highlights.*

GOLDIE TAUB CHERNOFF

WORK IN PROGRESS: Cloth Magic, a how-to-do-it book in poetry; *String-A-Long.*

SIDELIGHTS: Goldie Taub Chernoff has organized anti-pollution action programs in New York City and has testified at public hearings. She is a member of the Charlotte Gray Panthers and is active in behalf of improving public transportation in Charlotte and community action programs.

"I have recently returned from one of my idea-gathering world trips, this time on a freighter to East Asian countries.

"My ideas come from my experiences working with young people, my art education, my travels, and my exploring mind. I am always alert to new ways of using old materials and old ways of using new materials. My concern for the environment is reflected in my many books, where the use of discarded materials are emphasized."

FOR MORE INFORMATION SEE: Horn Book, April, 1974; *Teacher,* March, 1975.

These puppets are paper bags. ■ From *Puppet Party* by Goldie Taub Chernoff. Illustrated by Margaret Hartelius.)

CLIFFORD, Harold B.   1893-
(Burt Farnham)

PERSONAL: Born May 21, 1893, in Winthrop, Me.; son of Edwin T. (a salesman) and Stella Mae (Farnham) Clifford; married Gladys L. Mower, July 3, 1917; children: Stella Dorothy Clifford Gray, George Edwin, Flora Elsie Clifford Majumder. *Education:* Bates College, A.B., 1916, M.A., 1941. *Politics:* Independent. *Religion:* Methodist. *Home:* East Boothbay, Me.

CAREER: Elementary school teacher, Franklin, Me., and secondary school teacher, Afred, Me., 1912-13, 1916-17; school administrator in Hartland Union, Me., 1917-25, in Boothbay Union, Me., 1925-56. *Member:* National Education Association, American Association of School Administrators, Maine Teachers Association, Maine School Superintendents Association, Phi Beta Kappa, Rotary. *Awards, honors:* Ed.D., University of Maine, 1956; Distinguished Service Award, American Association of School Administrators, 1960.

WRITINGS: America My Home, Scribner, 1940; *Canada My Neighbor,* Scribner, 1944; *Yesterday in America,* American Book Co., 1949; *American Leaders,* American Book Co., 1953; *Maine and her People,* Wheelwright, 1957; *Boothbay Region, 1906 to 1960,* Wheelwright, 1961; *Exploring New England,* Follett, 1961; *You and Your Job in Maine,* Wheelwright, 1964; *Charlie York, Maine Coast Fisherman,* International Marine Publishing Co., 1974.

WORK IN PROGRESS: Clear Sailing; Sea Horse.

SIDELIGHTS: Charlie York, Maine Coast Fisherman has been taped for a Talking Book.

HOBBIES AND OTHER INTERESTS: Gardening, stamp collecting, music, history.

COHEN, Barbara   1932-

PERSONAL: Born March 15, 1932, in New Jersey; daughter of Leo Kauder and Florence (an innkeeper; maiden name, Marshall) Kauder Nash; married Eugene Cohen (an innkeeper), September 14, 1954; children: Leah, Sara, Rebecca. *Education:* Barnard College, B.A., 1954; Rutgers University, M.A., 1957. *Religion:* Jewish. *Home:* 540 Foothill Rd., Bridgewater, N.J. 08807.

CAREER: High school teacher of English in the public schools of Tenafly, N.J., 1955-57, Somerville, N.J., 1958-60, and Hillsborough, N.J., 1970—. *Member:* National Education Association, Authors Guild, League of Women Voters, Hadassah, New Jersey Education Association, Phi Beta Kappa.

WRITINGS–Juveniles: The Carp in the Bathtub, Lothrop, 1972; *Thank You Jackie Robinson* (ALA Notable Book), Lothrop, 1974; *Where's Florrie?,* Lothrop, 1976; *Bitter Herbs and Honey,* Lothrop, 1976. Contributor to *New Jersey Education Association Review.* Author of column, "Books and Things," in *Somerset Messenger-Gazette,* 1967—.

WORK IN PROGRESS: Another juvenile book.

Mama was a wonderful cook. It was well known that she made the finest chicken soup in Flatbush. Also very good tsimmis, noodle kugel, mondel brioh, and stuffed cabbage. ■ (From *The Carp in the Bathtub* by Barbara Cohen. Illustrated by Joan Halpern.)

BARBARA COHEN

SIDELIGHTS: "I think I'm a writer because I spent my childhood listening to my relatives tell stories about each other. I don't write the stories they told, but I absorbed atmosphere and the tale-telling habit from them. All my writing is in some way inspired by my experience, but is only now and then a direct recounting of that experience. I did not set out to write children's books. I write what I want to write and it turns out to be for children. At least that's what my publishers tell me."

COLE, Lois Dwight
(Caroline Arnett, Lynn Avery, Nancy Dudley, Allan Dwight, Anne Eliot)

PERSONAL: Born in New York, N.Y.; daughter of Charles Buckingham and Bertha Woolsey (Dwight) Cole; married Turney Allan Taylor; children: Turney Allan, Jr., Linda Dwight. Education: Smith College, B.A. Religion: Member of Congregational Church. Home: 181 East 73rd St., New York, N.Y. Agent: Claire Smith, Harold Ober Associates, 40 East 49th St., New York, N.Y.

CAREER: The Macmillan Co., New York, N.Y., associate editor; Whittlesey House, New York, N.Y., editor; G. P. Putnam's Sons, New York, N.Y., editor; William Morrow and Co., New York, N.Y., senior editor; Walker & Co., New York, N.Y., senior editor; free lance editor and writer. Member: P.E.N., Cosmopolitan Club (New York).

WRITINGS: Under pseudonym Caroline Arnett, Melinda, Fawcett, 1975; Clarissa, Fawcett, 1976.

Under pseudonym Lynn Avery: Cappy and the River, Duell, Sloan & Pearce, 1960; Mystery of the Vanishing Horses, Duell, Sloan & Pearce, 1963.

Under pseudonym Nancy Dudley: Linda Goes to the Hospital, Coward, 1953; Linda Travels Alone, Coward, 1954; Linda's First Flight, Coward, 1955; Linda Goes to a TV Studio, Coward, 1956; Linda Goes on a Cruise, Coward, 1957.

Under pseudonym Allan Dwight: (With husband Turney Allan Taylor) Spaniard's Mark, Macmillan, 1932; (with Taylor) Linn Dickson, Confederate, Macmillan, 1934; (with Taylor) Drums in the Forest, Macmillan, 1936; (with Taylor) Kentucky Cargo, Macmillan, 1938; The Silver Dagger, Macmillan, 1959; Guns at Quebec, Macmillan, 1962; Soldier and Patriot: The Life of General Israel Putnam, Washburn, 1965; (with Taylor) To the Walls of Cartagena, Holt, 1967.

Under pseudonym Anne Eliot: Dorie of Dogtown Common, Abingdon, 1962; Return to Aylforth (adult novel), Meredith, 1967; Shadows Waiting (adult novel), Meredith, 1969; Stranger at Pembroke (adult novel), Hawthorn, 1971; Incident at Villa Rahmana (adult novel), Hawthorn, 1972; The Dark Beneath the Pines (adult novel), Hawthorn, 1974.

SIDELIGHTS: "Sometimes it is impossible for an author to know whence came an idea that developed into a book and sometimes it is quite clear, at the moment or later. The Allan Dwight books all came from reading histories, some person or incident that had special appeal. Spaniards Mark grew from a visit to the coast of Georgia and the ruins there. Linn Dickson, Confederate came about because my husband's grandfather was a captain under Stonewall Jackson and we put Linn in the battles where he had fought. Drums in the Forest was sparked by reading the splendid volumes of Francis Parkman on the history of Canada, the heroic and fascinating figure of Count Frontenac and the colorful and exciting background of 1687-1691. Kentucky Cargo came from reading accounts of the ·1790's travellers down the Ohio and Mississippi and the Spanish plot to separate the west from the east. A footnote in a history of Connecticut mentioned that the siege of Havanna in 1762, was the last time the Colonial and British troops fought side by side until World War I—how could a boy be with them? The Silver Dagger was my answer to that question. Guns at Quebec again came from Parkman and the excitement of the siege under Wolfe. To the Walls of Cartagena took a Virginia boy from Williamsburg to Jamaica and to that siege during the War of Jenkin's Ear in 1739. The short biography of General Putnam was a tribute to an admirable and patriotic figure.

"We always went to see the locale of each book. Of the two Lynn Avery books, Cappy and the River came from the early travellers and their accounts. The Mystery of the Vanishing Horses grew from a memory of something heard when I was young, about an island in a swamp near the Erie Canal and the business of stealing horses, but I have no idea where that came from, it just floated up from the subconscious.

"The Nancy Dudley books about Linda started when my own small daughter had to go to the hospital, and had no idea what it would be like, and I thought other children

LOIS DWIGHT COLE

might like to know ahead of time. The other titles were first situations for a little girl, six to eight.

"As for the Anne Eliot novels—*Return to Aylforth* grew from the possibility that a nurse's suitcase might not be searched; *Shadows Waiting* started with the line 'The night has a thousand eyes'; *Stranger at Pembroke* came about because a three-greats grandfather was murdered on the Natchez Trace, at the time of the Revolution and his papers stolen; *Incident at Villa Rahmana* was a tribute to Morocco because of a stay there; *The Dark Beneath the Pines* came from many, many summers spent in the Adirondacks, though its time is before the time I first knew the lakes and mountains. Caroline Arnett's *Melinda* came from wondering what would take an American girl to regency London and what might happen to her there."

HOBBIES AND OTHER INTERESTS: Travel and history.

CORCOS, Lucille   1908-1973

PERSONAL: Born September 21, 1908, in New York, N.Y., daughter of Joseph and Amelia (Abrams) Corcos; married Edgar Levy (an artist, writer, and teacher), May 7, 1928; children: David C., Joel C. *Education:* Art Students League, New York, N.Y., student, 1927-31. *Home:* 167 South Mountain Rd., New City, N.Y. 10956. *Agent:* McIntosh & Otis, Inc., 475 Fifth Ave., New York, N.Y. 10017.

One winter's night, when all the plain was white with moonlight, there was seen crossing it a great tall black horse, ridden by a man also big and equally black, carrying before him on the saddle a woman and a child. ■ (From *The Little Lame Prince* by Dinah Maria Mulock Craik. Illustrated by Lucille Corcos.)

CAREER: Artist and illustrator, with work including paintings, murals, full-page color reproductions for *Life, Vogue, Fortune,* and other national magazines, and book illustrations. Had one-man shows in New York; paintings exhibited at museums throughout United States, in Europe, and South America; represented in permanent collections of Whitney Museum of American Art, Museum of Tel Aviv, and in corporate and private collections; murals include "Kaleidoscope" for Waldorf Astoria Hotel, 1945. *Member:* Artists Equity Association (director, New York chapter, 1964-66), Audubon Artists. *Awards, honors:* Honorable mention award, first Portrait of America Show, 1944; Grumbacher purchase award, Audubon Artists, 1956.

WRITINGS–All self-illustrated: *Joel Gets a Haircut,* Abelard, 1952; *Joel Spends His Money,* Abelard, 1954; *Joel Gets A Dog,* Abelard, 1958; *From Ungskah One to Oyaylee Ten: A Counting Book for all Little Indians,* Pantheon, 1965; *The City Book,* Western, 1972.

Illustrator: *Treasury of Gilbert and Sullivan* (Book-of-the-Month Club selection), 1941; *Chicikov's Journey,* Limited Editions Club, 1944; Dinah M. Craik, *Little Lame Prince,* Grosset, 1946; *A Treasury of Laughter,* 1946; *Follow the Sunset,* 1952; *Women Today,* 1953; *The Picture of Dorian Gray,* Limited Editions Club, 1958; *Songs of the Gilded Age* (Book-of-the-Month Club selection), 1960; *Grimm's Fairy Tales,* four-volume edition, Limited Editions Club, 1962.

FOR MORE INFORMATION SEE: Life, July 12, 1954; Illustrators of Children's Books, 1946-56, Horn Book, 1958; Illustrators of Children's Books: 1957-1966, Horn Book, 1968; Washington Post Children's Book World, November 5, 1972.

(Died August, 1973)

CORMIER, Robert Edmund 1925- (John Fitch IV)

PERSONAL: Born January 17, 1925, in Leominster, Mass.; son of Lucien Joseph and Irma (Collins) Cormier; married Constance B. Senay, 1948; children: Roberta S., Peter J., Christine J., Renee E. Home: 1177 Main St., Leominster, Mass.

CAREER: Radio station WTAG, Worcester, Mass., writer, 1946-48; Telegram & Gazette, Worcester, Mass., reporter, 1948-55; Fitchburg Sentinel, Fitchburg, Mass., reporter, 1955-59, wire editor, 1959-66, associate editor and human interest columnist under pseudonym of John Fitch IV, 1969—; free-lance writer, 1966—. Parent Teachers Association, president, 1959-60. Member: L'Union St. Jean Baptiste d'Amerique. Awards, honors: News writing, top prize, Associated Press in New England, 1959, 1973; best newspaper column, K. R. Thomson Newspapers, Inc., 1974.

WRITINGS: Now and at the Hour, Coward, 1960; A Little Raw on Monday Mornings, Sheed, 1963; Take Me Where the Good Times Are, Macmillan, 1965; The Chocolate War (ALA Notable Book), Pantheon, 1974. Numerous short stories. Book review column, Fitchburg Sentinel.

WORK IN PROGRESS: A novel.

SIDELIGHTS: "I am always writing, going to the movies, reading books, enchanted with my wife and son and daughters."

FOR MORE INFORMATION SEE: Library Journal, June 1, 1960; Leominster Daily Enterprise, July 28, 1960; Fitchburg Sentinel, August 2, 1960.

CORWIN, Judith Hoffman 1946-

PERSONAL: Born November 14, 1946, in New York, N.Y.; daughter of Harry (in investments) and Mary Hoffman; married Jules Arthur Corwin (a United Nations official), October 4, 1969; children: Oliver Jamie. Education: Pratt Institute, B.F.A., 1969. Home and office: 333 East 30th St., New York, N.Y. 10016.

CAREER: Western Publishing, New York, N.Y., experimental toy division, 1969; Cherry and Shackelford Design, New York, N.Y., design assistant, 1969-1970; Parks, Recreation, Cultural Affairs, New York, N.Y., graphic designer, 1970-1971; free-lance illustrator, 1971—. Exhibitions: Society of Illustrators "Illustrator's 16" National Exhibition, 1974, "Illustrator's 18," 1976. Awards, honors: Keuffel and Esser design award, 1969; national intern program, Hallmark, Inc., summer 1968; guest editor, Mademoiselle Magazine, summer, 1969.

JUDITH HOFFMAN CORWIN

Instead of the voice, the thought is told with the face, hands, and body. ▪ (From Red Light Says Stop! by Barbara Rinkoff. Illustrated by Judith Hoffman Corwin.)

ILLUSTRATOR: Barbara Rinkoff, *Red Light Says Stop,* Lothrop, 1974; Herbert Zim, *Medicine,* Morrow, 1974; *UNICEF Coloring Book,* UNICEF, 1974; Malcolm Weiss, *666 Jellybeans,* T. Y. Crowell, 1975; Jim Krayer, *Captain Kangeroo Activity Book,* Platt, 1976; Alice Gilbreath, *Weaving,* Morrow, 1976.

SIDELIGHTS: "My work is varied, though I best enjoy drawing and stitchery. I like vibrant colors and a firm, controlled line. The vitality and imagination of children are my inspiration."

FOR MORE INFORMATION SEE: Print Magazine, November-December, 1973.

DeARMAND, Frances Ullmann

PERSONAL: Born in Springfield, Mo.; daughter of William (a realtor) and Caroline (Block) Ullmann; married

IT'S APRIL FOOL'S DAY! Fooled you again...no! ■ (From *A Very, Very Special Day* by Frances Ullmann De Armand. Illustrated by Tom Vroman.)

David William DeArmand (now U.S. representative of British printing firms), June 20, 1942. *Education:* Drury College, student, one year; Wellesley College, B.A. *Politics:* Democrat. *Home:* 370 Central Park West, New York, N.Y. 10025. *Agent:* McIntosh & Otis, Inc., 475 Fifth Ave., New York, N.Y. 10017.

CAREER: National Parent-Teacher, New York, N.Y., executive editor, 1931-37; *Calling All Girls,* New York, N.Y., editor, 1941-47; *Child Study,* New York, N.Y., executive editor, 1949-51; Doubleday & Co., encyclopedia managing editor, 1951-54; Junior Literary Guild, New York, N.Y., 1954-69, executive editor, 1961-69; free-lance editor. *Member:* American Association for the United Nations, American Civil Liberties Union, Citizens' Union, League of Women Voters.

WRITINGS: (Editor) *Never to Be Forgotten,* Dodd, 1943; *Girl Alive!,* World Publishing, 1947, revised edition, 1957; (managing editor) *The Encyclopedia of Child Care and Guidance,* Doubleday, 1954, revised edition, 1963; *A Very, Very Special Day* (Junior Literary Guild selection), Parents, 1963; (compiler) *When Mother Was a Girl: Stories She Read Then* (Junior Literary Guild selection), Funk, 1964.

Pamphlets: *Getting Along with Brothers and Sisters,* Science Research Associates, 1950; *Life with Brothers and Sisters,* Science Research Associates, 1952.

Contributor to *Family Circle, Family Life, Better Living,* other magazines.

HOBBIES AND OTHER INTERESTS: Theater, art galleries, other metropolitan pursuits; travel.

DeJONG, David C(ornel)   1905-1967 (Tjalmar Breda)

PERSONAL: Born June 9, 1905, in Blija, Friesland, The Netherlands; came to United States as child; son of Remmeren R. and Jantje (DeJong-Cornel) DeJong; married Helen Elizabeth Moffit (a medical librarian), June 29, 1945. *Education:* Calvin College, A.B., 1929; Duke University, M.A., 1932; also studied at University of Michigan, University of Wisconsin, Brown University. *Home:* 106 Francis St., Providence, R.I. *Agent:* Russell & Volkening, Inc., 551 Fifth Ave., New York, N.Y. 10017. *Office:* 5 Hayes St., Providence, R.I.

CAREER: Was a teacher of creative writing and fiction technique at Brown University, Providence, R.I., University of North Carolina, Chapel Hill, 1953, University of Rhode Island, Kingston, 1954-55; conductor of writers' workshops, University of Rhode Island, 1956-58; novelist-poet in residence, Vernon Court College, summer, 1966; free-lance writer. *Awards, honors:* Houghton Mifflin fellowship, 1938, for *Old Haven;* University of Minnesota, Rhode Island College, and Ford Foundation fellowships for writing.

WRITINGS: Belly Fulla Straw (novel), Knopf, 1934; *Old Haven* (novel), Houghton, 1938; *Light Sons and Dark* (novel), Harper, 1940; *Day of the Trumpet* (novel), Harper, 1941; *Benefit Street* (novel), Harper, 1942; *Across the*

The squirrel tried to dodge away, but between them was the tall, upright, golden harp. Luke the cat jumped so hard and the squirrel dodged off so crookedly that they both got tangled in the strings... ■ (From *The Squirrel and the Harp* by David Cornel DeJong. Illustrated by Jo Spier.)

Board (poetry), Harper, 1943; *With a Dutch Accent* (autobiography), Harper, 1945; *Domination in June* (poetry), Harper, 1946; *Somewhat Angels* (novel), Reynal, 1947; *Snow on the Mountain* (short stories), Reynal, 1949.

Two Sofas in the Parlor (novel), Doubleday, 1951; *The Desperate Children* (novel), Doubleday, 1952; *The Unfairness of Easter* (short stories), Talisman, 1959; *The Seven Sayings of Mr. Jefferson* (juvenile), Parnassus, 1959.

The Happy Birthday Umbrella (juvenile), Atlantic-Little, Brown, 1960; *The Birthday Egg* (juvenile), Atlantic-Little, Brown, 1962; *Outside the Four Walls of Everything* (poetry), Linden, 1962; *Looking for Alexander*, Atlantic-Little,

Brown, 1963; *Around the Dom* (juvenile), Holt, 1964; *Alexander, the Monkey Sitter* (juvenile), Atlantic-Little, 1965; *The Squirrel and the Harp* (juvenile), Macmillan, 1966; *Still Travelling on Sunday* (poetry collection), Windfall Press, in press; *Stay Alive, Eleanor* (novel), Windfall Press, in press; *Deciphering the Elephant* (poems), Wagon and Star Press, in press; *The Clumsy Yellow Bees* (stories), Wagon and Star Press, in press. Contributor to magazines and newspapers; has done several translations from the Dutch and Flemish. Editor, *Smoke* (poetry journal) for five years.

WORK IN PROGRESS: A novel; two more juveniles; the translation of Frisian Folk Tales.

SIDELIGHTS: Because of a spinal injury, DeJong's writing was cut off for three years, then limited to shorter material. Spoke Dutch, Frisian, German.

(Died September 5, 1967)

DIETZ, David H(enry) 1897-

PERSONAL: Born October 6, 1897, in Cleveland, Ohio; son of Henry W. and Hannah (Levy) Dietz; married Dorothy B. Cohen, 1918; children: Doris Jean Turner, Patricia Ann Morris, David H., Jr. *Education:* Western Reserve U., B.A., 1919. *Home:* 2891 Winthrop Rd., Shaker Heights, Ohio 44120. *Office:* The Cleveland Press, Cleveland, Ohio 44114.

DAVID H. DIETZ

Medicine began in the days of the cave men of the Old Stone Age. It is easy to see why this was so. ■ (From *All About Great Medical Discoveries* by David Dietz. Illustrated by Ernest Kurt Barth.)

CAREER: Cleveland Press, Cleveland, Ohio, member of editorial staff, 1915—; Scripps-Howard Newspapers, science editor, 1921—, writer of daily column on science and medicine, 1923—. Western Reserve University, Cleveland, Ohio, lecturer in general science, 1927—. Consultant to Surgeon General, U.S. Army, during World War II. Shaker Heights (Ohio) Library board of trustees, president. *Military service:* U.S. Army, World War I. *Member:* National Association of Science Writers (charter member, first president), Sigma Xi, Sigma Delta Chi, Omicron Delta Kappa; Rowfant, Oakwood, Mid-Day, and Play House clubs (all Cleveland); National Press Club (Washington). *Awards, honors:* Pulitzer Prize in journalism, 1937; Goodrich Award for distinguished public service, 1940; Westinghouse Distinguished Science Writers Award, 1946; Lasker Medical Journalism Award, 1954; Ohioana Career Medal, 1958; Grady Medal of American Chemical Society, 1961; Litt. D. from Western Reserve University, 1948; LL.D. from Bowling Green State University, 1954.

WRITINGS: The Story of Science, Dodd, 1931; *Medical Magic,* Dodd, 1937; *Atomic Energy in the Coming Era,* Dodd, 1945; *Atomic Science, Bombs and Power,* Dodd, 1954; *The New Outline of Science,* Dodd, 1972.

Books for young people: *All About Satellites and Space Ships,* Random House, 1958; *All About Great Medical Discoveries,* Random House, 1960; *All About the Universe,* Random House, 1965; *Stars and the Universe,* Random House, 1968.

SIDELIGHTS: In 1946, Dietz accompanied joint Army-

Navy Task Force One to Bikini Atoll for atomic bomb tests as newspaper correspondent and radio commentator. His books for adults have been translated into seventeen languages for publication in Europe, South America, and Israel. His youth books have been translated into Chinese, Persian, Italian, Arabic and Burmese.

HOBBIES AND OTHER INTERESTS: Playing violin, travel.

DILLARD, Annie   1945-

PERSONAL: Born April 30, 1945, in Pittsburgh, Pa.; daughter of Frank and Pam (Lambert) Doak; married Richard Henry Wilde Dillard (a poet and novelist), June 5, 1965 (divorced). *Education:* Hollins College, B.A., 1967, M.A., 1968. *Agent:* Blanche Gregory, 2 Tudor City Place, New York, N.Y. 10017. *Office: Harper's,* 2 Park Ave., New York, N.Y. 10016.

CAREER: Harper's Magazine, New York, N.Y., contributing editor, 1973—. *Member:* Author's Guild, P.E.N., Thoreau Society, Thoreau Lyceum, Phi Beta Kappa.

WRITINGS: Tickets for a Prayer Wheel (poems), University of Missouri Press, 1974; *Pilgrim at Tinker Creek,* Harper's Magazine Press, 1974. Contributor to *Atlantic Monthly, Sports Illustrated, Prose, Cosmopolitan, American Scholar,* and others. Columnist, *Living Wilderness,* 1973-75; *Harper's Magazine,* 1975—.

SIDELIGHTS: Of *Pilgrim at Tinker Creek,* Melvin Maddocks wrote in *Time* magazine: "To an age hooked on novelty, variety and pluralism, her message is as clear as William Blake's: 'See a world in a grain of sand'—if you dare. . . . She sums up herself and perhaps her species thus: 'I am a frayed and nibbled survivor in a fallen world.' But what she has done is bear witness to her mystery as no leeched turtle (and few living writers) could—in a remark-

PILGRIM
AT
TINKER
CREEK

by Annie Dillard

I live by a creek, Tinker Creek, in a valley in Virginia's Blue Ridge. . . . It's a good place to live; there's a lot to think about. The creeks — Tinker and Carvin's — are an active mystery, fresh every minute. Theirs is the mystery of the continuous creation and all that providence implies: the uncertainty of vision, the horror of the fixed, the dissolution of the present, the intricacy of beauty, the pressure of fecundity, the elusiveness of the free, and the flawed nature of perfection. ■ (From *Pilgrim at Tinker Creek* by Annie Dillard. Line drawing by author.)

Something about the Author

ANNIE DILLARD

able psalm of terror and celebration."

FOR MORE INFORMATION SEE: Horn Book, October, 1974.

DOUGLAS, Marjory Stoneman   1890-

PERSONAL: Born April 7, 1890, in Minneapolis, Minn.; daughter of Frank Bryant and Lilian (Trefethen) Stoneman; divorced. *Education:* Wellesley College, B.A., 1912. *Home:* 3744 Stewart Ave., Coconut Grove, Fla.

CAREER: Miami Herald, Miami, Fla., reporter, editor, 1915-22, book editor, 1941-47; American Red Cross in France, publicity department, 1917-20; University of Miami, Coral Gables, Fla., instructor in department of English, 1925-29, editor of University of Miami Press, 1960-63, director emeritus of University of Miami Press, 1963—. Hurricane House Publishers, Coconut Grove, Fla., president. *Military service:* U.S. Naval Reserve, 1917-18, yeoman first class. *Member:* Friends of University Library (president, 1960-66), Florida Anthropological Society, Florida Historical Association, Society of Women Geographers (Washington, D.C.), Friends of the Everglades (president, 1970). *Awards, honors:* Barhour Medal for Conservation; honorary Litt.D., University of Miami; Horton Hollowell fellowship, Wellesley College, 1966-67; Florida Audubon Society award, 1975, for conservationist of the year; Florida Wild Life Federation, Governor's Award, for conservationist of the year.

WRITINGS: The Gallows Gate (play), Baker, 1928; *The Everglades: River of Grass,* Rinehart, 1947; *Road to the Sun* (novel), Rinehart, 1951; *Freedom River* (junior novel),

Scribner, 1953; *Hurricane,* Rinehart, 1958; *Alligator Crossing* (junior novel), John Day, 1959; *The Key to Paris* (junior history), Lippincott, 1960; *Florida: The Long Frontier,* Harper, 1967. Fiction writer for *Saturday Evening Post* and other national magazines, and writer of articles and book reviews, 1924-40.

WORK IN PROGRESS: A biography of W. H. Hudson.

DOW, Emily R.   1904-

PERSONAL: Born May 26, 1904, in Exeter, N.H.; daughter of Albert N. and Florence (Griffin) Dow; married Winslow Eddy (an engineer), November 8, 1947; children: Carolyn (stepdaughter; Mrs. William Timbers). *Education:* Wheelock College, graduate, 1924; special courses at Rachel McMillian Nursery School (London, England), Columbia University, Vesper George Art School. *Religion:* Episcopalian. *Home and office:* Brumble Farm, Walnut Ave., North Hampton, N.H. 03862.

CAREER: Nursery school and kindergarten teacher before marriage; writer of books for children. *Member:* New Hampshire Arts and Crafts Society, Saffron and Indigo Society, Rye Beach Club, Rye Beach-Little Boars Head Garden Club, Guild of Strawberry Banke.

*WRITINGS—*Self-illustrated: *What Can I Do Now?,* Aladdin Books, 1950; *How to Make Doll Clothes: A Book for Daughters, Mothers, and Grandmothers,* Coward, 1953; *Brooms, Buttons, and Beaux: A World of Facts for Girls in Their Teens,* Barrows, 1957; *Of Parties and Petticoats: A World of Wonderful Things for Girls in Their Teens,* Barrows, 1960; *Toys, Toddlers, and Tantrums: The Baby Sitters Book,* Barrows, 1962; *Crafts for Fun and Fairs,* Barrows, 1964; *Now What Shall We Do?: The Family Book of Things to Do and Games to Play,* Barrows, 1966.

EMILY R. DOW

JANE CAMPBELL EDWARDS

EDWARDS, Jane Campbell 1932-
(Jane Campbell)

PERSONAL: Born March 31, 1932, in Miles City, Mont.; daughter of Christopher M. and Josephine (Gast) Campbell; married Richard B. Edwards (now a department manager for a grocery chain), September 26, 1953; children: Linda, Richard, Andrew, Sheila, Patrick. *Education:* Attended schools in San Francisco, Calif. *Politics:* Democrat. *Religion:* Catholic. *Home:* 1531 Queenstown Ct., Sunnyvale, Calif.

CAREER: Writer for young people.

WRITINGS: What Happened to Amy?, Lothrop, 1961; *Lab Secretary*, Bouregy, 1964; *The Houseboat Mystery*, Bouregy, 1965 (reprinted as *The Affair of the Albatross*, Lancer, 1974); *Island Interlude*, Bouregy, 1969; (with Gilbert Martinez) *The Mexican-American: His Life Across Four Centuries* (history text for eighth graders, California approved for use in schools), Houghton, 1973. Authored two units on Malaysia in *People in Change*, Addison-Wesley, 1975. Contributor of short stories to *Young Miss* (formerly *Calling All Girls*).

Under pseudonym Jane Campbell: *Carol Stevens: Newspaper Girl*, Bouregy, 1964; *Believe No Evil*, Bouregy, 1969.

WORK IN PROGRESS: Kilgarrom (adult "Gothic" novel).

EINSEL, Naiad

PERSONAL: Naiad sounds like "dry-ad"; born in Philadelphia, Pa.; daughter of Samuel (a grocer) and Esther (Ap-

taker) Giblan; married Walter Einsel (a designer/illustrator/sculptor), June 20, 1953; children: Leslie (Mrs. John Paul Bastoni), Hilary. *Education:* Pratt Institute, Graduate Certificate, 1947. *Home and Office:* 26 South Morningside Drive, Westport, Conn. 06880.

CAREER: Illustrator. *Seventeen Magazine,* New York, N.Y., assistant art director (promotion), 1947-48; Weintraub Agency, New York, N.Y., associate art director, 1948-51; CBS Radio, New York, N.Y., assistant art director (promotion), 1951-54. *Exhibitions:* Society of Illustrators, American Institute of Graphic Artists, Art Directors Club of New York. *Member:* Society of Illustrators. *Awards, honors:* American Institute of Graphic Artists, certificate of excellence, 1954, 1955, 1956; Art Directors Club of New York, certificate of merit, 1957; Society of Illustrators, citation for merit, 1970 (two), 1972, 1974, 1976 (two).

ILLUSTRATOR: (With husband Walter Einsel) William North Jayme and Roderick Cook, *Know Your Toes,* Clarkson Potter, 1963; Carlo Collodi, *Adventures of Pinocchio,* Macmillan, 1963; Evelyn White Minshull, *Nine Fine Gifts,* Parents', 1962; Maurice Sagoff, *Shrinklits,* Doubleday, 1970. Illustrations have appeared in most of the major magazines; has done several book jackets, record album covers, TV commercials, TV titles, package designs, and movie posters.

SIDELIGHTS: "Before Walter and I met, we had both been aware of each other's work in print and admired one another's style, probably because they were similar. I was working as an art director in the promotion department at CBS and Walter had the identical position at NBC. We met when he came over to CBS to apply for an opening at a better salary. He didn't get the job. He got me instead. During our courtship, whenever Walter picked me up at the office everyone hastily covered up his work out of fear that the spy from NBC would take back ideas with him.

"We discovered we had similar tastes in almost everything—the furnishings and colors of our apartments were interchangeable—we liked the same foods, antiques, people, animals, cars, and politics. So we decided to combine all of this under one roof, and since we liked one another also, we decided on a practical and romantic working arrangement: marriage.

"As we worked side by side our styles grew more alike, reflecting the influence we had on each other. There were times when I struggled to draw a pose in a particular fashion and Walter was able to draw it for me. I would then incorporate his sketch into my drawing. Sometimes he would have difficulties with his assignments and I would be able to help him with a suggestion or a sketch. We soon found that we could work interchangeably on drawings. This turned out to be especially useful when one or the both of us were under the pressure of a heavy work load. A job would come in and we would discuss it, to come up with an idea. Sometimes the person with the idea would do a rough exploratory sketch. Or the other would do the sketch from a verbal description, adding a certain personal touch. Then one of us (whichever felt like it or had more time) would develop the drawing, designing it a little more carefully, researching details when necessary. Now we discuss the result, suggesting perhaps a change here or there. The other may then refine it even more. If we are both

Something about the Author

A thousand woodpeckers flew in through the window and settled themselves on Pinocchio's nose. They pecked and pecked so hard at that enormous nose that in a few moments, it was the same size as before. ■ (From *The Adventures of Pinocchio* by C. Collodi. Illustrated by Naiad Einsel.)

NAIAD EINSEL

satisfied one of us will trace it carefully with a hard sharp pencil onto vellum paper, improving and refining it still further. This is the most enjoyable stage of the drawing.

The next step, of inking, is rather mechanical. If it is a two or three color job one of us will do the color overlays, which is also mostly mechanical and sometimes quite tedious. The most fun is applying color on a full-color assignment. Walt usually does this because he has a steadier hand. I am lazy and afraid of botching up all that intricate drawing. We use felt markers most of the time. We used to mix our own colors (we lean toward what printers call off-beat colors) but markers now come in such a wide variety of hues and values that we find almost every color we need. We can alternate on any step along the way toward completing a finished piece of art. It's usually a matter of convenience.

"The really great thing about collaborating is the freedom one has when one doesn't feel the responsibility of the job. I always work with greater ease on Walter's assignments than on my own. "Actually, we receive most of our assignments individually and work on them from start to finish pretty much on our own. It is only when the job is too complex or if we're working on a number of jobs with tight deadlines that we employ what we call the 'leapfrog

method.' We sign the finished illustration according to who received the assignment. If we are told that either of us can do the job or if the client thinks of us as a team, we both get credit for it (or we both get blamed!) Walter seldom asks for help unless he is really jammed, but I am eager to accept assistance whenever it's offered because my time is divided between my career and the duties of running a large and active household, with children, pets and plants.

"Last summer, when Walter was working day and night on a mechanical sculpture for a television commercial, I was working day and night on a campaign of full-page ads for him along with my own free-lance assignments. Since we think so much alike and have such similar tastes, it's easy to fill in for each other at any stage.

"We work in a pleasant studio on the second floor of our Victorian farmhouse. Our desks are separated by an old U.S. Navy map file cabinet that's great for storing proofs. Cork panels cover most of the walls, holding clippings, photos, posters and mementos we have collected over the years. We like to work late at night when all is quiet. No phones. No meals. No animals.

"A number of years ago we fell into the habit of making elaborate Valentines and birthday cards for each other. They often took the form of collages, with lettering or rubber stamps and old decorations incorporated into the designs. Each year these efforts became more complex: flaps opening, moving parts, etc. Walter started making them in third dimension. The first was a fish made of thin strips of balsa wood bent and glued, painted black and resembling delicate wrought iron. Then he carved a figure with internal whirling disks, a bird with a flowing wire tail. He developed these objects with more and more complexity. A whirl-a-gig man who tips his hat as he kicks his legs when you turn a crank; a man who bounces up and down as the horse he is riding raises and lowers his head when the tail is cranked; a figure representing Barbara Fritchie whose head flips back when her hand is pulled down, a painted tin flag raises out of her neck while the strains of *'The Stars & Stripes Forever'* come from a music box, deep within her bosom.

"These figures have increased in their complexity and size over the years and they threaten to take over our house. A number of them are life-size or larger. They ring bells, they light up. The Statue of Liberty actually embraces you. One man comes completely apart right before your eyes and goes back together again with the turning of a knob. They are all painstakingly carved, and then assembled after their intricate mechanism has been designed and installed, edged with brass, painted or stained, sometimes outfitted with wigs, buttons or lace, waxed and perched on handsomely crafted cabinets or pedestals.

"One of the most elaborate is a life-size gum machine man (for a tv commercial). He stands on copper stove pipe legs and has three arms. One waves a flag, one holds a megaphone to his moustachioed mouth and the other operates a lever that dispenses a pack of gum into a milk-glass tray attached to the cabinet that is the figure's torso.

"Walter works in the basement under a network of pipes and furnace vents that often leave their mark on his brow. It is only recently that he's had the luxury of a beautiful old wood lathe with dozens of handsomely handled cutters and a drill press. Until now he's managed to get along with a band saw and hand tools. The peg board over his workbench hangs heavy with a wild assortment of old gears and tools chosen not only for their utility but their form as well.

"In addition to the figures in every room, our house is filled with a collection of country antiques, trade signs, weather vanes and Tiffany lamps. Every wall is adorned with kitchen utensils, old tools, wheels, lanterns and scales. We have an old pump organ that he electrified with a small vacuum cleaner motor. There is an old IBM time clock and cabinet that houses our hi-fi. There are assorted clocks, crocks, jars, tobacco tins and countless other reminders of the past, chosen for their shape, color or design.

"We have many ferns and hanging plants. I seem to have a way with them and know how to talk to them and encourage them to flourish. If we were asked to design a house, it would probably look like this one. All the objects and decor look like our drawings and vice versa. The colors and patterns are those we favor in our work. Our house reflects our interests and our personalities, naturally.

"We designed four commemorative postage stamps for the U.S. Government, *'Progress in Electronics'*. I designed a commemorative bicentennial quilt for the town of Westport, Conn."

HOBBIES AND OTHER INTERESTS: Playing guitar (folk), banjo, mandolin and songwriting.

EINSEL, Walter 1926-

PERSONAL: Born October 10, 1926, in New York, N.Y.; son of Philip John (a structural engineer) and Ethel (Davis; a librarian) Einsel; married Naiad Giblan (an illustrator), June 20, 1953; children: Leslie (Mrs. John Paul Bastoni), Hilary. *Education:* Parsons School of Design, graduate, 1949. *Home and office:* 26 Morningside Drive South, Westport, Conn. 06880.

CAREER: Designer, illustrator, sculptor. National Broadcasting Company, New York, N.Y., assistant art director, 1951-54; *New York Times,* New York, N.Y., assistant art director, 1954-57. *Exhibitions:* Museum of Contemporary Crafts, New York, N.Y., people figures, 1964; face coverings, 1970; "Man and His World" (one man show), Montreal, sculptures, 1973; Fairtree Gallery, New York, N.Y., sculptures, 1975. *Military service:* U.S. Navy, 1944-46. *Member:* Society of Illustrators. *Awards, honors:* Art Directors Club of New York, certificate of excellence; Society of Illustrators, awards of merit have been given from time to time over the past fifteen years.

WRITINGS—Self illustrated: Did You Ever See?, Young Scott, 1963.

Illustrator: (With wife Naiad Einsel), William North Jayme and Roderick Cook, *Know Your Toes,* Clarkson Potter, 1963; S. J. Sackett, *The Cowboy Song Book,* Young Scott, 1965. Einsel's illustrations have appeared in most of the

did you ever see a deer? steer? ■ (From *did you ever see?* by Walter Einsel. Illustrated by the author.)

WALTER EINSEL

major magazines and he has done several book jackets, record album covers, TV commercials, TV titles, package designs, and movie posters.

ERLICH, Lillian (Feldman) 1910-

PERSONAL: Born March 7, 1910, in Johnstown, Pa.; daughter of Abraham and Bessie (Ginsburg) Feldman; married John Jacob Erlich (a stockbroker), April 14, 1930; children: John Lewi, Nina Erlich Singer. *Education:* Studied at Cornell University, 1927-29, Columbia University, 1929-30. *Politics:* Democrat. *Home:* 9621 S.W. 77th Ave., Miami, Fla. 33156.

CAREER: During early career was free-lance writer and editor, contributing to magazines for both adults and children; Junior Literary Guild at Doubleday, associate editor, 1963-69, 1972-73; Child Study Association of America, director of publications, 1968-72; free-lance writer and editor, 1973—. *Member:* Authors Guild.

WRITINGS: (With Eleanor Clymer) *Modern American Career Women* (teenage), Dodd, 1959; *What Jazz is All About* (teenage), Messner, 1962, revised, 1975; (with other staff members) *You, Your Child and Drugs,* Child Study Association, 1971. Weekly column for *New York Post,* 1947-50.

SIDELIGHTS: "The big event of my childhood was that I fell in love with the written word. We lived, at the time, in Johnstown, Pennsylvania, near a good public library where I became a steady customer. What a marvelous world unfolded there, stretching far beyond the hills that encircled my small valley town. I devoured books and lived for days in trembling expectation of the arrival of a new copy of *St. Nicholas Magazine.* It was not long before I tried creating the same magic myself. I was soon turning out reams of words—poems, stories, plays. My most ambitious project, I remember was a book on how to bring up children. I reasoned that only a child could point out the grievous errors made by grownups in this department—and I carefully hid the manuscript under the mattress of my bed.

"When I was twelve, we moved to Atlantic City, New Jersey, where I spent my high-school years. There I acquired another lifelong addiction—the sea. I am never happier than when I am within sight and sound and smell of salt water. My younger sister and I spent long summer days swimming in the surf or fishing from rickety, barnacled piers (and what a triumphal procession when we each carried home a small flounder).

"There was a period, too, when I entered contests. All I had to know was that someone, somewhere, was offering a prize for an essay or a short story—and my pencil flew. My winnings didn't exactly put me through high school, but they bolstered my determination to become a writer.

"I entered Cornell in 1927, at the peak of the 'Roaring Twenties.' My English classes were particularly fine; one of my instructors went on to become a famous literary critic. During my freshman year, I met the young man who later became my husband. He was a native New Yorker and eventually returned to his home to enter a business career. I joined him there and became a New Yorker by marriage.

"During the depression years, I worked in a number of jobs, some of them related to writing. I was a reporter, for example, on a fashion trade paper, and an advertising copywriter in a Brooklyn department store. I also worked as a comparison shopper for a Fifth Avenue department store, a job that required the combined talents of a marathon walker and an F.B.I. agent. Later, I contributed articles to magazines, wrote a weekly newspaper column, and edited a children's periodical.

"As a reader, writer, and a natural-born gossip, I have always been fascinated by biography. I wrote *What Jazz is All About* because I have always loved this unique American music. My father sang black songs he had picked up in his travels about the country, and I had several musical uncles who collected jazz records—so I had an early introduction to the stirring new music that was evolving during my childhood. Later, in New York, I had the extraordinary good fortune to hear some of the greatest artists of jazz history—Louis Armstrong, Duke Ellington, Charlie Parker, and dozens more. I noted that there were no comprehensive histories of this music and its performers written especially for teenagers and young adults—a gap in the library shelves that I was eager to fill. The original book was published in 1962. When we moved to Florida, I had time once more to plunge into the world of jazz concerts, radio stations, and recording studios; and I completely updated the original book—right up to today's jazz-rock.

LILLIAN ERLICH

"Young people who are interested in becoming writers should know that it's hard but rewarding work. Someone once said that writing a book is like crossing the Atlantic Ocean in a rowboat. But what a lovely feeling when you reach the other shore. The best preparation is, of course, to read and write as much as possible. Also, learn to do research. There are endless sources beyond the usual dictionaries and encyclopedias on library shelves; and looking up an obscure bit of history or a little-known fact can be as interesting as unraveling a detective mystery."

EVANS, Mari

PERSONAL: Born in Toledo, Ohio; divorced. *Education:* Attended University of Toledo. *Home:* 750 West Tenth St., Indianapolis, Ind. 46202. *Office:* Afro-American Department, Memorial Hall West, Indiana University, Bloomington, Ind. 47401.

CAREER: Indiana University—Purdue University at Indianapolis, instructor in Black literature and writer-in-residence, 1970-71; Indiana University, Bloomington, assistant professor of Black literature and writer-in-residence, 1971-76. Producer, director, writer for television program, "The Black Experience," WTTV, Indianapolis, 1968-73. Visiting assistant professor, Northwestern University, 1972-73; has lectured and read at numerous colleges and universities. Consultant to Discovery Grant Program, National Endowment for the Arts, 1969-70; consultant in ethnic studies, Bobbs-Merrill Co., 1970-73. Member of literary advisory panel, Indiana State Arts Commission; chairman, State-

wide Committee for Penal Reform; member of Fall Creek Parkway YMCA Board of Management; board of directors, Marion County Girls Clubs of America. *Member:* Authors Guild, Authors League of America. *Awards, honors:* John Hay Whitney fellow, 1965-66; Woodrow Wilson Foundation grant, 1968; Indiana University Writers' Conference award, 1970, and Black Academy of Arts and Letters first annual poetry award, 1971, for *I Am a Black Woman;* Doctor of Humane Letters, Marion College, 1975; MacDowell fellow, 1975.

WRITINGS: Where Is All the Music? (poems), P. Breman, 1968; *I Am a Black Woman* (poems), Morrow, 1970; *J.D.* (juvenile), Doubleday, 1973; *I Look at Me* (juvenile), Third World Press, 1974; *Jim Flying High* (juvenile), Doubleday, in press. Poetry is represented in anthologies and textbooks including *A Rock Against the Wind,* Dodd,; *Black American Literature,* Glencoe Press; *Black Literature in America,* McGraw; *Black Out Loud,* Macmillan; *Black Poets,* Bantam; *Black Voices,* New American Library; *Understanding the New Black Poetry,* Morrow; *Dark Symphony,* Free Press; *Psyche,* Dial; *Premier Book of Major Poets,* Fawcett Premier Books; *Poetry of Black America,* Harper; *Major Black Writers,* Scholastic. Contributor to *Phylon, Okike, Black World* (formerly *Negro Digest*), *Iowa Review, Dialog,* and other periodicals.

SIDELIGHTS: Mari Evans, notes a *Virginia Quarterly*

MARI EVANS

Kicking the bottle is fun. The bottle takes you to all kinds of interesting places. Kicking a bottle is more fun than kicking a can. You have to be better to do it. J D could steer a bottle all the way from the grocery store home without breaking it. ■(From *J D* by Mari Evans. Illustrated by Jerry Pinkney.)

J D

Mari Evans

Doubleday

JD

by Mari Evans

Illustrated by Jerry Pinkney

Review writer, "is a powerful poet. Her craftsmanship does not interfere with the subject she treats with a fullness born of deep caring. She subtly interweaves private and public Black frustration and dignity with an infectious perception. Sparseness of speech belies a command of the language and knowledge of the Black experience.... We need to hear this authentic voice again and again, for there is strength in exquisitely revealing expressions of ghetto dynamics."

Ms. Evans' poetry has been used on record albums, television specials, and in two Off-Broadway productions: "A Hand Is on the Gate," and "Walk Together Children."

Her poems are included in the following record albums: "Beyond the Blues," Argo; "A Hand Is on the Gate," Folkways; "Walk Together Children," Spoken Arts; "Conflict," Holt; "Poetry, Song, Drama Level 3," Macmillan Gateway English; "Spectrum in Black," Scott, Foresman; "Black Poems, Black Images," Warren Schloat; "I've Got to Know," Kimbo Educational Records.

FOR MORE INFORMATION SEE: Library Journal, December 15, 1974.

FAIRMAN, Joan A(lexandra)   1935-

PERSONAL: Born April 11, 1935, in Philadelphia, Pa.; daughter of Alexander Daisley and Florence (Wenner)

He ran down the hill with his fishing equipment under his arm, food in a neat pack on his back, and Penny close at his heels.
■ (From *A Penny Saved* by Joan A. Fairman. Illustrated by Haris Petie.)

Fairman. *Education:* Peirce Junior College, graduate, 1953. *Politics:* Republican. *Religion:* Episcopalian. *Home:* 4147 Elbridge St., Philadelphia, Pa. 19135.

CAREER: Curtis Publishing Co., Philadelphia, Pa., executive secretary, 1953-70; Towers, Perrin, Forster & Crosby, Inc. (management consultants), Philadelphia, Pa., executive secretary, 1970—.

WRITINGS: (Contributor) Margaret Early, E. K. Cooper, Nancy Santeusanio, Marian Adell, editors, *Widening Circles,* Harcourt, 1970; *A Penny Saved,* Lantern Press, 1971. Contributor to national children's magazines, including *Jack and Jill* (author of "Baba Yaga" serial) and *Ranger Rick's Nature Magazine.*

WORK IN PROGRESS: Short stories for *Jack and Jill;* continuation of "Baba Yaga" serial.

FARR, Finis (King)   1904-

PERSONAL: Born December 31, 1904, in Lebanon, Tenn.; son of Finis King and Ethel (Riley) Farr. *Education:* Princeton University, A.B. (cum laude), 1926. *Agent:* Brandt & Brandt, 101 Park Ave., New York, N.Y. 10017.

CAREER: Free-lance writer. *Military service:* U.S. Army, Infantry, 1942-46; served in China, Burma, India Theater; became major. *Member:* Authors League of America.

WRITINGS: Frank Lloyd Wright: A Biography (British Book Society selection), Scribner, 1961; *Black Champion: The Life and Times of Jack Johnson* (American Heritage Book Club selection), Scribner, 1964; *Margaret Mitchell of Atlanta: The Author of "Gone With the Wind,"* Morrow, 1965; *The Elephant Valley* (novel), Arlington, 1966; *FDR* (biography), Arlington, 1969; *Chicago, A Personal History,* Arlington, 1970; *O'Hara* (biography), Little, Brown, 1973; *Fair Enough: The Life of Westbrook Pegler,* Arlington, 1975; *Rickenbacker's Luck* (biography), Houghton, 1976. Has contributed articles and fiction to *Saturday Evening Post, Sports Illustrated, National Review, Cosmopolitan, Town and Country, Ladies' Home Journal, McCall's, Diplomat,* other magazines.

SIDELIGHTS: Frank Lloyd Wright: A Biography was selected by the English-Speaking Union for distribution abroad and was placed in the White House Library by Booksellers of America. Farr's books have been translated throughout the world.

FELLOWS, Muriel H.

EDUCATION: University of Pennsylvania, B.S. (cum laude) and M.A.

WRITINGS—Books for children: The Land of Little Rain (Junior Literary Guild selection), Winston, 1936; *The Magic Painter* (Junior Literary Guild selection), Winston, 1938; *Ancient Aztecs,* Franklin Publishing, 1974.

By the fifteenth century, the Aztecs had conquered most of the tribes living in the valley of Mexico. ■ (From *Ancient Aztecs* by Muriel H. Fellows. Illustrated by the author.)

FERAVOLO, Rocco Vincent 1922-

PERSONAL: Born May 12, 1922, in Newark, N.J.; son of Michael R. and Angelina (DiCicco) Feravolo; married Beatrice Tartaglia, 1948; children: Angela, Michael. *Education:* Attended Seton Hall University, 1941-1943, University of Michigan, 1943-1944; Montclair State College, B.A. (magna cum laude), 1948, M.A., 1950; Rutgers University, graduate study. *Home:* Yardley Rd., Mendham, N.J. *Office:* George Washington School, Morris St., Morristown, N.J.

CAREER: Newark State College, Newark, N.J., fencing coach, 1942-43; Morris Plains Borough School, Morris Plains, N.J., teacher, 1948-52; Drew University, Madison, N.J., fencing coach, 1949-68; George Washington School, Morristown, N.J., teacher, 1952-53, principal, 1954-68; Lafayette School, Morristown, N.J., principal, 1953-54; Newark State College, Union, N.J., part-time instructor, 1956-64; Fairleigh Dickinson University, Madison, N.J., instructor, 1965-66; Morristown Public Schools, Morristown, N.J., assistant superintendent for curriculum, 1968-72; Morris School District, Morris, N.J., secondary supervisor, 1972—. *Military service:* U.S. Army, 1943-46, attaining rank of sergeant.

MEMBER: Authors' Guild, National Elementary Principals' Association, National Education Association, National Association for the Advancement of Colored People, National Fencing Coaches Association, National Association for Supervision and Curriculum Development, Aircraft Owners and Pilots Association, Amateur Fencing League of America, New Jersey Science Association, New Jersey Education Association, New Jersey Principals' Association, New Jersey Association for Supervision and Curriculum Development, Morris County Authors' Association, Morris County Education Association, Morris County Elementary Principals Association, Phi Lambda Pi, Kappa Mu Epsilon,. Salle D'Armes Santelli (New York). *Awards, honors:* National Science Teachers Award, 1956, for project "Elementary Astronautics for the Gifted Child in Science," New Jersey Teachers of English Award for *Around the World in Ninety Minutes.*

WRITINGS: Junior Science Book of Flying, Garrard, 1960; *Junior Science Book of Electricity,* Garrard, 1960; *Junior Science Book of Magnets,* Garrard, 1960; *Junior Science Book of Light,* Garrard, 1961; *Wonders of Sound,* Dodd, 1962; *Junior Science Book of Weather Experiments,* Garrard, 1963; *Wonders of Mathematics,* Dodd, 1963; *Junior Science Book of Heat,* Garrard, 1964; *Wonders of Gravity,* Dodd, 1965; *Junior Science Book of Water Experiments,* Garrard, 1965; Teachers Manual ("Science 3" textbook series), Silver Burdett, 1965; *Third Grade Science Book* (part of a new K-6 program), Silver Burdett, 1965; *Easy Physics Projects,* Prentice-Hall, 1966; *Wonders Beyond the Solar System,* Dodd, 1968; *More Easy Physics Projects,* Prentice-Hall, 1968; *Around the World in Ninety Minutes,* Lothrop, 1968. Contributor to *New Jersey Educa-*

Without gravity, one would drift in free orbit, enjoying the peacefulness of space. Of course, you would have a line attached to the station so that you wouldn't wake up and find that you had drifted into outer space. ■ (From *Wonders of Gravity* by Rocco Feravolo. Illustrated by Robert Bartram.)

tion Review, Children's Digest, Effective Reading.

WORK IN PROGRESS: Where Has All the Fresh Air Gone, a true story about pollution.

SIDELIGHTS: "Writing and painting have been 'hobbies' for many years, even back to my high school days. During my beginning years as a teacher, I was deeply concerned about making science teaching a 'work experience' for children. I conducted many science workshops that involved the students as the active participants in the learning process. It was this concern that gave me the initial impetus to write practical science books for children.

"Several years ago, I obtained my private pilot's license, and plan to use this experience to eventually write a book about what it takes to fly, from the first ride with the instructor to the private pilot's license. My love for flying and my ability as a writer will soon be coupled to provide a book that will be different.

"A writer must be active in many fields if he plans to write about them. My leisure time is usually spent in the cockpit of a plane or with a sword in my hand practicing one of my first loves—fencing. During the summer, I can usually be found on my twenty-seven-foot cabin cruiser scrubbing the deck or on the ocean blue."

Rocco Feravolo fenced in South America in 1960 in the Aruba Sports Olympics and won a silver medal in sabre and a bronze medal in foil. He was a member of the National Interscholastic Fencing Championship Team and the Eastern Intercollegiate Fencing Championship Team. His original manuscripts were selected to be part of the de-Grummond collection at the Southern Mississippi University library. His book, *The Wonders of Sound,* has been published in Portuguese, and is being used in Brazil in a cultural exchange program.

FOR MORE INFORMATION SEE: Christian Science Monitor, November 29, 1968.

FERN, Eugene A. 1919-

PERSONAL: Born September 29, 1919, in Detroit, Mich.; son of Joseph and Frances (Crystal) Fern; married Claire Ginsberg (a nursery school director), September, 1947; children: Marica, Arnold. *Education:* Columbia University, B.S., 1946, M.A., 1947. *Home:* 1085 McKinley St., Baldwin, Long Island, N.Y. *Agent:* McIntosh and Otis, 475 Fifth Ave., New York, N.Y. 10017. *Office:* New York City Community College, 13 Pearl St., Brooklyn, N.Y.

CAREER: First Machinery Corp., Bridgeport, Conn., machinist, 1940-42; New York City Community College, Brooklyn, N.Y., professor of art, 1947—; Fern Studios, Brooklyn, N.Y., artist, commercial illustrator and designer, 1950—. *Military service:* U.S. Army Air Forces, 1942-45; served in Alaska; became sergeant. *Member:* Committee on Art Education. *Awards, honors: Parents' Magazine* award for *What's He Been up to Now?,* 1961; painting awarded first honorable mention, Brooklyn Museum, 1950.

WRITINGS—Author, illustrator: *Pepito's Story* (Junior Literary Guild selection), Ariel Books, 1960; *The Most*

EUGENE A. FERN

Frightened Hero, Coward, 1960; *What's He Been up to Now?,* Dial, 1964; *The King Who Was Too Busy,* Farrar, Straus, 1966; *Birthday Presents,* Farrar, Straus, 1967; *Lorenzo and Angelina,* Farrar, Straus, 1968.

Illustrator: *The Little Bear's Mother,* Farrar, Straus, 1959; *The Library Mice,* Farrar, Straus, 1962; Lace Kendall, *The Mud Ponies,* Farrar, Straus, 1963.

Writer of television series for Leather Industries of America, 1960-62.

HOBBIES AND OTHER INTERESTS: All areas of creative expression, including music, dance, literature, and architecture.

FISCHBACH, Julius 1894-

PERSONAL: Born April 25, 1894, in Huntington, W.Va.; son of Julius Hoffman (a timekeeper) and Mary (Woody) Fischbach; married Mary Mildred Bibb, June 17, 1925; children: David Bibb, Mary Ellen (Mrs. William H. Heater). *Education:* University of Michigan, A.B., 1917; Southern Baptist Theological Seminary, Th.M., 1920. *Politics:* Republican. *Home:* 1122 North Genesee Dr., Lansing, Mich. 48915.

CAREER: Baptist minister at churches in Mount Hope, W.Va., 1920-25, Morgantown, W. Va., 1925-36, First Baptist Church, Lansing, Mich., minister, 1936-61, pastor emeritus, 1961—; Peoples Church, East Lansing, Mich., associate minister, 1972. Interim minister in Michigan, Rhode Island, Utah, Wisconsin, Minnesota, Washington, and California, 1961-66. Guest preacher in Scotland and England, 1951; preacher on world tour of missions, 1955. West Virginia Baptist Assembly, president, 1933-36; American Baptist Convention, member of general council, 1947-53, chairman of national advisory committee on juvenile

JULIUS FISCHBACH

protection, 1954-56; Michigan Baptist Convention, president, 1955-58; Trustee of Alderson-Broaddus College, 1932-36; Hillsdale College, 1945-54. Daily radio program, "Thought for the Day," 1950-63. *Member:* Kiwanis Club (president, Lansing, Mich., 1961), Inter-City Wranglers Club. *Awards, honors:* D.D., Hillsdale College, 1943; Legion of Honor, Kiwanis Club, 1971.

WRITINGS: Squaring Up, Judson, 1941; *Story Sermons for Boys and Girls,* Abingdon, 1947; *Sermonettes for Boys and Girls,* Revell, 1949; *Children's Sermons in Stories,* Abingdon, 1955; *Talks for Children on Christian Ideals,* Abingdon, 1959; (self-illustrated) *The Children's Moment,* Judson, 1966. Stories included in *A Treasury of Story Sermons for Children,* Harper. Contributor of articles to religious journals.

SIDELIGHTS: "To begin with, I am a Christian minister. I came to this profession by compulsion. In my younger days I had some experience in many vocations, having worked as secretary in the office of the American Car and Foundry Co., the DuPont Power Co., a law office, an architect's office and a bank. All of these had their attractive features but the *call* to the ministry was stronger than all the rest and, after an A.B. degree at the University of Michigan and a masters degree at the Southern Baptist Seminary in Louisville, Kentucky, I was ordained to the Christian ministry and have served in this capacity for fifty-seven years.

"I have always loved children and seem to have a natural ability to deal with them. It has been my conviction all through my ministry that children are perhaps the most important group in the church family. In all my pastorates I

have included a children's section in the morning worship service, calling the children down to the front for a story before sending them to their classes. I was led to write books of children's stories because I could not find the material I needed for my own program. Furthermore, I wished to make each children's story an integral part of the morning worship. Using the same bible text I had chosen for the adult sermon, I wove a story for the children as an illustration of this text. In this way I felt the family was being tied together in the worship service. As time went on and more and more stories were needed, I wrote more books. It has been my privilege to travel extensively in this country, in Europe, and around the world. Naturally many of my stories have been inspired by experiences and observations from near and far away.

"Since childhood I have enjoyed drawing and painting, particularly pen sketches and oils. I made sketches for one of my books, *The Children's Moment,* and was delighted that they were accepted and used by the publisher."

HOBBIES AND OTHER INTERESTS: "Fly fishing for trout, golf, oil painting, watching baseball and football games, tennis outdoors and volleyball indoors. The latter two have been dropped in recent years."

FOSTER, Doris Van Liew   1899-

PERSONAL: Born November 9, 1899, in Bellaire, Mich.; daughter of Leon Gray and Georgia (Knapp) Van Liew; married, 1922, divorced, 1946; children: Virginia Foster Springer, H. Max, Eleanor Foster Vloedman, Derk, Jr. *Education:* Western State Normal College (Kalamazoo, Mich.), student, 1918-20. *Politics:* Republican. *Religion:* Protestant. *Home:* 7421 S.W. 53rd Pl., Miami, Fla. 33143.

CAREER: Public schools, Jackson, Mich., teacher, 1921; Emergency Day Care Center, Indianapolis, Ind., teacher, 1944-45; Indianapolis Day Nursery, supervisor and teacher of branch nursery, 1945, until retirement in mid-1960's.

WRITINGS: Tell Me Little Boy, 1953, *Tell Me Mr. Owl,* 1957, *A Pocketful of Seasons* (Junior Literary Guild selection), 1961, *Honker Visits the Island,* 1962, *Feather in the Wind: The Story of a Hurricane,* 1972 (all published by Lothrop).

SIDELIGHTS: "I was born when the prevailing lifestyle in my small town was simple. A friendly neighborhood encompassed my child world. Nature played a prominent role. The changing seasons provided their accompany of activities and pleasures. All of nature was important to my well-being, it still is, along with daily reading, especially poetry.

"Living with children informally, such as a day nursery, was conducive to my attempting not to write a juvenile book but rather to talk to children. I was fortunate to be able to listen when at rare moments they revealed glimpses only pertinent to childhood. Such moments were at story time or on the play-yard. For instance, one day the bright sun was momentarily hidden by a dark cloud and a surprised child looking up into the sky asked 'Teacher who turned out the light?'

Sometimes the winds whip a frothy flounce
on a blue petticoat sea.
Or perhaps the winds stay hushed,
leaving the sailboat rocking helplessly. ■
(From *A Pocketful of Seasons* by Doris Van Liew Foster.
Illustrated by Talivaldis Stubis.)

"One of the charms of retirement (I loathe the word) is that I have the choice of taking many a beckoning path without a watch in my pocket. Time to have that leisurely cup of coffee mornings, time to change my mind at will without dire results, time to observe the world about me.

DORIS VAN LIEW FOSTER

"I am not a joiner but I treasure a few close friends, enjoy traveling and most important sharing in family activities be it camping, picnicking, whatever. I welcome the trust of my grandchildren, the family dogs and a neighborhood cat. I spend less and less time writing but this saying is above my desk: 'If I keep a green bough in my heart, the singing bird will come.'"

FOSTER, Elizabeth   1905-1963

PERSONAL: Born July 1, 1905, in Cleveland, Ohio; daughter of Maximilian (writer, playwright) and Elizabeth (Dickson) Foster; divorced; children: Mariana Mann Smith, Nancy Mann Israel. *Education:* Attended Miss Porter's School, Farmington, Conn., 1919-21, Art Students League of America, Columbia University. *Home:* Rangeley, Me. *Agent:* Howard Moorepark, 440 East 79th St., New York, N.Y. 10021; A. P. Watt & Son, Hastings House, Norfolk St., Strand, London, W.C.2, England.

CAREER: Free-lance writer. *Member:* Colony Club (New York, N.Y.).

WRITINGS: Singing Beach, Harper, 1941; *The Days Between,* Harper, 1942; *Dirigo Point,* Harper, 1943; *Gigi, The Story of a Merry-Go-Round Horse* (juvenile), Houghton, 1943; *Gigi in America* (juvenile), Houghton, 1945; *The Islanders,* Houghton, 1946; *The House at Noddy Cave* (juvenile), Houghton, 1947; *Children of the Mist,* Macmillan, 1961. Contributor to magazines.

(Died, 1963)

FRANCIS, Dorothy Brenner 1926-

PERSONAL: Born November 30, 1926, in Lawrence, Kan.; daughter of Clayton (a district judge) and Cecile (Goforth) Brenner; married Richard M. Francis (a professional musician), August 30, 1950; children: Lynn Ann, Patricia Louise. *Education:* University of Kansas, Mus.B., 1948. *Politics:* Republican. *Religion:* Methodist. *Home:* 1505 Brentwood Ter., Marshalltown, Iowa 50158.

CAREER: Band and vocal instructor in Orange, Calif., 1948-50, Pleasant Hill, Mo., 1950-51, Cache, Okla., 1951-52, and Gilman, Iowa, 1961-62; now teaches piano and trumpet privately, and directs a Methodist junior high choir. Community Chamber Orchestra, Marshalltown, board member, 1967. *Member:* Mystery Writers of America, P.E.O. Sisterhood, Marshalltown Tuesday Music Club (former president), Mu Phi Epsilon.

WRITINGS: Adventure at Riverton Zoo, Abingdon, 1966; *Mystery of the Forgotten Map,* Follett, 1968; *Laugh at the Evil Eye,* Messner, 1970; *Another Kind of Beauty,* Criterion, 1970; *Hawaiian Interlude,* Avalon, 1970; *Nurse on Assignment,* Avalon, 1972; *Studio Affair,* Avalon, 1972; *A Blue Ribbon for Marni,* Avalon, 1973; *Nurse Under Fire,* Avalon, 1973; *Murder in Hawaii,* Scholastic, 1973; *Nurse in the Caribbean,* Avalon, 1974; *Nurse in the Keys,* Avalon, 1974; *Golden Girl,* Scholastic, 1974; *Nurse of Spirit Lake,* Avalon, 1975; *Alamanda House,* Avalon, 1976; *Murder in the Balance,* Avalon, 1976; *The Flint Hills Foal,* Abingdon, 1976; *Two Against the Arctic* (novel, adapted from a "Wonderful World of Disney" TV script), Pyramid,

DOROTHY BRENNER FRANCIS

1976. Short stories included in Augsburg publications. Contributor of light verse to magazines.

WORK IN PROGRESS: A junior novel with a Key West background.

SIDELIGHTS: "I was born in Lawrence, Kansas while my father was in law school at the university. Shortly, we moved to Olathe, a small town in the eastern part of the state, where I lived until I was graduated from the University of Kansas.

"I was an only child and although I grew up during the depression I don't recall being poor. There was always coal for the stove and vegetables from the garden. Olathe was a quiet town until the government located a naval air station and a powder plant close by. Then Olathe was a war-time boom town. I met many different kinds of people at my summer jobs as clerk-typist at the air station.

"During my school years I had a major interest in music and spent much time practicing on the piano and the trumpet. I also read a lot and mystery books were my favorites.

"I majored in music in college, and after being graduated cum laude, traveled for a summer with an all-girl dance band, playing one-night stands throughout the midwest and Montana. This was a hard life and by summer's end I was ready to report for music teaching in California. While in California I lived on Balboa Island—a very deserted island during the winter months. I taught two years before marrying a musician and teacher. I taught two more years while he served as drum major for the Army band at Ft. Sill, Oklahoma.

"In 1952 we moved to Marshalltown, Iowa where our two daughters were born and where we have lived ever since. I didn't start writing until we moved to Iowa. I was amazed that editors would pay me for a four-line light verse. I also began to write stories for the children's weeklies, and soon decided to write a book. I wrote for five years before I received a contract for that book, and have been writing ever since.

"In recent years we have had opportunity to travel and we usually visit an island—Key West, St. Croix. In all my books I have tried to show an interesting background as well as tell a gripping story. My writing has always been based on people and places I have known. One of our daughters is a pianist and the other an artist and horsewoman. Following their interests has given me ideas for many of my books.

"I work three to four hours each day, usually in the morning. I can hear the mailman's truck two blocks down the street; he is my main link to New York, the publishing Mecca.

"For the past ten years I have attended the Writer's Conference at the University of Indiana under the direction of Dr. Robert Mitchner. This annual association with the greats of the literary world as well as with beginners in the field has taught me a great deal about the art and craft of writing. But there is only one way to learn to write and that is by writing—and, as someone once said, 'the first million words don't count.'"

I have a wooly blanket.
It's cuddly and it's pink.
And it is very dear to me,
More so than you would think. ■
(From *More Poems to Read to the Very Young*, selected by Josette Frank. Illustrated by Dagmar Wilson.)

FRANK, Josette   1893-

PERSONAL: Born March 27, 1893, in New York, N.Y.; daughter of Leo (a merchant) and Hattie (Brill) Frank; married Henry Jacobs; children: Judith Jacobs Rosen, Stephen Frank. *Home:* 201 West 54th St., New York, N.Y. 10019. *Office:* 50 Madison Ave., New York, N.Y. 10010.

CAREER: Child Study Association of America, New York, N.Y., director for children's books and mass media, 1923—. Editor, lecturer, and writer.

WRITINGS: What Books for Children?: Guideposts for Parents, Doubleday, 1937, revised edition, 1941; (with Clara Lambert) *From the Records: An Adventure in Teacher Training,* Play Schools, 1939; *Your Child's Reading Today,* Doubleday, 1954, 2nd revised edition, 1968; *Comics, TV, Radio, Movies: What Do They Offer Children?,* Public Affairs Committee, 1955; (compiler) *Poems to Read to the Very Young,* Random House, 1961; *Children and TV,* Public Affairs Committee, 1962; *Television: How to Use it Wisely With Children,* Child Study Association of America, 1965, revised edition, 1976; *More Poems to Read to the Very Young,* Random House, 1968.

Supervisory editor—All published by Random House: Anna Sewell, *Black Beauty,* 1949; Daniel Defoe, *The Life and Adventures of Robinson Crusoe,* 1952; David McDowell, *Robert E. Lee,* 1953; *Big Black Horse* (adaptation of *The Black Stallion,* by Walter Farley), 1953; Estelle Schneider, *King Arthur and the Knights of the Round*

Table (adaptation of *The Story of King Arthur and His Knights,* by Howard Pyle), 1954; Lewis Carroll (pseudonym of Charles Lutwidge Dodgson), *Alice in Wonderland,* 1955; Shirley Temple, compiler, *Storybook,* 1958; Andrew Lang, compiler, *Blue Fairy Book,* 1959. Advisory editor, *Children's Digest* and *Humpty Dumpty.*

FRANZÉN, Nils-Olof   1916-

PERSONAL: Born August 23, 1916, in Oxeloesund, Sweden; son of Frans Waldemar (an organizing secretary) and Elma (Loefstedt) Franzén; married Birgit Levihn (a civil servant), August 31, 1940; children: Berit (Mrs. Kjell Engdahl), Bo (son), Gerd (daughter). *Education:* University of Stockholm, B.A., 1942, M.A., 1960. *Home:* Luetzengatan 4, 115 23 Stockholm, Sweden.

CAREER: Sveriges Radio (Swedish Broadcasting Corp.), Stockholm, 1940—, began as announcer, staff of magazine, 1941-43, producer in talks department, 1943-49, head of talks department, 1950-55, director of radio, 1956-73.

WRITINGS: Se, daa kom daer en kvinna (historical novel about Don Juan), Ljus Foerlag, 1944; *Den aattonde doedssynden* (novel), Ljus Foerlag, 1945; *Hur stora foerfattare arbeta* (essays on authorship), Natur & Kultur, 1947; *Den groena manteln* (historical novel), Ljus Foerlag, 1948; *Rossini,* Bonnier, 1951; *Emile Zola,* Natur & Kultur, 1958; *Zola et la Joie de vivre* (thesis; published in French), Almqvist & Wiksell, 1958; *Moliere,* Natur & Kultur, 1960; *Brunkebergsmorden* (crime novel), Bonnier, 1971; *Doedens aengel* (crime novel), Bonnier, 1972; *Svea Soeder* (crime novel), Bonnier, 1973; *Stina* (easy-reader novel), Bonnier, 1974.

NILS-OLOF FRANZÉN

Within a few minutes, the room was filled with tobacco smoke, as Agaton Sax's wonderful mind worked methodically on the great mystery he now had to solve. . . . Any criminal, seeing him at this moment, would have trembled in every limb and throwing down his weapon, would have stammered: "I give up, sir!" ■ (From *Agaton Sax and the Scotland Yard Mystery* by Nils-Olof Franzén. Illustrated by Quentin Blake.)

Children's books—"Agaton Sax" series: *Agaton Sax klipper till,* Bonnier, 1955; *Agaton Sax och den ljudloesa spraengaemnesligan,* Bonnier, 1956, published as *Agaton Sax and The League of Silent Exploders,* Deutsch, 1974; *Agaton Sax och vita moess-mysteriet,* Bonnier, 1957, published as *Agaton Sax and the Haunted House,* Deutsch, 1975; *Agaton Sax och de slipade diamanttjuvarna,* Bonnier,

1959, translation by Evelyn Ramsden published as *Agaton Sax and the Diamond Thieves,* Deutsch, 1965, Delacorte, 1967; *Agaton Sax och det gamla pipskaegget,* Bonnier, 1961, his own translation published as *Agaton Sax and The Scotland Yard Mystery,* Dell, 1969; *Agaton Sax och Bykoepings gaestabud,* Bonnier, 1963, published as *Agaton Sax and the Criminal Doubles,* Deutsch, 1971; *Agaton Sax och Broederna Max,* his own translation published as *Agaton Sax and the Incredible Max Brothers,* Dell, 1970; *Agaton Sax och den bortkomne Mr. Lispington,* Bonnier, 1966, published as *Agaton Sax and the Colossus of Rhodes,* Deutsch, 1972; *Agaton Sax och de okontanta miljardaererna,* Bonnier, 1967; *Agaton Sax och den svaellande rotmos-affären,* Bonnier, 1970, published as *Agaton Sax and the London Computer Plot,* Deutsch, 1973 (all Deutsch translations by author and Pamela Royds).

Other children's books: *Sammansvaerjningen* (historical adventure), Raben & Sjoegren, 1955; *Den hemlighetsfulle ryttaren* (historical adventure), Raben & Sjoegren, 1956; *Goeran Ulv* (historical adventure), Bonnier, 1960; *Goeran Ulv och faangarna i Bastiljen* (historical adventure), Bonnier, 1962; *Herr Zippo och den tjuvaktiga skatan,* Bonnier, 1968; *Fred Y. och den farlige Dr. Snook,* Bonnier, 1968; *Herr Zippo och barnen i byn,* Bonnier, 1969.

Translator into Swedish: Grimmelshausen, *Der abentheureliche Simplicissimus,* Ljus Foerlag, 1944; *Le Sage: Gil Blas,* Ljus Foerlag, 1945; (translation and abridgement with wife, Birgit Franzen) Edward Gibbon, *Decline and Fall of the Roman Empire,* three volumes, Ljus Foerlag, 1946-50.

WORK IN PROGRESS: Another story in "Agaton Sax" series.

SIDELIGHTS: Some of the Agaton Sax adventures also have been published in Germany, Austria, Netherlands, Denmark, Finland, Norway, Poland, and Czechoslovakia.

HOBBIES AND OTHER INTERESTS: Listening to Mozart's music and reading books about the composer, whom he considers "mankind's most beautiful genius."

After a week in the warm oven, the eggs opened and two tiny dragons popped out, breathing smoke but no fire. Mr. Drackle was enchanted with the baby dragons. ■ (From *Mr. Drackle and his Dragons* by Elizabeth Hull Froman. Illustrated by David McKee.)

FROMAN, Elizabeth Hull   1920-1975

PERSONAL: Born April 26, 1920, in Minneapolis, Minn.; daughter of George Eliot (a civil engineer) and Elsie (Booth) Hull; married Robert Froman (a free-lance writer), May 30, 1942. *Education:* Attended Minnesota public schools. *Residence:* Tompkins Cove, N.Y. 10986.

WRITINGS: Eba, the Absent-Minded Witch, World Publishing, 1965; *Mr. Drackle and His Dragons,* Watts, 1971. Contributor to *Saturday Review* and *Atlantic Monthly.*

(Died January 11, 1975)

GELINAS, Paul J.   1911-

PERSONAL: Born July 17, 1911, in Woonsocket, R.I.; son of Edmond J. (an engineer) and Anna (Desaultnier) Gelinas; married Eva Jane MacFarlane, June, 1933; children: Robert P. *Education:* Acadia University, B.A., 1933; Columbia University, M.A., 1949; College of the City of New York (now City College of the City University of New York), M.Sc., 1950; New York University, Ed.D., 1954. *Politics:* Independent. *Religion:* Baptist. *Home:* 31 West Meadow Rd., Setauket, Long Island, N.Y. 11733.

CAREER: Reporter and feature writer, 1940-41; Setauket, N.Y., public schools, superintendent, 1942-60; adjunct professor of psychology at Adelphi University, Hofstra University, and Long Island University, 1942-60; psychologist, 1961—. *Military service:* National Guard, 1934-36. *Member:* National Education Association, New York State Psychological Association, Suffolk County Psychological Association. *Awards, honors:* The Paul J. Gelinas High School in Setauket, N.Y., was named in his honor.

WRITINGS—Mainly for young people: *The How and Why Wonder Book of Coins and Currency,* Wonder Books, 1965; *So You Want to be a Teacher,* Harper, 1965; *Geography of the World for Young Readers,* Grosset, 1965; (with Robert Scharff) *History of the World for Young Readers,* Grosset, 1965; *Frightened Women,* Tower, 1967; *Teenagers and Their Hangups,* Rosen, 1975.

With son, Robert P. Gelinas—all published by Rosen Press: *Your Future in School Psychology,* 1968; *The Teenager and Psychology,* 1971; *How Teenagers Can Get Good Jobs,* 1971; *The Teenager in a Troubled World,* 1972; *Teenagers Look at Sex in Nature,* 1973.

WORK IN PROGRESS: The Teenager and Social Action and *The Madness in All of Us.*

SIDELIGHTS: "Although I was born in Rhode Island, several of my early years were spent in northern Quebec and Ontario where at the time there were few children of my own age. And yet those years in the wilderness were not too lonely. My imagination was active enough to conjure up many fantasies, to people my world with wonders among the towering pines and the immensity of the forest. Accordingly, there was little formal education, merely tutoring and wide reading in both English and French. Years later, in college, I realized how well my poetry-writing mother had inculcated in me not only a love of reading, but also a sense of awe toward nature, and toward those strange, unpredictable creatures called human beings.

"Among the sorrows and tragedies, which is the lot of most growing children, was the loss of my faithful Great Dane, a dog who seemingly could read my own thoughts. Surely, a heaven must exist for animals such as he, his great size possibly alarming others of his species, but finally letting his great kindness and gentleness reach out to both man and beast. I was so glad that Noah had saved my pet's ancestors, later to have him gladden my days in the solemn forests of the northland.

"If my mother lent the delight of books and of literature, my father provided the down-to-earth stories of the masculine world where men fought for justice with the rough dignity of woodsmen, pitted against the odds of rushing rivers, of struggles to tame nature, to withstand the ruthlessness of storms, and even the frequent ugliness of the human spirit perverted in hatred and cruelty.

"Most of my writings have sprung from my desire to simplify and to make clear what is often hidden in scientific jargon. As a clinical psychologist, I have been fascinated with the popularization of the psychology, personality, and the motives of young people. Somehow, that seems more important to me than to engage in esoteric research largely for the benefit of other scientists.

"A book once written is like a child that has been born. It goes out into the world to enlarge life itself, to convey new

PAUL J. GELINAS

understanding, and new feelings. Ever since as a little boy I scribbled stories for my mother to read, I await the reactions of my readers. If they are made happy by something that I have written, then I feel that the project has been worthwhile.

"Much of my writing, including a newspaper column entitled *Psychologically Speaking,* is done in our summer cottage in St. Andrews, New Brunswick, Canada where the abrupt hills and the high tides form settings for the calls of seagulls over the Bay of Fundy or for the lonely cries of loons on the distant inland lakes.

"I like to encourage young people to become writers. Perhaps there are few callings which bring such a sense of achievement. To create, to evolve, to perform magic on the printed page is an elixir given to those who are really blessed with the urge to express themselves constructively for the welfare of mankind."

HOBBIES AND OTHER INTERESTS: Tennis, boating, golf, swimming—"and pleasant evenings by the fireplace with congenial friends."

GILBERT, (Agnes) Joan (Sewell) 1931-

PERSONAL: Given name is pronounced Jo-ann; born November 7, 1931, in Dixon, Mo.; daughter of Daniel Boone and Blanche Evelyn (Gilbert) Sewell; married Dewey Franklin Lipscomb, January 24, 1953; married second husband, Ira Joseph Gilbert, October 9, 1961. *Education:* Southwest Missouri State College, B.S. in Ed., 1954. *Home:* Box 326, Dixon, Mo. 65459.

CAREER: Columbia Daily Tribune, Columbia, Mo., women's editor, 1955-58; also wrote continuity for Radio

JOAN GILBERT

Ever since the first sponge touched him and he had his first whiff of shoe polish, he had been a different horse. His eyes had a new brightness and his head went higher, his ears moving busily. ■ (From *Summerhill Summer* by Joan Gilbert. Jacket illustration by Darrell Wiskur.)

Station KGBX, Springfield, Mo., worked in society department of newspaper in Springfield, and did public relations work for Gascosage Electric Cooperative; free-lance writer. Book chairman of Dixon library board. *Member:* Missouri Writer's Guild.

WRITINGS: Summerhill Summer (teen-age mystery), Bethany, 1967; *House of Whispers,* Paperback Library, 1971. Contributor of about three hundred articles to *Writer's Digest, Health, Calling All Girls, Ebony, American Girl, Missouri Farmer, Missouri Life, Saddle and Bridle, Norden News,* and *Management Quarterly,* newspapers, and religious weeklies for teen-agers. Contributing editor, *Management Quarterly;* recipe editor, *Today's Farmer;* book review editor, *Saddle and Bridle.*

WORK IN PROGRESS: Teen novels.

HOBBIES AND OTHER INTERESTS: Animals, outdoors, books, music.

GORDON, Esther S(aranga) 1935-

PERSONAL: Born March 29, 1935, in Boston, Mass.; daughter of Jacob and Fay (Barocas) Saranga; married Bernard L. Gordon (a college professor), July 19, 1959; children: Jocelyn Fay, Zimra Joy. *Education:* Boston University, A.B., 1957; Boston State College, Ed.M., 1958. *Home and office:* Old Colony Rd., Chestnut Hill, Mass. 02167.

CAREER: Elementary school teacher in Ashaway, R.I., 1958-59, and Stonington, Conn., 1959-60; Boston School Department, Boston, Mass., elementary school teacher,

ESTHER S. GORDON

1961—, teacher at James A. Garfield School, 1974—. *Member:* Boston Teachers Union.

WRITINGS—For children: *There Really Was a Dodo,* Walck, 1974; *Once There Was a Passenger Pigeon,* Walck, 1976.

WORK IN PROGRESS: Books about auks, hawks and other birds.

SIDELIGHTS: Esther Gordon writes to inform children about pollution, extinction, and conservation. She has traveled professionally to Paris, Moscow, and Jerusalem.

It was a strange, large bird that couldn't fly. But there aren't any dodos living on earth anymore, and there will never be another one. ■ (From *There Really Was a Dodo* by Esther S. and Bernard L. Gordon. Illustrated by Lawrence DiFiori.)

GRANSTAFF, Bill 1925-

PERSONAL: Born May 17, 1925, in Paducah, Ky.; son of William Lawrence and Frankie Bell (Hunsaker; an artist) Granstaff; married Joan McBride (a framer/print helper), June 27, 1947; children: William Frank, Ann Laurie. *Education:* Kansas City Art Institute, Kansas City, Mo., four years, graduate; American Academy of Art, Chicago, Ill., one year, post graduate. *Politics:* Republican. *Religion:* Baptist. *Home and office:* Rt. #2, Princeton, Ky. 42445. *Agent:* Heritage Gallery, 217 Rosemont Garden, Lexington, Ky. 40503.

CAREER: Baptist Publishers, Nashville, Tenn., staff illustrator, 1952-58; Famous Artist School, Westport, Conn., instructor (illustration), 1959-61; free-lance illustrator, Nashville, Tenn., 1963-73; print maker and painter, Princeton, Ky., 1973-75. *Exhibitions:* Suzannes Gallery, Murray, Ky., 1974; Stewarts, Louisville, Ky., 1975. *Military service:* Army Air Cadet, 1943-1946. *Member:* Audubon Society, Graphics Society, Flying Club (Caldwell Co.). *Awards, honors:* Robert Brackman Blue Ribbon, Nashville, Tenn., 1955.

ILLUSTRATOR: Webb Garrison, *What's In a Word?,* Methodist, 1954, Abingdon, 1965; Johana Wyss, *Swiss Family Robinson,* Grossett, 1960; Betty Swinford, *The White Panther,* Moody, 1964; Eula Crawford, *Together Is a Happy Way,* Broadman, 1968.

BILL GRANSTAFF

SIDELIGHTS: "I probably am an artist today due to the G.I. Bill Art School. Love to illustrate childrens' books. Also do realistic still life and loose watercolors. I was a student of Bill Mosby, Ross Braught, Ed Laning, and John Pike."

HOBBIES AND OTHER INTERESTS: Commercial pilot, ham radio operator, amateur photographer.

GRANT, (Alice) Leigh 1947-

PERSONAL: Leigh rhymes with "see"; born September 22, 1947, in Greenwich, Conn.; daughter of John Barrett (business executive) and Swan (McLean) Grant. *Education:* Hollins College, Roanoke, Va., B.A., art history, 1969; Pratt Institute, B.F.A., 1971. *Home and office:* 295 South Beach Ave., Old Greenwich, Conn. 06870. *Agent* (educational): Paige Gilles, Publishers Graphics, 611 Riverside Ave., Westport, Conn. 06880.

CAREER: Early Years Magazine, Darien, Conn., art director, part of 1973-74. *Exhibitions:* Society of Illustrators Show (New York City), 1974; Children's Book Art Show, Contemporary Arts Museum (Houston), 1975.

ILLUSTRATOR: Molly Burkett, *Year of the Badger,* Macmillan (England), 1972; Michael Hardcastle, *Games,* Heineman (England), 1972; Joan Nixon, *Secret Box Mystery,* Putnam, 1974; Norma Klein, *Naomi in the Middle,* Dial, 1974; Martha Hickman, *I'm Moving,* Abingdon, 1974; Barbara Hazen, *I Wish I Were an Only Kid Like Wigger,* Atheneum, 1975; Emily Hanlon, *What if a Lion Eats Me and I Fall Into a Hippopotamus's Mudhole,* Delacorte, 1975; Robert Burch, *The Jolly Witch,* Dutton,

LEIGH GRANT

Mommy came in to run our bath. "Bubble, pine, or regular?" she said.
"Reg," said Bobo.
Bobo never likes bubble anymore. She used to. I can only have a bubble now if I have it by myself. ■ (From *Naomi in the Middle* by Norma Klein. Illustrated by Leigh Grant.)

1975; Clyde Bulla, *Shoeshine Girl,* Crowell, 1975; Carrie Goddard, *Isn't It a Wonder,* Abingdon, 1976.

SIDELIGHTS: "I use a crowquill pen and work in either FW ink, Dr. Martin's Dyes, and/or Caran D'Ache pencils. My style is heavily influenced by etching which I studied at Pratt. I currently use cross-hatching as a major texture in my drawings.

"I have always been interested in art. My family has a small collection of paintings and my great-aunt was a student of Robert Henri.

"I have spent two years outside the United States, one in France (school) and one in England (working). I loved England—it was so beautiful and so diversified. I have travelled throughout Europe including Greece, Yugoslavia, Turkey, and the Soviet Union.

HOBBIES AND OTHER INTERESTS: Preservation of the wilderness-plant and animal; houseplants; gardening; archaeology; and raising finches. "I ride horses, ski, sail, and wind-surf."

FOR MORE INFORMATION SEE: Society of Illustrators Annual, 1974.

GROOM, Arthur William 1898-1964
(Graham Adamson, George Anderson, Daphne du Blane, Gordon Grimsley, Bill Pembury, John Stanstead, Maurice Templar, Martin Toonder)

PERSONAL: Born 1898, in Hove, Sussex, England; son of William Samuel and Emily Ann (Short) Groom; married Marjorie Helen Grimsley, 1928; children: Susan. *Education:* Attended Montrose College, 1908-12, Whitgift School, 1912-16. *Religion:* Church of England. *Home:* 3 Pembury Rd., Gloucester, England. *Agent:* A. M. Heath & Co. Ltd., Dover St., London, England; Howard Moorepark, 440 East 79th St., New York, N.Y. 10021.

CAREER: Bank of Scotland, England, clerk, 1916-19; Colonial Bank (now Barclay's), British West Indies and British Guiana, sub-manager, 1919-22; London's Underground Railways, London, England, editor of staff magazine, 1922-28; professional writer, 1928-64. Frequent lecturer. Vice-president, Gloucester Branch, International Friendship League; vice-president, Gloucester Branch, Y.M.C.A.; diocesan reader, Church of England, 1950-64. *Military service:* Pay Corps, 1940-45; became captain; awarded Certificate of Merit, made Birthday Honours List, 1945. *Member:* P.E.N., Society of Authors, Savage Club (London).

WRITINGS—Juvenile: Merry Christmas, Mills & Boon, 1930; *Collection of Tales for Children*, Birn, 1935; (with others) *Pamela's Pet* (stories), Birn, 1936; (with P. Megroz) *The Girls' Own Book*, Birn, 1936; *Our Friends Next Door*, Birn, 1947; *Tom Puss in Nursery Rhyme Land*, Marks & Spencer, 1948; *The Money Book*, Rockliff, 1948; *Farmyard Friends*, Birn, 1949; *Once Upon a Birthday*, Birn, 1950; *Gran'pop's Annual*, illustrated by Lawson Wood, Dean, 1950, reissued as *Lawson Wood's Annual*, Dean, 1951; *Around the Farm*, Birn, 1951; *The Book of Railways*, Birn, 1951; *The Boys' Book of Heroes*, Birn, 1951; *The Doll Dressing Books*, four parts, Birn, 1951; *The Wild West Book*, Birn, 1952; (adapter) Charles Kingsley, *Water-Babies*, Birn, 1952; *The Girls' Book of Heroines*, Birn, 1952; *The Wild West Book* (not the same as 1952 publication), Birn, 1953; *My Picture Book of Animals*, Dean, 1955; (adapter) Sir James Matthew Barrie, *Peter Pan and Wendy*, Birn, 1955; (adapter) *The Adventures of Robin Hood*, Dean, 1956; *My Picture Book of Trains*, Dean, 1956; *Marvell, the Amazing Magician*, Newnes, 1956; *The Adventures of Dilly Duckling*, Newnes, 1956; *The Wild West Book* (not the same as earlier publications), Birn, 1957; *Lone Ranger Adventure Stories*, Adprint, 1957; *Hopalong Cassidy Stories*, Adprint, 1957; *Champion, The Wonder Horse*, Daily Mirror, 1957; *Roy Rogers' Adventures*, Dean, *Number 1*, 1957, *Number 2*, 1958, *Number 3*, 1959; (adapter) Steve Frazee, *Zorro*, Daily Mirror, 1959; *Circus Boy*, Daily Mirror, 1959. Author of *Bubble and Squeek Annual*, Birn, 1950-53, and (with Madeline Collier) *Bobby Bear's Annual*, Dean, 1954-55.

Also author of *Little People of the Woods*, Birn, *Bedtime Stories*, Birn, *Tom Puss at the Panto*, Birn, *The Christmas Book*, Birn, *Leisure Hour Stories*, Birn, *School-Girl Stories*, Birn, *Wonders of the World*, Birn, (adapter, from a film of Walt Disney) *101 Dalmations*, Dean, *Dilly Duckling Painting Book*, Dean, *Noah's Ark Story Book*, Dean, *Queen Elizabeth's Little House*, Dean, *Butterflies and Birds*, Dean, *The Four Seasons Country Book*, Dean, *Picture Book of Road Travel*, Dean, *Disneyland Pop-Up Book*, Dean, (adapter, from a film by Walt Disney) *The Lady and the Tramp*, Dean, *Pussies and Puppies Book*, Dean.

Juvenile religious: *The Man Who Loved God*, Wheaton, 1959; *The Coat of Many Colours*, Wheaton, 1959; *Jacob's Happy Day*, Wheaton, 1959; *The Baby in the Bulrushes*, Wheaton, 1959; *The Burning Bush*, Wheaton, 1959; *Moses and the Hidden Spring*, Wheaton, 1959; *The Promised Land*, Wheaton, 1959; *The Walls of Jerico*, Wheaton, 1959; *The Prodigal Son*, Wheaton, 1959; *The Child Jesus*, Wheaton, 1961. Also author of *My Picture Book of Prayers* (2 volumes), *Dean's Picture Book of Prayers*, *Gold Medal Book About Jesus*, *My Picture Book About Jesus*, *Second Picture Book About Jesus* (all published by Dean).

Junior novels: *The Kidnapped Form*, Juvenile Productions, 1938; *The Ghost of Gregory*, Lunn, 1946; *Lords of the Isle*, Art and Educational Publishers, 1947; (under pseudonym, Gordon Grimsley) *Champion*, Lunn, 1947; *The Bearded Stranger*, Lunn, 1947; *Ken of the "Courier,"* Art and Educational Publishers, 1947; *The Adventure at Marston Manor*, Lunn, 1947; *The First Term at Tenmeade*, Art and Educational Publishers, 1948; *Tenmeade and Western Priory*, Boardman, 1948; *The Scarlet Runner*, Jarrold, 1948; *All Guns Ablaze!: A Story of Admiral Nelson*, Boardman, 1949; *The Smuggler's Secret: A Thrilling Tale of Cornwall in the Year 1870, With a Glimpse of the Days When Smugglers Held Sway*, Jarrold, 1950; *The Phantom Frigate: A Story of the Year That Followed Trafalgar*, Boardman, 1950; *The Headland Mystery*, Collins, 1950; *John of the Fair*, Warne, 1950; *I, Elizabeth Tudor*, Burke, 1954; (adapter) *The Adventures of Sir Lancelot*, Adprint, 1958; *The Young David*, Roy, 1962.

Juvenile nonfiction: *Continent for Sale: A Story of the Louisiana Purchase*, Winston, 1953; *How Money Was Developed*, Routledge & Kegan Paul, 1958; *This is the History of Money*, Archer, 1958; *Yellow Quiz Book*, Wheaton, 1960; *Red Quiz Book*, Wheaton, 1961; *How We Weigh and Measure*, Routledge & Kegan Paul, 1961; *Question and Answer Book*, Purnell, 1961; *Bible Quiz Book*, Pilgrim, 1962; *Green Quiz Book*, Wheaton, 1962; *Blue Quiz Book*, Wheaton, 1962; *Quiz Book of Sport*, Wheaton, 1964; *How Law is Kept*, Routledge & Kegan Paul, 1964. Also author of *Buffalo Bill Annual*, Boardman, 1949-55, and "Western Rangers" books, Progressive Press, 1949-64.

Adult novels: The "Jack Broughton V. C." Series, Newnes, 1940; *Wheels on the Western Front*, Newnes, 1940; *Montana Moon*, Progressive Press, 1946; *Buck McHarty Rides Again*, Progressive Press, 1946; *Ranch House Mystery*, Progressive Press, 1946; *Vengeance Rides West*, Progressive Press, 1946; *Death at the Crooked Y*, Progressive Press, 1946; *The Grinning Skull*, Progressive Press, 1946; *Ace High Jack*, Progressive Press, 1946; *The Boss of the Double Diamond*, Progressive Press, 1949; *The Sheriff of Angel County*, Progressive Press, 1949; *The Sheriff's Badge*, Foley, 1949; (as ghost writer for Captain Freddie Guest) *Escape from the Blooded Sun*, Jarrold, 1956.

Adult nonfiction: *Writing for Children*, Black, 1929; (editor) Jasper Maskelyne, *Maskelyne's Book of Magic*, Harrap, 1936; *Edward the Eighth, Our King*, Allied Newspapers,

1937; *Etiquette for Everyone*, Southern Editorial Syndicate, 1946; *The Power of Public Speaking*, Vawser & Wiles, 1946; *Western Omnibus*, Coordination Press, 1949; *His Late Majesty, King George VI*, Pitkin, 1952; (with Bella Austin) *Mother Christmas*, Parrish, 1961. Also editor of *Scouting in Europe*, Newnes.

SIDELIGHTS: Author of over four hundred books, many of which are not listed because "records of them were lost during bombing in World War II or subsequently" and because "it has been virtually impossible to keep a tag on all publications." He wrote original books based on TV Western programs, including Range Rider, Roy Rogers, Cheyenne, Circus Boy, Frontier Circus, Wagon Train, Rawhide, Champion the Wonder Horse, Davy Crockett, Hopalong Cassidy, Gene Autry, Lone Ranger, Buffalo Bill, Tenderfoot, Laramie, Klondike, Royal Canadian Mounted Police, Bonanza, and Wells Fargo. He also wrote original books on the following children's literature: *Pinocchio, B'rer Rabbit, Gulliver's Travels, Water-Babies, Sleeping Beauty, Peter Pan, Snowwhite and the Seven Dwarfs, Robin Hood, Alice in Wonderland, 20,000 Leagues under the Sea, Cinderella, Jack and the Beanstalk, The Toy Soldiers, Little Women, Sir Lancelot,* and *Sooty.* Several of his books have been adapted for television and screen.

Groom founded and wrote the *Buffalo Bill Wild West Annual*, 1946-51. Author of *Mickey Mouse Annual*, 1931-64. Founded and wrote all *Sunny Stories Annuals*, for Newnes, and wrote entire *Sunny Stories Weekly Magazine*, 1953-55. Wrote other annuals including *Donald Duck Annual, Gran'Pop's Annual, Pinky and Perky Annual, Bubble and Squeek Annual, Lenny the Lion Annual,* and *Brumas Annual.* Creator of Dilly and Dimple Duckling characters.

(Died September, 1964)

HAUSER, Margaret L(ouise)   1909-
(Gay Head)

PERSONAL: Born May 13, 1909, in High Point, N.C.; daughter of Charles Merrimon (a banker) and Annie (Tomlinson) Hauser. *Education:* Salem College, Winston-Salem, N.C., B.A. (magna cum laude), 1929; American Academy of Dramatic Arts, student, 1929-30. *Religion:* Quaker. *Home:* 30 East 38th St., New York, N.Y. 10016. *Office:* Scholastic Magazines and Book Services, 50 West 44th St., New York, N.Y. 10036.

CAREER: High Point Enterprise, High Point, N.C., feature writer, 1933-37; Scholastic Magazines and Book Services (educational publishers), New York, N.Y., 1937-46, editor of *Practical English*, 1946-62, editor of *Co-ed*, 1956-74, director of home economics and guidance, 1962-74, director of language arts, 1963-66.

WRITINGS—Under pseudonym Gay Head: *Boy Dates Girl: Question and Answer Book*, Scholastic Book Services, 1949, revised edition, 1952; *Hi There, High School: Tips on How to Be Counted in the Crowd, and How to Make Yourself Count in School Life*, Scholastic Book Services, 1953, revised edition, 1955; *Etiquette for Young Moderns: How to Succeed in Your Social Life*, Scholastic Book Services, 1954; *Dear Gay Head* (originally published as *You're Asking Me?*, 1958), Scholastic Book Services,

1958; (with editors of *Co-ed*) *Party Perfect*, Scholastic Book Services, 1959; (with editors of *Co-ed*) *The Co-ed Book of Charm and Beauty*, Scholastic Book Services, 1962; (editor) *First Love* (anthology of short stories), Scholastic Book Services, 1963.

HEGARTY, Reginald Beaton   1906-1973

PERSONAL: Born August 5, 1906, in Somerset, Mass.; son of William (a whaler) and Sarah C. (Parlow) Hegarty; married Georgiana Lawrence, February 18, 1933 (deceased); children: William Russell. *Education:* Attended high school in New Bedford, Mass. *Politics:* Republican. *Religion:* Congregationalist. *Home:* 77 Adams St., Fairhaven, Mass. 02719. *Office:* New Bedford Free Public Library, New Bedford, Mass. 02740.

CAREER: Grew up aboard whaleships, making three voyages (more than eight years at sea) before he was thirteen, and undergoing training in all phases of whaling during the final voyage; grocery store manager, 1927-40; machinist (precision grinder), 1940-45; worked in a shipyard, 1945-54; operator of New Bedford (Mass.) Public Library bookmobile, 1954; New Bedford (Mass.) Free Public Library, cu-

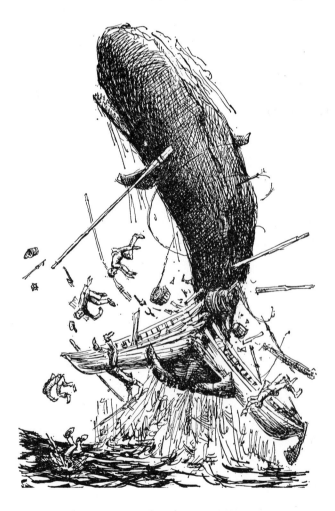

We could see the pieces of the boat and its gear falling all around the whale. He had cut that boat in two just as easy as a knife cuts through soft butter. ■ (From *The Rope's End* by Reginald B. Hegarty. Illustrated by Wallace Tripp.)

rator of Melville Whaling Room, 1962-73. Consultant to Kendall Whaling Museum, 1955-73, and Mystic Seaport. Member of town meeting, Fairhaven, Mass.

WRITINGS: Returns of Whaling Vessels Sailing from American Ports, 1876-1928, Reynolds Printing, 1959; *New Bedford and American Whaling* (fourth-grade textbook), Reynolds Printing, 1960; *Addendum to Starbuck and Whaling Masters,* Reynolds Printing, 1964; *Birth of a Whaleship,* Reynolds Printing, 1964; *Rope's End* (juvenile), Houghton, 1965. Contributor of articles to newspapers.

WORK IN PROGRESS: Five books, all pertaining to some phase of whaling.

SIDELIGHTS: The Melville Whaling Room is believed to house the largest and most comprehensive collection on whaling in existence. In recent years Hegarty had been occupied with indexing and cataloging some 67,000 items. One item alone, the crew lists, covers some 6,900 voyages representing about 160,000 names. "It is almost a certainty," he wrote, "that any family having four generations in this country had someone go whaling out of New Bedford."

(Died January 18, 1973)

HERMANSON, Dennis (Everett) 1947-

PERSONAL: Born January 1, 1947, in Enterprise, Ala.; son of Tenho Everett and Audrey Helen (Johnston) Hermanson. *Education:* Attended Syracuse University, 1965-67, New York University, 1967-69. *Home:* 357-B Pelham Road, New Rochelle, N.Y. 10805. *Office: Change Magazine,* NBW Tower, New Rochelle, N.Y. 10805.

DENNIS HERMANSON

He looked out over the bay, where pelicans were diving, accompanied by their tormentors, the gulls. The tide was going out, and with it a line of porpoises arching and sliding through the waves. ■ (From *Lands End* by Mary Stolz. Drawings by Dennis Hermanson.)

CAREER: Free-lance illustrator, designer. *Change Magazine,* New Rochelle, N.Y., art director, 1974—. *Exhibitions:* Swann Collection of Cartoon and Caricature, New York, N.Y.; editorial art of *The New York Times,* Bordeaux, France, 1974; numerous private collections.

ILLUSTRATOR: Mary Stolz, *Lands End,* Harper, 1973. Illustrations have appeared in *Business Week, National Lampoon, Social Policy, Boys' Life, Teacher, New York Times* and *Washington Post;* designs book jackets for major New York publishers.

WORK IN PROGRESS: Novel for teen-agers and a picture book.

SIDELIGHTS: "My direction might best be summed-up as . . . in new, special, sophisticated ways, I want to make the field of childrens' book illustration more exciting, more complex and thus create an interest in the modern child that can compete with the television's pace and changes. I personally feel children's books have continued to use illustration in old ways, and need to become more sophisticated, more sensorial and more up-to-date to get a child watching television or listening to Elton John interested in a still object he must take the time and effort to read.

"I would be most happy to consider working with publishers or editors committed to exciting, innovative approaches to the childrens' book field. My chief asset as an illustrator/designer is the ability to work in any style of illustration necessary, from Breugel to Batman, or even a combination of many styles in the same drawing. This is something few illustrators offer."

HODGES, Carl G. 1902-1964

PERSONAL: Born September 11, 1902, in Quincy, Ill.; son· of McClellan (a merchant) and Anna Fredricka (Lepper) Hodges; married Ruth Zuckswert, December 31, 1935. *Education:* Attended schools in Quincy, Ill. *Politics:* Republican., *Religion:* Lutheran. *Home and office:* 2431 Whittier Ave., Springfield, Ill.

CAREER: In furniture and oil business during early years; National Association of Petroleum Retailers, executive secretary, 1938-41; State of Illinois, Springfield, public relations for Department of Public Welfare, 1946, Illinois State treasurer, 1947-48; *Peoria Star,* Peoria, Ill., columnist, 1949-53; State of Illinois Information Service, Springfield, superintendent, 1953-61. Springfield Historical Monuments Commission, member, 1957-59. *Member:* Illinois State Historical Society (life member), Sangamon County Historical Society, Mystery Writers of America (Midwest vice-president, 1958, 1960-61), Springfield Civil War Round Table (president, 1962-63), Society of American Travel Writers, Springfield Advertising and Public Relations Club (president, 1964), Publicity Club of Chicago.

WRITINGS: Naked Villainy, Suspense Books, 1951; *Crime on My Hands,* Phantom Books, 1953; *Murder by the Pack,* Ace Books, 1953; *Baxie Randall and the Blue Raiders* (juvenile), Bobbs, 1962; *Dobie Sturgis and the Dog Soldiers,* Bobbs, 1963; *Benjie Ream* (juvenile), Bobbs, 1964; *Land Rush* (juvenile), Duell, Sloan & Pearce, 1965. Novelettes syndicated by Hearst Features; articles in motel and travel journals.

HOBBIES AND OTHER INTERESTS: Professional football fan, stamp-collector (U.S. mint singles), photography.

(Died November 25, 1964)

SANDY HUFFAKER

But I kept trying, lifting my fingers from the holes one at a time and in different combinations until I produced some sweet, soft notes. ■ (From *H. Philip Birdsong's ESP* by Harriet Lawrence. Illustrated by Sandy Huffaker.)

HUFFAKER, Sandy 1943-

PERSONAL: Born September 23, 1943, in Chattanooga, Tenn.; son of Hugh D. (in insurance) and Mary K. Huffaker; married Ann S., May, 1966 (divorced August, 1975); children: Susan, Sandy Jr. *Education:* University of Alabama, B.A., 1966. *Politics:* Democrat. *Home and office:* 67 East 11th St., New York, N.Y. 10003. *Agent:* Barbara Gordon, 165 East 32nd St., New York, N.Y. 10016.

CAREER: Free-lance illustrator. *The Birmingham News,* Birmingham, Ala., editorial artist, 1966-68; *The News & Observer,* Raleigh, N.C., political cartoonist, 1968-71. *Exhibitions:* Society of Illustrators, 1975, Andre Romy Gallery, 1975. *Member:* Society of Illustrators, National Association of Editorial Cartoonists. *Awards, honors:* National Society of Illustrators, citation for merit, 1974, 1975, 1976.

ILLUSTRATOR: Philip Birdsong's Magic Flute, Young Scott, 1969; Harriet Lawrence, *Philip Birdsong's ESP,* Young Scott, 1969; Preston Wilcox, *White Is,* Grove, 1970. Four textbooks for slow learners, Globe Books.

SIDELIGHTS: "I was working in pen and ink mostly, now in pencil and a lot of color work. I try to be as realistic and intricate as possible. Humor is what my work is about, although it can seem tragic at times; probably due to the political cartoon influence.

"I was influenced by about four hundred people, actually—anyone and everyone."

FOR MORE INFORMATION SEE: Advertising Techniques, September, 1974; *Chattanooga Free Press,* April 27, 1975.

JAUSS, Anne Marie 1907-

PERSONAL: Born February 3, 1907, in Munich, Germany; moved to Lisbon, Portugal, 1932, came to United States, 1946; daughter of Georg and Caroline (Hegeler) Jauss. *Education:* Attended state art school in Munich, Germany. *Home:* R.D. 1, P.O. Box 82H, Stockholm, N.J. 07460.

CAREER: Painter, illustrator, and writer. *Exhibitions:* Portraits, Inc., Suffolk Museum, Larcada Gallery, Old Custom House (Philadelphia, Pa.), Netherwood Arts (Hyde Park, N.Y.). *Member:* Wilderness Society. *Awards, honors:* New Jersey Association of Teachers of English author's award, 1968.

WRITINGS: Wise and Otherwise, McKay, 1953; *Legends of Saints and Beasts,* Aladdin, 1954; *Discovering Nature the Year Round,* Aladdin, 1955; *The River's Journey,* Lippincott, 1957; *Under a Green Roof,* Lippincott, 1960; *The Pasture,* McKay, 1968; (with Patricia Tracy Lowe) *The Little Horse of Seven Colors, and Other Portuguese Folk Tales,* World, 1970.

Illustrator: Peter Lum, *The Stars in our Heaven,* Pantheon, 1948; Christiane Grautoff, *The Stubborn Donkey,* Aladdin, 1949; Peter Lum, *Fabulous Beasts,* Pantheon, 1951; Joseph Gaer, *Holidays Around the World,* Little, Brown, 1953; J. Beatty, *In Came Horace,* Lippincott, 1954; Christiane Grautoff, *The Tale that Grew and Grew,* Sterling, 1955; M. F. Blaisdell, *Cherry Tree Children,* Little, Brown, 1957; Nelson F. Beeler and Franklyn M. Branley, *Experiments with a Microscope,* Crowell, 1957; Nelson F. Beeler and Franklyn M. Branley, *Experiments with Light,* Crowell, 1957; Duane Bradley, *Engineers Did It,* Lippincott, 1958; Tillie S. Pine and Joseph Levine, *Magnets and How to Use Them,* McGraw, 1958; Anita Hewett, *Think, Mr. Platypus,* Sterling, 1958; Anita Hewett, *Koala Bear's Walkabout,* Sterling, 1959; Patricia Lauber, *Our Friend, the Forest,* Doubleday, 1959.

ANNE MARIE JAUSS

(From *The Valiant Little Tailor* by Grimm. Illustrated by Anne Marie Jauss.)

M. F. Blaisdell, *Bunny Rabbit's Diary,* Little, Brown, 1960; Mary Phillips, *Dragonflies and Damselflies,* Crowell, 1960; Dorothy G. Spicer, *Forty Six Days of Christmas: A Cycle of Old World Songs, Legends and Customs,* Coward, 1960; Duane Bradley, *Time for You: How Man Measures Time,* Lippincott, 1960; Harry Milgrom, *Explorations in Science: A Book of Basic Experiments,* Dutton, 1961; Frances Toor, *The Golden Carnation,* Lothrop, 1961; Isabel Wyatt, *The Golden Stag,* McKay, 1962; S. Resnick, *Selections from Spanish Poetry,* Harvey, 1962; Laura Cathon and Thusnelda Schmidt, *Perhaps and Perchance Tales of Nature,* Abingdon, 1962; Edna M. Cameron, *Children of the Tundra,* Lippincott, 1963; Isabel Wyatt, *King Beetle Tamer and Other Lighthearted Wonder Tales,* McKay, 1963; Edward Frankel, *DNA: Ladder of Life,* McGraw, 1964; S. Resnick, *Selections from Spanish American Poetry,* Harvey, 1964; Froman, *Our Fellow Immigrants,* McKay, 1956; Alfred Duggan, *The Falcon and the Dove,* Pantheon, 1966; Jean Longland, *Contemporary Portuguese Poetry,* Harvey, 1966; Virginia Brock, *Pinatas,* Abingdon, 1966; Grimm Brothers, *The Valiant Little Tailor,* Harvey, 1967; Robert Froman, *The Science of Salt,* McKay, 1967; Homer E. Newell, *Space Book for Young People,* McGraw, 1968; Howard G. Smith, *Hunting Big Game in the City Parks,* Abingdon, 1969.

Hans Christian Andersen, *Nightingale and the Emperor,* Harvey, 1970; D. C. Whitney, *The Easy Book of Division,* Watts, 1970; Ester Wier, *The White Oak,* McKay, 1971; Lois J. Hussey and Catherine Pessino, *Collecting Small Fossils,* Crowell, 1971; Howard G. Smith, *Tracking the Unearthly Creatures of Marsh and Pond* (Christopher Award, 1973), Abingdon, 1972; D. C. Whitney, *The Easy Book of Numbers and Numerals,* Watts, 1973; Robert Gambino, *Easy to Grow Vegetables,* Harvey, 1975.

FOR MORE INFORMATION SEE: Illustrators of Children's Books, 1946-1956, Horn Book, 1958; *Illustrators of Children's Books: 1957-1966,* Horn Book, 1968.

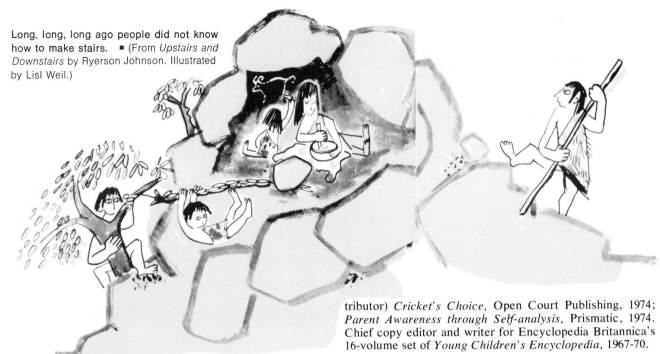

Long, long, long ago people did not know how to make stairs. ■ (From *Upstairs and Downstairs* by Ryerson Johnson. Illustrated by Lisl Weil.)

JOHNSON, (Walter) Ryerson 1901-

PERSONAL: Born October 19, 1901, in Divernon, Ill.; son of Simeon Ryerson (a physician) and Effie May (Potts) Johnson; married Lois Lignell (now an artist and package designer), May 10, 1939; children: Jennifer. *Education:* University of Illinois, B.S., 1926. *Politics:* Liberal. *Religion:* Liberal. *Residence:* Lubec, Maine. *Current address:* P.O. Box 116, Algonquin, Ill. *Agent:* Mauri Grashin, 8732 Sunset Blvd., Hollywood, Calif.

CAREER: Johnson worked as a coal miner while attending the University of Illinois, where he produced an English theme which turned out to be a salable short story, "and I haven't been good for much of anything except writing ever since." He held various jobs on the East Coast after graduation, and found himself in 1929 a warehouse manager for U.S. Gypsum Co., Boston, Mass., where, he says, "I got along so well it scared me." He quit, worked his way to and from Europe as a seaman, and worked his way across Europe with a musical saw. Aside from free-lancing, his jobs since have been: Popular Publications, New York, N.Y., editor, 1945; Adult Education Association of the U.S.A., Chicago, Ill., editor of *Adult Leadership* and staff writer, 1952-54. *Member:* Mystery Writers of America (former regional officer), Writers Guild of America (West), Authors League (former president, Pulp Writers section). *Awards, honors:* Jane Addams Award, Womens' International League for Peace and Freedom, 1963, for *The Monkey and the Wild Wild Wind.*

WRITINGS: Barb Wire, Sam Curl, 1947; *South to Sonora,* Arcadia House, 1948; *Naked in the Streets,* Fawcett, 1951; *Mississippi Flame,* Fawcett, 1952; *Lady in Dread,* Fawcett, 1953; *Gozo's Wonderful Kite,* Crowell, 1961; *The Monkey and the Wild Wild Wind* (juvenile), Abelard, 1962; *Upstairs and Downstairs,* Crowell, 1963; *Let's Walk Up the Wall,* Holiday, 1967; *The Mouse and the Moon,* R. Hale, 1968; *I Like Dinosaurs,* E. M. Hale, 1971; *A Pretty for Ma,* Ginn, 1972; *Susi Did It,* Ginn, 1972; (con-

tributor) *Cricket's Choice,* Open Court Publishing, 1974; *Parent Awareness through Self-analysis,* Prismatic, 1974. Chief copy editor and writer for Encyclopedia Britannica's 16-volume set of *Young Children's Encyclopedia,* 1967-70.

"Bob and Bee Blake" Series: *The Trail of the Golden Feather,* 1963, *The Trail of the Witchwood Treasure,* 1963, *The Trail of the Moaning Ghost,* 1963, *The Trail of the Deadly Image,* 1963 (all published by Crowell-Collier).

Wrote most of the fiction sections for *Westward the Nation* (fifth-grade reader), Franklin Publishing, 1965; both fact and fiction pieces for Science Research Associates "Comprehensive Reading Series"; materials for other textbook publishers. Also has ghosted novels. Contributor of some five hundred short stories, novelettes, and articles to periodicals.

RYERSON JOHNSON

WORK IN PROGRESS: Children's books illustrated by wife, with titles including *What If,* a fantasy, and *Who Will Play with Beebe?;* a new teen-age adventure-mystery series based on Hawaii; schoolbook materials.

SIDELIGHTS: "I moved into writing for children when our young daughter began to have observable growing-up problems. Free-lancing . . . working at home, I had a lot of time to spend with our growing daughter. And don't they grow fast . . . and change and change! When she'd have some developmental problem that seemed to me might be universal with children, I started dramatizing the problem in story or article form. I geared the stories to her age level. It got so that *Parents' Magazine* wrote me one time: 'What's Jennifer doing these days?' This continued from pre-school right on through high school when she'd come home from classes and look at what was coming hot from the typewriter on a teen-age adventure-mystery series: 'Oh, that's good, daddy,' or 'No, no; kids wouldn't say it like that.' She was my most dependable critic.

"It's fun writing for children because they are still creatively exploring, making unorthodox comparisons, asking irreverent questions. They still have a happy sense of wonder and expectation . . . still resisting our determination to put them into our rigid societal mold. In writing for children, you can move back and forth from the realist kind of realism to far-out fantasy."

Johnson feels he may have been too much of a "technique writer" in the past, but "in an age of specialization I have liked to remain something of a jack-of-all-trades. If you specialize you box yourself in—rule out too much of the rest of life.

"I believe in the one-world concept, while at the same time waving the flag for individualism. It has been important to be my own boss to the greatest extent possible, and stay free for travel or for change. This maybe explains why I chose freelancing as a way of making a living. It leaves you time for friends, travel, study, loafing. It does, if you hold down the fixed charges.

"Adventures into personality are important, but so are physical experiences. Before I was married, I made a kind of bumming trip through Europe from the Channel to the Dardanelles. One summer we opened up two copper mine tunnels on the 7,000 foot top edge of a mountain in Montana. We didn't find much copper but it was fun looking.

In the past few years Johnson has moved more and more into textbook writing, teaming with educators in the preparation of school materials.

JOHNSON, Shirley K(ing)   1927-

PERSONAL: Born March 18, 1927, in Adair County, Iowa; daughter of Roland E. (a farmer) and Gladys (Evans) King; married Thomas G. Johnson, June 2, 1946; children: Elaine, Evan; Barry and Bryan (twins). *Education:* Attended schools in Cumberland, Iowa. *Home:* 4118 Randolph St., Lincoln, Neb. 68510.

WRITINGS: A Dog Named Chip, Zondervan, 1964.

SHIRLEY K. JOHNSON

WORK IN PROGRESS: A juvenile fiction book set in New Zealand, *Land of the Long White Cloud.*

SIDELIGHTS: "I write because I enjoy it; I write for children because I was so bored as a youngster and a good book made life bearable. I write from experience, from ideas I get from reading other stories. I plan the theme first—What will my character *learn?* The setting second and then the characters take shape. I write it out in longhand, type it roughly, then type it once more. Usually I go over each sentence five or six times. I want it to go smoothly. If the reader must back up and go over a phrase twice, it's not well done."

Shirley Johnson enlivened a farm childhood by writing adventure stories, and has been turning out fiction, on and off, since then.

JONK, Clarence   1906-

PERSONAL: Born July 16, 1906, near Raymond, Minn.; son of Willem John (a carpenter, mason, farmer) and Delia (Molenaar) Jonk; married Virginia Frances Dunn; children: Nancy Jonk Crowe, Dolly Jonk Morstad, William, Ginger Jonk Irwin, Byron, Richard, Robert, Rodney, Shelley, Daniel, Jennifer. *Education:* Studied at University of Minnesota, University of Texas. *Politics:* Liberal-Progressive. *Religion:* Humanistic. *Mailing address:* Box 398, Bodega Bay, Calif. *Agent:* Bertha Klausner, International Literary Agency, 130 East 40th St., New York, N.Y.

CAREER: Riverman and carpenter on locks and dams, Mississippi River, 1933-39; lockman-farmer, 1937-40;

worker in munitions plant, 1940-45; carpenter, building contractor, quarry operator, 1945-56; full-time writer, and inventor of toys and games, 1956—.

WRITINGS—Poetry: *Sonnets to Celeste*, Ramsey Co., 1933; *Tracks, Fields and Home*, privately published, 1944; *The Summer House*, privately published, 1949; *Black Lace* (collection of love poems), Pageant, 1953; *The Hour was Late*, Falmouth, 1953; *Whimsies*, Branden Press, in press.

Non-fiction: *River Journey*, Stein & Day, 1964.

Juvenile: *Jimmy, a Little Pup*, Denison, 1959; *Ma Poos and the Fabulous Whimplegoose*, Denison, 1959; *Old Angus, the Unhappy Baker*, Denison, 1959; *Yami and His Unicycle*, Faber, 1962.

WORK IN PROGRESS: Remember Pa?, adult non-fiction; *This Year 13*, juvenile.

SIDELIGHTS: "Although I am a writer, first; I am also a farmer, a gardener, and (preferred) a dweller-by-water. Once it was the Mighty Mississippi, where for seven years I moved about in a houseboat; then in a steamboat of my own making, partially recorded in my book, *River Journey*.

"Then I lived on land, twenty years upon the banks of the St. Croix River in Wisconsin. Now I live next to the Pacific Ocean; specifically, in the seaside village of Salmon Creek. Living in a small shingled cottage with a daughter, Jennifer, two cats, three canaries, and a garden that surrounds the house.

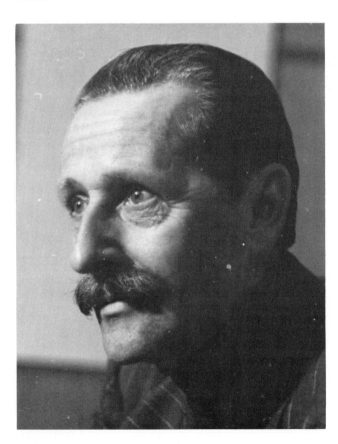

CLARENCE JONK

"I am adding a room; into which will go my typewriter, books, manuscripts (a pile 12' high), a chair, table, a record player; because I need background music, regardless of what I am writing: poetry needs certain music, whereas children's stories need other kinds of music—I can't explain what kind, anymore than I can explain what kind of a children's story I am going to write next.

"A writer's memory is a stern disciplinarian, but it also stops poetry from being born, which comes out of passionate idleness."

Copies of all Jonk's published juveniles, plus galley proofs and original manuscripts have been donated to the Kerlan Collection, University of Minnesota Library, Minneapolis, Minnesota.

FOR MORE INFORMATION SEE: Minneapolis Sunday Tribune, December 25, 1949; *Sunday Pioneer Press*, St. Paul, Minn., January 6, 1952; *St. Paul Dispatch*, October 14, 1959; *Look*, November 22, 1960.

KABDEBO, Thomas 1934-
(Tamas Kabdebo)

PERSONAL: First name is sometimes listed as Tamas; born February 5, 1934, in Budapest, Hungary; naturalized British citizen, 1963; son of Bela and Klara (Kelen) Kabdebo; married Agnes Wohl (an architect), July 27, 1959; children: Lilian Claire, Andrea Mary. *Education:* Attended University of Budapest, 1952-56; University of Wales, B.A., 1960; University of London, Dip. Lib., 1962, M.Phil., 1969. *Religion:* Roman Catholic. *Home:* 61 Gowan Ave., London S.W.6, England. *Office:* Main Library, University of Manchester, Manchester, England.

CAREER: University of London, University College, London, England, assistant librarian, 1961-69; University of Guyana, Georgetown, Guyana, university librarian, 1969-72; City of London Polytechnic, London, England, librarian, 1973-74; University of Manchester, Manchester, England, Social Sciences librarian, 1974—. *Member:* P.E.N., Library Association (London). *Awards, honors:* World Poetry Society Award, 1968, for *Hungarian Love Poems of the Twentieth Century*.

WRITINGS: (With Glynn Mills Ashton) *Gemau Hwngaria* (Hungarian short stories in Welsh; title means "Treasures of Hungary"), Gee & Sons (Denbigh, N. Wales), 1962; *Fortified Princecriptions on Poetry* (poetry satires), privately printed, 1965; *Erettsegi* (novel; title means "Maturity"), Feher Hollo (London), 1971; *Two-hearted* (poems in English and Hungarian), Poetry Seminar Workshop, University College, London, 1973; *Magyar Odisszeuszok* (short stories in Hungarian; title means "Odysseus Patronius"), Dario Detti (Rome), 1974.

Editor: (And translator) Attila Jozsef, *Poems*, Danubia, 1966; (and contributor) *University College Poetry*, Poetry Seminar Workshop, University College, London, 1967, 1969, 1973; (with Paul Tabori, and translator) *A Tribute to Gyula Illyes: Poems*, Occidental Press, 1968; (and translator) *Selected Poems of Gyula Illyes*, Chatto & Windus, 1971. Also editor of anthologies, *Hungarian Love Poems of the Twentieth Century*, 1967, and *British Poets*, 1969, published as special issues of *Poet* magazine (Madras).

THOMAS KABDEBO

Translator of books for children: Eva Janikovsky, *Basil and Barnabas,* Chatto & Windus, 1971; Ferenc Mora, *The Chimney-Sweep Giraffes,* Chatto & Windus, 1971. Contributor of articles or translations to periodicals, including *justforallthat, New Hungarian Quarterly, Image, Poetry Singapore,* and *Resurgence.* Editor of *justforallthat,* 1969-72.

WORK IN PROGRESS: A guide to the literature of the Amerindians of Guyana; "Without Him," a play.

SIDELIGHTS: Because he tried to cross the Hungarian-Czech frontier, Kabdebo was imprisoned for six months on political charges in 1955. Upon his release from prison, he worked for six months in a coal mine. A member of the National Guard and a newspaper reporter during the 1956 Hungarian Revolution, he finally emigrated to England when the revolution was crushed.

"My travels have taken me around Europe, North and South America, Australia, and a good many islands where I have tried to fish above and under the water. In some capacity or another—refugee, research worker, conference delegate, reporter, interpreter, guide, tourist or fisherman—I have been to thirty-eight countries. My urban relaxation is trying out as many swimming pools as I can (I used to be a swimming international) and looking at as many good pictures as I can find. Apart from my native language Hungarian, and my adopted tongue English, I used to be able to cope with Russian and still can do Italian."

KAPLAN, Irma   1900-

PERSONAL: Born June 17, 1900, in Gothenburg, Sweden; daughter of Mathias (managing director of a textile factory) and Selma (Friedland) Kaplan. *Education:* Etisk-Pedegogiska Institutet, Uppsala, student, 1922-23; studied at University of Hamburg, Germany and University of London, England, 1924, 1925. *Home:* Jakobsdalsgatan 3, Gothenburg 412 68, Sweden.

CAREER: On her return from studying languages abroad in 1925, she began entertaining children from neighboring villas with story evenings, and arranged a children's theater; after the death of her father in 1927, was employed as a governess for a number of years; teacher of English and German at a girls' boarding school in Sweden, 1942-44; teacher of Swedish, English, and German at another private school in Sweden, 1944-47; teacher of Swedish history and English at Nye Elementarskolan (first grade through examinations to a university), Stockholm, Sweden, 1948-69.

WRITINGS: (Retold from a collection of folk tales originally compiled by Gunnar O. Hylten-Vavallius and George Stephens), *Swedish Fairy Tales,* Muller, 1953, published in America as *Fairy Tales from Sweden,* Follett, 1967; (compiled, translated, and retold) *Old European Fairy Tales,* Muller, 1969; (translated) Zacharias Topelius, *The Sea King's Gift and Other Stories from Finland,* Muller, in press; *Heroes from Kalevala* (retold selections from the folk epic "Kalevala"), Muller, in press.

Children's plays in Swedish, both published by Barnbiblioteket saga: *Paask Haxorna* (title means "The Easter Witches"), first produced at Barnteatern (Children's Theatre), 1941; *Kvaellen foere Julafton* (title means "The Night Before Christmas"), first produced at Barnteatern, 1943.

WORK IN PROGRESS: Stories from East and West; Legends from Three Epochs.

IRMA KAPLAN

SIDELIGHTS: "I really do not consider myself an author. I have always had my greatest pleasure entertaining children of any age. The very best way has been telling them stories, and the very best stories have been those based on folklore. Nowhere can we find the same mystery or thrilling adventures connected with magic spells and nature inhabited by fairy creatures and talking animals. And all these things were reality to the people who inhabited the world centuries ago.

"I was a very busy teacher; some years I taught up to thirty-six pupils which meant heaps of books to correct every evening. There was really no time for writing books. In 1948, on my summer holiday, I visited England for the first time after the war. I went by boat and happened to sit beside an English publisher. He showed me a Norwegian storybook based on folklore. I told him I knew quite a lot about folklore and that ours was much the same and perhaps even more interesting. He recommended that I write some stories and send them to him in London.

"A year later I met with an accident which resulted in a serious fracture of my jaw and prevented my working at school for two months. That was how I started writing Swedish fairy tales and later when I retired from teaching I continued to write stories and entertain children. I also studied folklore from various other countries."

KAPLAN, Jean Caryl Korn 1926-
(Jean Caryl)

PERSONAL: Born March 28, 1926, in Mount Vernon, N.Y.; daughter of Louis (a businessman) and Hannah

JEAN CARYL KAPLAN

As for the sports, swimming and sailing were pure relaxation, but not tennis! Hank was a martinet on the courts. The counselor had been serious about shaping him into a tennis champ. ■ (From *Bones and the Smiling Mackerel* by Jean Caryl. Illustrated by Jessica Zemsky.)

(Kahn) Korn; married Ira Kaplan (a retail executive), July 3, 1948; children: Ellen, Robert, Lori. *Education:* Mount Holyoke College, student, 1943-44; New York University, B.S., 1965, M.A., 1970. *Home:* 27 Brite Ave., Scarsdale, N.Y. *Agent:* Muriel Fuller, P.O. Box 193, Grand Central Station, New York, N.Y. 10017.

CAREER: Presently an elementary school teacher, White Plains, N.Y.

WRITINGS—All under name Jean Caryl: *Bones and the Black Panther,* Funk, 1963; *Bones and the Smiling Mackerel* (Junior Literary Guild selection), Funk, 1964; *Bones and the Painted House,* Funk, 1968. Contributor to *Trails for Juniors.*

KARLIN, Eugene 1918-

PERSONAL: Born December 15, 1918, in Kenosha, Wis.; son of Isadore and Sarah Karlin; married Evelyn Wolfe (a professor), June 26, 1943; children: Lorie, Nina. *Education:* Attended Chicago Professional School of Art; Art Institute, Chicago, Ill., Art Students League, New York, N.Y., Colorado Springs Fine Art Center. *Home and office:* 3973 48th St., Sunnyside, N.Y. 11104.

CAREER: Free-lance illustrator. *Fortune Magazine*, New York, N.Y., staff artist, 1943-45; Parsons School of Design, New York, N.Y., teacher, 1948; Workshop School of Advertising and Editorial Art, teacher, 1949-58; Pratt Institute, Brooklyn, N.Y., teacher, 1955-64; School of Visual Arts, New York, N.Y., teacher, 1954—. *Exhibitions:* Art Institute, Chicago, Ill.; Pennsylvania Academy; Corcoran Gallery, Washington; San Francisco Museum; Los Angeles Museum, Oakland, Calif.; Metropolitan Museum, New York, N.Y.; Philadelphia Art Alliance; U.S. State Department Travelling Exhibit, "Graphic Arts—U.S.A.", Eastern Europe; Society of Illustrators; Art Directors Club of New York. *Awards, honors:* Art Institute, Clyde M. Carr prize, Flora Meyer Witkowsky prize; Art Director's Club of New York, award for distinctive merit, 1953-57, 1961; American Institute of Graphic Arts, certificate of excellence, 1955-57; Society of Illustrators, award for excellence, 1959, 1962-64, award for merit, 1959-66, 1970-73, 1974-75; *Herald Tribune*, childrens book award for *Adventure in the Desert*, 1961; *Communication Arts Magazine*, award for excellence, 1961, award for distinctive merit, 1962; Advance Club of Springfield, Mass., honorable mention, 1970.

(From *The Iliad and the Odyssey of Homer* retold by Alfred J. Church. Illustrated by Eugene Karlin.)

EUGENE KARLIN

ILLUSTRATOR: Herbert Kaufmann, *Adventure in the Desert*, Astor-Honor, 1961; *First Date*, Random House, 1962; Alfred J. Church, *The Aeneid for Boys and Girls*, Macmillan, 1962; Marianne Moore, *Fairy Tales*, Macmillan, 1963; Alfred J. Church, *The Iliad and the Odyssey of Homer*, Macmillan, 1964; *The Rubaiyat of Omar Khayyam*, T. Y. Crowell, 1964; *Elmira*, Houghton, 1966; H. E. Davis, *The Sayings of Jesus*, Golden Press, 1967; *Plato* (dialogues), Limited Editions Club, 1968; Wallace Kirkland, *The Lure of the Pond*, Regnery, 1969; Lois Wyse, *Poetry 2*, Doubleday, 1972. Illustrations have appeared in *Seventeen, Look, Family Circle, Sports Illustrated, Avant-Garde, Redbook, Town and Country, Mademoiselle, Todays Living, McCall's* and other well-known magazines.

SIDELIGHTS: "I have been painting and drawing since age ten. The past few years, my work has become linear and I have concentrated on pen-and-ink contour drawings. My work is direct and spontaneous and I make no preliminary sketches. As a youth I was influenced by Orozco and Picasso. I enjoy travel and tennis."

FOR MORE INFORMATION SEE: *American Artist Magazine*, March, 1966; *Idea*, Number 84, 1967, Number 100, 1970; *Illustrators of Children's Books: 1957-1966*, Horn Book, 1968; Diana Klemin, *The Art of Art for Children's Books*, Clarkson Potter, 1966; Diana Klemin, *The Illustrated Book*, Clarkson Potter, 1970.

ISAMI KASHIWAGI

KASHIWAGI, Isami   1925-

PERSONAL: Born July 17, 1925, in Onomea, Hawaii. *Education:* Attended Pennsylvania Academy of Fine Arts, 1947-52. *Religion:* Protestant. *Home:* Mileses, New York 12761.

CAREER: Free-lance illustrator, painter and beekeeper. Hankins Volunteer Fire Company, Hankins, N.Y., volunteer fireman, 1968—. *Military service:* U.S. Army, 1945-47. *Awards, honors:* Pennsylvania Academy of Fine Arts, Cresson prize.

ILLUSTRATOR: David Severn, *Dream Gold,* Viking, 1952; Vanya Oakes, *Desert Harvest,* Winston, 1953; Keith Robertson, *Outlaws of the Sourland,* Viking, 1953; Willy Ley, *Engineers' Dreams,* Viking, 1954; Nancy Webb and Jean Francis Webb, *The Hawaiian Islands,* Viking, 1956; William Knowlton, *Let's Explore Beneath the Sea,* Knopf, 1957; Alice Geer Kelsey, *Tino and the Typhoon,* Longmans, 1958; Vanya Oakes, *Hawaiian Treasure,* Archway.

SIDELIGHTS: "There was no real challenge to me in the sugar plantation in Hawaii, where I was born. As I went about my chores as a child I grew up with a close attachment to the soil and nature. To become an artist or a beekeeper preoccupied me.

"I was illustrating books in Philadelphia and New York and all this time I yearned for a country life surrounded by woods. I finally bought an old farm house in Sullivan County, New York some ten years ago.

"The illustrations I enjoy doing most have dealt with the outdoors. I enjoy the changes in seasons and especially the exposure to the raw winters. Here I have delved into painting the mountainous Catskills, keeping bees for honey production and the many facets of country living including doing all the house repairs and remodeling myself. In recent years, many young people from the cities have come out to the country and feel it important to live in close affinity to the soil."

KAYE, Geraldine (Hughesdon)   1925-

PERSONAL: Born January 14, 1925, in Watford, Hertfordshire, England; daughter of Gerald (a surveyor) and Dorothy (White) Hughesdon; married Barrington L. B. Kaye (now a lecturer and writer), April 16, 1948 (divorced, August, 1975); children: Miranda Jane, Jennifer Sarah, Matthew Edward. *Education:* London School of Economics

GERALDINE KAYE

Yvette read the story of Little Red Riding Hood very fast and after a bit Joannna didn't listen, but just told the story to herself in her head. Anyway it was very nice of Yvette to read a story Joanna thought, and you couldn't expect a French girl to know that she was much too big for a story like that, when Mummy didn't even know she was too big for dolls. ▪ (From *Joanna All Alone* by Geraldine Kaye. Illustrated by Mary Dinsdale.)

and Political Science, University of London, B.Sc. (second class honors), 1949. *Home:* 39 High Kingsdown, Bristol BS2 8EW, England. *Agent:* A. M. Heath & Co. Ltd., 35 Dover St., London W.1, England.

CAREER: Teacher at secondary school in Singapore, 1952-54, and at Mitford Colmer School, London, England, 1962-64. *Military service:* Women's Royal Naval Service, 1943-46.

WRITINGS—Juveniles: *The Boy Who Wanted to Go Fishing*, Methuen, 1960; *Kwasi Goes to Town*, Abelard, 1962 (also published as *Great Day in Ghana*, Abelard, 1962); *Kofi and the Eagle*, Methuen, 1963; *Koto and the Lagoon*, Deutsch, 1966, Funk & Wagnalls, 1969; *The Raffle Pony*, Brockhampton, 1966; *Chik and the Bottle-House*, Nelson, 1966; *Tail of the Siamese Cat*, Nelson, 1966; *The Blue Rabbit*, Brockhampton, 1967; *The Sea Monkey*, Longmans Young, 1967, World, 1968; *Tawno, Gypsy Boy*, Brockhampton, 1968; *Bonfire Night*, Macmillan, 1969; *Eight Days to Christmas*, Macmillan, 1970; *Runaway Boy*, Heinemann, 1971; *In the Park*, Macmillan, 1971; *Rainbow Shirt*, Macmillan, 1971; *Ginger*, Macmillan, 1972; *Nowhere to Stop*, Brockhampton, 1972; *The Rotten Old Car*, Brockhampton, 1973; *Tim and the Red Indian Headress*, Brockhampton, 1973; *Marie Alone*, Heinemann, 1973; *The Yellow Pom-Pom Hat*, Brockhampton, 1974;

Joanna All Alone, David E. Charles, 1974, Nelson, 1975; *Goodbye Ruby Red*, Brockhampton, 1974, Children's, 1976; *Billy Boy*, Brockhampton, 1975; *A Nail, a Stick and a Lid*, Brockhampton, 1975, Children's 1976; *Children of the Turnpike*, Hodder & Stoughton, 1976. Author of a number of school readers for use in Africa, all published by Oxford University Press. Writer of children's programs for British Broadcasting Corp. and Radio Malaya.

SIDELIGHTS: "I write mostly about children who are caught up in a cross-culture situation, as I have lived abroad a great deal and this is something which moves and interests me."

Geraldine Kaye has lived in Africa and Malaya and writes about children of those countries.

FOR MORE INFORMATION SEE: Times Literary Supplement, December 6, 1974.

KEATING, Leo Bernard 1915- (Bern Keating)

PERSONAL: Born May 14, 1915, in Fassett, Quebec, Canada; son of John Julian (an engineer) and Laure (Lalonde) Keating; married Marian Frances West (a photographer), June 10, 1939; children: John Geoffrey, Kate Maulding (deceased). *Education:* Student at New York University; University of Arkansas, B.A. (summa cum laude), 1938. *Politics:* Democratic Party (liberal branch). *Religion:* None. *Address:* Bayou Rd. 141, Greenville, Miss. 38701.

CAREER: Full-time professional writer; has worked as reporter for a newspaper and a radio station. *Military service:* U.S. Naval Reserve, 1941-46; became lieutenant. *Member:* Society of Journalists and Authors, Authors Guild, Society of American Travel Writers, Overseas Press Club, Outdoor Writers of America.

WRITINGS—Under name Bern Keating: *The Mosquito Fleet*, Putnam, 1963; *The Horse that Won the Civil War* (juvenile), Putnam, 1964; *Life and Death of the Aztec Nation* (juvenile), Putnam, 1964; *Zebulon Pike: Young America's Frontier Scout* (juvenile), Putnam, 1965; *The Invaders of Rome* (juvenile), Putnam, 1966; *Chaka, King of the Zulus* (juvenile), Putnam, 1968; (photographs by Dan Guravich) *The Grand Banks*, Rand McNally, 1968; *Alaska*, National Geographic Society, 1969; *The Northwest Passage: From the Mathew to the Manhattan, 1497-1969*, Rand McNally, 1969; *Florida*, Rand McNally, 1972; *The Gulf of Mexico*, Viking, 1973; *Illustrated History of the Texas Rangers*, Rand McNally, 1975. Ghost writer of other books under various pseudonyms. Regular contributor to *National Geographic, Travel and Leisure, Smithsonian,* and other magazines.

WORK IN PROGRESS: A novel on the Mississippi slave revolt of 1835; continuing research on world population-food problems; books for National Geographic special publications department.

SIDELIGHTS: Keating has traveled in more than eighty-four countries and circled the globe four times. Speaks "native-level French, good Spanish."

Most of the tribes did treat the voyagers kindly — even too kindly. for they insisted on gorging them with feasts of dogmeat so fat and greasy, it turned even the fur trader's stomach. ■ (From *Famous American Explorers* by Bern Keating. Illustrated by Lorence Bjorklund.)

KELLOGG, Jean 1916-
(Sally Jackson, Gene Kellogg)

PERSONAL: Born December 28, 1916, in Chicago, Ill.; daughter of Donald (a lawyer) and Florence (Baker) Defrees; married James H. Kellogg (a manufacturer), November 4, 1939 (died February 15, 1967); children: Frances (Mrs. George Smith), James M. *Education:* Smith College, B.A. (highest honors), 1939, University of Chicago, M.A. (honors in English), 1965, Ph.D., 1969. *Politics:* Independent. *Religion:* Catholic. *Home:* 179 East Lake Shore Dr., Chicago, Ill. 60611.

CAREER: Henry Regnery Co., Chicago, Ill., assistant editor, 1950-1955, associate editor, 1955-1959, editor-in-chief, 1959-1964; Mundelein College, Chicago, Ill., assistant professor, English department, 1969-1971; Rosary College, River Forest, Ill., assistant professor, English department, department of Religious studies, 1971-1972, associate professor, English department, department of Religious studies, chairman of the Humanities division, 1972-1974; Mundelein Graduate School of Religious Studies, Chicago, Ill., visiting professor, 1971-74; University of Chicago divinity school, Chicago, Ill., associate professorial lecturer in religion and literature, 1975—. *Member:* Women's National Book Association, Children's Reading Round Table, American Catholic Philosophical Association, American Academy of Political and Social Science, College Theology

JEAN KELLOGG

Society, American Academy of Religion. *Awards, honors:* Sophia Smith Scholar, Honor Society for Excellence in the Arts.

WRITINGS—All published by Reilly & Lee, except as indicated: (Adapter) L. Frank Baum, *The Wizard of Oz* (juvenile), 1961; (adapter) Baum, *The Land of Oz* (juvenile), 1961; (adapter) Baum, *Dorothy and the Wizard in Oz* (juvenile), 1961; (adapter) Baum, *Ozma of Oz* (juvenile), 1962; *Hans and the Winged Horse* (juvenile), 1964; *The Rod and the Rose* (juvenile), 1964.

Juveniles under pseudonym Sally Jackson: *The Littlest Star,* Reilly & Lee, 1960; *The Littlest Skater,* Reilly & Lee, 1961; *Here We Go,* Reilly & Lee, 1961; *Is This Your Dog?,* Reilly & Lee, 1962.

Under pseudonym, Gene Kellogg: *The Vital Tradition,* Loyola University Press, 1970; *Dark Prophets of Hope,* Loyola University Press, 1975. Contributor to *Christian Century, America, Thought, Cross Currents.*

WORK IN PROGRESS: The metaphysical novel in the Nineteenth Century.

KEMPNER, Mary Jean   1913-1969

PERSONAL: Born in 1913 in Galveston, Tex.; daughter of Daniel W. Kempner (a businessman and philanthropist); first husband was Oakleigh L. Thorne (a banker); married Alan Pryce-Jones (a literary critic), October 26, 1968; children: (first marriage) Daniel Kempner Thorne. *Home:* Sintra, Portugal.

CAREER: War correspondent accredited to the Navy during World War II, reporting for *Vogue* and Newspaper Enterprise Association from China, Japan, Okinawa, and the Pacific; following the war was on the staff of *Vogue* until 1952; free-lance writer, contributing chiefly to *Harper's, Harper's Bazaar,* and *House Beautiful,* 1952-69.

WRITINGS: Invitation to Portugal (young adult book), introduction by Alan Pryce-Jones, Atheneum, 1969.

(Died September 11, 1969)

KEMPTON, Jean Welch   1914-
(Jean-Louise Welch)

PERSONAL: Born April 3, 1914, in Vineland, N.J.; daughter of Howard Gow (a fund raiser) and Etta (Roat) Welch; married Donald Eugene Kempton (a psychologist), June 25, 1952. *Education:* Attended Cornell University, 1932. *Religion:* Presbyterian. *Address:* Route 2, Box 191, Horse Shoe, N.C. 28742.

CAREER: Womens Home Companion, designed dolls and stuffed animals, 1942; F.A.O. Schwartz, New York, N.Y., designed and made dolls, 1943; Doubleday & Co., Inc., Garden City, N.Y., correspondent, 1943-48; writer of children's educational radio and television series in Garden City, N.Y., 1948-49; director of religious education for churches in Garden City, N.Y., 1949-51, and Hagerstown, Md., 1951-52. State coordinator of Women in Community Service, 1964-70; education chairman of North Carolina

JEAN WELCH KEMPTON

Extension Homemakers, 1969. *Member:* North Carolina Mental Health Association (member of board of directors, 1968-71; state chairman, Operation Santa Claus, 1968), Cornell Womens Club, Hendersonville Mental Health Association.

WRITINGS: (Under name Jean-Louise Welch) *The Animals Came First* (children's book), Oxford University Press, 1948, 2nd edition, Walck, 1963; *Living with Myasthenia Gravis: A Bright New Tomorrow,* C. C Thomas, 1972. Contributor to *Child Life, International Journal of Religious Education* and *Newsday.*

WORK IN PROGRESS: Nutritional approach to the treatment of myasthenia gravis.

SIDELIGHTS: "Childhood memories are filled with illness and long hours spent by myself. During these periods, I often amused myself by making up stories and sometimes acting them out with my dolls and pets. My father read to me a great deal and helped me acquire a love of reading.

"My school attendance was so irregular that when I graduated from grammar school, my total attendance was only two years. Mother tutored me at home. I did manage to keep up well during high school years but my education was again interrupted when I was at Cornell University. I developed a rare neuro-muscular disease called myasthenia gravis.

"At that time so little was known about treating the illness that I was expected to die. A resident physician in the hospital where I spent many months tried a new drug which saved my life and opened the door of hope to all victims of the disorder. I became the human guinea pig for the oral form of the drug and worked along with the doctors on medical research.

And so the donkey with the cat on his back, the cow and the ox started in the direction of the low, sweet sound and the dim light. ■ (From *The Animals Came First* by Jean Louise Welch. Illustrated by Ruth Carroll.)

"Frustrated by a long period of inactivity, I began writing some of the stories I made up to fill my loneliness. My father always encouraged me to write, to use my imagination constructively. It really was to please him that I attempted to sell one of my stories. It was gratifying that he lived to see some of them published.

"Although I prefer to write for children, on the urging of the doctors of the Bowman Gray School of Medicine in Winston-Salem, I am now concentrating on writing about myasthenia gravis, from which I have completely recovered. It means long hours of research and scientific consultations but my goal is to enable others to become as well as I am. I also am assisting with research being conducted at the medical school.

"My husband and I retired on forty acres on the side of Forge Mountain near Asheville, North Carolina. Community projects keep interrupting my writing but I hope to complete the medical writing soon, and to get back to writing children's stories."

KISINGER, Grace Gelvin (Maze)   1913-1965

PERSONAL: Surname is pronounced *Ki*-singer, first syllable as in "kite"; born May 14, 1913, in Ridgway, Pa.; daughter of Henry Riley and Labelle (Sutton) Maze; married Harry Elliott Kisinger (a businessman), April 16, 1938, deceased. *Education:* Indiana State College, Indiana, Pa., B.S., 1934. *Home:* 920 College Ave., Pittsburgh, Pa. *Agent:* Ruth Cantor, 156 Fifth Ave., New York, N.Y.

CAREER: Worked in sales promotion and selling, principally with West Penn Power Co., Pittsburgh, Pa., and Ringgold Corp., Kittanning, Pa., 1936-55; began to write verse for greeting cards in 1944 and sold more than five hundred items to about ten different firms; switched to short stories and articles, and then to novels for teen-age girls.

WRITINGS: The Enchanted Summer, Random House, 1956; *More than Glamour,* Nelson, 1957; *The New Lucinda* (Junior Literary Guild selection), Nelson, 1958; *Bittersweet Autumn,* Macrae Smith, 1960; *Too Late Tomorrow,* Macrae Smith, 1962. Contributor to periodicals.

WORK IN PROGRESS: A novel for teenage girls, about student nursing.

(Died, December 7, 1965)

KISSIN, Eva H.   1923-

PERSONAL: Born February 12, 1923, in New York, N.Y.; daughter of Samuel A. (an architect) and Rose (Rubenstein) Hertz; married Benjamin Kissin (a medical doctor and professor), July 1, 1950; children: Ruth. *Education:* Syracuse University, B.A. (magna cum laude), 1943; New York University, M.A., 1949, M.A., 1973. *Home:* 25 Grace Ct., Brooklyn Heights, N.Y. 11201. *Agent:* Curtis Brown Ltd., 60 East 56th St., New York, N.Y. 10022.

CAREER: Teacher in public schools of New York, N.Y., 1946-52; Ramaz School, New York, N.Y., English teacher, 1973—. Brooklyn Museum, Brooklyn, N.Y., consultant on

EVA H. KISSIN

junior membership, 1961-69, vice-president of community committee. *Member:* Phi Beta Kappa.

WRITINGS: (Editor) *Stories in Black and White* (juvenile), Lippincott, 1970.

WORK IN PROGRESS: A second short story anthology.

SIDELIGHTS: "I decided to compile *Stories in Black and White* after reading Bernard Malamud's *Black Is my Favorite Color.* It seemed to exemplify·the distances between the two groups as well as the will to bridge them. As a teacher I could see the real need for a source that would present similar situations seen from both black and white perspectives. I felt it would be of genuine classroom value."

FOR MORE INFORMATION SEE: Library Journal, June 15, 1970.

KLIMOWICZ, Barbara   1927-

PERSONAL: Surname is pronounced Klim-o-wits; born September 11, 1927, in Mansfield, Ohio; daughter of Everett K. (a mechanical engineer) and Dorothy (Hunter) Tingley; married Charles H. Klimowicz (now a petroleum engineer), October 20, 1951; children: Mark, Lynn. *Education:* Ohio State University, B.F.A., 1949, B.S. in Ed., 1951. *Religion:* Presbyterian. *Home:* Rumbai, Sumatra, Indonesia.

BARBARA KLIMOWICZ

I grabbed her braids and managed to tie them good and tight to a branch of the Northern Spy.
"So long, kid," I snarled, like Jack would have done. ■ (From *The Great Green Apple War* by Barbara Klimowicz. Illustrated by Lee J. Ames.)

CAREER: Kindergarten teacher in Salem, Ill., 1960-65, and remedial reading teacher, 1967, teacher of art and science in Tulsa, Okla., 1968.

WRITINGS: Fred, Fred, Use Your Head, Abingdon, 1966; *Strawberry Thumb,* Abingdon, 1968; *The Word-Birds of Davy McFifer,* Abingdon, 1970; *My Sister, the Horse,* Abingdon, 1971; *When Shoes Eat Socks,* Abingdon, 1971; *The Great Green Apple War,* Abingdon, 1973; *Ha, Ha, Ha, Henrietta,* Abingdon, 1975.

SIDELIGHTS: "I guess if I had to state the one thing in the world that interests me most, it would be words—words in all sizes, in all situations. To me they hold a special fascination that makes me want to do things with them—work crossword puzzles, play Scrabble, rhyme them, enjoy the sounds of them in various combinations. But most of all I enjoy building stories with them.

"As a kindergarten teacher, I soon learned the importance of story time to my small pupils. It was interesting to note that some stories held them spellbound while others floated past them out the school windows and meant nothing. It made me want to find what that something was that made children forget all distractions and listen. I am still searching and experimenting with words. There are always children to try my stories on—even in the Sumatran jungle where I am now living."

KOHNER, Frederick 1905-

PERSONAL: Born September 25, 1905, in Trnovany, Czechoslovakia; son of Julius and Helene (Beamt) Kohner; married Fritzie Klein, 1930; children: Ruth Kohner Drenick, Kathy Kohner Zuckerman. *Education:* Studied at Sorbonne; University of Vienna, Ph.D., 1929. *Home:* 12046 Coyne St., Los Angeles, Calif. *Agent:* William Morris Agency, 1350 Avenue of the Americas, New York, N.Y. 10019.

CAREER: Newspaper reporter, screenwriter, novelist, lecturer, playwright, since coming to United States in 1936; lecturer in film department at University of Southern California, 1961-63, and University of California, Los Angeles. *Member:* Writers Guild of the Authors League of America.

WRITINGS: Gidget, Putnam, 1957; *Cher Papa,* Putnam, 1959; *Gidget Goes Hawaiian,* Bantam, 1961; *The Continental Kick,* Bantam, 1962; *Mister, Will You Marry Me?,* New American Library, 1963; *Affairs of Gidget,* Bantam, 1963; *Gidget Goes to Rome,* Bantam, 1964; *Gidget in Love,* Dell, 1965; *The Gremmie,* New American Library, 1966; *Gidget Goes Parisienne,* Dell, 1966; *Kiki of Montparnasse,* Stein & Day, 1967; *Gidget Goes to New York,* Dell, 1968; *The Magician of Sunset Boulevard,* Droemer-Knaur, 1975; *Amanda,* Droemer-Knaur, 1975.

Plays: (With Albert Mannheimer) "The Bees and the Flowers," 1946; "Stalin Allee"; "The Woman of My Life." Author of about twenty screenplays for major producers,

FREDERICK KOHNER

Based on *"Gidget"* by Frederick Kohner.

and "Gidget" series, American Broadcasting Co. television network, 1965.

WORK IN PROGRESS: The Delights of Olding, a vademecum for the aging.

SIDELIGHTS: "Gidget," a name Kohner coined from "girl" and "midget," has become popular with teen-age readers. The Gidget books have been translated into ten languages. His doctoral thesis, *The German Film,* is a widely-used reference book in Germany.

A musical based on his book *Kiki of Montparnasse* is in preparation, written by Dale Wasserman, music by Michel Legrand.

KOSSIN, Sandy (Sanford) 1926-

PERSONAL: Born June 4, 1926, in Los Angeles, Calif.; son of Leo (a plumbing contractor) and Clara (Klur) Kossin; married Josephine Koscomb (a teacher), May 21, 1954; children: David, James. *Education:* Attended Jepson Art Institute, Los Angeles, Calif. *Home and office:* 143 Cow Neck Rd., Port Washington, N.Y. 11050.

CAREER: Illustrator. Parson's School of Design, New York, N.Y., teacher. *Exhibitions:* Permanent collection at MacArthur Museum, Norfolk, Va.; United States Airforce Art Museum. *Military service:* U.S. Navy, sonarman second class, 1944-46. *Member:* Society of Illustrators. *Awards, honors:* Society of Illustrators, certificates of merit, 1963-65, 1967, 1968, 1970-74; Art Directors Club Exhibition, 1962, 1965, 1968.

ILLUSTRATOR: Robyn Supraner, *Think About It, You Might Learn Something,* Houghton, 1973; Jonah Kalb, *The Kid's Candidate,* Houghton, 1975.

WORKS IN PROGRESS: "Several are in the works at this time (titles unknown)."

SIDELIGHTS: "Cartoon illustration, to me, is a very strong means of portraiture—in spite of my being best known for dramatic realism in other adult orientated areas, such as advertising and editorial illustration which has been used in such magazines as: *Saturday Evening Post, Life,*

SANDY KOSSIN

Illustrated by Sandy Kossin

Old Thunder Thighs, Mrs. Turtletaub, came charging across the room and got whipped-cream topping right in the middle of her forehead. ■ (From *Think About It, You Might Learn Something* by Robyn Supraner. Illustrated by Sandy Kossin.)

Redbook, Good Housekeeping and others. But I found my strongest feelings were in finding and depicting, humorously, life around me; children (my own) and people I've known.

"I tend to work in line drawings and apply paint, when color is necessary, in a semi-opaque manner using Winson Newton designer colors and Liquitex or even a combination of markers and watercolors.

"Although my drawings are humorous, I don't like being called a 'cartoonist.' I'm basically an *illustrator* who sees with a smiling eye. A student of Rico Lebrun, I find my work has strong 'fine arts' attitudes which has given it its strength.

"My interests away from the studio include tennis, which is rapidly becoming an obsession, and sailing. I have a twenty-foot sloop."

FOR MORE INFORMATION SEE: American Artist Magazine, May, 1969.

KROLL, Francis Lynde   1904-1973

PERSONAL: Born November 9, 1904, in Fairbury, Neb.; son of August (a farmer and politician) and Maude (Lynde) Kroll; married Viola Hathaway, August 17, 1926; children: Francis L., Jr., Stanley H., Keith D. *Education:* University of Nebraska, student, 1923-26; Chadron State College, A.B., 1959, M.A., 1962; University of Wyoming, graduate study. *Politics:* Democrat. *Religion:* Presbyterian. *Home:* 927 B St., Fairbury, Neb. 68352. *Agent:* Lurton Blassingame, 10 East 43rd St., New York, N.Y. 10017.

CAREER: Teacher in Helvey, Parks, Dodge, Valentine,

and Crawford, Neb., 1927-42, 1955-64; U.S. Department of Agriculture, Meat Inspection Service, Omaha, Neb., inspector, 1942-55; Sunol (Neb.) Consolidated School, superintendent, 1964-65; Palisade (Neb.) public schools, superintendent, 1965-68; Orleans (Neb.) public schools, superintendent, 1968-71. *Member:* National Education Association, Nebraska State Teachers Association, Nebraska Writers Guild (vice-president, 1954-55), Sigma Nu.

WRITINGS: Young Sioux Warrior (Junior Literary Guild selection), Lantern, 1952; *Young Sand Hills Cowboy,* Lantern, 1952; *Young Crow Raider,* Lantern, 1953; *Young Medicine Man,* Lantern, 1956; *Top Hand,* McKay, 1965. Author of fifty one-act plays for children. Contributor to *Encyclopaedia Britannica;* contributor of about fifty short stories and a few articles to *Story Parade, Plays, Stag, Man's Life,* and other magazines and newspapers.

WORK IN PROGRESS: Juvenile fiction about settlement of Nebraska near the Oregon Trail; a historically-based novel about the Sioux; a basketball sports story.

SIDELIGHTS: Kroll's first book grew out of one of his short stories, widely reprinted in anthologies and in the *Tokyo Times,* portraying the Sioux Indians apart from their contact and conflict with white men.

"I am trying to find a plane between the Romantics and those now termed Realists, aiming to portray life more nearly as it is. A story-teller's task is to tell a story."

Kroll's writing is collected at the Oregon University Research Library in Eugene, Ore.

(Died November 12, 1973)

It was a steep slope and the ground was loose, giving the horse poor footing.
■ (From *Young Sioux Warrior* by Francis Lynde Kroll. Illustrated by Charles H. Geer.)

But sometimes the bird was too fast.
It might climb up the tree, using its
wing claws to grab onto branches.
Or it might fly to another tree.
■ (From *Dinosaur Story* by Joanna Cole.
Illustrated by Mort Kunstler.)

KÜNSTLER, Morton   1927-
(Mutz)

PERSONAL: Born August 28, 1927, in Brooklyn, N.Y.; son of Thomas L. and Rebecca (Weitz; a teacher) Künstler; married Deborah Goldberg (an interior designer), November 4, 1951; children: David, Amy, Jane. *Education:* Attended Brooklyn College, 1943-45, University of California, Los Angeles, 1945-46, Pratt Institute, New York, N.Y., 1947-50. *Home and office:* Twin Ponds Lane, Syosset, N.Y. 11791. *Agent:* Lavaty, 45 East 51st Street, New York, N.Y. 10022.

CAREER: Illustrator. *Awards, honors:* Society of Illustrators, certificates of merit.

ILLUSTRATOR: Alfred Ollivant, *Bob, Son of Battle,* Grosset, 1960; Ernest Thompson Seton, *King of the Grizzlies,* Scholastic, 1970; Robert Froman, *The Wild Orphan,* Scholastic, 1972; Joanna Cole, *Dinosaur Story,* Scholastic, 1974; Betsy Haynes, *Spies on the Devil's Belt,* Scholastic, 1975. Illustrations have appeared in many books, magazines, advertising, paintings for galleries, museums, and covers for *Mad Magazine* (under pseudonym Mutz).

WORK IN PROGRESS: Poster for movie, *The Hindenburg;* series of farm paintings for Hesston Corporation; series of paintings for Frame House Gallery in Louisville, Kentucky.

SIDELIGHTS: "I speak Spanish and have lived and traveled extensively in Mexico. Paint and draw mostly historical and adventure subject matter. Enjoy animal and wildlife painting. Have made many trips all over the United States for research for historical paintings."

FOR MORE INFORMATION SEE: Vlanoff, *Illustrated History of World War I in the Air,* Arco, 1971.

MORTON KÜNSTLER

LAMB, G(eoffrey) F(rederick) (Balaam)

PERSONAL: Born in London, England; son of Frederick William (an accountant) and Elizabeth (Kendall) Lamb; married Olga Heckman, July 10, 1943; children: Christopher John, Anthony Stuart. *Education:* Kings College, London, B.A., 1932, M.A., 1939. *Home:* Penfold, Legion Lane, Kingsworthy, Winchester, Hampshire, England.

CAREER: Teacher of English in schools in England, 1933-45; Camden Training College, London, England, lecturer in English, 1946-50; author, 1950—. *Member:* Society of Authors, Children's Writer's Group (honorary secretary, 1963-68), National Book League, Magic Circle (London).

WRITINGS: (Editor) *Valiant Deeds in Life and Literature,* Harrap, 1942; (editor) *United States and United Kingdom,* Harrap, 1944; *Tales of Human Endeavour,* Harrap, 1946; *Six Good Samaritans,* Oxford University Press, 1947; (with C. C. Fitz-Hugh) *Precis and Comprehension,* Harrap, 1947; *Commentaries on Galsworthy's Plays,* Pitman, 1948; *Questions Answered About Teaching,* Jordan, 1949.

(Editor) *The English at School,* Allen & Unwin, 1950; (editor) *Other People's Lives,* Harrap, 1951; (editor) *All Over the World,* Harrap, 1951; *Modern Action and Adventure,* Harrap, 1952; (with Fitz-Hugh) *Introductory Precis and Comprehension,* Harrap, 1952; (editor) *All Kinds of Adventure,* Harrap, 1952; *Your Child at School,* F. Watts, 1953; (editor) *Essays of Action,* Macmillan, 1953; (under pseudonym Balaam) *Chalk in My Hair* (autobiography), Benn, 1953; *English for General Certificate,* Harrap, 1954; *The Spirit of Modern Adventure,* Harrap, 1955; (editor) *Short Stories of Action,* Allen & Unwin, 1955; (under pseudonym Balaam) *Chalk Gets in Your Eyes,* Benn, 1955; *English for Middle Forms,* Harrap, Volume I, 1956, Volume II, 1963; *Franklin—Happy Voyager,* Benn, 1956; *English for Lower Forms,* Harrap, Volume I, 1957, Volume II, 1960; *Thrilling Exploits of Modern Adventure,* Harrap, 1957; *The South Pole,* Muller, 1957; (under pseudonym Balaam) *Come Out to Play,* M. Joseph, 1958; (editor) *Living Dangerously,* Allen & Unwin, 1958; (editor) *Stirring Deeds,* Harrap, 1958; *The Happiest Days,* M. Joseph, 1959; *Great Exploits of World War II,* Harrap, 1959.

Thrilling Journeys of Modern Times, Harrap, 1962; *Punctuation for Schools,* Harrap, 1962; *Modern Adventures in Air and Space,* Harrap, 1964; *Look at Schools,* Hamish Hamilton, 1964; (editor) *Story and Rhythm,* Harrap, 1966; *Composition and Comprehension for CSE,* Harrap, 1968; *The Pegasus Book of Magicians,* Dobson, 1968; *Practical Precis and Comprehension,* Harrap, 1969; *One Hundred Good Stories,* Wheaton, Books 1-4, 1969, Books 5-6, 1970.

Modern Adventures at Sea, Harrap, 1970; *Wonder Book of the Seashore,* Transworld, 1970; *Your Book of Card Tricks,* Faber, 1972, Nelson, 1973; *Your Book of Mental Magic,* Nelson, 1973; *Your Book of Table Tricks,* Faber, 1974, Nelson, 1975; *Discovering Magic Charms and Talismans,* Shire Publications, 1974; *More Good Stories,* Wheaton, 1975; *Your Book of Secret Writing Tricks,* Nelson, 1975.

WORK IN PROGRESS: Victorian Magic for Routledge.

SIDELIGHTS: "When I was young I wanted to be a conjurer, and took lessons from a well-known magician. Then I decided to be a writer. I couldn't make a living at this so I became a teacher. In due course, I found myself an education college lecturer, teaching other people (mostly ex-service men) to be teachers. This was an extremely interesting job, but the training college ultimately closed down.

"By this time I'd published quite a few books, so I decided to have another go at earning my living as a writer. This time I was more successful, and I've been a full-time writer ever since. My teaching experience was now very useful, as a number of my books were written for children. Some were educational books, and two or three were based on my experiences as a teacher. Others were true-adventure books, biography, or social history.

"A few years ago I renewed my early interest in conjuring, and several of my recent books are connected with magic, especially magic for young people. This means that I now combine my two early interests of conjuring and writing, so I suppose I'm more or less back where I started! It's not a bad place to be.

"I'm a Londoner. I now live in a country town about sixty miles away, but I was born in London, educated there, and did most of my teaching in the London area. I wouldn't want to live there again, but I like to feel that it's near enough to reach."

G. F. LAMB

LAMB, Lynton 1907-

PERSONAL: Born April 15, 1907, in Nizaamabad, India; son of Frederick and Annie (Brown) Lamb; married Barbara Morgan, 1933; children: James, Andrew. *Education:* Attended Kingswood School, L.C.C. Central School of Arts and Crafts, both in England. *Home:* Sandon, near Chelmsford, Essex, England.

CAREER: Artist. Member, The Arts Council of Great Britain, 1951-54; member, Council of Industrial Design, 1952-55. *Military service:* Royal Engineers, 1940-45, becoming captain. *Member:* Royal Society of Arts (fellow), Society of Industrial Artists (fellow; president 1952-53), Society of Authors, London Group Double Crown Club. *Awards, honors:* Gold Medal of the International Philatelic Society, 1961; Royal Society of Arts award (Royal Design for Industry), 1975, for book illustration and design.

WRITINGS: The Purpose of Painting, Oxford University Press, 1936; *County Town,* Eyre & Spottiswoode, 1950; *Preparation for Painting,* Oxford University Press, 1954; *Cat's Tales,* Faber, 1959; *Drawing for Illustration,* Oxford University Press, 1962; *Materials and Methods of Painting,* Oxford University Press, 1970; *Worse Than Death,* Gollancz; *Death of a Dissenter,* Gollancz. Contributor to *Signature, Alphabet and Image, Motif, Chambers's Encyclopedia,* on art subjects.

ILLUSTRATOR: Thomas Hardy, *Our Exploits at West Poley,* Oxford University Press, New York, 1952; George Eliot, *Silas Marner,* Limited Editions, 1953; Charlotte Bronte, *Jane Eyre,* Coward, 1955; William Mayne, *Member for the Marsh,* Oxford University Press, 1956; Henri Bosco, *Boy and the River,* Oxford University Press, 1956, Pantheon, 1957; Edith Nesbit, *Railway Children,* Dover, 1957; William Mayne, *Grass Rope,* Dutton; also illustrated H. G. Wells' *Tono-Bungay.*

WORK IN PROGRESS: Editor with Quentin Bell of a new series of art paperbacks for Oxford University Press, and writing a book in the series, *Materials and Methods of Painting;* an autobiography.

SIDELIGHTS: "I may say that, although I have always been a painter by instinct and training, I was also brought up, at school, to want to write; and in my early years as a book designer at Oxford University Press, London, met the late Charles Williams, a great and sympathetic man, who was to encourage me in the exact usage of the English language to express only what could properly be said in words and to eschew anything that could not.

"As for my illustrations, I have tried, likewise, to compliment the author's meaning by the creation of images that use the language of the painter coming in on a parallel course to the author's. As both author and illustrator, therefore, I can say with confidence that this was achieved in my *Cat's Tales.*"

HOBBIES AND OTHER INTERESTS: Playing cricket.

FOR MORE INFORMATION SEE: Illustrators of Children's Books: 1946-1956, Horn Book, 1958; *Illustrators of Children's Books: 1957-1966,* Horn Book, 1968; Diana Klemin, *The Illustrated Book,* Clarkson Potter, 1970.

LANDAU, Elaine 1948-

PERSONAL: Born February 15, 1948, in Lakewood, N.J.; daughter of James and May (a department store manager; maiden name, Tudor) Garmiza; married Edward William Landau (an electrical engineer), December 16, 1968. *Education:* New York University, B.A., 1970; Pratt Institute, M.L.S., 1975. *Religion:* Jewish. *Home:* 46-01 39th Ave., Queens, N.Y. 11104.

CAREER: Reporter on community newspaper in New York, N.Y., 1970-72; Simon & Schuster, New York, N.Y., editor, 1972-73. *Member:* National Organization for Women, Women's Equity Action League, American Library Association.

WRITINGS: (With Jesse Jackson) *Black in America: A Fight for Freedom,* Messner, 1973; *Woman, Woman! Feminism in America,* Messner, 1974; *Hidden Heroines: Women in American History,* Messner, 1975. Contributor of reviews to *New York Times Book Review.*

WORK IN PROGRESS: A children's book about death.

SIDELIGHTS: "I wrote my first book at the age of nine in the children's room of my local library. I spent a lot of time in that room, reading and growing, while remaining safely hidden from a mother, older sister, and aunt who assured me that to dream of becoming an author was an unrealistic career aspiration.

ELAINE LANDAU

"But no matter. The relative hasn't been born who can dampen the magic of a well-spun story. Besides, I was a very determined little girl. So determined that by the time I was fifteen, I had written over two dozen books—the longest of which was a full nine pages!

"At twenty-five I finally found a publisher. Although being a 'real' author is often a very lonely occupation (you can't entertain friends while completing a chapter), it is also my greatest joy. I've always loved the idea of reaching out to share my thoughts and feelings with others, and I still can't think of a better way to do so."

HOBBIES AND OTHER INTERESTS: Botany.

LANE, Carolyn 1926-

PERSONAL: Born June 4, 1926, in Providence, R.I.; daughter of Harry T. (president, Blocker Air Conditioning Corp.) and Margaret (Breitenfeld) Blocker; married M. Donald Lane, Jr. (an architect), April 28, 1951; children: Jay Donald. *Education:* Connecticut College, B.A., 1948. *Home:* Ward Rd., Salt Point, N.Y. 12578.

CAREER: Artist and writer. Has been a professional greeting card designer, paints, and does silk screen work; during the past ten years has designed and executed eight sets for local theatrical organizations, three of them for productions of her own plays. *Member:* Authors Guild. *Awards, honors:* Community Children's Theatre, Kansas City, Mo., 12th annual merit award, 1963, and Pioneer Drama Service award, 1967, both for *Turnabout Night at the Zoo;* Pioneer's Best Children's Play, 1969, for *The Wayward Clocks;* Theatre Guild of Webster Groves, Mo., one-act play contest, first prize, 1969, for *The Last Grad.*

WRITINGS—Juvenile books: *Uncle Max and the Sea Lion,* Bobbs, 1970; *Turnabout Night at the Zoo,* Abingdon, 1971; *The Voices of Greenwillow Pond,* Houghton, 1972; *The Winnemah Spirit,* Houghton, 1975.

Plays: *Turnabout Night at the Zoo* (juvenile), Pioneer Drama Service, 1967; *The Wayward Clocks* (juvenile), Pioneer Drama Service, 1969; *The Last Grad* (one-act adult drama), Baker's Plays, 1970; *Child of Air* (one-act adult drama), Pioneer Drama Service, 1972.

WORK IN PROGRESS: Several children's books, a monthly book review column for *Hudson Valley* magazine.

SIDELIGHTS: "Many authors of children's books write their stories specifically for their own children, or for other children they know—but I write mine for the child I once was myself. That, after all, is the child I know the best, and since children haven't changed much over the years, I like to think my readers are very much like me.

"What sort of stories did I like way back then? I liked fantasy, for one thing—but only if it was believable. The characters had to seem real and likeable, the settings had to be described so well that I could see them, and the stories themselves had to sound as though they might really have happened. I believed every word of the *Mary Poppins* books, for example, and though I knew all those marvelous happenings were really not possible in our own humdrum world, they were entirely believable to me while I was reading about them. The Banks' house on Cherry Tree Lane seemed a warm and lovely place to be, and it was as familiar to me as my own home. It still is.

"Right now I am working on a ghost story, and though I don't normally 'believe' in ghosts, I believe in *this* ghost,

"Frederick," he said soberly, "plainly it's time you and I had a little talk about your proper duties as a grown-up frog. Do you know what frogs are for?" ■ (From *The Voices of Greenwillow Pond* by Carolyn Lane. Illustrated by Wallace Tripp.)

CAROLYN LANE

because I have given him such a distinct personality that he seems absolutely real to me. I am, also, writing a story about an abandoned cat, and because I feel so genuinely sad about her plight, I almost expect her to show up—all bedraggled and lonely—on my front porch some rainy night!

"I was raised by a mother and father who had delightful senses of humor, and this humor seems to have been passed along to me. I cannot write even the saddest story without injecting a note of laughter here and there, and over the years I've discovered that life is never wholly sad or happy—it's a combination. No matter what terrible thing happens, there is always a funny side to it, and no matter how funny something is, there's always an undertone of sadness in it. My own books are more humorous than otherwise, but I think a few serious thoughts emerge in each one of them.

"I also liked (and still like) real stories about real people, and believe it is characters, not plots, that make the best stories. If the characters are stiff and unbelievable, the most intriguing plot in the world will not make the story come alive. This applies to both fantasy and reality. In a truly good story it doesn't matter whether the main character is a lion, a boy, a frog, or a ghost—if he is not made real and likeable by the author, then his story is not worth reading.

"My own childhood was a happy one, and I hope this happiness shines for other children through my books. I am always pleased when an editor or a librarian likes my work, but the real reward is knowing that even one child, somewhere, has enjoyed reading something I wrote."

LARSON, William H.   1938-

PERSONAL: Born June 3, 1938, in La Crosse, Wis.; son of George H. and Mabel (Carlsson) Larson; married Karen Nelsestuen, July 30, 1960; children: Christopher William, Andrew Joseph, Daniel James. *Education:* Wisconsin State University at La Crosse, B.S., 1960. *Home:* 2321 James Blvd., Racine, Wis. 53403. *Office:* Western Publishing Co., Inc., 1220 Mound Ave., Racine, Wis. 53404.

CAREER: High school English teacher in Racine, Wis., 1960-64; Western Publishing Co. Inc., Racine, Wis., editorial assistant, 1964-67, director of publishing services, 1967-68, editor, 1968-73, senior editor, 1973—.

WRITINGS: (Editor) *Stand By for Adventure,* Whitman Publishing, 1967; (editor) *Seven Great Detective Stories,* Whitman Publishing, 1968; (editor with N. Gretchen Greiner) *Adventure Calling,* Whitman Publishing, 1969; *Let's Go to Animal Town,* Golden Press, 1975.

LEE, Robert J.   1921-

PERSONAL: Born December 26, 1921, in Oakland, Calif.; son of Jewel E. (a railroad engineer) and Hattie (Ingersoll) Lee; married Lucille Theilacker, November 14, 1943; children: Stephanie (Mrs. Robert Hanson), Robin. *Education:* Attended Academy of Art College, San Francisco, Calif., 1940-41, 1946; studied privately with Richard Guy Walton, Richard Stephens, and Hamilton Wolf. *Agent:* Estelle Mandel Company, 65 East 80th St., New York, N.Y. 10021. *Office:* Marymount College, Tarrytown, N.Y. 10591.

CAREER: Academy of Art, San Francisco, Calif., instructor, 1946-47, 1949; Pratt Institute, Brooklyn, N.Y., instructor, 1955-56; Marymount College, Tarrytown, N.Y., associate professor, 1962—. *Exhibitions*—group: Smithsonian Institution, Palace of Legion of Honor (San Francisco), Chicago Art Institute, National Academy of Design, Springfield Museum of Fine Art (Mass.), New York City Center, Butler Institute of Fine Arts (Youngstown, Ohio), St. Louis Museum, Oklahoma Museum of Art, Rue de Lamar Gallery (Austin), Naples Art Gallery (Fla.), Marymount College; one-man shows: Long Island University, Academy of Art (San Francisco), Queens College (Charlotte, N.C.), The Gallery (Palm Springs), Knox-Campbell (Tucson), Centenary College (New Jersey), Rue de Lamar Gallery, Naples Art Gallery. *Military service:* U.S. Air Force, corporal, 1942-45. *Member:* Society of Illustrators, Graphic Artists Guild. *Awards, honors:* Allied Artists, first prize, Gold Medal of Honor, Lillian Cotton Award for Oil Painting; Springfield Museum of Fine Art, Purchase Award; Society of Illustrators, ten citation of merit awards, award of excellence; Society of Publication Designers, certificate of merit, 1971, 1974.

ILLUSTRATOR: Polly Curren, *This is a Town,* Follett, 1957; *Twenty White Horses,* Holt, 1964; Manuel Komroff,

ROBERT J. LEE

Heroes of the Bible, Golden Press, 1965; *Tales of the Arabian Nights,* Whitman, 1965; Helen McCully and Dorothy Crayder, *The Christmas Pony,* Bobbs, 1967; Selma G. Lanes, *The Curiosity Book,* Platt, 1968; Edith Eckblad, *A Smile is to Give,* Rand, 1969; Kenneth Grahame, *Wind in the Willows,* Dell, 1969; Sophia H. Fenton, *Ancient Egypt: A Book to Begin On,* Holt, 1971; Alfred D. Laurence, *Homer Pickle, The Greatest* (book jacket), Platt, 1971; Bill Martin, Jr., *Old Devil Wind,* Holt, 1971; Sarah Keyser, *Who Lives Here?,* Platt, 1972; Louis Untermeyer (editor), *Men and Women: The Poetry of Love,* American Heritage, 1973; Thornton Wilder, *Our Town,* Limited Editions, 1974; Millicent Selsam, *Questions and Answers About Horses,* Scholastic, 1974; William Faulkner, *A Fable,* Franklin Library, in press.

SIDELIGHTS: "I work in all mediums but prefer oils. I work six or seven days a week. Always knew I wanted to be an illustrator and painter. As a boy and young man in California I worked as a field hand, cannery worker, loaded box cars, and rode horse patrol for the forest service. At present I am doing a series of paintings from research in Spain and Portugal during my sabbatical from Marymount College. I was influenced by Hamilton Wolf, Richard Guy Walton and Richard Stephens. I have traveled in Haiti and other Caribbean Islands."

FOR MORE INFORMATION SEE: American Artists Magazine, January, 1968.

LEGUM, Colin 1919-

PERSONAL: Born January 3, 1919, in Kestell, South Africa; the son of Louis Samuel (hotel owner) and Jay (Horwitz) Legum; married Margaret Roberts (an economist), July 25, 1960; children: David, Kate, Elizabeth, Josephine. *Education:* Attended Kestell Government School, Orange

Free State, South Africa. *Home:* 15 Denbigh Gardens, Richmond, Surrey, England. *Office: The Observer,* 160 Queen Victoria St., London, E.C.4, England.

CAREER: Sunday Express and *Daily Express,* political and parliament correspondent, Johannesburg, South Africa, 1935-39; *Forward* and *The Mineworker,* Johannesburg, editor, 1939-43; *Illustrated Bulletin,* Johannesburg, editor, 1943-47; *The Observer,* London, associate editor and commonwealth correspondent, 1949—. Television and publishing consultant. Staff member, Tavistock Institute of Human Relations, London, 1949-52; honorary general secretary, South African Labour Party, 1946-49; Johannesburg city councillor, 1941-48; honorary secretary, Southern African Labour Congress; trustee, Africa Education Trust, Africa Publications Trust. *Member:* Commonwealth Writers' Association, Institute of Race Relations, Royal Institute of International Affairs.

WRITINGS: (With others) *Attitude to Africa,* Penguin, 1951; *Must We Lose Africa?,* W. H. Allen, 1954; *Bandung, Cairo, and Accra,* Africa Bureau (London), 1958; *Congo Disaster,* Penguin, 1960; (editor) *Africa—A Handbook to the Continent,* Praeger, 1961, revised edition, 1966; *Pan-Africanism—A Brief Political Guide,* Praeger, 1962; (editor and author of introduction) *The Congo, My Country,* by Patrice Lumumba, Praeger, 1962; (with Margaret Legum) *South Africa—Crisis for the West,* Praeger, 1964; (with Margaret Legum) *The Bitter Choice* (Child Study Association book list), World, 1967. Editor, "Praeger Library of African Affairs."

WORK IN PROGRESS: Africa Contemporary Record (annual volume).

HOBBIES AND OTHER INTERESTS: African and primitive art; Africana books; photography.

COLIN LEGUM

DELORES LEHR

LEHR, Delores 1920-

PERSONAL: Surname is pronounced Leer; born December 22, 1920, in Dallas, Tex.; daughter of Robert Powers and LaNette (Mims) Lehr. *Education:* Southern Methodist University, student, 1944-45. *Politics:* Republican. *Religion:* Presbyterian. *Home:* 3017 Mahanna Springs Dr., Dallas, Tex. 75235.

CAREER: Farm and Ranch (magazine), youth editor, 1945-50; Wyatt Advertising Agency, San Antonio, Tex., radio-television director, 1951-56; Monte Rosenwald & Associates (advertising agency), Amarillo, Tex., account executive, 1956-60; Wyatt Advertising Agency, radio-television director, 1960-68; Dallas Market Center, Dallas, Tex., vice-president, public relations and advertising, 1968—. *Member:* National Multiple Sclerosis Society, Public Relations Society of America (North Texas chapter), Dallas Press Club, Texas Teenage Library Association (honorary), Theta Sigma Phi (chapter president, 1951, 1961). *Awards, honors:* Headliner Award, Theta Sigma Phi (San Antonio), 1964, (Dallas), 1974.

WRITINGS: The Tender Age, Lothrop, 1961; *Turnabout Summer,* Doubleday, 1964. Contributor of about seventy teen-age short stories to magazines, including *Ingenue, American Girl, Catholic Miss,* and *Venture.*

WORK IN PROGRESS: A third teen-age novel; short stories.

HOBBIES AND OTHER INTERESTS: Swimming, reading, and travel.

LLOYD, (Mary) Norris 1908-

PERSONAL: Born September 1, 1908, in Greenwood, S.C.; daughter of Robert Brown and Corrie (Van Diviere) Norris; married William Bross Lloyd, Jr., 1933; children: William B. III, Roberta Lloyd, Lola Lloyd Horwitz, Christopher. *Education:* Attended Barnard College, Anderson College; Antioch College, A.B.; graduate studies at University of Chicago. *Religion:* Religious Society of Friends. *Home:* 806 Rosewood Ave., Winnetka, Ill. 60093.

CAREER: Settlement house work, teacher, housewife, and writer. Antioch College, trustee, 1960-62; Community Music Center of North Shore, trustee, 1954-61; active in Parent-Teacher Association. *Member:* Midland Authors. *Awards, honors:* Friends of Literature Award for Fiction, 1962; Society of Midland Authors Distinguished Service Award, 1973.

WRITINGS: Desperate Dragons, Hastings, 1960; *A Dream of Mansions,* Random, 1962; *Billy Hunts the Unicorn,* Hastings, 1964; *Katie and the Catastrophe,* Reilly and Lee, 1968; *The Village that Allah Forgot,* Hastings, 1974. Author of short stories and poems.

SIDELIGHTS: "I was the youngest of nine children but I never had the feeling of being the 'baby' as my mother filled our house with young children who needed to be cared for. They stayed sometimes for months or even for years. My father was a 'railroad man' and we lived in three small southern towns in the years before I went away to college at sixteen. I would often visit my father at work in the depot; he would get very busy as train time approached. It seemed that the trains were the only excitement in those towns; I thought they were dull places and wanted to get on a train and ride away—somewhere, anywhere. I filled my head with happenings from books; thank goodness we had in our bookcase collections of myths, fairy tales, adventure stories as well as the *Bible* and *Pilgrim's Progress.* However, those years in towns where it seemed nothing ever happened laid down a rich sediment from which springs my most creative work.

"I wanted to be a writer but I, also, wanted to love and be loved, to marry and have children. I suppose I thought I could do both but marriage and children and new scenes crowded out the writing for a while. Not completely, for I always had something going, a poem, a story, or most important, a notebook with descriptions of people and places, recollections, dreams. As my children grew up my notebook grew. My first book, *Desperate Dragons,* was given to me by my younger son, then attending kindergarten. He had heard stories of dragons and I think he found them very scary. He asked, 'Couldn't there be some dragons on a small far-away island?' When the idea bloomed into a story and was published I agreed to give him a percentage of royalties.

"My childhood in small southern towns grew into my first novel for adults, *A Dream of Mansions.* The main character is a thirteen-year-old girl and the time is the time I was growing up in the South. Still the work is definitely fiction, but given warmth and reality from the memory of the sights and sounds and smells and tensions of my childhood.

NORRIS LLOYD

"During the time I was more concerned with marriage and children, perhaps too happy to be a writer, we traveled and lived two years in Geneva, Switzerland and at a later time a year in Tunisia. In the summers we lived in Vermont. My second book for young people is set in Vermont. *Billy Hunts the Unicorn* sounds like fantasy but it isn't; it's a story of an American boy who had lived in Europe until he was nine years old adjusting to America and particularly to Vermont.

"In my next book I return to the South—Walhalla, South Carolina. *Katie and the Catastrophe* is only slightly embroidered reality; I lived this story or something very similar to it.

"I am very proud of *The Village That Allah Forgot*. During the year we lived in Tunisia I was busy with other writing. I did not plan to write a book about Tunisia; I thought I didn't know enough. When we returned home and I talked to schools about our year there, I realized that most young people know very little about the countries of North Africa. Africa south of the Sahara was becoming better known. Tunisia, Algeria, Morocco and Libya, inhabited mostly by Moslems and Arab-speaking people, had recently gone through their own struggle for independence as we had in the United States two-hundred-years ago. Since no one else seemed to be writing a book about Tunisia I plunged in, using everything I had seen and heard. I couldn't forget the picture of a boy standing beside a country road holding up one egg for sale. This boy is the hero of my story. Luckily I had Tunisian friends in the United States who corrected me when my imagination went wrong.

"I often talk to young people who want to be writers. I say to them, keep a notebook; not a diary, but a big, cheap, lined notebook with space to write one line or six pages. Begin that notebook today with descriptions of faces, streets, flowers, animals. Write poems and read poems. Use your childhood. Sad, happy, or dull it is your own, unique to you. And finally I say, you can't dream a book; it has to be written. Writing requires discipline; a bell on the typewriter should ring for you to write at the same hour every morning."

He climbed up on the rock and Bee said, "One-two-three-go," and they dived in together.
■ (From *Billy Hunts the Unicorn* by Norris Lloyd. Illustrated by Robin Lloyd Papish.)

Something about the Author

LOCKE, Lucie 1904-
(Lucie Locke Price)

PERSONAL: Born February 22, 1904, in Valdosta, Ga.; daughter of Stevens Thomas (a physician) and Caroline (a teacher; maiden name, Haygood) Harris; married David Roger Locke, September 9, 1926 (died January, 1960); married Armstrong Price (a geological expert on shorelines), February 27, 1962; children: (first marriage) Brent (Mrs. Carrol Laverne Riley), Elizabeth (Mrs. David Crilley Clarke), David Roger, Jr. *Education:* Attended Newcomb College Art School of Tulane University. *Politics:* Independent. *Religion:* Unitarian-Universalist. *Home:* 401 Southern St., Corpus Christi, Tex. 78404.

CAREER: Art teacher in public schools of El Paso, Tex., 1924-25; art curator for Corpus Christi (Tex.) Centennial Museum, 1937-40; artist, poet. *Member:* Southwest Sculpture Society, Poetry Society of Texas, Texas Fine Arts (member of board of directors, 1947-48), South Texas Art League (member of board of directors). *Awards, honors:* First prize in landscape painting from Eagle Pass International Exposition, 1942, for ''With Head Unbowed''; Avalon presidential citation for excellence in poetry, 1969, for ''The Spiral''; Diploma di Benemerenza for *Seize the Ring* and ''Moon-Pulled,'' 1972.

WRITINGS: (Self-illustrated) *Naturally Yours, Texas* (children's poems), Naylor, 1949; *Seize the Ring* (poems), von Boeckmann-Jones Press, 1972. Poems represented in anthologies, including *Bouquet of Poems,* 1968, and *Masters of Modern Poetry,* 1974, both published by Centro Studi e Scambi Internazionali. Art critic for *Corpus Christi Caller-Times,* 1940-70.

WORK IN PROGRESS: Poems; *Caroline and I, Or 'Summer Brook' and Other Poems,* childhood reminiscences of life in Highlands, N.C.; poems on scientific and other subjects.

SIDELIGHTS: ''I have taken an active part in the development of art organizations in this area since 1939. I began my active writing career in the 1940's and have been a 'pioneer' in this section in both areas. I attended the Southwest Writer's Conference every year (except two) from 1945 until its demise in 1966 (now revived in Houston, Tex.) and won awards each year, as well as in the Colony Writers (which I helped establish). I am still an active writer of poetry at age seventy, and am also doing miniature nudes in terra cotta.''

LOEPER, John J(oseph) 1929-
(Jay Lowe, Jr.)

PERSONAL: Surname is pronounced *Low*-per; born July 9, 1929, in Ashland, Pa.; son of Peter H. (a jeweler) and Mary (Monaghan) Loeper; married Jane B. Knawa, June 13, 1959. *Education:* Pennsylvania State University, A.B.S.; Trenton State College, B.S., M.A.; Protestant Episcopal University, London, Ph.D. *Religion:* Roman Catholic. *Residence:* New Hope, Pa. *Agent:* James Brown Associates, Inc., 22 East 60th St., New York, N.Y. 10022.

CAREER: Teacher in Lambertville, N.J., 1952-56, and Princeton, N.J., 1956-59; Hatboro (Pa.) public schools, guidance counselor, 1959-61, administrator, 1961—. New Hope-Solebury Board of Education, president. New Hope Public Library, member of board of directors. *Member:* National Education Association, Pennsylvania State Education Association. *Awards, honors:* American Educators Medal from Freedoms Foundation, 1965; guest lecturer, 1975, at Bergische Universitat, West Germany.

WRITINGS: Men of Ideas (juvenile), Atheneum, 1970; *Understanding Your Child Through Astrology,* McKay, 1970; *Going to School in 1776,* Atheneum, 1974; *The Flying Machine,* Atheneum, 1975. Contributor of articles to education journals and to *Gourmet, Coronet,* and *Cats Magazine;* has done drama reviews for newspapers.

WORK IN PROGRESS: The Solid Gold Doghouse.

SIDELIGHTS: ''I have been writing since my elementary school days. My very first story was about a boy who lost his dog. I still have it, filed away with the many things never published. There are usually hundreds of stories, poems and ideas an author has that are never printed.

''My first published story appeared in a college magazine. It was a long time after that before another reached print. Yet the years in between were spent in writing. The secret of successful writing is patience and practice. A writer must keep his imagination and ingenuity active and sharpen his writing skills. And he must be willing to wait until his efforts are accepted.

''My greatest pleasure comes from the letters I receive from my readers, especially the young readers. These let

LUCIE LOCKE

JOHN J. LOEPER

you know that your writing is being appreciated and enjoyed. And there is always pleasure in seeing your work in print. It makes the work and the waiting worthwhile."

HOBBIES AND OTHER INTERESTS: Oil paintings of American primitives.

FOR MORE INFORMATION SEE: Library Journal, July, 1970.

LONERGAN, (Pauline) Joy (MacLean) 1909-

PERSONAL: Born December 5, 1909, in Toronto, Ontario; married John Lonergan. *Education:* Denison University, B.A., 1932; Syracuse University, M.A., 1933. *Home:* 651 East 14th St., New York, N.Y. 10009.

CAREER: High school teacher, New York State, 1934-38; Prentice-Hall, Inc., New York, N.Y., publicity director, 1942-44; Brentano's, New York, N.Y., children's books, 1949-51; United Transformer Corp., New York, N.Y., bookkeeper, 1956-70; The Seabury Press, New York, N.Y., editorial secretary, Clarion Book, 1972-75, now retired. *Member:* Authors Guild.

WRITINGS: When My Mother Was a Little Girl, Watts, 1961; *When My Father Was a Little Boy,* Watts, 1961; *Pretend ABC,* Watts, 1962; *There You Are,* Watts, 1962; *Brian's Secret Errand,* Doubleday, 1969.

MacLEOD, Beatrice (Beach) 1910-

PERSONAL: Born January 15, 1910, in Brentwood, Long Island, N.Y.; daughter of William De'Verne and Edith (Waldo) Beach; married Robert Brodie MacLeod (a professor of psychology), October 17, 1936 (died, 1972); children: Ian Fullerton (died, 1972), Alison Stuart. *Education:* Swarthmore College, B.A., 1931; Yale University, M.F.A., 1934. *Home:* 957 East State St., Ithaca, N.Y. *Office:* Telluride Association, 217 West Ave., Ithaca, N.Y.

CAREER: Director of summer stock players, "Forty-Niners," Whitefield, N.H., 1933-41; Swarthmore College, Swarthmore, Pa., director of dramatics, 1934-46; Montreal Negro Theatre Guild, Montreal, Quebec, director, 1946-48; Ithaca College, Ithaca, N.Y., assistant professor of drama, 1949-51; Tompkins County Society for Mental Health, Ithaca, N.Y., executive secretary, 1955-58; Telluride Association, Ithaca, N.Y., executive secretary, 1959—. Children's Theatre Workshop, Ithaca, N.Y., director, 1957-61. *Member:* Phi Beta Kappa.

WRITINGS: On Small Wings (juvenile), Westminster, 1961.

MADDISON, Angela Mary 1923- (Angela Banner)

PERSONAL: Married name legally changed from Parsons to Maddison, 1968; born May 14, 1923, in Bombay, India; daughter of Sydney Howard (an engineer) and Iris Lydia (MacDiarmid) Phipps-Lincke; married Lionel Parsons (an army officer), March 24, 1941; children: John Lincke Maddison, Danne Mary Diarmid Maddison. *Education:* Attended boarding schools in England. *Politics:* Liberal. *Religion:* Roman Catholic. *Home:* 24 Cranley Mews, South Kensington, London, England. *Office:* Ant & Bee Partnership, c/o Grindlay's Bank Ltd., 13 St. James's Sq., London S.W.1, England.

CAREER: Author and illustrator of children's books. *Member:* Hurlingham Club.

WRITINGS—Children's books; all under pseudonym Angela Banner: *Mr. Fork and Curly Fork,* Edmund Ward, 1956.

"Ant and Bee" series: *Ant and Bee: An Alphabetical Story,* Edmund Ward, 1950, Watts, 1958; *More Ant and Bee,* Edmund Ward, 1956, Watts, 1958; *One, Two, Three with Ant and Bee,* Edmund Ward, 1958, Watts, 1959; *Around the World with Ant and Bee,* Watts, 1960; *More and More Ant and Bee,* Edmund Ward, 1961, Watts, 1962; *Ant and Bee and the Rainbow,* Edmund Ward, 1962, Watts, 1963; *Ant and Bee and Kind Dog,* Edmund Ward, 1963, Watts, 1964; *Happy Birthday with Ant and Bee,* Watts, 1964; *Ant and Bee and the ABC,* Watts, 1966; *Ant and Bee Time,* Watts, 1969; *Ant and Bee and the Secret,* Watts, 1970; *Ant and Bee and the Doctor,* Watts, 1971; *Ant and Bee Big Buy Bag,* Kaye & Ward, 1971; *Ant and Bee Go Shopping,* Watts, 1972.

"Kind Dog" series: *Kind Dog on Monday,* Ant & Bee Partnership, 1972; *Kind Dog Up and Down the Hill,* Ant & Bee Partnership, 1972.

And then Ant and Bee made *all this* with their bricks! ■ (From *Ant and Bee Go Shopping* by Angela Banner. Illustrated by the author.)

"Which Two" series: *Fayida, Pierre, Khesoo, Carlos,* Ant & Bee Partnership, 1972.

WORK IN PROGRESS: Private study of law.

SIDELIGHTS: "No child is too young to 'read' a few words from memory in return for praise and this leads to reading confidence (too often destroyed by educating adults). I believe that children make the best reading teachers so I make books for shared-reading between children of different ages. Having said all that, and feeling as strongly as I do on the subject of children reading together, I can hardly bear to dilute those words with further words about myself, but here goes. . . . I had a wonderful wonderful childhood till the age of ten when I first went to school. I can never remember how many calendars I had in order to cross off each school day more than once.

"I began my first book, which was an exposé of British boarding schools, at the age of thirteen. The next year my parents came home on leave from India and my father read what I had written. He took me away from school the same term at the age of fourteen, and when six months later my parents returned to India, I went back with them. Without delay I must say that I was to blame and not my school which is still doing quite well. Any school would have been my prison. I pine when I am trapped in a hospital. I avoid small islands and airplanes, and in all my hardworking life I have never been caught in regular employment.

"I consider any routine to be a restriction on freedom, but I bow to the monotonous disciplines of life, such as tooth washing after meals (eaten at irregular hours). I hate repetitive music and seeing the same show twice. I shall always be short of time, and my beloved husband Lionel is kept twice as busy as most men because between us we undertake too many projects."

HOBBIES AND OTHER INTERESTS: Painting.

FOR MORE INFORMATION SEE: Margery Fisher, *Who's Who in Children's Books,* Holt, 1975.

MANCHEL, Frank 1935-

PERSONAL: Born July 22, 1935, in Detroit, Mich.; son of Lee and Olga (Fluhr) Manchel; married Sheila Wachtel, 1958; children: Steven Lloyd, Gary Howard. *Education:* Ohio State University, A.B., 1957; Hunter College (now Hunter College of the City University of New York), M.A., 1960; Teachers College, Columbia University, Ed.D., 1966. *Home:* 5 Cranwell Ave., South Burlington,

FRANK MANCHEL

In the 1957 French version of *The Hunchback of Notre Dame,* Anthony Quinn played the bell-ringer. It hardly compared to the previous classic combination of spectacle and horror created by Chaney and Laughton. ■ (From *Terrors of the Screen* by Frank Manchel.)

Vt. 05401. *Office:* Department of Communication and Theatre, University of Vermont, Burlington, Vt. 05401.

CAREER: High school instructor in English, New Rochelle, N.Y., 1958-64; Southern Connecticut State College, New Haven, assistant professor of English, 1964-67; University of Vermont, Burlington, associate professor of English, 1967-71, professor of communication and theater, 1971—, director of La Mancha Project in Composition (cooperative program with Vermont high schools, exploring techniques in improving writings skills). University of Bridgeport, visiting professor, summer, 1967; chairman of the Governor's Committee on Children and Youth, 1973. *Military service:* U.S. Army, Medical Corps, 1957. U.S. Army Reserve, 1957-63. *Member:* University Film Association, Professors for Peace in the Middle East, American Federation of Film Societies (chairman of executive board), Society for Cinema Studies (treasurer), American Film Institute, British Film Institute. *Awards, honors:* Simmonds Foundation grant for research in England, 1971.

WRITINGS: Movies and How They are Made, Prentice-Hall, 1968; *When Pictures Began to Move,* Prentice-Hall, 1968; *When Movies Began to Speak,* Prentice-Hall, 1969; *Terrors of the Screen* (Junior Literary Guild selection), Prentice-Hall, 1970; (contributor) Sheila Schwartz, editor, *Readings in the Humanities,* Macmillan, 1970; *Cameras West* (Junior Literary Guild selection), Prentice-Hall, 1972; *Film Study: A Resource Guide,* Fairleigh Dickinson University Press, 1973; *Yesterday's Clowns: The Rise of Film*

Comedy, Watts, 1973; *The Talking Clowns,* Watts, 1976; *Far Out: The Science Fiction Film,* Watts, 1976.

Contributor of articles and reviews to film and other professional journals.

SIDELIGHTS: Referring to his book *Yesterday's Clowns: The Rise of Film Comedy,* Frank Manchel explains that ''the demand for comedy of all kinds seems to be a permanent fixture of society. When life goes sour, people want to laugh. It is not unusual, therefore, that the most popular figures in film history have been the great jesters. The great comics of the cinema show us as we are, and to a great degree, argue for reforms; they appear to say to their audiences, 'Revolt! Society needs to change and these are the reasons why.' The comedian's art is based on the differences between what is and what is possible. Through scorn and sarcasm, with irony and satire, they reduce the existing customs and institutions to ruins. Through their comedy they show us as human beings who sometimes take ourselves too seriously or not seriously enough. Their aim, which has been the aim of all great comedy since the beginning of time, is to criticize the world in the belief that things can be better.''

Terrors of the Screen was nominated for a National Book Award. *Cameras West* was chosen as an ''Ambassador Book'' by the English Speaking Union. Manchel's earlier book, *Movies and How They Are Made,* has been published in Portuguese translation.

MANISCALCO, Joseph 1926-

PERSONAL: Born October 12, 1926, in San Francisco, Calif.; son of Vincent (a truck driver) and Linda (Montalbano) Maniscalco; married Shirley D'Arcy, 1951; children: Glen, Christine, John. Education: La Sierra College, B.A., 1950; San Jose State College, M.A., 1952; attended Art Center School, Los Angeles, Calif., 1952. Religion: Seventh Day Adventist. Home and office: 82 Hillcrest Dr., Angwin, Calif. 94508.

CAREER: Loma Linda Medical School, Loma Linda, Calif., medical artist, 1949-50; Pacific Union College, Angwin, Calif., art teacher, 1950-54; Pacific Press Publishing Association, Mountain View, Calif., staff artist, 1954-56; free-lance artist, Grass Valley, Calif., 1956—. Military service: U.S. Army, 1945-46; became staff sergeant.

WRITINGS: Nenook the Polar Bear, Pacific, 1957; Animals of the Bible, Southern, 1958; Our Wonderful Birds, Southern, 1960; Marty the Marmot, Southern, 1961; Elmer the Squirrel, Pacific, 1962; Baby Animals of the Sierra, Pacific, 1963; Birds of the Sierra, Pacific, 1963; Bible Animals, Warner, 1963; Tantor the Elephant, Pacific, 1964; Creatures of the Sea, Pacific, 1964; God's Other Book, Southern, 1965; Birds, Review & Herald, 1965; Trees Every Child Should Know, Pacific, 1965; Billy Bison, Pacific, 1965; The Waldenses, Southern, 1965; How to Draw Bears, Foster, 1965; Creepy Crawly Creatures, Pacific, 1966; Reptiles and Amphibians, Pacific, 1966; Flowers and Insects, Pacific, 1966; Martin Luther, Southern, 1966; Happy Hippo, Southern, 1967.

JOSEPH MANISCALCO

The Art of Painting Portraits and Features, M. Grumbacher, 1974; The Story of a Good Shepherd, Standard Publishing, 1974; Paul, Standard Publishing, 1975; Jesus, Standard Publishing, 1975; Joseph, Standard Publishing, 1975; Moses, Standard Publishing, 1975; Bible Hero Stories, Standard Publishing, 1975; Nebuchadnezzar, Mighty King of Babylon, Review & Herald, 1975; Symbology–Pagan and Christian, Pacific Union College, 1975. Has written and illustrated over 200 stories for various periodicals, and illustrated over 200 books.

WORK IN PROGRESS: Series for Reformation; correspondence course on how to draw; two books, In Search of Winged Serpents and The Unveiling.

SIDELIGHTS: "For the past five years I have been traveling and studying ancient cultures around the world. I have traveled thirty-four countries shooting sixteen-millimeter movie film as well as taking stills and painting. I hope to compile the complete study shortly. In my past travels I have visited Europe three times, the Middle East twice, and the Orient, South Pacific, Australia and New Zealand, as well as Central America.

"For a number of years I was an illustrator and as I read the books selecting pictorial material I thought I would try writing. I have painted a number of murals which hang in different cities throughout the United States. My major interests have been religious, historical and wildlife subjects.

"I am very much interested in healthful living. I am careful of my diet and exercise regularly. In 1944 I was awarded several athletic scholarships. I have also won several art awards, the latest was first place in an international poster contest for Liberty magazine."

HOBBIES AND OTHER INTERESTS: Skiing, backpacking, lifting weights, gymnastics, photography.

MANNHEIM, Grete (Salomon) 1909-

PERSONAL: Born May 14, 1909, in Celle, West Germany; came to United States, 1949; daughter of Oscar (a businessman) and Nanny (Schloss) Salomon; children: Hanna (Mrs. Joe Baer), Susan (Mrs. Norman Tanen). Education: Seminar Frobelhaus, Berlin, Germany, degree in nursery school teaching, 1928; Reiman Art School, Berlin, student, 1930. Home: 2609 Ave. L, Brooklyn, N.Y. 11210.

CAREER: Nursery school teacher in Berlin, Germany for eight years; operated studio specializing in child photography in Johannesburg, South Africa, 1936-49; free-lance photographer in New York, N.Y., 1949—. Camp Airy (boys' summer camp), Thurmond, Md., teacher of photography, 1952-75. Photographs have appeared in exhibitions, and in magazines and advertising. Awards, honors: Awards for photography in national and international competitions.

WRITINGS: (Author, and illustrator with photographs) Farm Animals, Knopf, 1964; Touch Me–Touch Me Not, Knopf, 1965; Feather or Fur, Knopf, 1967; Two Friends, Knopf, 1968; The Geese Are Back, Parents' Magazine Press, 1968; The Baker's Children, Knopf, 1970; The Veterinarian's Children, Knopf, 1971.

Nancy and Jenny went into a quiet corner and talked. ■ (From *The Two Friends* by Grete Mannheim. Photos by the author.)

Illustrator with photographs: Elisabeth S. Helfman, *Patsy Pat*, Dutton, 1958; Blossom Budney, *My Pony Joker*, Knopf, 1961. Articles on photography in *Popular Photography, Camera 35;* photographs in *Ladies' Home Journal, Parents Magazine, Youth News, American National Red Cross*, other national magazines.

WORK IN PROGRESS: Two books for children on travel and nature.

SIDELIGHTS: "I find the company of children the most rewarding, inspiring and enjoyable in my life, that's why I chose to be a nursery-school teacher, child's photographer, and mother. I see my four grandsons as the biggest bonus in my life.

"I always enjoyed story telling to children. Now I communicate with printed words and photographs in my books. I do use my camera as observer and recorder for my illustrations. I will never force the children or animals into unnatural situations. I mostly start with the picture story and then write the words to form the complete book. I make my own layout to bring a successful marriage to photo and word.

"Ideas for picture stories and children's books can be everywhere. I met a little boy on his horse and we got into a conversation. We had the same type of humor. He was full of pep and I asked him (with his mother's permission) if he would like to be photographed on his horse. He was so full of ideas about what to do with and on his horse that the photos soon gave me material for a book, *My Pony Joker.*

GRETE MANNHEIM

86   Something about the Author

"My first book was *Patsy Pat, a Duck's Story*. I met the duck in a garage in Maryland. She said 'quack, quack' and got water to drink from a hose. She said 'quack, quack' again and got part of the mechanic's sandwich. I saw her walking side by side with the mechanic's wife and children. I never had seen a pet duck before and was amazed. I asked for permission to photograph her and the children. First the children and the duck were very shy. I turned the session into an interesting game; the duck looked grimy gray, so I suggested that she needed a bath. The kids looked at me astonished, 'Who ever gives a duck a bath?' they asked. But mother, children and duck soon cooperated. They had a lot of wet fun and I got a fine picture story book."

Grete Mannheim's work is represented in the Kerlan Collection, University of Minnesota.

MANNING, Rosemary 1911-
(Mary Voyle)

PERSONAL: Born December 9, 1911, in Weymouth, England. *Education:* University of London, B.A. in classics, 1933. *Home:* 20 Lyndhurst Gardens, London N.W.3, England.

CAREER: Sometime teacher and business woman; now writer.

ROSEMARY MANNING

WRITINGS—Adult books: (Under pseudonym Mary Voyle) *Remaining a Stranger*, Heinemann, 1953; (under pseudonym Mary Voyle) *A Change of Direction*, Heinemann, 1955; *The Shape of Innocence*, Doubleday, 1960 (published in England as *Look, Stranger*, J. Cape, 1960); *The Chinese Garden*, J. Cape, 1962, Farrar, Straus, 1964; *Man on a Tower*, J. Cape, 1965.

Children's books: *Green Smoke*, Doubleday, 1957; *Dragon in Danger*, Constable, 1957, Doubleday, 1959; *The Dragon's Quest*, Constable, 1961, Doubleday, 1962; *Arripay*, Constable, 1963, Farrar, Straus, 1964; *Heraldry*, A. & C. Black, 1966; *Boney Was a Warrior*, Hamish Hamilton, 1966; *A Grain of Sand*, Bodley Head, 1967; *The Rocking Horse*, Hamish Hamilton, 1970. Short stories in *Horizon, Cornhill, Cosmopolitan, Mademoiselle*.

WORK IN PROGRESS: Dragon in the Harbor; an adult novel; an anthology called *Railways and Railwaymen*, about the lives and work of railwaymen from 1825 up to the present.

SIDELIGHTS: "I was born in Weymouth, Dorset a seaside town in the south of England, much of it dating from the eighteenth century, with a beautiful old harbour. I have recently bought a small two-hundred-year-old house right on the quay, where I hope I shall one day live. I find it a good place to write and have returned to writing adult fiction after the long gap of over ten years.

"The three dragon books came about like this: I spent several weeks in the summer of 1956 with old friends, who had a small girl, called Sue. She adored books and being read to, so I began *Green Smoke*, and read it to her chapter by chapter. I think the dragon is more or less based on myself, though I hope I am not so greedy. The other two dragon books followed quickly, and later, *Arripay*, a rather bloodthirsty novel about a real pirate of the early fifteenth century. His name was actually Harry Paye, but his French and Spanish enemies reduced this to 'Arripay'.

"*Heraldry* is a subject I love, and often give talks about, both to grown-ups and children. *A Grain of Sand* is a selection of poems by William Blake. It was written for young people over eleven or twelve. The other two books, however, *Boney* and *The Rocking Horse*, were written for really young children, sixes and sevens. Both are set in or near Weymouth.

"I have lived in London most of my grown-up life and love it too much to leave it, even for my harbour house."

HOBBIES AND OTHER INTERESTS: Music, books, the country.

FOR MORE INFORMATION SEE: Children's Literature in Education/11, APS Publications, Inc., May, 1973.

MARCHER, Marion Walden 1890-

PERSONAL: Born December 16, 1890, in Racine, Wis.; daughter of Eugene Wilson and Harriet Salisbury (Walden) Marcher. *Education:* Belmont College, student, 1910-11; Northwestern University, B.S. in Education, 1936; Columbia University, M.A. in Education, 1939. *Religion:*

Presbyterian. *Home:* 2429 East Bradford Ave., Milwaukee, Wis. 53211.

CAREER: Public school, West Allis, Wis., kindergarten director, 1914-17; Humbolt Park School, Milwaukee, Wis., kindergarten director, 1917-48; now retired. *Awards, honors:* Graphic Arts Award for *Monarch Butterfly.*

WRITINGS: Bob's Summer Sleighride, Aladdin, 1951; *Monarch Butterfly,* Holiday, 1954. Formerly contributor to children's magazines.

WORK IN PROGRESS: Sher Singh: Boy of India.

SIDELIGHTS: Marion Marcher is interested in nature, nature sciences, and travel. She thinks India "is the most fascinating country today [and] the least understood." Before writing *Monarch Butterfly,* she raised and observed butterflies for a decade.

MAVES, Mary Carolyn 1916-

PERSONAL: Born April 30, 1916, in Hooker, Okla.; daughter of H. J. (a banker) and Margaret (Pittman) Hollman; married Paul B. Maves (a clergyman and professor), September 10, 1939; children: Margaret A. (Mrs. Allan K. Hansell), David H. *Education:* University of Nebraska, B.Sc. in Ed., 1938. *Religion:* United Methodist Church. *Home:* 4614 Finley Ave., Apt. 31, Los Angeles, Calif. 90027.

CAREER: Volunteer teacher in church schools. Member of Task Group on Religious Education and Hearing-Impaired Persons, National Council of Churches. *Member:* American Association of University Women.

WRITINGS—Children's books, with husband, Paul B. Maves: *Finding Your Way through the Bible,* Abingdon, 1971; *Learning More about the Bible,* Abingdon, 1973; *Exploring How the Bible Came to Be,* Abingdon, 1973; *Discovering How the Bible Message Spread,* Abingdon, 1973. Co-author with husband of a curriculum unit for fifth and sixth grade children of the Methodist Church, "Being a Christian," Graded Press, 1965, revised edition, 1967, 2nd revised edition published as "Followers of the Way," 1970. Editor and contributor to a kit for church school teachers of deaf children for National Council of Churches, 1975. Contributor to *Christian Home.*

WORK IN PROGRESS: Religious education materials for deaf children.

SIDELIGHTS: "I have always loved to read. When I was growing up in a little town in Oklahoma I read all the children's books in our little town library and then most of the grown-up books. Of course we had books at home, too. One of my very favorites was a book of Bible stories. Over and over I read it, again and again. Moses became as familiar to me as if he had lived on the same street. No matter how often I read the story, I was always excited and delighted when the Israelites escaped from Pharaoh's army and crossed the Red Sea to safety. Other characters became real friends—Abraham, Ruth, Samuel, and of course David! Who could forget David, the shepherd boy who became a king! The stories of Jesus, too, became real. I almost thought that I was there.

PAUL AND MARY MAVES

"It was the most natural thing in the world that, when I grew up, I would enjoy learning more about the Bible and would teach church school classes. The boys and girls in my classes often acted out Bible stories, putting scarves on their heads to help them pretend, making scrolls to read from, and molding lamps and bowls out of clay. We even made bread for Biblical meals.

"My husband's and my names appear as authors of our books about the Bible for children. Really, a lot of other names ought to be there, too, names of our children's friends who helped us to write. Sarah and Julie; Tim, Tom, and Mark; Becky and Suzanne; Brad and David—all these and others came to our house and read what we were writing as we went along. If they did not understand what we were trying to explain, they would say so. Then we would change a few words, or even paragraphs. One time Renee told us, 'That's not kid English.' So we kept changing until the children were satisfied."

MAVES, Paul B(enjamin) 1913-

PERSONAL: Surname rhymes with "saves"; born April 21, 1913, in Burwell, Neb.; son of Benjamin C. and Ellen Alverda (Craun) Maves; married Mary Carolyn Hollman (a writer), September 10, 1939; children: Margaret Alverda Maves Hansell, David Hollman. *Education:* Nebraska Wesleyan University, A.B., 1936; Drew University, B.D., 1939, Ph.D., 1949; also studied at New York University, 1945-46, and Harvard University, 1957-58; Columbia University, visiting scholar, 1964-65. *Politics:* Democrat. *Home:* 4614 Finley Ave., Apt. 31, Los Angeles, Calif. 90027. *Office:* Kingsley Manor, 1055 No. Kingsley Dr., Los Angeles, Calif. 90029.

CAREER: Pastor of Methodist churches in Albany, N.Y., 1940-42, and Middlebury, Vt., 1942-45; New York University, New York, N.Y., instructor in education, 1945-46; Federal Council of Churches of Christ in America, research associate, 1946-48, acting executive secretary of department of pastoral services, 1948-49; Drew University, Madison, N.J., adjunct professor of human relations, 1948-49, assistant professor, 1949-51, associate professor, 1951-56, George T. Cobb Professor of Religious Education, 1956-67; National Council of Churches of Christ, New York, N.Y., associate executive director of department of educational development, 1967-70; St. Paul School of Theology, Kansas City, Mo., director of field education, 1970-1975; Kingsley Manor, Los Angeles, Calif., administrator, 1975—. Staff associate, National Training Laboratories, Inc., 1960-70; delegate to White House Conference on Aging, 1961; member of board of directors, National Council on Aging; member of certification council, Board of Health and Welfare Ministries of United Methodist Church, 1964-72.

WRITINGS: (With J. Lennart Cedarleaf) Older People and the Church (Religious Book Club selection), Abingdon, 1949; Christian Service to Older People (pamphlet), Women's Division of Christian Services, Methodist Church, 1949; (editor) The Practical Field in Theological Education (pamphlet), Department of Pastoral Services, Federal Council of Churches of Christ in America, 1949; The Christian Religious Education of Older People, Department of Pastoral Services, Federal Council of Churches of Christ in America, 1950; (editor) Anxiety in Religious Work and Medical Practice (pamphlet), Clifton Springs Sanitarium, 1950; (contributor) J. Richard Spoon, editor, Pastoral Care, Abingdon, 1951; They Shall Bring Forth Fruit in Age (pamphlet), National Council of the Protestant Episcopal Church, 1951; The Best Is Yet to Be, Westminster, 1951; (editor) The Church and Mental Health (Religious Book Club selection), Scribner, 1953; Understanding Ourselves as Adults, Abingdon, 1959.

(Contributor) Marvin Taylor, editor, Religious Education: A Comprehensive Survey, Abingdon, 1960; (contributor) Clark Tibbitts, editor, A Handbook of Social Gerontology, University of Chicago Press, 1960; On Becoming Yourself (for seventh grade students), Graded Press, 1962; (with Charles Stewart) Christian Faith and Emotional Health, Abingdon, 1962; (with wife, Mary Carolyn Maves) Finding Your Way Through the Bible, Graded Press and Abingdon, 1971; (with Mary Carolyn Maves) Learning More About the Bible, Abingdon, 1973; (with Mary Carolyn Maves) Exploring How the Bible Came to Be, Abingdon, 1973; (with Mary Carolyn Maves) Discovering How the Bible Message Spread, Abingdon, 1973.

Author of curriculum materials for the Methodist church. Contributor to Encyclopedia for Church Group Leaders. Contributor of about fifty articles and reviews to church publications and theology and other journals, including Church School, Child Guidance, Workers on Youth, Adult Teacher, Mature Years, and International Journal of Religious Education. Guest editor, Pastoral Psychology, September, 1954.

WORK IN PROGRESS: Senior Citizens in the Household of God.

HOBBIES AND OTHER INTERESTS: Writing poetry.

MAYBERRY, Florence V(irginia Wilson)

PERSONAL: Born in Sleeper, Mo.; daughter of William Everett and Myrtle (Foose) Wilson; married David Maurice Mayberry, August 1, 1936; children: Michael David. Education: Ventura Junior College, A.A. Politics: Non-partisan. Religion: Baha'i World Faith. Home: P.O. Box 155, Haifa, Israel 31-100.

CAREER: Chamber of Commerce, Santa Paula, Calif., secretary-manager, two years; now volunteer lecturer for Baha'i Faith, traveling throughout Western hemisphere. Member: Business and Professional Women's Club (Santa Paula, Calif.; president, two years).

WRITINGS: The Dachshunds of Mama Island, Doubleday, 1963. Contributor of mystery-psychological short stories and poetry to national magazines and anthologies.

WORK IN PROGRESS: A children's book, Pobrecito and the Princesa; three short stories.

SIDELIGHTS: "My husband and I changed residence from California to Israel in 1973. In California he owned his own building materials business, and is now retired. Here in Haifa, Israel, we both are engaged in volunteer service to the Baha'i Faith. My particular function is as a member of the Baha'i International Teaching Centre, with title of counsellor which engages me in international service.

FLORENCE V. MAYBERRY

"Regarding the juvenile book *The Dachshunds of Mama Island*, as a Baha'i speaker I have made fifteen trips to Alaska which is the background for this book. One of the most beautiful spots of Alaska—or, for that matter, in the world—is Sitka, which is the specific background of the book. While there at one time I met a family who owned an island and, also, who owned a number of Dachshunds, a rather unusual little dog for a cold climate. Much later I acquired a beautiful Dachshund of my own and then conceived the idea of using the personality of my Dachshund multiplied in various ways to dwell in an island of my imagination with a family, also of my imagination. Thus, the background is real, the dogs and people are fictitious.

"I intend to write another juvenile using the background of Mexico, where my husband and son and I lived for over two years. I speak Spanish. Actually I have many fascinating backgrounds to draw upon since I have traveled around the world as well as intensively in the Western Hemisphere. And now, of course, I live in Israel, another fascinating area."

McCALLUM, Phyllis 1911-

PERSONAL: Born April 5, 1911, in Pacific Grove, Calif.; daughter of Henry Garfield (a judge) and Mae (an artist; maiden name, Hull) Jorgensen; married George Alexander McCallum (a college professor), December 20, 1936; chil-

PHYLLIS McCALLUM

dren: Alexsan (Mrs. Paul L. Dillon, Jr.), Michael Douglas. *Education:* Stanford University, B.A., 1936. *Politics:* Republican. *Religion:* United Methodist. *Home:* 1187 Clark Way, San Jose, Calif. 95125.

CAREER: Author, playwright. Member of advisory board of Pioneer Drama Service, 1970—; San Jose Junior Theatre, member of advisory board, 1951—, president, 1967-69; vice-president of San Jose Entertainment Commission, 1971, and Council of Arts, Greater San Jose Area, 1974-75. *Member:* National League of American Pen Women (president of Santa Clara County branch, 1972-74; national letters board, 1974-76), Chi Omega.

AWARDS, HONORS: Seattle Junior Programs national playwriting contest first prize, 1958, for *The Pale Pink Dragon;* Community Children's Theatre, Inc., playwriting first prize, 1963, for *Kangalou,* second prize, 1967, for *The Tough and Tender Troll;* Pioneer Drama Service second prize, 1967, for *The Tough and Tender Troll;* National League of American Pen Women national letters contest first prize, 1974, for *Hansel and Gretel and the Golden Petticoat,* and third prize, 1974, for *Williamsburg Won't;* Children's Theatre of Richmond playwriting contest fourth prize, 1974, for *The Pudgy Pony of Pompeii.*

WRITINGS—Plays, all published by Pioneer Drama Service: *The Pale Pink Dragon* (three-act; first produced in 1967), 1966; *The Tough and Tender Troll* (three-act; first produced at Yuba College Theatre, December 1, 1967), 1967; *The Vanilla Viking* (three-act; first produced in Santa Clara, Calif., at Haman School, April 10, 1970), 1967; *The Gratefull Griffin* (three-act), 1968; *Hansel and Gretel and the Golden Petticoat* (one-act; first produced in Jonesboro, Ark., at Dudley Elementary School), 1973; *Crumple, Rumpelstiltskin* (one-act), 1974. Also author of *The Uniform Unicorn* (three-act; first produced in Wilmington, N.C., at City Children's Theatre, 1968), published by Pioneer Drama Service. Contributor of plays, stories, and articles to *Eleusis, Pen Woman, Lutheran, Vista, Instructor,* and *Plays.*

WORK IN PROGRESS: A children's play for San Jose's Bicentennial titled *The Dignified Donkey of New Almaden; Jack and the Butter Beanstalk;* a musical dramatization of "Pollyanna."

SIDELIGHTS: "I grew up next to the forest in Pacific Grove, where I was sure fairies and elves danced at night. Because I was a rather frail little girl (now in my sixties I swim a quarter of a mile a day during the summer), I lived in the world of imagination and started writing stories at an early age and writing plays for the neighborhood. My first success was winning an essay contest on John Adams in the seventh grade. My teachers always praised my writing and encouraged me to write my Senior class play in high school. It was a three-act comedy titled 'Yes Girl.' Every one, even the butler and the maid, got married. I've always believed in happy endings.

"I write plays rather than books because I even dream in dialogue and prefer the dramatic format. My two children were actors in plays of such inferior writing that our audience was bored, shuffling their feet and running up and down the aisles. I thought, 'I'll write a play that will hold them' and put together all the things that held them in their seats—action, color, humor, the unusual. *The Pale Pink*

Dragon, still my most popular play, had a dragon, three witches, six bears, a fierce white cat, a dragon fly, and dancing flowers. The audience didn't move an eyebrow and when my daughter as Princess Pinkie sang a love song to the prince, the little boy in back of me called out 'Kiss her!' I knew that I'd discovered the perfect formula for a children's play.

"One of my greatest thrills was taking my two grandsons to see *The Pale Pink Dragon* eighteen years after their mother and uncle had been in the original cast. I've dedicated my plays to the members of my family—each one has a different play. *The Vanilla Viking* is dedicated to 'Bill who shares his wife with a typewriter.'

"When my mother and sister returned from Norway declaring 'Your next play has to be about trolls.' I resisted for a long time, because trolls are so evil, smelly, and downright scarey; but, because surgery kept me from my usual activities for nearly a year, I had time for research. One day, the idea of a troll who was both good and wicked popped into my mind, and Foss, the little boy who was kidnapped by the trolls and trained to be bad in spite of his kindly human nature, was born. *The Tough and Tender Troll* is my publisher's favorite play.

"My publisher and his family flew in from Denver last summer to visit us at our summer home at Fallen Leaf Lake, and he told my husband that he considers me the number one playwright for children in the United States. As we drove into our driveway I said 'Welcome to my Caladar.' Caladar is the magic kingdom in four of my plays—only love and peace prevail there. When they awakened in the morning to find our sparkling lake at their feet they said, 'This really is a magic kingdom.'

"Fallen Leaf *is* magic for me. I do a great deal of my writing there, wrestling with the plot as we hike for the mail and then returning to my typewriter under the blue umbrella and rescuing my hero from the machinations of the villain. I consider myself a fairly nice person, but my fingers fly over the keys when I'm giving lines to my villains. Strangely enough, most of them are lady villains: Queen Malduvia, Queen Contemptua, Queen Abrupta, Princess Snively, Princess Pea-Green, Madam Upbraida, and Ponderosa. I usually write four hours a day, two in the morning and two after lunch.

"My favorite play is *The Grateful Griffin,* one of the Caladar plays. Another is *The Pudgy Pony of Pompeii* (unpublished) which I researched on the very streets of Pompeii. Research is a fun part of writing. I've never been to Williamsburg, but my prize winning one act, *Williamsburg Won't,* was so thoroughly researched that I think that I know where every building stands. I wrote *The Tough and Tender Troll* before ever setting foot in Norway, but when I did I picked out the very spot where my farm on the fjord should be and had the joy of standing on the steps of the stabbur in act one.

"The greatest delight in writing plays is that it combines the creative effort of the playwright, the director, the technical director, the costume designer, the actors, and the audience itself. No two productions of my plays are alike, and that pleases me. If you've written a book, you never know when someone is enjoying it, but with a play you hear the laughter and feel the pleasure of the audience on the spot.

"My other enthusiasms are running my church library, traveling with and studying the out-of-doors with my biologist husband, researching future plays."

McCARTY, Rega Kramer 1904-

PERSONAL: Born January 8, 1904, in Batavia, Iowa; daughter of James Perry and Allie Myrtle (Walker) Kramer; married Frederick Neal McCarty, 1926; children: Mark Thomas. *Education:* Attended Monmouth College, one year, and Iowa State Teachers College. *Religion:* Protestant. *Home:* 4601 Sixth Ave., Tacoma, Wash. 98406. *Agent:* John Payne, Lenniger Literary Agency, 437 Fifth Ave., New York, N.Y. 10016.

CAREER: Teacher at elementary schools in Keswick, Iowa, 1921-22, Sigourney, Iowa, 1922-26; buyer or member of personnel staff at retail stores in Iowa and Washington State, at intervals, 1930-42; public relations work, Washington State, 1959-65. Teacher of creative writing, 1957—. Formerly trustee of Northwest Writers' Conference; and board member of Family Service Agency of Tacoma. *Member:* National League of American Pen Women, Seattle Free Lances, Tacoma Writers Club (former president; honorary life member).

WRITINGS: Brenda Becomes a Buyer, Messner, 1960; *Lorna Evans, Social Worker,* Messner, 1961.

REGA KRAMER McCARTHY

Published plays: *Pioneer Christmas, The Return, Home for Christmas, Carol Finds Christmas, Longing for Christmas, Blake's Decision, And There Found They Christ, But This I Know, The Broken Arc, The Cross on the Hill,* (with Mary Werner Hall) *My Son Lives, The Easter Spirit, Unexpected Guest* (all published by Rodeheaver Hall Mack Co., 1950-61). Other plays published in same period: *The Morning Came,* Nazarene Publishing; *Friendship Has a Language,* Nazarene Publishing; (author of script and song lyrics) *The Children's Bible,* Lorenz Publishing; *The Extra Gift,* Standard Publishing. Contributor of short verse, adult and juvenile short stories, and articles to magazines.

WORK IN PROGRESS: A book on writing fiction and one on writing nonfiction; short stories, articles, and verse.

SIDELIGHTS: "When we were young children in Iowa, my mother would gather all six of us around the table with the lighted lamp, and read to us. Perhaps this is when my love of stories began, though stories were not what I wrote first but poems and essays.

"In school, any subject that had to do with reading or writing interested me. I recall well my first experience as a ghost-writer. In the eighth grade, my brother and I among the others in the class, were assigned to write a Thanksgiving story. I had what seemed to me a sparkling idea and worked very hard at the writing. A day before the stories were due, my brother begged me to write a story for him, since he hadn't been able to come up with one. Because I loved him dearly, I dashed off a story in a humorous vein, thinking it so different from mine that the teacher wouldn't be able to identify it as my writing. And she didn't identify it. But when it came to voting the best story, guess whose story won first. You're right; 'his' story was way out in front. We both learned a lesson. He could scarcely force himself to go up for the prize. I swore never again to ghost write; and I haven't.

"In high school, I printed by hand a 'newspaper' of humorous news items to circulate among my friends, as well as some poetry I did *not* show to my friends. In college, I hoped someone would tell me how to go about writing properly, but no one did. My English professor assigned us a story to write, but did not give us any guidelines for writing it.

"It was not until after I was married that I decided it was time I began to write in earnest. I bought myself a typewriter and, from the typing chart that came with it, I learned which fingers should hit which keys and laboriously learned to type. Before long I had some poetry published and a few filler items. Yet any real knowledge of fiction techniques eluded me.

"When I came to Tacoma, Washington with my husband to open a business, I finally found a group of aspiring writers who invited me to join them. Through study and what information we could glean as to techniques, several of the group went on to become professional writers. During these years, I began to gather notes and material that would one day be used in helping others to learn writing. This wasn't a conscious plan in the beginning, but because I had been a teacher, no doubt, the half-formed idea lay in the back of my mind that there should be an easier way to learn the basic techniques of writing, without which a writer is lost.

"Not many years after I began publishing, I was asked to teach a class in writing. One class led to another, and for some twenty years I have been teaching creative writing. It has been a pleasure to see many of my students become professional writers. Teaching has led to the books I am presently working on—one on the techniques of fiction and one on writing nonfiction.

"Since my husband is a business man, it was natural that I assist him in stores we owned for a number of years. It was natural too that when I looked about for subject matter for my first book, a girl who wanted to become a buyer for a department store would walk into the story. For the second book I chose the field of social work in which I had become very interested. I have two nieces who are social workers.

"Earlier I had published juvenile fiction, most of it during the years my son, Mark, was growing up. His problems and interests offered good story material. I'm afraid I was guilty of 'conning' him into helping me with the dishes by suggesting that we make up a story. He became very good at it.

"When I moved into book writing, I was inclined toward the teen-age group of readers. Since many of my college students were still in their teens, I felt an identity with their problems and activities. By this time, too, my son was in college and I came to know his group of friends well. At the same time I was writing books, I was also writing confession stories, many of them involving teen-agers in rebellion. I write for religious markets, and publish program material and plays. I have written feature articles, and at one time had my own column in a weekly newspaper. It is this versatility, I believe, that has caused writing to remain so interesting to me.

"I believe that everything an author writes has in it some grain of his experience, and that something of the author goes into everything he writes. A very personal kind of communication takes place between the author and his reader. Perhaps few vocations are more lonely or more difficult, but in few are the personal rewards as great."

McDONALD, Lucile Saunders 1898-

PERSONAL: Born September 1, 1898, in Portland, Ore.; daughter of Frank Mathew and Rosa (Wittenberg) Saunders; married Harold Dewey McDonald, December 25, 1922; children: Richard Keith. *Education:* University of Oregon, student, 1915-17; writing courses at Columbia University, 1923, 1939, 1940, University of Washington, 1942, 1943. *Home:* 3224 109th Ave. S.E., Bellevue, Wash. 98004.

CAREER: Started newspaper career in Oregon, working for the *Eugene Daily Guard, Bend Bulletin, Salem Statesman, The Oregonian,* 1916-1920; *Buenos Aires Herald,* Buenos Aires, Argentina, reporter, 1921; United Press Association, night editor in Buenos Aires, 1921, reporter in New York, N.Y., 1922; Standard News Association, New York, N.Y., rewrite desk, 1923; *Morning World,* New York, N.Y., reporter; *Cordova Daily Times,* Cordova, Alaska, news editor, 1927-28; *New York Times,* staff writer in Istanbul, Turkey, 1930-31; *Seattle Times,* Seattle, Wash., feature writer on Sunday Magazine, 1942-66, now occasional contributor to *Seattle Times Sunday Magazine.*

LUCILE SANDERS McDONALD

MEMBER: Women in Communications, Seattle Free Lances, Authors League of America, Pacific Northwest Writers Conference, Puget Sound Maritime Historical Society (honorary lifetime membership), Washington State Historical Society, Western Writers of America. *Awards, honors:* National Headliner Award of Theta Sigma Phi for distinguished service in the field of journalism; Washington Presswomen Torchbearer award.

WRITINGS: Dick and the Spice Cupboard, Crowell, 1936; *Jewels and Gems* (Junior Literary Guild selection), Crowell, 1940; *The Giant with Four Arms,* Nelson, 1941; *Sheker's Lucky Piece* (British Children's Book Club), Oxford University Press, 1942; *Bering's Potlatch,* Oxford University Press, 1944; *Washington's Yesterdays,* Binfords, 1953; *Search for the Northwest Passage,* Binfords, 1958; *Coast Country* (adult), Binford, 1966; *Where the Washingtonians Lived* (adult), Superior, 1969; *The Look of Old Time Washington* (adult), Superior, 1971; *Swan Among the Indians* (adult), Binford, 1972; *Garden Sass: The Story of Vegetables* (juvenile), Nelson, 1972; *The Arab Marco Polo: Ibn Battuta* (juvenile), Nelson, 1975.

With Zola Helen Ross: *The Mystery of Catesby Island* (Junior Literary Guild selection), Nelson, 1950; *Stormy Year,* Nelson, 1952; *Friday's Child* (Junior Literary Guild selection), Nelson, 1954; *The Mystery of the Long House,* Nelson, 1956; *Pigtail Pioneer,* Winston, 1956; *Wing Harbor* (Junior Literary Guild Selection), Nelson, 1957; *The Courting of Ann Maria,* Nelson, 1958; *Assignment in Ankara* (Junior Literary Guild selection), Nelson, 1959; *Winter's Harvest,* Nelson, 1960; *The Sunken Forest,* Weybright & Talley, 1968; *For Glory and the King,* Meredith, 1969. Onetime regular contributor to *Matrix,* Methodist youth magazines, travel and outdoor publications. Also on editorial board of the Puget Sound Maritime Historical Society and contributor to its quarterly, "Sea Chest."

WORK IN PROGRESS: Several books.

SIDELIGHTS: "My husband died in 1971 and I moved away from the lake-shore home we had occupied for twenty-eight years. Now I live four blocks from my son's home, but still can look at my beloved Lake Washington from my windows. One of my as-yet-unpublished manuscripts is about the lake and *The Sunken Forest* was a story based on a mystery that had that body of water as its setting.

"Most of my writing has been related to places I have actually seen. The *Ibn Battuta* book came out of my having lived in Turkey, where I discovered that the only account of it in mediaeval times was by the Arab traveler. I couldn't get him out of my mind and made several false starts over the years before I finally settled on a straight biography to tell his story. Right now I am dabbling with another idea that was associated with the same material though it relates to a fictional character who might have lived one hundred years earlier.

"All my life I have written—there is nothing else that I do reasonably well. I began writing stories for the school monthly in high school. Also, I wrote school news for *The Oregonian* the last year before graduation. I went on to journalism school and after leaving the campus stuck to newspaper work almost completely until after my son was born. By that time I was moving around in the wake of my husband who had become European sales manager for the Caterpillar Tractor Company.

"Dick, as a little boy, became fascinated by the windmills we saw in our travels and this prompted me to write *The Giant with Four Arms.* It was actually my first attempt at juveniles, though not the first one I sold. My story ideas seemed to grow up along with my son until I reached a teen level for the books I co-authored with Zola Ross. When we worked together I furnished backgrounds and most of the characters and Zola did the heavy plotting. We were often asked how we worked together. It was a real partnership—always the same day with two typewriters going in two rooms at one of our houses. We generally completed the rough draft of two chapters at a sitting, then stopped and read aloud to make certain the sequences were smooth and the descriptions of people and places were not mismatched.

"We are again endeavoring to work on a book, but now we live fifteen miles apart instead of four miles and cannot be together as often. Meanwhile, I plunged in and completed some volumes on my own, all of which involved considerable research. The last one was aimed at young adult level.

"As to the way I write when I work alone—I have a special room for my workshop. It is lined with reference books and I own five filing cabinets full of notes and material I can consult. I am always at my typewriter by nine o'clock and stay with it until lunchtime or later. The nice thing about being retired is that one doesn't have to watch the clock or meet a deadline unless it is a proofreading or indexing one for a publisher.

"I have covered all the continents in my travels, most recently visiting Australia and New Zealand."

HOBBIES AND OTHER INTERESTS: History of the Pacific Northwest.

McDONNELL, Lois Eddy   1914-

PERSONAL: Born June 20, 1914, in State College, Pa.; daughter of Milton W. (a professor) and Rebecca (Reiley) Eddy; married Fred V. McDonnell (a banker), June 12, 1943 (died August 1, 1965); children: Mary McDonnell Harris, Milton Eddy. *Education:* Dickinson College, A.B., 1935; Columbia University, M.A., 1936. *Politics:* Republican. *Religion:* United Methodist. *Home:* 123 Parker St., Carlisle, Pa. 17013.

CAREER: Public schools, Carlisle, Pa., elementary teacher, 1936-43, 1958-66; Shippensburg State College, Shippensburg, Pa., teacher in Rowland Center for Young Children, 1966—. Methodist Church leadership and laboratory schools in East and Middle West, teacher, 1940—.

LOIS EDDY McDONNELL

Angered, Susan picked up the board and threw it on the floor. "It was my game," she cried. "I had more kings." ■ (From *Susan Comes Through the Fire* by Lois Eddy McDonnell. Illustrated by Jim Walker.)

Member: National Education Association, National Council of Teachers of English, Pennsylvania State Education Association, Delta Kappa Gamma.

WRITINGS—Juvenile: *Hana's New Home,* Friendship, 1957; *Stevie's Other Eyes,* Friendship, 1962; *Susan Comes Through the Fire,* Friendship, 1969.

Texts: *Friends at Home and in the Community,* Abingdon, 1943; *Everyone Needs a Church,* Abingdon, 1951; revised, 1959; *The Home and Church: Partners in the Christian Education of Children,* Abingdon, 1961.

Teacher's guides: *Children of the Congo,* Abingdon, 1952; *Primary Teacher's Guide to India, Pakistan, and Ceylon,* Friendship, 1954; *Primary Teacher's Guide on Indian Americans,* Friendship, 1955; *Finding Christian Friends in the Philippines,* Abingdon, 1956; *Primary Teacher's Guide on Japan,* Friendship, 1957; *Primary Teacher's Guide on Good News to Share,* Friendship, 1960; *Primary Teacher's Guide on Persons of Special Need,* Friendship, 1962; *Primary Teacher's Guide for Susan Comes Through the Fire,* Friendship, 1969. Graded courses published by Graded Press, 1949; more than one hundred articles in religious education periodicals; script for filmstrip "Next Steps in Religion," Traco.

SIDELIGHTS: "It was teaching children that got me into writing for children. It is a pleasure to share books with girls and boys. I like helping girls and boys express their thoughts in written form. It is fun to write stories for children to read and enjoy.

"For each book I have written, there were ever so many things I needed to know. I have found it best to go to places where I could be among people I was writing about. When I was writing *Stevie's Other Eyes,* I spent time at schools where blind children were learning to read and write. I even went to a camp where I hiked trails, gathered blueberries, and boated with sightless campers. When I was writing *Susan Comes Through the Fire,* I made visits to the children's room at the Johns Hopkins Hospital and got to know children with burns.

"At the time I began to write books for girls and boys, my two children were the first to hear them. Their questions and comments gave me good ideas. I wonder how many girls and boys stop to think how much authors gain from readers."

McGAW, Jessie Brewer 1913-

PERSONAL: Born October 17, 1913, in Montgomery County, Tenn.; daughter of L(ewis) Vernon and Birdie (Basford) Brewer; married H. F. McGaw, 1939 (divorced, 1958); children: Miriam Katherine, Vernon Howard. *Education:* Duke University, A.B., 1935; Peabody College, M.A., 1940; Columbia University, postgraduate study, 1948-50; American Academy in Rome, study under Fulbright Grant, 1959. *Religion:* Methodist. *Home:* 2405 Dickey Pl., Houston, Tex. *Office:* University of Houston, Cullen Blvd., Houston, Tex. 77004.

JESSIE BREWER McGAW

CAREER: Clarksville High School, Clarksville, Tenn., teacher, 1936-38; Ward Belmont School, Nashville, Tenn., teacher of Latin, 1938-40; Lausanne School, Memphis, Tenn., teacher of history, 1941-42; University of Houston, Houston, Tex., teacher, 1952-62. Board member of Houston Civic Music Association, 1956-58; Houston Day Care Association, 1957-62, Young Women's Christian Association, 1957-59. *Member:* American Association of University Women, Texas Institute of Letters, South Central Modern Language Association, American Classical Association, Texas Classical Association, Delta Kappa Gamma, Texas Folklore Society, Writers' Club, Kappa Kappa Gamma, League of Women Voters. *Awards, honors:* Cokesbury Book Store Award of Texas Institute of Letters for *How Medicine Man Cured Paleface Woman,* 1957; Theta Sigma Phi book award, 1958, for *Painted Pony Runs Away;* University of Houston Latin research grant, 1963; Delta Kappa Lambda research grant to study in Greece, 1972.

WRITINGS: How Medicine Man Cured Paleface Woman, W. R. Scott, 1956; *History of Houston YWCA,* Wetmore, 1957; *Painted Pony Runs Away,* Nelson, 1958; *Little Elk Hunts Buffalo,* Nelson, 1961. Contributor to Campfire Girls magazine, Texas Folklore Society Journal.

WORK IN PROGRESS: Translation into English (from the Latin) of Pico della Mirandola's *Heptaplus;* research for a juvenile book on Aztec petroglyphs.

SIDELIGHTS: "The first juvenile was written to solve a home need: to encourage my son to read. It was written for him about his favorite subject—Indians. I used an easy-reader format with words appearing below the Plains Indian pictographs I drew as nearly as possible like those I found from my research, mostly in the Smithsonian and from bound volumes of the American Ethnology Association, etc.

"Since I am a language major and have an intense interest in the primitive, pictorial style of many early languages, upon moving to Texas, I naturally began to study the pictorial language of the Plains Indians, who, according to their nomadic life-style, roamed the Western plains on their painted ponies hunting the buffalo that represented their whole economy of life: food, shelter and clothing. As there were many dialects spoken among the various tribes, it was necessary for them to communicate with those encountered on their hunting trips through a gesture language not unlike that used by deaf mutes. When written communication was needed for signing a petition to Washington, settling a peace treaty, recording history, giving directions, and the like, the pictographic written language was used.

"I soon learned from my research that some of the drawings for abstract ideas resembled the Egyptian hieroglyphics and early Chinese characters. For instance, although these cultures were miles and years apart, all three used a picture of two hands joining to represent *friendship* (unarmed). In the book called *Painted Pony Runs Away* I have a chart on similar drawings."

HOBBIES AND OTHER INTERESTS: Archaeology, music, art.

FOR MORE INFORMATION SEE: Illustrators of Children's Books: 1957-1966, Horn Book, 1968.

MEAD, Russell (M., Jr.) 1935-

PERSONAL: Born January 1, 1935, in Pueblo, Colo.; son of Russell M. (a salesman) and Marjorie (Moreno) Mead; married Florence Guyer, September 12, 1956; children: Judith Ann, Roger William, Michael Evin. *Education:* Dartmouth College, A.B., 1956. *Agent:* Brandt & Brandt, 101 Park Ave., New York, N.Y. 10017.

CAREER: Concord Academy, Concord, Mass., teacher of English, 1962-71, headmaster, 1971—. *Member:* Association of American Rhodes Scholars. *Awards, honors:* Rhodes Scholar, 1956; fellow in juvenile literature, Bread Loaf Writers' Conference.

WRITINGS: If a Heart Rings—Answer (teen-age novel), Dutton, 1964; *Tell Me Again About Snow White* (teenage novel), Dutton, 1965.

WORK IN PROGRESS: The Tales Men Tell, contemporary mythology.

MELCHER, Marguerite Fellows 1879-1969

PERSONAL: Born September 2, 1879, in Boston, Mass.; daughter of Otis Dwight (a grain dealer) and Florra Belle

MARGUERITE FELLOWS MELCHER

(Johnson) Fellows; married Frederic G. Melcher, June 2, 1910 (deceased); children: Daniel, Nancy (Mrs. J. A. Diemand, Jr.), Charity (Mrs. Del Travis). *Education:* Attended Smith College. *Politics:* Democrat. *Religion:* Unitarian Universalist.

CAREER: Writer. Democratic committeewoman, Montclair, N.J., 1959, 1961. *Member:* Dramatists Guild of Authors League of America, Democrats for Good Government, League of Women Voters, Smith College Club.

WRITINGS: (Translator from the French) De Segur, *Memoirs of a Donkey,* Macmillan, 1938; (translator) *Sophie: The Story of a Bad Little Girl,* Knopf, 1938; *Offstage,* Knopf, 1938; *The Shaker Adventures,* Princeton University Press, 1941; *Lost Pond,* Viking, 1956; *Catch of the Season,* Little, Brown, 1960; *Why Don't You Draw A Dog?,* Little, Brown, 1962.

Plays produced: "Private Practice," 1946; "Rose in the Wilderness," 1949; "He Went Sailing," 1951; "The Unicorn," 1951. Several one-act plays have also been produced. Other writings include radio scripts.

WORK IN PROGRESS: A small book of poems, tentatively titled *I Wonder Why;* a book for young people, tentatively titled *The Rose Computor.*

(Died, 1969)

MELIN, Grace Hathaway 1892-1973

PERSONAL: Surname pronounced Meh-leen; born February 19, 1892, in Columbus, Ohio; daughter of William (a painter) and Elizabeth (Martin) Hathaway; married Carl G. Melin (a chemist, retired), August 23, 1939. *Education:* Attended Columbus Normal School, 1910-12, and Oregon State College (now University), 1918-19; George Washington University, B.A., 1941. *Politics:* Independent. *Religion:* Protestant. *Home:* R.F.D., Clarksville, Md.

CAREER: Public school teacher in Columbus, Ohio, 1912-18; reporter for *Benton County Courier,* Corvallis, Ore., 1919-23; public school teacher in Washington, D.C., 1941-43, Edmonston, Md., 1943-46, and Laurel, Md., 1946-62; retired. *Member:* National Education Association, Maryland Teachers Association, Delta Kappa Gamma. *Awards, honors:* Third prize for a travel article in *Instructor,* 1949.

WRITINGS: Maria Mitchell, Girl Astronomer, Bobbs, 1954; *Dorothea Dix, Girl Reformer,* Bobbs, 1963; *Henry Wadsworth Longfellow: Gifted Young Poet,* Bobbs, 1968; *Carl Sandburg: Young Singing Poet,* Bobbs, 1973. Author of four plays published in *Instructor.*

HOBBIES AND OTHER INTERESTS: Reading, nature study, travel.

FOR MORE INFORMATION SEE: Washington Post, December 5, 1973.

(Died December 1, 1973)

The women inside were criminals, drunkards, or poverty stricken. They milled about the dark room. ■ (From *Dorothea Dix* by Grace Hathaway Melin. Illustrated by Vic Dowd.)

MELLERSH, H(arold) E(dward) L(eslie) 1897-

PERSONAL: Born May 28, 1897, in London, England; son of F. H. (an insurance secretary) and Florence (Parker) Mellersh; married Margot Sadler, August, 1921; children: Jacqueline (Mrs. Tony Nayman), Sally, Nicholas, Angela (Mrs. Robert Myers). *Education:* University of London, B.Sc., 1921. *Religion:* Church of England. *Home:* 6 Hill St., Stogumber, Taunton, England. *Agent:* Peter Janson-Smith, 31 Newington Green, London N16 9PU, England.

CAREER: Civil servant with Ministry of Supply until 1957; author. *Military service:* British Army, 1915-19; served in France; became lieutenant. *Member:* Linnean Society of London (fellow), West Country Writers' Association.

WRITINGS: Let Loose (novel), Selwyn & Blount, 1926; *Ill Wind* (novel), Chapman & Hall, 1930; *The Salt of the Earth,* Chapman & Hall, 1931; *The World and Man: A Guide to Modern Knowledge,* Hutchinson, 1952; *The Story of Life,* Hutchinson, 1957, Putnam, 1958; *The Story of Man: Human Evolution to the End of the Stone Age,* Hutchinson, 1959, published as *The Story of Early Man: Human Evolution to the End of the Stone Age,* Viking, 1960; *From Ape Man to Homer: The Story of the Beginnings of Western Civilization,* R. Hale, 1962, Taplinger,

1963; *Soldiers of Rome,* R. Hale, 1964, published as *The Roman Soldier,* Taplinger, 1965; *Minoan Crete,* Putnam, 1967; *FitzRoy of the Beagle,* Hart-Davis, 1968, Mason & Lipscomb, 1974; *The Destruction of Knossos: The Rise and Fall of Minoan Crete,* Weybright, 1970.

Children's books: *Finding Out About Ancient Egypt,* Muller, 1960, Lothrop, 1962; *Finding Out About Stone Age Britain,* Muller, 1961; *Saxon Britain,* Weidenfeld & Nicolson, 1961; *Finding Out About the Trojans,* Muller, 1962; *Carthage,* Weidenfeld & Nicolson, 1963; *Charles Darwin: Pioneer of the Theory of Evolution,* Arthur Barker, 1964, published as *Charles Darwin: Pioneer in the Theory of Evolution,* Praeger, 1969; *The Boys' Book of the Wonders of Man and His Achievements,* Roy, 1964; *Imperial Rome,* John Day, 1965 *Sumer and Babylon,* Wheaton, 1964, Crowell, 1965; *Archaeology: Science and Romance,* Wheaton, 1966; *The Discoverers: The Story of the Great Seafarers,* Wheaton, 1969; *The Explorers: The Story of the Great Adventurers by Land,* Wheaton, 1969.

Contributor to *Reader's Digest Dictionary* and to *New Statesman, Fortnightly,* and *Contemporary Review.*

WORK IN PROGRESS: A short history of Peru.

SIDELIGHTS: "Having gone straight into the Army in the first world war—and having luckily survived, though wounded three times—I went and got myself married to a girl more lovely than I deserved. She had an almost equally delightful young niece and nephews and to these I found myself telling stories, or, rather, one long story that went on and on until I had my own children and then my grandchildren to tell it to.

"But I had also come out of the war remarkably ignorant and I set about re-educating myself. Particularly I had to do so in things that they hadn't taught me much about at school, such as ancient history. That subject fascinated me; Stone Age man, the Sumerian, the boy or girl in ancient Rome. They had really lived in a world different from ours and yet, no doubt, feeling that their world was as modern as we think our own. I began to write about them for grown-ups.

"Then my literary agent approached a publisher of a series of books that not only covered the ancient history of people, but also sought to show how that history had been discovered. So they let me write, *Finding Out About Ancient Egypt.*

"I really knew very little about ancient Egypt, and I, too, had to 'find out.' I think my ignorance was almost an advantage. I could, perhaps, make things more easily clear for others who didn't know much about the subject either—not that I recommend ignorance as a good recipe for writing!

"Since then, I have gone on writing for children. Some books have been less successful than *Finding Out About Ancient Egypt,* but what makes one book successful and another not, I cannot tell. I have at any rate tried never to write down to children, assuming that they were just as intelligent as their seniors, if not more so. That has always seemed a good idea.

H. E. L. MELLERSH

"To have visited the country whose ancient people one is going to write about certainly helps, though I have not always managed it. For the rest, it is a matter of reading and reading. I live in the country now, but I get my books from and pretty often go to visit the London Library, a wonderful institution that always seems to have what I want. When looking for the right book I don't mind 'skipping,' nor do I persevere if the book seems too dull for words; I may have missed something, but I should probably not have taken it in anyway...."

MISKOVITS, Christine 1939-

PERSONAL: Born July 17, 1939, in Elizabeth, N.J.; daughter of John, Jr. (a millwright) and Stella (Smolen) Sabora; married Walter J. Miskovits (a customer service agent for Delta Airlines), February 7, 1959; children: Daniel, Ronald, Michael, Eric. *Education:* Attended Rutgers University, 1957-59; additional study in an external degree program. *Religion:* Roman Catholic. *Home:* 28 Hurden St., Hillside, N.J. 07205.

CAREER: St. Elizabeth Hospital, Elizabeth, N.J., technician, 1970—.

WRITINGS: Where Do Insects Go in Winter? (juvenile), Denison, 1973. Contributor to *Highlights, Weekly Reader, Young World, Accent on Youth, My Pleasure, Junior Trails, Friend, Young Miss, Golden, Child Life, Primary Treasure, Wee Wisdom,* and *Kindergartner.*

WORK IN PROGRESS: A juvenile adventure novel, tentatively titled *From the Fire and the Ashes.*

SIDELIGHTS: "I have always loved the feel and smell of a brand new book; and can recall thinking—even as a young child—that someday I, too, would write a book. Writing came to me, though, not as a planned career, but rather as a hobby—something I simply liked to do.

"My stories began as simple, character building lessons for tiny tots, based on experiences I'd had with my own four young children. Yet from the first day I sat down at a typewriter and began filling an empty page with words, ideas and people, I was hooked!

"Where do my stories come from? From everywhere and anywhere. A person, a phrase, an incident—any one of these can be a springboard to a story. In fact, my biggest problem has always been not in what to write, but in selecting the one story or article I feel I can write best at that particular time.

"I've never adhered to the advice given to most authors, 'Write only about what you know.' I write about things I would like to know—things I feel others might want to learn with me.

"Sometimes this learning experience comes out as an article, sometimes a story, even a fact-based book. But there is, in everything I write, something I've learned that I want to share."

MITCHELL, (Sibyl) Elyne (Keith) 1913-

PERSONAL: Born December 30, 1913, in Melbourne, Australia; daughter of Harry George (a soldier) and Sibyl (Keith-Jopp) Chauvel; married Thomas Walter Mitchell (a grazier and member of Victoria Parliament), November 4, 1935; children: Indi (Mrs. John Hill), Walter-Harry (deceased), Honor, John. *Education:* Educated in Melbourne, Australia. *Religion:* Anglican. *Home:* Towong Hill, Corryong, Victoria, Australia 3707. *Agent:* Curtis Brown Ltd., 1 Craven Hill, London, England.

CAREER: Writer of children's books. Works with her husband on their cattle ranch. *Member:* Lyceum Club, Alexandra Club, Ski Club of Australia, Ski Club Arlberg.

WRITINGS: Australia's Alps, Angus & Robertson, 1942, revised edition, 1962; *Speak to the Earth,* Angus & Robertson, 1945; *Soil and Civilization,* Angus & Robertson, 1946; *Images in Water,* Angus & Robertson, 1947; *Flow River, Blow Wind,* Harrap, 1953; *Black Cockatoos Mean Snow,* Hodder & Stoughton, 1956.

For children: *Silver Brumby,* Hutchinson, 1958, Dutton, 1959; *Silver Brumby's Daughter,* Hutchinson, 1960, published as *The Snow Filly,* Dutton, 1961; *Kingfisher Feather,* Hutchinson, 1962; *Winged Skis,* Hutchinson, 1964; *Silver Brumbies of the South,* Hutchinson, 1965; *Silver Brumby Kingdom,* Hutchinson, 1966; *Moon Filly,* Hutchinson, 1968; *Jinki: Dingo of the Snows,* Hutchinson, 1970; *Light Horse to Damascus,* Hutchinson, 1971; *Silver Brumby Whirlwind,* Hutchinson, 1973; *The Colt at Taparoo,* Hutchinson, 1975.

ELYNE MITCHELL

Contributor to *Age* (Melbourne newspaper) and *Walk-about*.

WORK IN PROGRESS: Text for *Snowy Mountains,* a book of photographs of Australia; another Brumby story.

SIDELIGHTS: "I had wanted to write since I was seven and always made up stories for myself. Added to this, I love adventuring. Being brought up in the Army, we rode horses a great deal. I also loved being in the country—the Australian bush.

"When we married, my husband was Australian Ski Champion, so I had to learn to ski—and skis and skiing became the real way to adventure in Australia, in New Zealand, in Chile's Andes, in the Rockies of Canada, in many mountains of the United States and in Europe's Alps.

"Here, at home, the way to get into the Snowy Mountains use to be on horseback, with our skis in a sling from our shoulders, like a rifle and our gear on a pack horse. We would ride to the snowline and then get on to our skis. (Now there are roads into the mountains.)

"Adventuring and writing came together in my first book, *Australia's Alps,* which was mainly written about a lot of ski exploration of the Western Face of the Snowy Mountains, which several of us did in one magnificent winter.

"All that wandering in the mountains is the basis of the *Silver Brumby* series, as also, of course, is the work I do here, riding after cattle, so that one learns a great deal about horses and ponies and there have been many that we have loved dearly.

"A cousin, Ethel Anderson, who wrote beautiful prose and poetry, helped me a lot. It was she who made me carry a notebook so that I could always write down the *exact* description of what I saw . . . notebook balanced on the pummel of the saddle.

"I wrote *The Silver Brumby* for my eldest daughter, Indi, when I was giving her 'correspondence school work' here, because we live in an isolated place, and I wanted to give her a story that really interested her. Then I wrote books for them all, *Winged Skis* for my eldest son, Harry, *Silver Brumbies of the South* for Honor, *Moon Filly* for John and others for all of them. *The Colt at Taparoo* is for Indi's first child.

"In *Light Horse to Damascus,* I tried to give young people the excitement of that Middle-Eastern theatre of World War I. My brothers and myself had heard all of my father's stories and loved them and found them so exciting, when we were children. I wove those stories about imaginary horses, though some of the horses were real, like my father's little mare. Karloo, the hero-horse, is imaginary.

"Skiing is really my great joy. I ski in the mountains near our home, at Thredbo and go to Europe to ski whenever the opportunity occurs.

"So there is always the desire for action and adventure, and the desire to weave the height and depth of all one experiences and all one loves together into a story or a narrative which re-creates and communicates something of these things."

MORGAN, Shirley   1933-

PERSONAL: Born December 11, 1933, in Dorset, England; daughter of Leslie M. and Margaret (Andrews) Morgan; married James J. Kiepper (a professor), March 31, 1955 (divorced); children: Stephanie, Christopher. *Education:* University of New Hampshire, B.A., 1955; State University of New York at Oneonta, M.S., 1965. *Politics:* Independent. *Religion:* Episcopalian. *Home:* 17 Brockley Dr., Delmar, N.Y. 12054.

CAREER: Robert Freeman Advertising, London, England, fashion copywriter, 1955-56; George Dawson Advertising, Concord, N.H., copywriter, 1957-58; kindergarten teacher in Valatie, N.Y., 1962-66, and Guilderland, N.Y., 1966-71; Montessori teacher in Loudonville, N.Y., 1971-72; Emma Willard Children's School, Troy, N.Y., teacher, co-director, 1972— . *Member:* National Education Association, National Association for the Education of Young Children, English Speaking Union, Society of Children's Book Writers.

WRITINGS: Rain, Rain, Don't Go Away (juvenile), Dutton, 1972. Contributor of articles to education journals and newspapers.

WORK IN PROGRESS—For children: *Love to a Very Special Valentine; The Biggest Bike in the World; The Witch and I;* an adult novel.

SIDELIGHTS: "I was born and brought up in England by parents who both read a great deal. It was natural that my sisters and I read and loved books as much as they did. We also spent enjoyable hours together in imaginary worlds of families we invented. Our families were peopled by our teddy bears and dolls, who we pretended were our children.

"We lived outside a country village in Dorset, in a big house surrounded by lawns, flowers, and vegetable gardens, and criss-crossed with paths. We had two huge gold fish pools we loved (and frequently fell into).

"In the summers we spent long holidays at the beach in Cornwall, and this is where I began a life-long love of the sea. As a child I also enjoyed ballet classes and horseback riding.

"While World War II raged around Europe, I was in boarding school, immersing myself in books and discovering with delight everything Charles Dickens ever wrote, as well as the Brontë sisters and Jane Austen. I often memorized passages of prose or poetry which struck me as particularly beautiful.

"Life was more enjoyable because I could read and write. I wrote constantly—letters home, as well as essays and little stories for my younger sister. I tried to draw too, but I was sure I could never write a children's book for publication because I didn't draw well.

"My family moved to America in 1948, and I finished high school and went to the University of New Hampshire. Although English and American people share a similar language, in many other ways life was different and foreign to us. We all learned as we adjusted to a new country.

"Here I discovered a great many exciting American writers, and my reading and writing broadened. I also discovered the glories of New England beaches, and the fun of

Carefully, the boy put his steamship in the river flowing by the edge of the road and he watched the water carry it along. His sister splashed along behind it with her blue-flowered umbrella high above her head. ■ (From *Rain, Rain Don't Go Away* by Shirley Morgan. Illustrated by Edward Ardizzone.)

watching and studying people. I found myself listening to conversations on buses and in public places, and then making up fictional lives based on fragments of people's talk.

"After college I married and had two children. I worked as a fashion copywriter for an advertising agency in London and then in New Hampshire. Meanwhile, I continued to write and read. I read to my own two children every day, and typed stories and articles for both adults and children. None of these pieces of writing really pleased me until I wrote my first published book for children, *Rain, Rain, Don't Go Away.*

"The idea for this book came to me as I watched my children enjoy the sight of heavy spring rains seen through our living room window. I wrote the original manuscript in the middle of the night (although I am a morning person and normally do my best work in the morning). The story was re-written at least twenty times before I was satisfied with it and sent it to the publisher. I like to re-write my work as much as I like to write an original, first-draft. It's exciting to sense how to make a sentence or a paragraph better, and to know when I have done it as well as I possibly can.

"My present job directing a school for young children and teaching them, means I continue to read a great many children's stories, even though my own two are now grown up.

"Many of my story ideas come from conversations I have with the children I teach."

FOR MORE INFORMATION SEE: Albany Times Union, May 11, 1972.

MORRAH, David Wardlaw, Jr. 1914-
(Dave Morrah)

PERSONAL: Born March 27, 1914, in Atlanta, Ga.; son of David Wardlaw and Phyllis (Linderman) Morrah; married Patricia Turbiville, 1947; children: Elizabeth. *Education:*

SHIRLEY MORGAN

North Carolina State College, B.S. in Architectural Engineering, 1935. *Religion:* Presbyterian (ruling elder). *Home:* 1411 Whilden Pl., Greensboro, N.C. 27408.

CAREER: North Carolina State College, Raleigh, wrestling coach, 1935-37; Piggly Wiggly Stores, Greensboro, N.C., sales manager, 1937-40; Bradham and Co. (advertising), Greensboro, N.C., art director, 1947-55; Guilford College, Greensboro, N.C., development director, 1957-65, assistant to president, 1966-74. *Military service:* U.S. Army, five years; became captain. *Member:* Civitan Club, Tau Beta Pi, Sigma Phi Epsilon.

WRITINGS: Cinderella Hassenpfeffer, Rinehart, 1948; *Fraulein Bo-Peepen,* Rinehart, 1953; *Heinrich Schnibble,* Rinehart, 1955; *Sillynyms,* Rinehart, 1956; *Alice in Wunderbarland,* Rinehart, 1957; *Who Ben Kaputen Der Robin?,* Doubleday, 1960; *Me/And The Liberal Arts,* Doubleday, 1962; *Der Wizard in Ozzenland,* Doubleday, 1962; *Our Honor the Mayor,* Doubleday, 1964. Regular contributor to "Post Scripts" in *Saturday Evening Post,* 1946-62; columnist, *Greensboro Sunday News,* 1957-65; contributor to *Argosy,* 1965-69, *Liberty, Parade, Look, American Magazine,* and *Christian Science Monitor.*

WORK IN PROGRESS: A novel, *Hellmire,* for Doubleday.

HOBBIES AND OTHER INTERESTS: Wood carving, azalea culture.

MULLINS, Edward S(wift) 1922-

PERSONAL: Born February 25, 1922, in Sanford, Me.; son of Ernest Allen (a businessman) and Josephine (Swift) Mullins; married Mary Kilkenny (now an artist), May 26, 1944; children: Sheila (Mrs. Arnold Farese), David, Paul,

EDWARD S. MULLINS (SELF-PORTRAIT)

Nicholas. *Education:* New England School of Art, diploma, 1942; University of London, special courses in fine arts, 1951; Boston University, B.S., 1953. *Religion:* Roman Catholic. *Home:* 31 Green St., Milford, Conn. *Office:* 54 Broad St., Milford, Conn. 06460.

CAREER: Instructor in art at New England School of Art, Boston, Mass., 1947-54, and Milford (Conn.) High School, 1954-56; artist and planning director, Norcross Greeting Card Co., New York, N.Y., 1956-61; free-lance artist and writer, Milford, Conn., 1961-64; Norcross Greeting Card Co., artist, 1964-66; director of Milford School of Art and Gallery on the Green, both Milford, Conn., 1966—. *Military service:* U.S. Army, Signal Corps, 1942-45. *Member:* Milford Art League (past president). *Awards, honors:* Various prizes for oil paintings and water colors.

WRITINGS: Animal Limericks (juvenile; self-illustrated), Follett, 1966; *The Big Book of Limericks* (juvenile; self-illustrated), Platt & Munk, 1969. Columnist, "Thinking Out Loud," in *Milford Citizen,* 1956-58. Poems included in anthologies.

WORK IN PROGRESS: A novel; a children's book.

SIDELIGHTS: "Since I am an artist as well as a writer, one of my main interests in bringing a book into existence is doing the illustrations. I try to make them interesting by

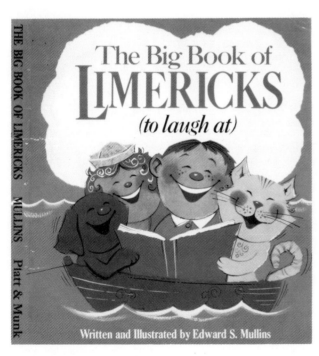

(From *The Big Book of Limericks* by Edward S. Mullins. Illustrated by the author.)

using different techniques and materials. In the case of *Animal Limericks,* for example, I was very daring. I cut animal shapes out of magazine pages and cemented them down. A grasshopper was cut out of an ear of corn, a cat emerged from a lady's gray hair, and a seal came to life in a sleek and slippery-looking piece of black marble. I enjoyed all this enormously, but Follett Publishing Company was not quite as thrilled about it, since a magazine page is extremely difficult to reproduce. They did a wonderful job with it, however, and the illustrations are very beautiful.

"In *The Big Book of Limericks,* the illustrations were made from torn pieces of tissue paper, which was really a very difficult technique when there were so many illustrations to do. Before I was finished, I found myself wishing I had used a simpler approach, like watercolor. Something that didn't stick to my fingers and get lost under the table all the time.

"I have written so many limericks in my life that my ordinary conversations almost fall into that verse form. I have discovered that the best approach (for me, at any rate) is to first visualize an amusing situation and then begin to play around with words until said situation has been best described.

"I've written all kinds of poetry, some of it very serious, but a limerick, due to the nature of the verse form, has to be amusing and fun in order to be successful. Writing one is very much like playing a game with words."

HOBBIES AND OTHER INTERESTS: Philosophy, world affairs, politics, theater, extrasensory perception (in all its forms), and gardening.

MURPHY, Robert (William)   1902-1971

PERSONAL: Born August 27, 1902, in Ridley Park, Pa.; son of William Robert (an engineer) and Mary Elizabeth (Bryant) Murphy; married Jean Warfield Whittle, March 22, 1946; children: Robert Shane, Molly Jean. *Education:* Friends Central School, Philadelphia, Pa., graduate, 1921; attended Washington and Lee University. *Politics:* Independent. *Religion:* Presbyterian. *Home:* 321 Skyline Dr., Prescott, Ariz. 86301. *Agent:* Harold Ober Associates, Inc., 40 East 49th St., New York, N.Y. 10017.

CAREER: Saturday Evening Post, Philadelphia, Pa., began as associate editor, became senior editor, 1942-62. Has conducted courses in writing at University of Indiana, University of Colorado, and University of Michigan Writers' Conferences. *Member:* Explorers Club (New York). *Awards, honors:* Dutton Animal Book award, 1964, for *The Pond.*

WRITINGS: Murder in Waiting (novel), Scribner, 1938; (with Helen Wills Moody) *Death Serves an Ace,* Scribner, 1939; *The Warm Hearted Polar Bear,* Little, Brown, 1957; *The Haunted Journey,* Doubleday, 1961; *The Peregrine Falcon,* Houghton, 1963 (published in England as *Varda, the Flight of a Falcon,* Cassell, 1964); *The Pond,* Dutton, 1964; *The Golden Eagle,* Dutton, 1965; *Wild Geese Calling,* Dutton, 1966; *The Phantom Setter, and Other Stories,* Dutton, 1966; *A Certain Island,* M. Evans, 1967; *Wild Sanctuaries: Our National Wildlife Refuges,* Dutton, 1968; *A Heritage Restored: America's Wildlife Refuges* (juvenile

Their clear gabbling came back to him as he watched them rise above the trees, their clean and dusky shapes cut sharp against the sky, close together and diminishing in the direction that the wedge had gone. ■ (From *Wild Geese Calling* by Robert Murphy. Illustrated by John Kaufmann.)

edition of *Wild Sanctuaries*), Dutton, 1969; *The Haunted Journey* (juvenile edition), Farrar, Straus, 1969; *The Mountain Lion,* Dutton, 1969; *The Stream,* Farrar, Straus, 1971. Contributor of forty-four short stories and numerous articles to *Saturday Evening Post* and other magazines, and to anthologies.

SIDELIGHTS: Wild Geese Calling was made into a television film.

HOBBIES AND OTHER INTERESTS: Nature, photography, falconry, hunting, fishing, conservation, and travel.

FOR MORE INFORMATION SEE: Young Reader's Review, December, 1966; *Best Sellers,* April 1, 1969, April 1, 1971; *New York Times Book Review,* February 15, 1970; *Antiquarian Bookman,* August 2-9, 1971.

(Died July 13, 1971)

MYERS, Hortense (Powner)   1913-

PERSONAL: Born July 15, 1913, in Indianapolis, Ind.; daughter of Walter Joseph Powner, Sr., and Stella (Smith) Powner; married Stanley M. Myers, 1947; children: Mark. *Education:* Butler University, B.S., 1953. *Religion:* Methodist. *Home:* 7839 West 56th St., Indianapolis, Ind. 46254. *Office:* United Press International, Indianapolis, Ind.

Something about the Author

CAREER: Old Trail News, Indianapolis, Ind., assistant editor, 1934-42; International News Service, Indianapolis, Ind., assistant bureau chief, 1942-58; United Press International, Indianapolis, Ind., statehouse reporter, feature writer, 1958—. Marion County Mental Health Association, past vice-president; Indiana Lincoln Foundation, member of board of directors. *Member:* Women in Communication (past president, Indianapolis alumnae), Woman's Press Club of Indiana (past president, past vice-president), National Federation of Press Women (president), Indianapolis Press Club (president), Society of Professional Journalists, Sigma Delta Chi (past president, Indiana chapter), Zonta Club (Indianapolis). *Awards, honors:* Frances Wright Award from Theta Sigma Phi and Frances Rabb Award from Woman's Press Club of Indiana, both for outstanding contribution to journalism; Women in Communication National Headliner award; Woman of Achievement citation from National Federation of Press Women.

WRITINGS: (Co-author with Ruth Burnett) *Carl Ben Eielson: Young Alaskan Pilot,* Bobbs, 1961; (with Robert Thompson) *The Brother Within: Robert Kennedy,* Macmillan, 1962; (with Burnett) *Cecil DeMille: Boy Dramatist,* Bobbs, 1963; (with Burnett) *Vilhjalmur Stefansson: Young Arctic Explorer,* Bobbs, 1966; *Edward R. Murrow: Young Newscaster,* Bobbs, 1969; *Vincent Lombardi: Young Football Coach,* Bobbs, 1971; *Joseph Pulitzer: Boy Journalist,* Bobbs, 1975.

HORTENSE MYERS

The plane sped down the runway at sixty, seventy, then eighty miles an hour. It missed first one high bank of snow and then the other. It lifted, hung sickeningly, and touched the icy ground again. At last, the plane soared smoothly into the air. ■ (From *Carl Ben Eielson* by Hortense Myers and Ruth Burnett. Illustrated by Gray Morrow.)

SIDELIGHTS: "My favorite subjects in school were those about people. I still have a silver bracelet that was my prize for a composition I wrote in elementary school. Not long after graduation from Ben Davis High School (Indianapolis, Indiana) I went to work for a weekly newspaper. It was on-the-job training for a lifetime career in what is often called communications. That is a term including not only writing for newspapers and magazines, but also writing for radio and television, writing books, plays and poetry and other ways we have of using language to convey information and ideas to other people.

"I also enrolled in college classes at night while I was working in the daytime. This is a slow way to get a college degree but it can be done. It took me twenty years. By that time I was married and had a little boy. When he saw his mother marching in a line of graduates at Butler University, he slipped away from his father and started to run across the football field yelling, 'Mommie, Mommie!'

"After working on the weekly newspaper, I began work for a wire service, United Press International, a world-wide organization providing news for newspapers, radio and television stations. Mostly I write about politics and government but I sometimes write about other happenings such as fires, tornadoes, explosions and crime.

"Writing books for the *Childhood of Famous Americans* series is just another way of communicating with people. The same skills acquired in getting facts for a news story can be used in getting facts upon which to base the episodes that go into these books.

"Things that happen to us when we are children often affect the way we think and act when we become adults. We can better understand people if we know some of the experiences they have had.

"Sometimes I say I would rather write books than newspaper articles because people usually keep books but newspapers are thrown away in a day or two."

NAYLOR, Penelope 1941-

PERSONAL: Born January 13, 1941, in New York, N.Y.; daughter of Lester Owen and Elaine (Connolly) Naylor. *Education:* Attended Smith College; also studied sculpture with Otto Georg Hitzberger, 1960. *Residence:* New York, N.Y.

CAREER: Professional painter, 1963—. Creative director of a New York travel marketing and publishing firm, 1973-74; incorporated own co-publishing company, 1975. Has exhibited paintings and drawings in New York, Pennsylvania, Africa, Spain, and Portugal. *Awards, honors:* Chi-

PENELOPE NAYLOR

When a wasp locates a spider, it swoops down and stings the spider with poison until the victim is paralyzed. ■ (From *The Spider World* by Penelope Naylor. Illustrated by the author.)

cago *Tribune* Spring Book Award, 1973, for *Black Images;* American Institute of Graphic Arts, certificate of excellence, children's book show, 1974.

WRITINGS—Juvenile: *Sculpture: The Shapes of Belief,* Watts, 1971; (self-illustrated) *Spider World,* Watts, 1972; *Black Images: The Art of Africa,* Doubleday, 1973.

Illustrator: Laura Baker, *A Tree Called Moses,* Atheneum, 1966; Bernice Kohn, *Ferns: Plants Without Flowers,* Hawthorn, 1968; Francine Klagsbrun, *The First Book of Spices,* Watts, 1968; D. X. Fenten, *Plants for Pots,* Lippincott, 1969; Alvin and Virginia Silverstein, *Bionics: Man Copies Nature's Machines,* McCall Publishing, 1970; Fred Warren and Lee Warren, *The Music of Africa,* Prentice-Hall, 1970.

WORK IN PROGRESS: Projects involving adult nonfiction, masks, symbols, art and visual experience, film scripts.

SIDELIGHTS: "My greatest interests are art, nature and travel, which I have spent the better part of my adult life pursuing. My only ambition in life is to continue to learn—and to convey some of the beauty, excitement and relevance of what I discover to others."

NEE, Kay Bonner

PERSONAL: Born in Plummer, Minn.; daughter of David Thomas (a teacher) and Helena (Franken) Bonner; married William J. Nee (engaged in public relations), April 19, 1947; children: Christopher, Nicole, Lisa, Rachel. *Education:* College of St. Catherine, B.A., 1941; University of Minnesota, graduate study, 1947. *Politics:* Democrat. *Religion:* Roman Catholic. *Home:* 219 Logan Park Way, Fridley, Minn. 55432. *Office:* Minnesota Association of Voluntary Social Service Agencies, Griggs-Midway Bldg., 1821 University Ave., St. Paul, Minn. 55104.

CAREER: Dayton Co., Minneapolis, Minn., emcee of radio show, 1945-50; Manson-Gold-Miller, Inc., Minneapolis, radio-television director, 1951-53; WCCO-TV, Minneapolis, writer, director, and producer, 1954-56; White-Herzog-Nee, Inc., Minneapolis, radio and television writer and producer, 1956-65; North State Advertising Agency, Minneapolis, president, 1966-70; Minnesota Association of Voluntary Social Service Agencies, St. Paul, executive director, 1972—. Television director of McCarthy for President campaign, 1968, and director of television and radio

KAY BONNER NEE

for other political campaigns. Member of Minnesota Governor's Committee on Status of Women, 1966. *Member:* American Federation of Television and Radio Artists, Delta Phi Lambda.

WRITINGS: (With husband, William Nee) *Eugene McCarthy: United States Senator,* Gilbert Press, 1964; *Powhatan* (juvenile), Dillon, 1971.

Children's one-act plays: "Rhymes Ago-go," produced in 1967; "Land of the Moogazoos," 1969; "The Winner," 1971; "Hey Joe!," 1972. Writer of weekly radio show, "Soda Set," 1945-50, ten-episode television series, "Your Child's World," 1967-68, eleven-episode television series, "Preparing Children for the 21st Century," 1973, and twelve-episode television series, "Living Married," 1975. Former columnist in *Catholic Miss.*

WORK IN PROGRESS: My Mother the Mayor, a children's book on political campaigning; editing *Proven Plays for Young Productions.*

SIDELIGHTS: "Writing can take many forms. I was writing long before I knew how to put it down on paper. As a young child we lived on a farm. There was no radio, no television, not even a movie house within twenty-five miles. My brother and I use to make up stories—serials which we added to by the day. I remember his main character was Leaks Lard and mine was Ken Lear. These two had wild adventures. We really stretched our imaginations. The television my children watch is many times mild in comparison to the dangers and cliff-hanging situations that were faced by Leaks and Ken. I often wonder what happened to these two. Where did we leave them? I hope they escaped whatever their last complication was and are living happily.

"When I was in the sixth grade I entered a national essay contest. Mine was entitled 'Sherman's March to the Sea' and it won me the first prize of a five-dollar gold piece. What a victory!

"In high school I was most fortunate. A unique and marvelous woman, Miss Abigail O'Leary, taught creative writing. She was the only person I have ever known who could actually 'teach' creative writing. Under her tutelage I was able to develop my writing style. My junior and senior years I entered contests and won prizes. Writing began to look like something real—something you did for more than just the fun of it. This was reinforced in college by another wonderful woman, Sister Alice, a poet herself and a great inspiration to fledging writers to keep writing in any form.

"I was delighted, when after graduation from college, I was able to earn a living as a script writer for radio and later television. My early experience with Leaks and Ken gave me a flair for dialogue that I might not otherwise have had—even though my adult scripts were tame in comparison to those early adventures.

"My own children have been most helpful in giving me an insight into what young people like to read. They have also acted as friendly critics. They can tell me in a minute (and do) if I sound phoney, hokey or have missed the point. My husband, who is a writer himself, has a real talent for editing, for cutting out unessentials and asking that all important question, 'What was it you really wanted to say?'

Certain techniques are necessary for writing, of course, but I think possibly the real ingredient is the desire to say something to your readers; to tell a story, to express an idea, and to do this in the most interesting way you know how."

NEWMAN, Shirlee Petkin 1924-

PERSONAL: Born February 16, 1924, in Boston, Mass.; married Jackson J. Newman (an automotive dealer), June 25, 1946; children: Paula, Jeffrey. *Education:* Attended high schools in Massachusetts and California, Boston Center for Adult Education, Cambridge Centre for Adult Education. *Home:* 34 Roosevelt Rd., Newton Centre, Mass. 02159.

CAREER: Copywriter for advertising agencies in Los Angeles, Calif., 1941-45, New York, 1945-46; associate editor, *Child Life,* Newton Centre, Mass, 1962-63; taught writing for children, Cambridge Center for adult education, Cambridge, Mass., 1975-76.

WRITINGS: Liliuokalani, Young Queen of Hawaii, Bobbs, 1960; *Yellow Silk for May Lee,* Bobbs, 1961; (adapter) *Folk Tales of Latin America,* Bobbs, 1962; (adapter) *Folk Tales of Japan,* Bobbs, 1963; *The Shipwrecked Dog,* Bobbs, 1963; (with Diane Sherman) *About People Who Run Your City,* Melmont, 1963; (with Diane Sherman) *About Canals,* Melmont, 1964; *Marian Anderson: Lady From Philadelphia,* Westminster, 1966; *Ethel Barrymore: Young Leading Lady,* Bobbs, 1966; *The Story of LBJ,* Westminster, 1967; *Mary Martin on Stage,* Westminster, 1969. Fiction, non-fiction, and photography has appeared in *American Girl, Calling All Girls, Jack and Jill, Scholastic,* education and trade journals.

WORK IN PROGRESS: Weekly half-page "Hooray For Kids" to be syndicated in newspapers; (with Jean Corcoran) working on historical fiction book about abolitionist period.

SIDELIGHTS: "I was born and brought up in Brookline, Massachusetts, a suburb of Boston, until the age of thirteen, when, because of my father's death, my mother took my older sister, younger brother and me to southern California. Transplanted, I returned from whence I came ... the public library. Almost my whole life has been spent in libraries, especially boys' and girls' sections. My favorite reading has always been books for young people, from picture books to young adults'. Some say I've never grown up. 'You're just a big kid,' they say. Perhaps. Know what? Hope I never do. And now that my own children are grown, I have a two-year-old granddaughter, with whom to identify ... and to see from her eyes, hear with her ears, feel as she feels is life's greatest joy.

"High school in California wasn't much fun for me until I became a 'staffer' on the Beverly Hills high school paper, and as a senior, talked my neighborhood weekly into letting me write 'gossip' about kids from all the surrounding high schools. 'Campus Chatter' it was called, and to my embarassment it earned me the name 'Mrs. Walter Winchell.' (Who was it said—literature is just gossip with style?)

"Once out of high school, with no funds for college, I held various jobs ... starting from a helper in a department store advertising department, to work in advertising; and marriage, to settle down in Brookline, Massachusetts, again. Even after marriage and housewifery (which I must say I took very seriously) I never stopped writing something ...

Finally the day of the wedding came. Lydia was helping Bernice get dressed. How lovely she looked in the long white bridal gown that Mrs. Cooke had made! ▪ (From *Liliuokalani* by Shirlee Petkin Newman. Illustrated by Leslie Goldstein.)

articles for trade journals and business publications ... pieces for local papers, etc. Until my daughter began reading children's magazines. ... Could I? I wondered. A course at Boston Center for adult education, and another at Cambridge Center for adult education, showed me I could. After many long hours, days, weeks, months, of writing, re-writing, re-writing, re-writing, I began to sell ... then on to books, and eventually, associate editorship of *Child Life*.

"Now that my own children are grown (my son works on a national weekly), I have more time to wander about, doing *live* research: from going through old houses, to windjamming on a high-masted schooner along the New England seacoast. All of my books have involved research of one sort or another, even my books of fiction.

"*Yellow Silk for May Lee* was set in Chinatown, San Francisco, near where I lived for a while during my advertising agency days. When I wrote the book many years later, I still read every scrap I could about Chinatown. *The Shipwrecked Dog* started by watching a freighter being towed off a sandbar one summer, but involved research about Portuguese people here in this country, and much looking into how rescue operations are carried out. The live research was getting a puppy and bringing it up.

"The most fun of all my work is receiving letters from boys and girls ... knowing they're out there, reading my books."

SHIRLEE PETKIN NEWMAN

Something about the Author

HOBBIES AND OTHER INTERESTS: Yoga, bird-watching, nature study, guitar, folk-singing, bike-riding. "Whatever takes my fancy—maybe ESP or psychic phenomena next."

NORTON, Frank R(owland) B(rowning) 1909-
(Browning Norton)

PERSONAL: Born March 5, 1909, in Parkman, Ohio; son of Melvin H. (a school superintendent) and Ruby (Browning) Norton; married Agnes Cluse (a psychologist), April 28, 1941; children: John Melvin, Mary Browning (Mrs. David C. White). *Education:* Ohio Wesleyan University, B.A., 1930; Westminster College, New Wilmington, Pa., M.S.Ed., 1957. *Politics:* "Disgusted Citizens of America." *Home and office:* 2853 Northwest Blvd., Columbus, Ohio 43221.

CAREER: High school teacher and basketball coach; Walter L. Main Circus, advance press agent; advertising salesman; insurance salesman; *Painesville Telegraph,* Painesville, Ohio, reporter and sports editor, 1941-43; *Youngstown Vindicator,* Youngstown, Ohio, reporter, 1944-58, Sunday editor, 1953-57; Ohio State University, Columbus, Ohio, professor of journalism, 1959-71; writer, 1971—. *Member:* Mystery Writers of America.

WRITINGS: (With J. Eugene Haas) *Human Response:*

FRANK R. B. NORTON

The Great Alaska Earthquake of 1964 Human Ecology, National Academy of Sciences, 1970.

Under name Browning Norton: (With Charles Landolf) *I Prefer Murder,* Graphic, 1956; *Tidal Wave,* Ace, 1960; *Johnny/Bingo,* Coward, 1971; *Help Me, Charley Buoy,* Coward, 1974.

Contributor to mystery magazines and popular periodicals, including *McCall's, Playboy, Adventure* and *Redbook.* Stories have been anthologized in *The Queen's Awards,* Little, Brown, 1953, *The Permanent Playboy,* Crown, 1959, *With Malice Toward All,* Putnam, 1968. His short stories have been published in England, Australia, Malaya, South Africa, Sweden, Denmark, Italy, Norway and Finland.

WORK IN PROGRESS: A third juvenile book and an adult suspense novel.

SIDELIGHTS: In 1965, Norton on leave from the School of Journalism at Ohio State University, became an investigator and writer for the Alaska earthquake project at OSU's Disaster Research Center. The project involved collecting data and writing narrative reports on effects of the 1964 earthquake in thirteen south-central Alaska towns and native villages, the response of the stricken communities to the trauma of disaster, and early efforts toward, and patterns of recovery.

HOBBIES AND OTHER INTERESTS: Travel, golf, reading, convivial friends.

OAKLEY, Helen (McKelvey) 1906-

PERSONAL: Born February 10, 1906, in New York, N.Y.; daughter of Ralph Huntington (an artist) and Helen (Fairchild) McKelvey; married Walter T. Oakley (now a publisher), August 6, 1938; children: Valerie Thurston (Mrs. Charles R. Atherton, Jr.), Deborah Huntington (Mrs. Kenneth Bodner). *Education:* Attended Shipley School; Bryn Mawr College, A.B., 1928. *Politics:* Republican. *Home:* 128 Park Ave., Manhasset, N.Y. 11030; and Shepherdstown, W.Va. 25443.

CAREER: Week-End Book Service, Inc., New York, N.Y., president and manager, 1929-41; writer. Has done book condensation work for *Liberty* Magazine; paints, and has taught art at Vincent Smith School, Port Washington, N.Y., and an adult education class in creative writing, Manhasset, N.Y.; para-professional library assistant, Manhasset Junior High School; librarian at Buckley Country Day School, Roslyn, N.Y., 1970-75. Trustee of Manhasset Public Library. *Member:* Authors Guild, Bryn Mawr Association of Long Island (founder-chairman), Manhasset Art Association, Christopher Morley Knothole Association (president, 1971-75).

WRITINGS—Fiction for young girls: *The Horse on the Hill,* Knopf, 1957; *The Ranch by the Sea,* Knopf, 1958; *The Enchanter's Wheel,* Norton, 1962; *ABCD: An Alphabet of Christmas Words,* Oxford University Press, 1966; *Freedom's Daughter,* Norton, 1968.

WORK IN PROGRESS: Three Hours for Lunch: The Life and Times of Christopher Morley, for Watermill Publishers.

HELEN OAKLEY

OFFIT, Sidney   1928-

PERSONAL: Born October 13, 1928, in Baltimore, Md.; son of Barney and Lillian (Cohen) Offit; married Avodah Crindell Komito (a doctor), August 8, 1952; children: Kenneth, Michael Robert. *Education:* Attended Valley Forge Military Academy; Johns Hopkins University, B.A., 1950. *Politics:* Democrat. *Religion:* Jewish. *Home:* 23 East 69th St., New York, N.Y. 10021.

CAREER: Mercury Publications, New York, N.Y., member of editorial staff, 1952-53; Macfadden Publications, New York, N.Y., member of editorial staff, 1954; freelance writer, 1954—; New York University, New York, N.Y., adjunct associate professor of creative writing of Division of Continuing Education, 1964—; New School for Social Research, New York, N.Y., member of writing workshops faculty, 1964—; *Intellectual Digest,* New York, N.Y., co-founder and senior editor, 1971-74; Lexington Democratic Club, New York, N.Y., member of executive committee, 1958-62; 19th Precinct Community Council, chairman, 1962—; school board selection committee, 1963. *Military service:* U.S. Army Reserve; became captain. *Member:* P.E.N. (vice-president, 1971-74; delegate to international executive board meetings, Yugoslavia, 1970, Berlin, 1973, Jerusalem, 1974), Authors Guild (executive council, 1971), Century Association. *Awards, honors:* Distinguished alumni award from Valley Forge Military Academy, 1961, for achievement in letters.

WRITINGS: (Compiler) *The Best of Baseball,* Putnam, 1956; *He Had It Made* (adult novel), Crown, 1959; *The*

Boy Who Won the World Series (teenage fiction), Lothrop, 1960; *Cadet Quarterback* (teenage fiction), St. Martins, 1961; *The Other Side of the Street* (adult novel), Crown, 1962; *Soupbone* (fantasy), St. Martins, 1963; *Cadet Command* (teenage fiction), St. Martins, 1963; *Cadet Attack* (teenage fiction), St. Martins, 1964; *Topsy Turvy* (fantasy), St. Martins, 1965; *The Adventures of Homer Fink* (juvenile), St. Martins, 1966; *The Boy Who Made a Million* (juvenile), St. Martins, 1968; *Not All Girls Have Million Dollar Smiles* (young adult), Coward, 1971; *Only a Girl Like You* (young adult), Coward, 1973. Contributed short stories to western pulp magazines, 1950-53; articles and stories in *New Leader, Saturday Evening Post, Columbia Journalism Review, Johns Hopkins Magazine* and others.

WORK IN PROGRESS: A novel.

SIDELIGHTS: "When I was in the sixth grade, the principal of our school was always visiting our class to tell us what a collection of geniuses we were. I knew she wasn't talking about me. My math grades kept me humble. Besides, the rest of my report card was no cause for celebration and certainly not pride. Then, at the end of the school year on a lazy afternoon when the books were put away and the teacher had run out of activities to educate us, someone suggested a story-telling hour. As I stood before

SIDNEY OFFIT

THE ADVENTURES OF
HOMER FINK

by SIDNEY OFFIT

Paul Galdone drew the pictures

THE ADVENTURES OF HOMER FINK

OFFIT

St. Martin's

"If I hadn't remembered Diogenes I would never have thought of hiding in a barrel. Diogenes tried to live his life with the barest essentials," Homer went on, "that way he was able to think without distraction about the governing of men. You know it works." ■ (From *The Adventures of Homer Fink* by Sidney Offit. Illustrated by Paul Galdone.)

my classmates—that audience of certified genius—I began, 'One dark and stormy night . . .' I have been a storyteller ever since.

"Most of my books for young readers were written for Ken and Mike, our sons. The stories are either autobiographical to tell my boys something of what my childhood was like or pure fantasy to let them in on their old man's daydreams. I have written books for my wife, too. I suppose I was trying to tell her what a wise and sensitive man she married.

"Although I have had periods in which writing was my primary occupation, time does not seem to have a correlation to the quantity or quality of my work. One of my most rewarding periods of composition was during the time my wife returned to college to study for her medical degree. It was then I wrote *The Adventures of Homer Fink*, the story of a young classicist who comes to terms with love and beauty and power."

FOR MORE INFORMATION SEE: New York Times, August 30, 1959, November 12, 1972; *Baltimore News-Post,* December 28, 1962; *Saturday Review,* January 19, 1964; *Baltimore Sun,* February 21, 1965.

ORLEANS, Ilo   1897-1962

PERSONAL: Born February 24, 1897, in London, England; son of Hirsch and Sara Orleans; married Friede C. Katchen, 1920; children: Judith Orleans Wahler, Julian. *Education:* Columbia University, B.A., 1916, journalism student, 1917, LL.B., 1919. *Home:* 134 Vassar Ave., Newark, N.J. *Office:* 225 Broadway, New York, N.Y. 10007.

ILO ORLEANS

CAREER: Falk & Orleans (law firm), New York, N.Y., partner, 1922-61, counsel, 1961-62. U.S. Selective Service System, government appeal agent during World War II. *Member:* American Bar Association, New York County Lawyers Association, Poetry Society of America. *Awards, honors:* Hayil Honor Award for contribution to devotional writing for youth, 1956.

WRITINGS: Funday, Kendall, 1930; *Father Gander,* Kendall, 1933; *Wonder Book of Fun,* Grosset, 1951; *The First Rainbow,* Union of American Hebrew Congregations, 1954; *This Wonderful Day,* Grosset, 1958; *Animal Orchestra,* Simon and Schuster, 1958; *The Zoo That Grew,* Walck, 1960; *I Watch the World Go By,* Walck, 1961; *Within Thy Hand,* Union of American Hebrew Congregations, 1961; *Gingerbread Children: Poems,* Follett, 1973. Contributor to periodicals for teachers, children, and parents, including *The Instructor, Jack and Jill, Child Life, Highlights for Children, Grade Teacher.*

SIDELIGHTS: "My literary work has largely been for children—poetry, both secular and religious—for about forty years. Some five hundred items have been put to music. Over twenty-five anthems have been published. . . . Over two hundred items of mine have appeared in school books, texts, teachers manuals, song books, television and radio series, anthologies in the United States and abroad."

Orleans' poems appear in hundreds of anthologies including Louis Untermeyer's *Rainbow in the Sky* and in children's magazines in the United States, Australia, England, and Canada. His work has also been published in braille.

(Died September 26, 1962)

OSMOND, Edward   1900-

PERSONAL: Born May 6, 1900, in Orford, Suffolk, England; son of Percy Herbert (a clergyman, Church of England) and Agnes (Sadler) Osmond; married Constance M. Biggs (an author and artist under name Laurie Osmond), November 12, 1927; children: Christine Gillian. *Education:* Educated privately; studied art at The Polytechnic, London, England, 1917-24, Art Teachers Diploma, 1924, Diploma in Art History, 1924. *Home:* Downland Cottage, Lullington Close, Seaford, Sussex, England.

CAREER: Free-lance illustrator, 1928—; author, illustrator, and designer of children's books. Part-time art teacher at Hastings College of Technology, Sussex, England, and at Hornsey College of Art, London, England. *Member:* Society of Industrial Artists, Society of Authors. *Awards, honors:* Carnegie Medal of Library Association, for outstanding children's book of the year by a British subject, 1954, for *A Valley Grows Up.*

WRITINGS—All self-illustrated, some also designed: *A Valley Grows Up,* Oxford University Press, 1953; *Houses,* Batsford, 1956; *Villages,* Batsford, 1957; *Towns,* Batsford, 1958; *From Drumbeat to Ticker Tape,* Hutchinson, 1960; *The Artist in Britain,* Studio Books, 1961; *People of the Desert,* Odhams, 1963; *People of the Jungle Forest,* Odhams, 1963; *People of the Grasslands,* Odhams, 1964; *People of the Arctic,* Odhams, 1964; *People of the High Mountains,* Odhams, 1965; *People of the Lonely Islands,* Odhams, 1965; *Animals of Central Asia,* Abelard-Schu-

Seals and sea-lions often have their "nurseries" on lonely islands, where their helpless babies can spend their first weeks of life on shore. ■ (From *People of the Lonely Islands* by Edward Osmond. Illustrated by the author.)

man, 1967; *Exploring Fashions and Fabrics,* Odhams, 1967. Also author of "Animals of the World" series, Clarendon Press, 1953-56, and of "Animals of Britain" series, Clarendon Press, 1959-62.

Illustrator: Jean Bothwell, *Vanishing Wildlife of East Africa,* Abelard, 1967; Maurice Burton, *Animals,* Watts, 1968; Wendy Boorer, *Dogs: Selection-Care-Training,* Grosset, 1971; George Cansdale, *Book of Pets,* Merry Thoughts.

WORK IN PROGRESS: Participating in a large work, *The Arts of Mankind,* to be published by Collins; a projected book on domestic animals.

SIDELIGHTS: Osmond writes for children of eight years and older. His theory of children's books is that they should be produced while the writer is, himself, learning about their subject matter—that this imparts some hidden excitement which may infect the reader. He thinks that ideally the book should be written, illustrated, and designed by the same person.

FOR MORE INFORMATION SEE: Illustrators of Children's Books: 1946-1956, Horn Book, 1958.

OUSLEY, Odille   1896-

PERSONAL: Born October 19, 1896, in Macon, Ga.; daughter of Thomas R. (a farmer) and Maymie T. (Hertel) Ousley. *Education:* George Peabody College for Teachers, B.A., M.A.; summer study at Columbia University and University of Virginia. *Religion:* Methodist. *Home and office:* 407 Landover Dr., Decatur, Ga. 30030.

CAREER: Supervisor of student teaching at Atlanta Normal School, Atlanta, Ga., and State Teachers College, Slippery Rock, Pa.; University of Georgia, Athens, reading specialist; University of Georgia and Emory University, Atlanta Area Teacher Education Service, specialist in reading and children's literature. *Member:* National Society

for Teachers of English, Association of Childhood Education, Association of Supervisors and Curriculum Directors, Delta Kappa Gamma, Kappa Delta Pi.

WRITINGS—All published by Ginn: (With David Russell and others) "Ginn Basic Readers" series, 1948, revised edition, 1961; (with Russell and others) "Ginn Basic Enrichment Readers" series, 1953-59; *My ABC Book,* 1962; *Mr. Bear's Bow Ties,* 1964; (compiler) *V Is for Verses* (anthology), 1964; *Cowboy Bill and the Big Umbrella,* 1965; *The Little Pig Who Listened,* 1966.

PAICE, Margaret   1920-

PERSONAL: Surname rhymes with "race"; born in 1920, in Brisbane, Queensland, Australia; daughter of Sydney (an engineer) and Violet (Burman) Cantle; married Hubert W. Paice, January 10, 1941 (died, 1956); married Wilfred L. Harriss (a high school teacher), January 16, 1960 (died, 1975); children: (first marriage) Jeannette (Mrs. Peter Lloyd), Peter W.; (second marriage) Christopher. *Education:* Studied at National Art School, Sydney, for one year, and at Royal Art Society School for one year. *Home:* 4 Paulwood Ave., Winmalee 2777, New South Wales, Australia.

CAREER: Commercial artist with firm in Sydney, Australia, 1957-60; illustrates and writes books for children. *Member:* Australian Society of Authors, New South Wales Children's Book Council, Fellowship of Australian Writers, Society of Women Writers, V.I.E.W. Club, Blue Mountain Gardening and Beautification Group.

WRITINGS—All self-illustrated for children: *Mirram,* Angus & Robertson, 1955; *Namitja,* Angus & Robertson, 1956; *Valley in the North,* Angus & Robertson, 1957; *The Lucky Fall,* Angus & Robertson, 1958; *A Joey for Christmas,* Angus & Robertson, 1960; *The Secret of Greycliffs,* Angus & Robertson, 1961; *Over the Mountain,* Angus & Robertson, 1964; *The Bensens,* Collins, 1968; *They Drowned a Valley,* Collins, 1969; *The Morning Glory,* Collins, 1971; *Run to the Mountains,* Collins, 1972; *Dolan's Roost,* Collins, 1974; *Colour in the Creek* (novel), Collins, in press; *Jackey-Jackey* (Australians in History series), Collins, in press. Contributor of short stories to magazines.

Illustrator: Anne E. Wells, *Tales from Arnhem Land,* Angus & Robertson, 1959; Clarice Morris, *A Handbook of Australian Wild Flowers,* Angus & Robertson, 1961; Stella Sammon, *The Lucky Stone,* Methuen, 1969; Anne E. Wells, *Rain in Arnhem Land,* Angus & Robertson, 1961; Anne E. Wells, *Skies of Arnhem Land,* Angus & Robertson, 1964.

WORK IN PROGRESS: A new book to be set in the Queensland cane country in the year 1933.

SIDELIGHTS: "I was born in Brisbane, Queensland, and my first few years were spent in New Guinea. After our return from the islands in 1924 my father never really settled down, consequently my education and that of my younger brothers was a rather scrappy affair, mainly by means of the Primary Correspondence School. I was by nature a rather solitary child, but I was an avid reader and when a book I enjoyed came to an end I continued the story in my mind, adding adventure after adventure, and additional characters to carry them out. I can remember doing this from the age of eight, perched up in a tree which was my favorite thinking place. Later I was greatly influenced by L. M. Montgomery's 'Anne' books, but these were all too perfect to 'add' to.

MARGARET PAICE

"Yet at no stage during my childhood did I think of becoming an author; I wanted to be an artist. I drew constantly, illustrating my unwritten stories and sketching anyone who would stay long enough once I appeared with pencil and paper. I won prizes in country shows with my drawings, and my big dream was somehow, someday to have art lessons. This, in outback Queensland, was an almost impossible dream at that time as art schools were only to be found in the capital cities.

"When it became necessary for me to leave home and earn my own living it was soon obvious that not only could I not do so as an artist, but that I wasn't trained for anything at all. It was 1939, and the war had just begun. I decided to join the newly formed Women's National Emergency Legion, but to do this I had to get to Brisbane first. I had to work my way down the line, as a mother's helper, and as a waitress at various hotels along the way, but I did reach the capital, obtained a live-in job as a housemaid in a guest house, and set about joining the W.N.E.L. Much later after General MacArthur made his headquarters in Brisbane, these girls became rather a glamour unit, driving American staff cars; but it didn't take me or my instructors long to discover that I had no mechanical sense at all, and it was suggested that I might like to serve my country in some other way—the land army perhaps? So I became a cook on an outback sheep station, a job I enjoyed.

"I stayed there two years, until on holiday I met and married Hubert Paice. We were transferred to Townsville, North Queensland, which was to become my home for the next fifteen years. We had two children and I made up stories to amuse them at times, and occasionally had a short story or poem published, but I was still hankering after art training, which in Townsville was further away than ever. Then I had the idea of writing a small children's book and illustrating it, hoping the drawings might catch the eye of some publisher in need of an illustrator. I put a tremendous amount of work into those drawings, then sent the whole thing off. I was amazed when shortly I received a letter from the children's editor saying he liked the story and offering to publish the book, illustrations included. The news would have been much more exciting had it not been for the fact that my husband was by then very ill. He died before *Mirram* was published.

"As a sort of emotional therapy I went on to write *Valley in the North,* which is based on the story of my husband's childhood, and dedicated to him and his family. Meanwhile *Mirram* had been commended and the education department had ordered a special edition for a supplementary school reader, so my publisher asked me to do a companion book. *Namitja* was the result. Now, it seemed, was the time for those art lessons, especially since I had to start life over again. I wrote to the National Art School in Sydney, New South Wales, and was accepted as a full time student in an illustration course.

"I left the children—now aged twelve and eight—in boarding schools, rented my house for a year, and left for Sydney. I studied hard for that year, in a class with students half my age (they were wonderful to me) but it became obvious that I couldn't afford to go on being just a student. I was still writing at night but I had to get a paying job. I was terribly lucky to obtain a good commercial art job doing illustrating and sales promotion, so I decided to sell the house and bring the children to Sydney to live. I bought another house in a pleasant riverside suburb, not realising that it was going to take me three hours a day simply going to and from work. I had no car and wouldn't have had the nerve to drive in city traffic anyway.

"In 1960 I married a high-school teacher and was able to give more time to my writing and painting. We had a son, Christopher, now a high-school student, and have made our home in the Blue Mountains fifty miles west of the city of Sydney. I am still writing, and paint sometimes, and enjoy travelling overseas whenever possible.

"During Book Week each year I visit schools and enjoy talking to and with young people. My method of writing is to do the first draft quickly in longhand, then comes the solid work of revising and polishing, and finally the typing. I research my material carefully as I feel youngsters are very discerning and will soon pick out shoddy work or any insincerity. I must always know the setting for a book intimately, which is probably why all my stories have been set in the Australian bush."

The Bensens, They Drowned a Valley, and *Run to the Mountains,* have all been dramatized by ABC Radio. A German edition of *Run to the Mountains* was published in 1975 and a Danish edition will be out in the near future.

HOBBIES AND OTHER INTERESTS: Reading, painting, drawing and gardening.

PARKER, Nancy Winslow   1930-

PERSONAL: Born October 18, 1930, in Maplewood, N.J.; daughter of Winslow Aurelius (a textile executive) and Beatrice (Gaunt) Parker. *Education:* Mills College, B.A., 1952; also studied at Art Students League, 1956, 1957, and School of Visual Arts, New York, N.Y., 1966-67. *Home:* 51 East 74th St., New York, N.Y. 10021.

NANCY WINSLOW PARKER

And put him in a bunk,
And then we'll let him go! ∎
(From *Oh, A-Hunting We Will Go* by John Langstaff. Illustrated by Nancy Winslow Parker.)

CAREER: NBC-Television, New York, N.Y., sales promoter, 1956-60; New York Soccer Club, New York, N.Y., sports promoter, 1961-63; Radio Corp. of America (RCA), New York, N.Y., sales promoter, 1964-67; Appleton, Century, Crofts, Inc. (publishers), New York, N.Y., art director, 1968-70; Holt, Rinehart & Winston, Inc. (publishers), New York, N.Y., graphic designer, 1970-72; free-lance writer and illustrator of children's books, 1972—. *Member:* Bichon Frise Club of America (past member of board of directors), Mills College Club of New York.

WRITINGS—Juvenile: *The Man with the Take-Apart Head,* Dodd, 1974.

Illustrator: John Langstaff, *Oh, A-Hunting We Will Go!,* Atheneum, 1974; Carter Houck, *Warm as Wool, Cool as Cotton,* Seabury, 1975.

WORK IN PROGRESS: Research for a children's book on American history; several fictional works for children; illustrating a children's book on natural fibers; making five wood constructions combining oils, wood carving, and construction.

SIDELIGHTS: "I cannot remember when I have not been interested in children's literature. As a writer, the field has limitless potential for fantasy and the joy of creation. As an illustrator, the opportunity to let yourself go in wild interpretation is an artist's dream come true.

"My background in American corporate business life was invaluable for the human experience it offered. However, the philosophy of the human condition as expressed by the surrealists and its protege René Magritte have been a profound influence on my thinking and creating. My life, my writing and my art are devoted to these expressions of time, space and reality.''

HOBBIES AND OTHER INTERESTS: Travel (Hawaii, West Indies, France), all things French (history, theater, literature, language, painting, architecture), carpentry, breeding and showing Bichon Frise, tennis, gardening.

FOR MORE INFORMATION SEE: Junior Literary Guild Catalog, September, 1974.

PARKS, Edd Winfield   1906-1968

PERSONAL: Born February 25, 1906, in Newbern, Tenn.; son of Edward Winfield and Emma (Wallis) Parks; married Aileen Wells (writer of juvenile books), November 3, 1933. *Education:* Harvard University, A.B., 1927; Vanderbilt University, M.A., 1929, Ph.D., 1933. *Home:* 555 West Cloverhurst, Athens, Ga. *Office:* Department of English, University of Georgia, Athens, Ga.

CAREER: Began teaching career at Vanderbilt University, Nashville, Tenn.; Cumberland University, Lebanon, Tenn., professor of English, 1933-35; University of Georgia, Athens, 1935-68, started as assistant professor of English, 1946. Was visiting professor at Duke University,

The two boys drew themselves erect, "Good morning, Mrs. Fish," they said. Each lifted his hat with a flourish. ■ (From *Teddy Roosevelt* by Edd Winfield Parks. Illustrated by Gray Morrow.)

summers, 1936, 1938, 1939, University of Brazil, 1949-50, University of North Carolina, 1953; Fulbright Professor at University of Copenhagen, 1955, University of Brazil, 1958; visiting lecturer in South America, 1950, Denmark, Norway, Finland, 1955, Venezuela, 1961; Lamar Lecturer, Mercer University, 1964. *Military service:* U.S. Military Intelligence, 1943-46; became captain; received Commendation Medal. *Member:* Modern Language Association, South Atlantic Modern Language Association (president, 1958-59), Southeastern American Studies Association (president, 1961-62), Southern Humanities Conference (chairman, 1962-63). *Awards, honors:* Carnegie fellow, 1948, 1952.

WRITINGS: (Editor with James Smith) *The Great Critics: An Anthology of Literary Criticism,* Norton, 1932, 3rd edition, 1951; (editor with Richmond Croom Beatty) *The English Drama: An Anthology, 900-1642,* Norton, 1935; (editor, and author of introduction, bibliography, and notes) *Southern Poets,* American Book Co., 1936, Phaeton Press, 1970; *Sut Lovingood Travels with Old Abe Lincoln,* Black Cat Books, 1937; *Segments of Southern Thought,* University of Georgia Press, 1938; *Charles Egbert Craddock* (Mary Noailles Murfree), University of North Carolina Press, 1941, Kennikat Press, 1972; (editor) *Essays of Henry Timrod,* University of Georgia Press, 1942; *Predestinate Iron* (poems), University of Georgia Press, 1948; *A Modern American Sampler,* [Rio de Janeiro], 1950; *Backwater* (novel), Twayne, 1957; *William Gilmore Simms as Literary Critic,* University of Georgia Press, 1961; *Ante-Bellum Southern Literary Critics,* University of Georgia Press, 1962; *Nashoba* (novel), Twayne, 1963; *Henry Timrod,* Twayne, 1964; *Edgar Allan Poe as Literary Critic,* University of Georgia Press, 1964; (editor with A. W. Parks) *The Collected Poems of Henry Timrod,* University of Georgia Press, 1965; (with A. W. Parks) *Thomas MacDonagh: The Man, the Patriot, the Writer,* University of Georgia Press, 1967; *Sidney Lanier: The Man, the Poet, the Critic,* University of Georgia Press, 1968.

Youth books: *Long Hunter,* Farrar & Rinehart, 1942; *Pioneer Pilot: A Boy's Story of the First Steamboat Voyage from Pittsburgh to New Orleans,* Bobbs, 1947; *Little Long Rifle,* Bobbs, 1949; *Safe on Second: The Story of a Little Leaguer,* Bobbs, 1953; *Teddy Roosevelt, All-'Round Boy,* Bobbs, 1953.

Contributor: *Culture in the South,* University of North Carolina Press, 1934; *Essays in Value,* Appleton, 1938; *Fighting Words,* Lippincott, 1943; *A Vanderbilt Miscellany,* Vanderbilt University Press, 1944; *Tennessee Old and New,* Tennessee Historical Commission, 1946; *A Southern Vanguard,* Prentice-Hall, 1947; *Studies in Shakespeare,* University of Miami Press, 1953; *Southern Renaissance,* Johns Hopkins Press, 1953; *South Atlantic Studies for Sturgis E. Leavitt,* Scarecrow, 1953; *Essays in Honor of Walter Clyde Curry,* Vanderbilt University Press, 1955; *A Southern Reader,* Knopf, 1955. Contributor to anthologies, literary journals, and magazines. Member of editorial board, *American Quarterly,* 1957-58, and *Mississippi Quarterly,* 1963-68.

WORK IN PROGRESS: Editing with A. W. Parks, *Selected Poems of William Gilmore Simms.*

(Died May 7, 1968)

PARR, Lucy 1924-
(Laura Carroll)

PERSONAL: Born July 25, 1924, in Kanab, Utah; daughter of Eustace Josiah (a rancher) and Geneva (Esplin) Chamberlain; married Robert Emmet Parr (a retired college professor; author), May 21, 1945. *Education:* Attended Utah schools. *Politics:* Republican. *Religion:* Mormon. *Home:* 845 Garfield Ave., Salt Lake City, Utah 84105.

CAREER: Writer and homemaker; worked as a cashier for several years in Hollywood, Calif., and Salt Lake City, Utah. *Awards, honors:* Instructor stories for children award, 1965, for "That Pesky Crow."

WRITINGS: Pioneer and Indian Stories (for children and young people), Bookcraft, 1969; *Family Christmas Stories,* Bookcraft, 1973; *Not of the World: A Living Account of the United Order* (adult), Horizon, 1975. Contributor of more than 250 stories, some articles (including "Picking Fish From a Ladder" in the *Encyclopedia Britannica* "Language Experiences in Reading" program) and some verse to over fifty juvenile, teen and adult magazines, some of them published under the pseudonym Laura Carroll; "The Last Ticket," reprinted in *Stories of Fun and Adventure,* Copp Clark Publishing Company, 1964, is used in Canadian Schools.

WORK IN PROGRESS: A book of true pioneer stories, short stories and articles.

SIDELIGHTS: "I was born at my grandmother's home in Kanab, Utah, an interesting old home that has been restored as a historic site for others to visit and enjoy. My twin sister, Lillian, and I were seventh and eighth in a family of nine children. We lived in the small town of Orderville in southern Utah during the nine school months. The town is in a small valley with massive white mountains on the east, high tree-covered hills and cliffs north and west. It was a beautiful, interesting place in which to grow up.

"We considered summers to be best of all, when we lived on our father's ranch fifteen miles from town. We worked hard, each one sharing in the tasks that must be done. We girls helped with the housework and with canning, drying, and preserving fruits and vegetables. We also helped to plant, weed, water and harvest large gardens and orchards. Sometimes we went to the fields to help Dad and our two brothers, especially at planting and harvesting time. We spent many hours herding cows around the ranch, watching to keep them out of the fields, a tedious task made more interesting by invented games and pretended adventures. We each felt a share of responsibility in providing for the family, and it was a good life.

"Our parents had grown up together and had been childhood sweethearts. We had the security of knowing that our home was filled with the love of our parents for each other and for every one of their children.

"Our city cousins coaxed to stay with us at the ranch, so our house was always full. Though we worked hard, there was time for play. We hiked, we rode horses, we went swimming in the reservoir, we searched the hillsides for Indian arrowheads and pottery. There were several other ranches within a few miles of ours and during summer months large groups would get together for 'corn roasts' and 'melon busts' and the fun of games and contests and visiting. The grown-ups entertained us with stories of when they were children, and true stories which their parents and grandparents had told to them of pioneer times.

"There was no electricity at our ranch, and so no radio. We learned the fun of inventing our own games and entertainment. We all loved to read and frequently took turns reading aloud while we worked at preparing food for canning, or in the evening when the whole family gathered. Evenings together were anticipated by all of us. Frequently we had programs for just our family, which sometimes included 'shadow shows' illuminated by a kerosene lantern. Dad always gave the funniest performances. Many evenings we all went to the hill to cook our supper 'Indian style' over a campfire or in a pit of hot coals.

"I can't remember a time that I was not fascinated by stories, whether from a book or magazine or a true story told by others. I could hardly wait to be old enough for school and learning to read. I 'made up' stories for my younger sister, and later for nieces and nephews, which was the beginning of my desire to share stories with others.

"When I was a child, many of the early settlers of the Southwest were still living. I loved to talk with them about 'the old days.' We were not far from several Indian reser-

LUCY PARR

vations and saw the Indians when they came through our town, particularly Navajos and Paiutes. Each year a group of Indians from the Paiute reservation at Moccasin, just over the Arizona border, would come a day or two before Christmas and camp north of town. On Christmas morning, they came to some of our homes to ask for 'Kismas gifts' of food and clothing. From the early days in our valley close friendships were formed with the Indians.

"It was natural that my first interest in story telling was to pass on my knowledge of the pioneers and Indians. This is the sort of book and story which I most enjoy reading, and the sort which I most enjoy writing. I have done extensive research about American history and the American Indian, particularly the history and Indians of the Southwest.

"For me, writing is a combination of pleasure and hard work. I feel that I am the person I am writing about, and I have many fine imaginary adventures. I have always been careful about facts in my stories, and have spent several hours searching for one detail about a weapon or utensil or home used by Indians or pioneers. I believe that authors have a responsibility to their readers to tell the truth even in small details. So research takes a large part of my writing time . . . but research, itself, can be fun.

"Homemaking and writing take most of my time now, but I do enjoy amateur oil painting of landscapes, birds and butterflies and flowers.

"My husband is an engineer and retired college professor. He writes about engineering subjects and aviation history. We help each other with writing projects. We enjoy hiking and taking pictures in our beautiful Utah mountains."

PAVEL, Frances 1907-

PERSONAL: Born February 26, 1907, in Bethlehem, Pa.; daughter of Johann and Cecilia (Svantner) Kvacky; married Otto J. Pavel, February 16, 1945. *Education:* West Chester State Teachers College, B.S. in Ed., 1935; Columbia University, M.A. in Ed., 1941; other graduate courses at University of California, Los Angeles, and California State College at Los Angeles. *Home:* 4913 Alhama Dr., Woodland Hills, Calif. 91364.

CAREER: Southampton (Pa.) public schools, elementary teacher and principal, 1935-40; Mansfield State Teachers College, Mansfield, Pa., demonstration teacher in laboratory school, 1941-42; Inglewood (Calif.) public schools, elementary teacher, 1944-49, principal, 1949-63; retired, 1963. Consultant, Silver Burdett Co., 1942-44.

WRITINGS—"Read It Myself" series; adaptations: *The Wolf and the Seven Little Kids, Goldilocks and the Three Bears, Little Red Riding Hood, Jack and the Beanstalk, Peter and the Wolf, The Frog Prince, The Ugly Duckling, The Elves and the Shoemaker, Hansel and Gretel, Snow White and the Seven Dwarfs, The Golden Goose, Rumpelstiltskin* (all published by Holt, 1961-62; all published in paperback by Franska Publishing House, 1975); *Archelon and the Sea Dragon,* Childrens, 1975.

WORK IN PROGRESS: Research in reading activities and experiences of the beginning reader, as a basis for writing supplementary reading materials.

FRANCES PAVEL

SIDELIGHTS: "I was born in Bethlehem, Pennsylvania of immigrant parents who left Czechoslovakia and came to America in the early 1900's. Two of my brothers and two sisters were born in the 'old country.' Then two more sisters, another brother and I were born in the 'new country.' My father—we called him 'pop,' until we all grew up, then we called him 'popsey'—was an avid reader and the best story teller in the world! I can still remember how we would sit on his lap when we were little, with his arms around us, or sit on the floor—listening—spellbound and fascinated by the folklore of Czechoslovakia. This was my first introduction to the wonderful world of literature.

"I can't recall exactly when I did start to write. I may have been writing as soon as I learned to speak, read and write the English language in school. At the elementary grade level I do remember getting 'prizes' for writing essays. During high school and college I continued to write such things as biographies for yearbooks, school papers, periodicals, etc.

"After graduating with honors from a teachers college in Pennsylvania—that was during the depression of the 30's—I was one of the few lucky graduates to get a position as a first grade teacher. At that particular time there were very few textbooks available for children who were beginning to learn to read. So I adapted their favorite fairy tales—as well as writing original stories for them—using vocabulary geared to the level of the average six-year-old child. That was the birth of the *Read it Myself* books.

Archelon is born! ■ (From *Archelon and the Sea Dragon* by Francis K. Pavel. Illustrated by Jim Lamb.

"When I became an elementary school principal, some of the primary grade teachers used these fairy tales in their classrooms. The children liked the stories so much that I finally submitted them for publication.

"*Archelon and the Sea Dragon* is a story about a huge sea turtle and other fantastic prehistoric sea creatures. The largest and most ferocious sea creature that ever lived, was a scaly swimming lizard that looked like a sea dragon. Millions and millions of years ago, these ancient sea creatures actually lived in the waters that covered many parts of the world, including some parts of North America. It took over three years of research and writing to do this story—but I loved every minute of it."

PETIE, Haris 1915-

PERSONAL: Born June 26, 1915, in Boulder Creek, Calif.; daughter of William Henry (in lumber business) and Isobel (Harris) Pfafflin; married Robert Petty (deceased); children: Isobel Read Petty, Virginia Moffett Petty. *Education:* Attended Rochester Institute of Technology, and Otis Art Institute. *Residence:* North Bergen, N.J. *Agent:* Florence Alexander, 50 East 42nd St., New York, N.Y. 10017.

CAREER: Artist and illustrator of children's books, fashion artist, advertising artist, designer of children's clothes. *Member:* Museum of Natural History, Smithsonian Institution.

WRITINGS—All self-illustrated: *Billions of Bugs,* Prentice-Hall, 1975; *The Seed the Squirrel Dropped,* Prentice-Hall, 1976.

Illustrator: Jim Breetveld, *Getting to Know Lebanon,* Coward, 1958; Regina Tor, *Getting to Know the Philippines,* Coward, 1958; Henry H. Collins Jr., *Earth Around Us,* Dial, 1960; Sam Olden, *Getting to Know Nigeria,* Coward, 1960; Sam Olden, *Getting to Know Argentina,* Coward, 1961; Sam Olden, *Getting to Know Africa's French Community,* Coward, 1961; Barnett D. Laschever, *Getting to Know Venezuela,* Coward, 1962; Blanche Saunders, *Dog Training for Boys and Girls,* Howell, 1962; Charles R. Joy, *Getting to Know the Sahara,* Coward, 1963; Ted Phillips, *Getting to Know Saudi Arabia,* Coward, 1963; Jim Witker, *Getting to Know Scandinavia: Denmark, Norway and Sweden,* Coward, 1963; Blanche Saunders, *Dog Care for Boys and Girls,* Howell, 1964; Grace Halsell, *Getting to Know Colombia,* Coward, 1964; Regina Sauro, *Too-Long Trunk,* Lantern, 1964; Eric Robins, *Getting to Know the Congo River,* Coward, 1965; Katharine V. Nespojohn, *Animal Eyes,* Prentice-Hall, 1965; Dorothy M. Broderick, *Training a Companion Dog,* Prentice-Hall, 1965; Lillie D. Chaffin, *Tommy's Big Problem,* Lantern, 1965; Sabra Holbrook, *Goat That Made a Boy Grow Big,* Coward, 1965; Vee Cawston, *Matuk, the Eskimo Boy,* Lantern, 1965.

Sabra Holbrook, *Getting to Know the Two Germanys,* Coward, 1966; Navin Sullivan, *Animal Timekeepers,* Prentice-Hall, 1966; Phyllis L. Berk, *Duke's Command,* Lantern, 1966; Mary Dana Rodriguez, *Hawaiian Spelling Bee,* Lantern, 1967; Linda Alexander, *Job Well Done,* Lantern, 1967; D. S. Halacy, Jr., *Energy and Engines,* World, 1967; Lorraine Henroid, *I Know a Postman,* Putnam, 1967; Virginia F. Voight, *I Know a Librarian,* Putnam, 1967;

Then he sat down for a moment, pulling Kunik and Tupak close to his side to keep them quiet. Matuk waited, listening and hoping that a seal would bark. ■ (From *Matuk the Eskimo Boy* by Vee Cawston. Illustrated by Haris Petie.)

Robert Whitehead, *First Book of Eagles,* Watts, 1968; Edward Jablonski, *Ladybirds: Women in Aviation,* Hawthorn, 1968; Edward Kurkul, *Tiger in the Lake,* Lantern, 1968; Kurt Unkelbach, *Both Ends of the Leash: Selecting and Training Your Dog,* Prentice-Hall, 1968; Daniel Cohen, *Vaccination and You,* Messner, 1969; Margaret Rau, *Yellow River,* Messner, 1969; Helen V. Stone, *Pablo the Potter,* Lantern, 1969; Martin L. Keen, *Lightning and Thunder,* Messner, 1969; Carla Greene, *Manuel, Young Mexican-American,* Lantern, 1969; Blanche Saunders, *Dog Care for Boys and Girls,* Howell, 1969; Blanche Saunders, *Dog Training for Boys and Girls,* Howell, 1969.

Peter Z. Cohen, *Morena,* Atheneum, 1970; Daniel Cohen, *Night Animals,* Messner, 1970; John F. Waters, *Saltmarshes and Shifting Dunes,* Harvey, 1970; Goldie B. Despain, *Tiny Ant Who Scared a Horned Toad,* Lantern, 1970; Kurt Unkelbach, *Catnip,* 1970; Jo Carr, *Trouble with Tikki,* Lantern, 1970; D. J. Chaconas, *Danger in the Swamp,* Lantern, 1971; Burke Davis, *Getting to Know Thomas Jefferson's Virginia,* Coward, 1971; David R. Collins, *Great American Nurses,* Messner, 1971; Chika Iritani, *I Know an Animal Doctor,* Putnam, 1971; Joan Fairman, *Penny Saved,* Lantern, 1971; Mabel Watts, *The Basket that Flew Over the Mountain,* Lantern, 1972; Barbara Ford, *Can Invertebrates Learn?,* Messner, 1972; Katherine Nespojohn, *Worms,* Watts, 1972; Seymour Simon, *From Shore to Ocean Floor: How Life Survives in the Sea,* Watts, 1973; Mabel Watts, *The Knights of the Square Table,* Lantern, 1973; Peter R. Limburg, *Watch Out, It's Poison Ivy,* Messner, 1973; Barbara Rich, *Let's Go to a Jet Port,* Putnam, 1973; Phyllis Perry, *Let's Learn About Mushrooms,* Harvey, 1974; Martin L. Keen, *The World Beneath Our Feet: The Story of Soil,* Messner, 1974; Anabel Dean, *Animals that Fly,* Messner, 1975.

SIDELIGHTS: Haris Petie has lived in California, Columbus, Ohio, Cleveland, Ohio, Rochester, New York, New York City, and for four years in Paris, France. Her works are represented in the Kerlan Collection, University of Minnesota.

FOR MORE INFORMATION SEE: Kirkus Reviews, April 15, 1975; *Wilson Library Journal,* June, 1975.

PHILLIPS, Loretta (Hosey) 1893-

PERSONAL: Born April 17, 1893, in Southbridge, Mass.; daughter of William Joseph (a building contractor) and Katherine (Dempsey) Hosey; married Prentice Phillips (now an artist and writer), December 23, 1917. *Education:* Attended Connecticut public schools and Norwich Art School, Norwich, Conn. *Politics:* Independent. *Religion:* Catholic. *Home:* 1060 Main St. Apt. 317, Worcester, Mass. 01603.

CAREER: One-time fashion artist and illustrator of books for children; now writer-illustrator in collaboration with husband, Prentice Phillips.

WRITINGS: (With husband, Prentice Phillips) *Two Silly Kings,* Steck, 1965. Illustrator, with husband, of more than twenty books for children. The Phillips' also are creators of a panel feature, "They Made the Headlines," which has been running on alternate weeks in *Worcester Sunday Telegram* for twenty years, and contributors of other illustrated features to Boston daily and Sunday newspapers, and to juvenile publications.

WORK IN PROGRESS: Two Phillips' collaborations, *New Englander's Good Bad and Indifferent,* and *Mr. Caps and Hairdos.*

PHILLIPS, Mary Geisler 1881-1964

PERSONAL: Born May 13, 1881, in Philadelphia, Pa.; daughter of William Henry and Mary Catherine (Dickes) Geisler; married Everett Franklin Phillips, October 27, 1906; children: Everett Franklin, William Taylor, Howard Geisler. *Education:* University of Pennsylvania, B.S., 1902. *Religion:* Protestant. *Home and office:* Westminster Manor, 81 South St., Auburn, N.Y.

CAREER: Girls' High School, Philadelphia, Pa., teacher of biology, 1902-06; *Botanical Abstracts,* Ithaca, N.Y., assistant editor, 1926-27; radio script writer for A. and P. broadcasts, 1926-27; Cornell University, New York State College of Home Economics, Ithaca, N.Y., radio script writer, 1926, assistant editor, 1934-35, professor and editor. Friends of Ithaca Public Library. *Member:* National League of American Pen Women, American Association of University Women, Art Association of Ithaca, Writers Group of Ithaca, Alumni Association of New York State College of Home Economics, American Red Cross, Kappa Kappa Gamma (province president), P.E.O. Sisterhood.

Millions of years before man appeared on earth, and millions of years before even the earliest mammal worked on dry land, the air of this planet was filled with the whirr of insect wings. Among them were those of giant relatives of today's dragonflies. ■ (From *Dragonflies and Damselflies* by Mary Geisler Phillips. Illustrated by Anne Marie Jauss.)

WRITINGS: Honey Bees and Fairy Dust, Macrae Smith, 1926; *Ant Hills and Soap Bubbles,* Macrae Smith, 1927; *Spider Webs and Sunflowers,* Macrae Smith, 1928; (editor with William Henry Geisler) *Glimpses Into the World of Science,* Heath, 1929; (co-author) *Nature—by Seaside and Wayside,* Heath, 1936; *Things That Go,* Rand McNally, 1937; *Little Lamb's Hat,* Rand McNally, 1952; *The Makers of Honey,* Crowell, 1956; *Dragonflies and Damselflies,* Crowell, 1960. Contributor to periodicals.

WORK IN PROGRESS: Book on the woodchuck, for young people.

HOBBIES AND OTHER INTERESTS: Painting in oils and water colors, and travel.

(Died January 25, 1964)

PHILLIPS, Prentice 1894-

PERSONAL: Born May 15, 1894, in Plainfield, Conn.; son of Warren Winfield (a farmer) and Flora Bertha (Card) Phillips; married Loretta Hosey (a free-lance artist and writer), December 23, 1917. *Education:* Attended public schools in Plainfield, Conn. *Politics:* Independent. *Religion:* Catholic. *Home:* 1060 Main St., Apt. 317, Worcester, Mass. 01603.

PRENTICE AND LORETTA PHILLIPS

CAREER: Commercial artist, owner and operator of art studio and advertising agency; free-lance writer and illustrator; former lecturer and teacher of cartooning and commercial art at Worcester Junior College, Worcester, Mass.

WRITINGS: (With wife, Loretta Phillips) *Two Silly Kings,* Steck, 1964. Illustrator with wife of more than twenty books for children. The Phillips' also are creators of a panel feature "They Made the Headlines," which appeared on alternate weeks in the *Worcester Sunday Telegram* for twenty years, and contributors of other illustrated features to Boston daily and Sunday newspapers and to juvenile publications.

WORK IN PROGRESS: Two picture books for children, *Daisy May to the Rescue* and *Mr. McTwid;* also articles for *New England Galaxy* and *Good Old Days* (magazines).

PILKINGTON, Roger (Windle)   1915-

PERSONAL: Born January 17, 1915, in St. Helens, Lancashire, England; son of Richard Austin and Hope (Cozens-Hardy) Pilkington; married Miriam Jaboor, 1937; married Ingrid Geiger, 1973; children: Cynthia, Hugh. *Education:* Freiburg University, student, 1933; Magdalene College, Cambridge University, M.A., 1937, Ph.D., 1942. *Home:* La Maison du Côti, Mont Arthur, St. Aubin, Jersey, C.I. *Agent:* A. M. Heath & Co., 35 Dover St., London, W.1, England.

CAREER: Cambridge University, Cambridge, England, research associate, 1937-45; free-lance writer, 1945—; Macmillan & Co., Ltd., London, science editor, 1960—. Freeman, City of London; delegate, World Council of Churches, New Delhi, India, 1961.

WRITINGS: Males and Females, Delisle, 1948; *Stringer's Folly,* Yates, 1949; *Sons and Daughters,* Allen & Unwin, 1951; *Biology, Man and God,* Lutterworth, 1951; *Revelation Through Science,* Lutterworth, 1954; *Thames Waters,* Lutterworth, 1956; *Small Boat Through Belgium,* Macmillan, 1957; *Small Boat Through Holland,* Macmillan, 1958; *Robert Boyle, Father of Chemistry,* J. Murray, 1959.

Small Boat to the Skagerrak, 1960; *Small Boat Through Sweden,* Macmillan, 1961; *Small Boat to Alsase,* Macmillan, 1961; *Small Boat to Bavaria,* Macmillan, 1962; *Small Boat Through Germany,* Macmillan, 1963; *Heavens Alive,* Fontana, 1964; *Small Boat Through France,* Macmillan, 1964; *Small Boat in Southern France,* Macmillan, 1965; *Small Boat on the Thames,* Macmillan, 1966; *Small Boat on the Meuse,* St. Martins, 1967; *Small Boat to Luxembourg,* Macmillan, 1967; *Small Boat on the Moselle,* Macmillan, 1968; *Small Boat to Elsinore,* Macmillan, 1969; *Small Boat in Northern Germany,* Macmillan, 1969; *Small Boat on the Lower Rhine,* 1970; *Small Boat on the Upper Rhine,* Macmillan, 1971; *Waterways in Europe,* John Murray, 1973.

Children's books: *The Facts of Life,* British Medical Association, 1955; *Jan's Treasure,* Macmillan, 1955; *In the Beginning,* Independent Press, 1955; *The Chesterfield Gold,* Macmillan, 1957; *The Great South Sea,* Macmillan, 1957; *The Ways of the Sea,* Routledge, 1957; *The Missing Panel,* Macmillan, 1958; *The Dahlia's Cargo,* Macmillan, 1959; *How Boats Go Uphill,* Abelard, 1959; *Don John's Ducats,* Macmillan, 1960; *World Without End,* Macmillan, 1960; *Who's Who and Why,* Delisle, 1961; *The Ways of the Air,* Routledge, 1961; *Nepomuk of the River,* Macmillan, 1962; *Boats Overland,* Abelard, 1963; *The Eisenbart Mystery,* Macmillan, 1963; *How Ships Are Navigated,* Routledge, 1963; *The River,* Oliver & Boyd, 1964; *Glass,* Oliver & Boyd, 1965; *The Boy from Stink Alley,* Macmillan, 1965, published in United States under the title, *I Sailed on the Mayflower,* St. Martins, 1968; *The Ormering Tide,* Deutsch, 1974; *The Face in the River,* Deutsch, 1976. Contributor to various magazines.

WORK IN PROGRESS: To Sweden with Love.

SIDELIGHTS: "I didn't start out as a writer. Not a bit. I began as a research scientist, and I did operations on very small banana flies, moving bits from one fly to another to see what happened. I had to write up the results for important scientific papers, and this had to be done in a special way, using the longest words possible and never saying 'I.' Like doctors, scientists always had to look very clever and mysterious. But when I began writing stories it took me a long time to get out of the habit and say 'I saw a pigeon' and not 'an individual specimen of an unidentified species of the order *columbiformes* was observed.'

"Now, I had always liked boats, which was strange because I was not brought up by the sea. I bought a small boat which the Royal Navy had finished with, and we had family week-ends on the Thames. My children loved it, and it gave them quite a new way of exploring the world. It also

ROGER PILKINGTON

gave me the idea of writing an exciting story about children on a boat being chased by crooks. This was *Jan's Treasure*, and I still think it was a rattling good tale.

"Well, after fifteen years my old *Commodore* grew too old, and was replaced by a young sister-ship. Between them they have produced thirty books, nineteen for grown-ups and about the places they took me to, and eleven for younger readers. It was fun writing the detective stories, because I knew every sandbank and quay and lockside where the adventures happened. This was good, because children are much more alert than grown-ups, and spot at once if an author doesn't know his background.

"A girl reader in the United States once took such a liking to Peter, the oldest of the children in the family I had invented, that she wrote and asked me to arrange for her to meet him when she came to London with her parents. I liked this, because it meant that she had really been carried away by the story. It became real, and that was what I wanted.

"I like other writing too, especially for children. I think the best I ever wrote was *The Boy from Stink Alley* which in the United States was called *I Sailed on the Mayflower*. It was the story of that great adventure told by one of the boys who actually went on it. (Did you know that half of the Pilgrim Fathers were teenagers?) I felt strongly about religious freedom and was brought up as a 'dissenter' so the

story appealed to me. It meant lots of digging about in dusty libraries to find the details.

"More recently I have written other books of quite different kinds. *The Ormering Tide* is a mysterious tale about the beautiful island of Jersey where I now live, and *The Face in the River* is about a girl who sees (or doesn't see?) a mermaid, who is her one real friend. She nearly made me cry, and that is a good sign.

"I always know if a book is going to be good. Sometimes the characters take control of it and make it up as they go. All I have to do is to write fast until my eyes are sore and I go out with my wife for a walk where the tide has left the beach bare under the stars. It's best when the characters do it for me like that. If I have to sit blankly and try a line or two and cross it out again—well, then it's not much use.

"And, of course, I'm mostly a winter writer, when the rain is falling and the gales howling round the rocks. In the summer I'm more likely to be out on the sea, or chugging away on some river or waterway in Europe."

FOR MORE INFORMATION SEE: Books and Bookmen, April, 1962.

PLIMPTON, George (Ames) 1927-

PERSONAL: Born March 18, 1927, in New York, N.Y.; son of Francis T. P. (a lawyer and former U.S. deputy representative to the United Nations) and Pauline (Ames) Plimpton; married Freddy Medora Espy (a photography studio assistant), March 28, 1968. *Education:* Phillips Exeter Academy, graduated, 1944; Harvard University, class of 1948, B.A., 1950; King's College, Cambridge, B.A., 1952, M.A., 1954. *Politics:* Democrat. *Religion:* Unitarian Universalist. *Home:* 541 East 72nd St., New York, N.Y. *Agent:* Russell & Volkening, 551 Fifth Ave., New York, N.Y. 10017.

CAREER: Editor of *The Lampoon* while at Harvard. Principal editor of *Paris Review,* 1953—, publisher, with Doubleday & Co., of Paris Review Editions (books), 1965-72. Instructor at Barnard College, 1956-58; associate editor, *Horizon,* 1959-61; contributing editor, *Sports Illustrated,* 1967—; contributing editor, *Sportsweek,* 1975—. Adviser on John F. Kennedy Oral History Project. *Military service:* U.S. Army, 1945-48; became 2nd lieutenant. *Member:* Century Association; Brook, Piping Rock, and Raquet and Tennis Clubs; Travellers Club (Paris). *Awards, honors:* Associate fellow, Trumbull College, Yale; distinguished achievement award, University of Southern California, 1967; D.H.L., Franklin Pierce College, 1968.

WRITINGS: The Rabbits's Umbrella (juvenile), Viking, 1955; *Out of My League* (experiences with baseball), Harper, 1961; *Paper Lion* (experiences with football), Harper, 1966; *The Bogey Man* (experiences with golf), Harper, 1968; (editor with Peter Ardery) *The American Literary Anthology,* Number 1, Farrar, Straus, 1968, Number 2, Random House, 1969, Number 3, 1970; *Mad Ducks and Bears,* Random House, 1973; *One For the Record,* Harper, 1974. (Editor) *Writers at Work,* Viking, Volume 1, 1957, Volume 2, 1963, Volume 3, 1967.

GEORGE PLIMPTON

WORK IN PROGRESS: A book on boxing; a book on the Celtics; a book on tennis; a book on his experiences with the New York Philharmonic; possible plans include a minor role with the Metropolitan Opera and playing hockey with the Boston Bruins.

SIDELIGHTS: The same man who edits the world's most successful literary quarterly and knows all the right people, literary and otherwise, has also fought in a bullfight staged by Ernest Hemingway in 1954; fought three rounds with the then light heavyweight champion, Archie Moore, in 1959; lost a tennis match, 6-0, to Pancho Gonzales; engaged in a swimming meet against Don Schollander; played a rubber of bridge with Oswald Jacoby as his partner; pitched to eight players in a post-season All-Star game at Yankee Stadium (see *Out of My League*); joined the Detroit Lions, 1963, as a third-string rookie quarterback and, after training, played one exhibition game in Pontiac, Michigan, where he lost 29 yards in five plays (see *Paper Lion*), played quarterback with the world champion Baltimore Colts, 1968; played golf in three pro-am tournaments (see *The Bogey Man*); sat in as a percussionist with the New York Philharmonic Orchestra for one month in 1967, toured with the orchestra in Canada, then appeared with it on television on the "Bell Telephone Hour," February 2, 1968; made his film acting debut as one of the Bedouin extras in "Lawrence of Arabia," 1962, had a small part in "The Detective," 1968, played the mayor in Norman Mailer's film, "Beyond the Law," 1968, and played Bill Ford in "Paper Lion," United Artists, 1968, while Alan Alda played Celluloid Plimpton.

Plimpton doesn't compete to win, but rather to experience at first hand what it feels like to actually be a participant. "I'm a writer, not an athlete," he says. Bud Shrake, an editor of *Sports Illustrated,* believes that, "if George ever concentrated on one thing, God knows what he could do." But this is not his ambition; rather, as one friend noted, it is "to know everyone of his time who is famous, interesting or talented, and to be wherever they are. Like Oscar Wilde, he wants to make a work of art out of his life." Such a life engenders feelings of envy, even from the successful. Another close friend, the late Robert Kennedy, once said: "If I wanted to be President, which of course I don't, I'd still *rather* be George Plimpton."

"There are people who would perhaps call me a dilettante," says Plimpton, "because it looks as though I'm having too much fun. I have never been convinced there's anything inherently wrong in having fun. You can still be totally committed to what you're doing."

FOR MORE INFORMATION SEE: New York Herald Tribune, April 21, 1961; *Book Week,* October 23, 1966; *New York Post,* November 9, 1966; *New York Times Magazine,* January 8, 1967; *Carleton Miscellany,* spring, 1967; *Time,* April 7, 1967, November 8, 1968; *Life,* June 30, 1967, November 15, 1968, November 29, 1968; *Commentary,* October, 1967; *Book World,* March 17, 1968; *New York Times,* November 4, 1968; *Newsweek,* November 11, 1968; *Atlantic,* December, 1968; *National Observer,* December 2, 1968.

Unfortunately, getting the dog home was easier said than done, as Mr. Montague soon discovered. The great dog had never been in the outside world before. ■ (From *The Rabbit's Umbrella* by George Plimpton. Illustrated by William Péne du Bois.)

POSTEN, Margaret L(ois) 1915-

PERSONAL: Born March 28, 1915, in Villisca, Iowa; daughter of Harry C. (a farmer) and Glenna (Fisher) Williams; married C. Leonard Posten (a building contractor and farmer), February 21, 1936; children: Pamela Ann (Mrs. Robert Abel), Johnnie L. *Education:* Tarkio College, associate degree in elementary education (highest honors), 1933; Northwest Missouri State College, B.S. (honors), 1968. *Religion:* Methodist. *Residence:* Villisca, Iowa 50864.

CAREER: Teacher in public schools in Iowa, 1933-56, Villisca Community School, Villisca, Iowa, elementary teacher, 1956—. 4-H Club leader and Sunday school children's superintendent, 1951-56, 1972-73. *Member:* Progress Club, Book Forum (vice-president, 1969-71, president, 1971—), Auxiliary of Good Samaritan Nursing Home, Wesleyan Service Guild. *Awards, honors:* Teacher of the Year, 1970, Villisca Community Schools, Iowa.

WRITINGS—All juvenile; all published by Denison, except as indicated: *This is the Place: Iowa,* Iowa State University Press, 1965, 3rd edition, 1970; *Lucky You!,* 1966; *The Gold Seekers: The Story of Hernando de Sota,* 1967; *Maggie and Friend,* 1969; *Symbols of Democracy,* 1971; *Skill Sheets for Individualized Reading,* Denison, 1976. Contributor to *Villisca Review* and *Encyclopedia Britannica* reading series.

There were eighteen ships that sailed away from Estramadura, Spain, that April morning in 1514. They were heavily loaded with animals and supplies. There were soldiers for fighting, cannon, equipment for warfare, gentlemen dressed in silks, the servants to the gentlemen, and the Franciscan friars who were sent to teach the Christian religion and convert the natives of the new land to Christianity. ■ (From *The Gold Seekers* by Margaret L. Posten. Illustrated by Howard Lindberg.)

SIDELIGHTS: "I was born on an Iowa farm where life was primitive and every member of the family worked to the best of one's ability. I loved farm life, the animals; especially the horses. From the time I was three years old I rode a horse. (In fact, *Maggie and Friend* is actually my own story.) I spent hours riding the countryside. I was the girl who carried the water in a jug to the neighborhood threshing crews, and the girl who led the horse that pulled the huge fork lifts of hay to the hay loft. All that life seems far away and nearly a dream in contrast to my ultramodern farm life of today.

"While I was in high school and college I was a reporter for the school paper. I enjoyed writing stories in my English classes, and in my early married life I told hundreds of stories to my children. Little did I realize that my material I gathered about Iowa for use in my own classroom would be published and now used by thousands of kids in Iowa! This opened the door to further writing.

"I love to travel! My husband and I have traveled in all the fifty states. We have loved hiking over two-hundred miles of trails in Glacier National Park, Montana. We have been in all the Provinces of Canada, have toured Mexico, and have been to eleven countries of Europe. We hope to travel much now.

"I have enjoyed my years of teaching and I hope I have been able to impress upon my pupils the greatness of the philosophy of a democracy, and that our democracy can survive only if our youth assume the responsibility for the future—they have a big job ahead!"

RANADIVE, Gail 1944-

PERSONAL: Surname is pronounced Ra-na-*dee*-vee; born February 16, 1944, in Boston, Mass.; daughter of Fred Leach (supervisor for Western Electric) and Audrey J. (Steeves) Collins; married Manmohan V. Ranadive (a physician in the U.S. Army), August 23, 1964; children:

[Grandmother] brought you something special, a pair of shiny silver anklets to slip over your chubby feet. Little silver decorations make a jingling sound with each step you take. You want to walk and walk just to make that sound. ▪ (From *If You'd Been Born in India* by Gail Ranadive. Illustrated by Paul Frame.)

Something about the Author

Nina M., Shawna M. *Education:* Lawrence General Hospital School of Nursing, R.N., 1964; student at Antioch College, Baltimore, Md., 1973-74. *Politics:* Independent. *Religion:* Unitarian-Universalist. *Residence:* Fort Leavenworth, Ky.

CAREER: Free-lance writer. *Member:* Society of Children's Book Writers, International Organization of Women Pilots, 99's Inc.

WRITINGS: If You'd Been Born in India, Albert Whitman, 1973.

WORK IN PROGRESS: Putting her own experiences as part of mixed-race, -religion, -nation family into fantasy form.

SIDELIGHTS: "I didn't start out with the idea of becoming a writer, though I did win school essay contests and have pieces published in the school newspaper. I don't think I really connected books with PEOPLE writing them; I was too busy simply enjoying the books themselves. Reading made me want to do and see and experience everything in the whole world, and all at once! Of course, the adults in my life tried to warn me that 'life isn't like that'; as exciting and patterned and complete with happy endings as books are.

"I became a nurse, because nurses can go anywhere and do all kinds of things and meet all kinds of people. I did meet an interesting person, a doctor from Bombay, India, and I married him. I worked as a nurse until our daughter Nina was nearly two years old. Then I discovered two things: 1. Being a nurse left little time to do all the other things I wanted to do. 2. Two-year-old children are great companions when you want to experience the world, because they see and hear and smell and feel things that adults miss.

"So I looked around for a profession I could do at home, and with (and sometimes in spite of) having a two year old around. Writing suggested a simple answer. I took a correspondence course in non-fiction writing and began investigating many things that had interested me, with the idea of writing about them. It wasn't to work out that way; I found I got too involved in these things to have the time to sit down to write about them! I had a lot of growing to do before I would discover that what I really wanted was to write for children.

"My husband was busy being a college student again, and had a three month summer vacation coming up. We decided to spend it in India, so that Nina and I could meet his family for the first time. Now, I had read everything I could get my hands on about India and Indian people, but nothing had given me any clue to what I would really find myself doing there; like sleeping on the floor, eating with my fingers, trying to take a bath in a bucket of boiled water. I suffered what is usually called 'cultural shock,' (not to mention dysentery). Yet Nina, three years old, had no problems adjusting at all. That's when I knew I wanted to write for that something special inside children that adults somehow don't have; I think you could call it 'optimism.'

"But it was to take three more years and another trip to India before I would finally write a book. Meanwhile, a second daughter, Shawna, arrived and I found myself having a good excuse to stay home and write. My first

GAIL RANADIVE

published efforts were greeting card verses. When we went back to India, Shawna had just had her first birthday. It was because of her and my husband's little niece, Beena, that my book was born. Beena's mother was going to have a baby, and for many days four-year-old Beena followed my Shawna around the apartment in Bombay. Finally, she went to her mother and demanded that she go to America to get the new baby, because 'American babies don't make puddles all over the floor.' You see, Shawna was wearing diapers and rubber pants, which Indian babies don't have; and suddenly I saw all of our cultural differences in a whole new way; that eating with fork or fingers were simply two different ways of doing the same 'human' things! That became the theme of my first book, *If You'd Been Born in India.*

"Now I am trying to work other experiences I have had into other books. It is like having an enormous hunk of clay before you and trying to find the best form to put it into in order to show what you feel and think and hope. Because real life IS as exciting as any found in books, and the people I have met during my trips to India, Nicaragua, Panama, Hawaii and Kashmir are even more fascinating than any I ever met in a book. For me, writing means LIVING, first, and sharing this living later, through books."

Gail Ranadive is a private pilot and a former operations officer of the U.S. Army Edgewood Flying Club, the first woman and first student pilot to hold this position in the club's history. Photographs taken on a visit to her husband's family in Bombay were used by the artist to illustrate *If You'd Been Born in India.*

RAPAPORT, Stella F(read)

PERSONAL: Born August 7, in New York, N.Y.; daughter of Abraham and Mollie (Rudolph) Fread; married Irving S. Rapaport (a lawyer), June 23, 1931; children: Myron S., Robert D. *Education:* Attended Hunter College, 1927-31, Art Students League, 1928-31, 1945-46. *Religion:* Jewish. *Home:* 36 Malvern Lane, Scarsdale, N.Y. 10583.

CAREER: Author and illustrator of children's books. *Member:* Authors League of America. *Awards, honors: A Whittle Too Much* chosen one of hundred best books of 1955 by *New York Times; The Bear—Ship of Many Lives* received *Boys' Life*-Dodd, Mead writing award, 1962.

WRITINGS—All self-illustrated: *A Whittle Too Much* (Catholic Children's Book Club selection), Putnam, 1955; *Reindeer Rescue,* Putnam, 1955; *Binkley's Bottleneck,* Putnam, 1956; *Horse Chestnut Hideaway,* Putnam, 1958; *The Bear—Ship of Many Lives,* Dodd, 1962; *Philip and the Ninety-Nine Frogs,* Macmillan.

SIDELIGHTS: "I enjoy painting, traveling and the study of nature. Every place I've visited has become a source of interest leading to a story or a painting. I traveled in Alaska where the real-life events of two books took place. I checked the original logs of the ship 'Bear' in the National Archives in Washington, and visited the famous ship in Nova Scotia. I drove up and down the hills of the Gaspé in Canada and *A Whittle Too Much* was created.

"I followed closely the building of the New York thruway—and the tiny old fashioned ferry on Lake Champlain—and *Binkley's Bottleneck* was written.

"For *Horse Chestnut Hideaway* I had only to look back into my own childhood and our house in the country. And *Philip* was just pure fun!

"I've enjoyed the personal contacts with children—giving over a hundred talks in schools and libraries."

RAZZI, James   1931-

PERSONAL: Born August 20, 1931, in New York, N.Y.; son of Guido (a waiter) and Marie (Cicatelli) Razzi; married Lis Rutzou, March 9, 1956 (divorced, July 17, 1962); married Hedi Studiger, June 1, 1963 (died May 2, 1970); married Mary Mooney, January 29, 1971; children: Signe, Christina, Jennifer. *Education:* Attended University of Florence, School of Visual Arts, and Art Students League. *Residence:* Brooklyn, N.Y.

CAREER: Commercial artist for a variety of concerns, 1956-67; free-lance commercial artist, 1967—. *Military service:* U.S. Navy, 1949-51.

WRITINGS—Juvenile: *Simply Fun!,* Parents' Magazine Press, 1968; *Easy Does It!,* Parents' Magazine Press, 1969; *Bag of Tricks!,* Parents' Magazine Press, 1971; *Don't Open This Box,* Parents' Magazine Press, 1973; *Just For Kids,* Parents' Magazine Press, 1974. Activities consultant to *Humpty-Dumpty.*

JAMES RAZZI

WORK IN PROGRESS: A pun and puzzle book for Scholastic Book Services; *Extra! 1,* a school magazine teaching aid, for Macmillan.

SIDELIGHTS: "To be honest about it, I sort of fell into writing the long way around. I started out being a commercial artist and wanting to specialize in illustration. As I progressed in my art career, I found myself stuck doing general art studio work. (Paste ups, mechanicals, layouts, et cetera.) It looked as if I wasn't going to make it as an illustrator because no one was beating down the door for my work.

"One day I happened to buy a *Humpty Dumpty* magazine for my daughter and I looked through it myself. I was fascinated by the cut-out pages where you cut out different items and made a toy or an animal or where you pulled a tab and the monkey did tricks. I also realized that I could invent things of that sort, also. I used to make all kinds of things out of scrap material when I was a kid. They had no rhyme or reason to them, I would just think them up out of my head and make whatever the material would lend itself to. A paper cup became a small pilgrim's hat, two ice-cream sticks crossed became an airplane and so on. I, also, liked pop-up books and toys that were punched out of cardboard and assembled and I would spend hours putting tabs A into slots A.

"Getting back to *Humpty Dumpty,* I worked up some ideas of my own to show to the art director there. One was a horse that galloped when you pulled the tab and the other was a lion that opened it's mouth when you pulled the tab. Duncan Morrison, the art director, is a great guy and always giving young artists a chance to show their work. He liked my ideas and bought the both of them. I guess you could say I haven't looked back since. One thing led to another and I did my first activity book for Parents' Magazine Press. The book was a great success and I just kept on doing them and Parents' kept on publishing them.

Everyone shouts, "Good luck!" as the pilot waves . . . . He's up, up and away! ■ (From *Simply Fun!* by James Razzi. Illustrated by the author.)

"I don't think of myself as a writer per se. I am really an 'idea' man. That is, I may come up with an idea for a book of punch-out toys. The only writing involved in that is the instructions. The rest is illustration and designing the toys. Another one of my areas is puzzle books. (Brain teasers, mazes, crossword puzzles, et cetera.) Again, it is more a matter of thinking up riddles and word puzzles than getting a story line. To bear this out, the only story book I ever did was *Don't Open this Box!* All the rest were activity books and puzzle books. I have just had a pop-up book published and a punch-out toy book.

"Now many people have asked me how or where I get my ideas. That's a hard question to answer. It's like asking a musical composer where he gets the ideas for his melodies. I don't really know how I get my ideas. Sometimes, I see something or hear something and suddenly I get an idea for something altogether unrelated to what I have just seen or heard. Sometimes, I consciously sit down and THINK of an idea. What I mean is that I will say to myself that I want to think of an idea for my next project and then I will start to think of what it might be. Another puzzle book? Another activity book? A game? And then I will think if it should or could have a special format. A good example is *Pirate Puzzles* which I did for Scholastic Book Services. I was always interested in pirates and piracy so I did some research on the subject. I wanted to do a factual book on pirates but I could never get it off the ground. One day I was fooling around with riddles and jokes and I said to myself, 'Why did the dirty pirate jump overboard?' and the answer, 'Because he wanted to be washed ashore.' After a chuckle or two to myself, I decided that I was going to take

my pirate material and use it in a funny puzzle book. So that's how I got the idea for *Pirate Puzzles*.

"I like to make people laugh if I can. I'm probably a frustrated 'stand-up' comic. So I try and make my illustrations as humorous as possible. The kids seem to like them and with three daughters of my own around the house, I can always test out my ideas on them first. But I'm afraid that after all these years of seeing created ideas before their eyes, they take it all in stride."

HOBBIES AND OTHER INTERESTS: Travel.

RENDINA, Laura Cooper 1902-

PERSONAL: Born November 9, 1902, in Northampton, Mass.; daughter of Edward Lincoln and Emma (Burckes) Jones; widow; children: (first marriage) Eveleth Cooper (Mrs. John C. Cowles), David Cooper, Judith Cooper (Mrs. Charles M. Chamberlain), (second marriage) Laura Rendina (Mrs. James Eadens), Mario Rendina. *Education:* Attended Smith College, two years, and Yale Art School. *Politics:* Independent. *Religion:* Unitarian. *Home:* 606 Calle del Otono, Sarasota, Fla. 33581.

CAREER: Writer, mainly of books for young people.

WRITINGS: Roommates (Junior Literary Guild selection), Little, Brown, 1948; *Debbie Jones*, Little, Brown, 1950; *Summer for Two*, Little, Brown, 1952; *My Love for One*, Little, Brown, 1955; *Lolly Touchberry*, Little, Brown,

1957; *Trudi,* Little, Brown, 1959; *World of Their Own* (Junior Literary Guild selection), Little, Brown, 1963; *Destination Capri* (Junior Literary Guild selection), Little, Brown, 1968. Contributor of short stories to *Ladies' Home Journal* and *Seventeen.*

WORK IN PROGRESS: A juvenile novel about the unicorn.

SIDELIGHTS: Has lived in Europe, principally in Italy, at intervals; speaks some Italian and French.

HOBBIES AND OTHER INTERESTS: Working with youth groups.

FOR MORE INFORMATION SEE: More Junior Authors, edited by Muriel Fuller, H. W. Wilson, 1963.

RICCIUTI, Edward R(aphael)   1938-

PERSONAL: Born May 27, 1938, in New York, N.Y.; son of Edward Albert (a psychologist) and Inez (a teacher; maiden name Gatti) Ricciuti; married Mercedes Margarita Hogan, October 26, 1962; children: Anna Maria Cristina Teresa, James Edward. *Education:* University of Notre Dame, B.A., 1959; Columbia University, University Cer-

That night, Donald and his father went out for hamburgers.
■ (From *Donald and the Fish that Walked* by Edward R. Ricciuti. Illustrated by Syd Hoff.)

tificate, 1965. *Politics:* Democrat. *Religion:* Roman Catholic. *Home address:* RFD 3, Box 39, Roast Meat Hill Rd., Killingworth, Conn. 06417. *Agent:* Curtis Brown Ltd., 60 East 56th St., New York, N.Y. 10022. *Office:* New York Zoological Society, Bronx, N.Y. 10460.

CAREER: Copy boy for *New York Mirror,* New York, N.Y., reporter on *Independent,* Rockland, N.Y., and *Herald-News,* Ridgewood, N.J., 1959-60; *Record,* Hackensack, N.J., reporter and science writer, 1960-64; associate editor of *Science World* and *Senior Science,* and contributing editor of *Junior Scholastic,* New York, N.Y., 1965-67; New York Zoological Society, Bronx, associate curator, 1967-68, editor and curator of publications and public relations, 1968-71. Consultant on nature and science to Connecticut Audubon Society, American Littoral Society, Beardsley Park Zoo, Conn., New York Zoological Society, New England Aquarium, Mystic Marinelife Aquarium; consultant to American Museum of Natural History, 1964-65; president of Connecticut Zoological Society, 1969, and American Alligator Council; conservation commissioner in Fairfield, Conn., 1969-70; producer of television announcements for Wildlife Management Institute; member of the cast of "Patchwork Family," WCBS-TV, New York, N.Y. *Military service:* U.S. Marine Corps Reserve, 1957-63. *Member:* Society of Magazine Writers. *Awards, honors:* Public education citation by the Animal Care Panel, 1964, for "Monkeys, Mice and Medicine."

WRITINGS: Animals and Atomic Research, U.S. Atomic Energy Commission, 1967; *Catch A Whale By The Tail,* Harper, 1969; (contributor) Laurance Pringle, editor, *Discovering the Outdoors,* Natural History Press, 1969; *An Animal for Alan,* Harper, 1970; *Shelf Pets,* Harper, 1971; *The American Alligator: Its Life In The Wild,* Harper, 1972; *Dancers on the Beach,* Crowell, 1973, *Killers of the Seas,* Walker, 1973; *Donald and the Fish That Walked,* Harper, 1974; *Do Toads Give You Warts?,* Walker, 1975. Contributor to *World Almanac, Parade, Family Health,*

EDWARD R. RICCIUTI

Argosy, Genesis, National Wildlife, Steelways, Computing Report, Science World, Scholastic Teacher, Signature, and *Audubon.* Newspaper column for Enterprise Science News; contributing editor, *Science World,* Scholastic Magazines, Inc.

WORK IN PROGRESS: Two books on natural history for Harper and Crowell.

SIDELIGHTS: Ricciuti has studied wild animals in many places, including Africa, Bialowieza Forest of Poland, Middle East, the Everglades, the Okefenokee Swamp, the Caroni and Nariva Swamps of Trinidad, and the Luquillo Forest of Puerto Rico. He has participated in expeditions to collect whales in Hudson Bay and sharks off the Atlantic and Pacific coasts. He is interested in the life of the sea, and has spent considerable time on the water and under the surface, especially in the Caribbean and the Long Island Sound area, as well as off both the East and West coasts, and the Red Sea.

"I believe strongly in basing popular books and articles about nature on personal observation and field work, in addition to using knowledge accumulated in scientific literature. This conviction has led me to many parts of the world, from the northern regions of Hudson Bay to the tropics, into the mountains and under the sea. However, while I have studied wildlife in places such as Africa, the Red Sea, Puerto Rico and the Bialowieza Forest of Poland, I consider the wild animals at our doorstep just as interesting as animals in exotic places. Some of the most fascinating episodes of nature I have ever seen have occurred within a few feet of my home."

FOR MORE INFORMATION SEE: Christian Science Monitor, November 6, 1969; *New York Times Book Review,* May 27, 1973; *Library Journal,* December 15, 1974; *Kirkus Reviews,* December 15, 1974; *Scientific American,* December, 1974; *Booklist,* January 1, 1975; *Publishers' Weekly,* January 6, 1975.

RICH, Josephine (Bouchard) 1912-

PERSONAL: Born June 27, 1912, in Tamora, Neb.; daughter of Joseph Napoleon and Carrie (Russell) Bouchard; married James Sears Rich (a physician specializing in radiology), April 27, 1935; children: Thomas Sears, Jeanne Bouchard. *Education:* Washington Boulevard Hospital School of Nursing, Chicago, Ill., R.N., 1933. *Politics:* Republican. *Religion:* Presbyterian. *Home:* 1855 McDonald Rd., Lexington, Ky. 40503.

CAREER: Scrub nurse for orthopedic surgeon, Davenport, Iowa, 1933; Washington Boulevard Hospital, Chicago, Ill., director of X-Ray and emergency departments, 1934-35. Member, board of directors of Community Chest agencies, American Red Cross, Commonwealth of Kentucky Social Service Committee, Central Kentucky Concert and Lecture Series, Auxiliary to Kentucky State Medical Association, Federation of Churchwomen. *Awards, honors:* Lexington's Outstanding Woman of 1958 Award from Beta Sigma Phi; Freedoms Foundation Honor Certificate, 1961, for article, "So You Want to Duck Jury Duty!," *Presbyterian Survey Magazine,* July, 1960.

*WRITINGS—*Youth books: *Jean Henri Dunant, Founder of the International Red Cross,* Messner, 1956; *Pioneer*

JOSEPHINE RICH

Surgeon, Dr. Ephraim McDowell, Messner, 1959; *The Doctor Who Saved Babies: Ignaz Semmelweis,* Messner, 1961; *Women Behind Men of Medicine,* Messner, 1967. Contributing editor, *M.D.'s Wife* Magazine.

WORK IN PROGRESS: James Lind, the Scurvy Man.

RIVOLI, Mario 1943-
(Seymour Marasmus, H.M. Koutoukas)

PERSONAL: Born January 31, 1943, in New York, N.Y.; son of Mario (a beautician) and Hedwig (Matulonis; an embroiderer) Rivoli. *Education:* Attended School of Visual Art, New York, N.Y., one year, Art Students League, New York, N.Y., one year, Newvillage School for Clowns, New York, N.Y., 1960-65. *Home and Office:* 175 MacDougal Street, New York, N.Y. 10011. *Agent:* McIntosh & Otis, 475 Fifth Ave., New York, N.Y. 10017.

CAREER: Artist. Tunnel of Love, New York, N.Y., proprietor, 1966-68; Glass Palace Studio, New York, N.Y., assistant director, 1974; Triptych Gallery, New York, N.Y., 1974—. *Awards, honors:* Society of Illustrators Award, 1966; Washington Square Outdoor Art Exhibit honorable mention, 1975, for *Chimps Do Not Have Tails.*

ILLUSTRATOR: Barbara Wersba, *A Song for Clowns,* Atheneum, 1965; Barbara Wersba, *Do Tigers Ever Bite Kings?,* Atheneum, 1966; Louise Young, *Best Foot Forward,* Van Nostrand, 1967.

MARIO RIVOLI

WORK IN PROGRESS: She Never Knew She Was a Rabbit, a psychological drama for children; *High Individuals,* portraits of artists, writers, and dancers; "Children" a modular mural to be completed in 1978.

SIDELIGHTS: "I suppose I am happiest when I am traveling, organizing junk and taking slides with my Rolleflex.

"Born in a broken home, struck with polio when I was seventeen months old, in a section of New York City called 'Hell's Kitchen,' I did a splendid job of creating my fantasy. My mom told me that when I was two, she put a crayon around my neck and I would draw on the linoleum all day. I still draw all day. I hated school until art school—made friends with humor and decided to go off on my own at seventeen.

I've been to England, Spain, Portugal, and Morocco. Last summer, not able to afford far away places, I made sojourns to the Bronx and abandoned piers of the west side of New York City. I was thrilled to be as excited on my home ground and realized a newness of New York. I spent days at the garbage dump on Gansevort Pier collecting objects for assemblages. I would like to reproduce sections of sidewalks for a show.

"I have no interest in politics and big business. I adore games and transvestites. I know sign language. I would like to write and illustrate my own book. The kind of book one reads at four and comes true at sixteen.

"I love television, my friends and the thought of being a student of life for the rest of my life."

FOR MORE INFORMATION SEE: Publishers' Weekly, Volume 189, Number 4; *Junior Literary Guild Catalog,* September, 1965; *Illustrators of Children's Books: 1957-66,* Horn Book, 1968.

ROGERS, Frances   1888-1974

PERSONAL: Born in Grand Rapids, Mich. in 1888. *Education:* Attended public and private schools in Grand Rapids, Mich., The Art Institute, Chicago, Ill.; also studied in Wilmington, Del., and at the Boston Museum of Fine Arts. *Home:* 5 Broadway Rd., Woodstock, N.Y.

CAREER: Illustrator and cover designer for books and leading magazines until 1933; then a writer for adults and juveniles.

WRITINGS: Picture Puzzle Posters, Ray Long & Richard Smith, 1933; (with Alice Beard) *Heels, Wheels and Wire,* Stokes, 1936, 3rd edition, 1966; (with Beard) *Fresh and Briny,* Stokes, 1936; (with Beard) *5000 Years of Glass,* Stokes, 1937; *Big Miss Liberty,* Stokes, 1938; (with Beard) *5000 Years of Gems and Jewelry,* Stokes, 1940; *Indigo Treasure,* Stokes, 1941; (with Beard) *Old Liberty Bell,* Stokes, 1942; (with Beard) *Paul Revere: Patriot on Horseback,* Stokes, 1943; (with Beard) *Birthday of a Nation,* Lippincott, 1945; (with Beard) *Jeremy Pepper* (Junior Literary Guild Selection), Lippincott, 1946; *Mr. Brady's Camera Boy,* Lippincott, 1951; *Fire Engine Boy,* Lippincott, 1953; *Lens Magic,* Lippincott, 1958; *Painted Rock to Printed Page,* Lippincott, 1960; *5000 Years of Stargazing,* Lippincott, 1964; *The History of a Small Town Library,* Vanguard, 1974.

(Died June 6, 1974)

During the Centennial year Liberty Bell came into its own. It was peered at and acclaimed by the visiting throngs. ■ (From *Old Liberty Bell* by Frances Rogers and Alice Beard. Illustrated by Frances Rogers.)

FRANCES ROGERS

RONGEN, Björn 1906-

PERSONAL: Born July 24, 1906, in Voss, Norway; married Charlotte Schanche Olsen, March 9, 1940; children: Thana (Mrs. Ola Bredeveien), Ole. *Education:* Attended University of Oslo. *Religion:* None. *Home:* Skogvegen 22, Dröbak, Norway, 1440.

CAREER: Author and free-lance journalist. *Member:* Den norske Forfatterforening, Ungdomslitteraturens forfatterlag, P.E.N. *Awards, honors:* Several literary prizes.

BJÖRN RONGEN

The men pulled him up very slowly, and carefully. The fact that tears came into Olaf's eyes when he saw the valley and the sky and the snow-topped mountains and the green earth was only because he could not bear the full light all at once. ■ (From *Olaf and the Echoing Cave* by Björn Rongen. Illustrated by Ralph Pinto.)

WRITINGS—Novels: *To semester*, O. Norli, 1934, reissued, Samlaget, 1966; *Embetsfolk*, Gyldendal, 1935; *Stille smil*, Gyldendal, 1936; *Det drar ifra Vest*, Gyldendal, 1939; *Nettenes natt*, Gyldendal, 1940; *Tolv liv*, Gyldendal, 1946; *Hun moeter deg alltid*, Gyldendal, 1946; *Fager er lien*, Gyldendal, 1948; *Kunnskapens tre*, Gyldendal, 1949; *Driftekarens hoest*, Gyldendal, 1951; *Kvinnen og pisken*, Gyldendal, 1953; *Ragnhilds rike*, Gyldendal, 1955; *Toget over vidda*, Gyldendal, 1956; *I joekulens skygge*, Gyldendal, 1957; *Klart for tog*, Gyldendal,1958; *Store Ma*, Tiden, 1960; *Nei men Johanne*, Gyldendal, 1962.

Juvenile books: *Bergtatt I Risehola*, Damm, 1953, translation by Evelyn Ramsden published as *Olaf and the Echoing Cave*, McGraw, 1968; *Anne Villdyrjente*, Gyldendal, 1956, translation by Evelyn Ramsden published as *Anna of the Bears*, Methuen, 1965, Farrar, Straus, 1967; *Utvandrer-*

gutten: Knute Nelsons Saga, Gyldendal, 1959; *Fem Doegn paa isfjell: Tegninger av Arne Johnson*, Aschehoug, 1959; *De hemmelige flyktningene*, Gyldendal, 1962; *Den store brannen*, Norsk Barneblad, 1967; *Ola den heldige*, Norsk Barneblad, 1970. Also author of *Slalaam for livet*. Author of radio plays, several hundred short stories and approximately fifty translations.

FOR MORE INFORMATION SEE: Young Readers Review, February, 1969.

SAINT, Dora Jessie 1913-
(Miss Read)

PERSONAL: Born April 17, 1913, in Surrey, England; daughter of Arthur Gunnis and Grace (Read) Shafe; married Douglas Edward John Saint (now a schoolmaster), July 26, 1940; children: one daughter. *Education:* Homerton College, student, 1931-33. *Address:* C/o Michael Joseph Ltd., 26 Bloomsbury St., London, W.C. 1, England.

CAREER: Teacher and writer. Justice of the Peace for Newbury Borough, Berkshire, England. *Member:* Society of Authors.

WRITINGS—All under pseudonym Miss Read: *Village School,* M. Joseph, 1955, Houghton, 1956; *Village Diary,* Houghton, 1957; *Hobby Horse Cottage* (juvenile), M. Joseph, 1958; *Storm in the Village,* M. Joseph, 1958, Houghton, 1959; *Thrush Green,* Houghton, 1959; *Fresh From the Country,* M. Joseph, 1960, Houghton, 1961; *Winter in Thrush Green,* M. Joseph, 1961, Houghton, 1962; *Miss Clare Remembers,* M. Joseph, 1962, Houghton, 1963; (compiler) *Country Bunch,* M. Joseph, 1963; *Over the Gate,* M. Joseph, 1964; *Chronicles of Fairacre,* M. Joseph, 1964; *Village Christmas,* Houghton, 1966; *Market Square,* Houghton, 1966; *Howards of Caxley,* Houghton, 1967; *Fairacre Festival,* Houghton, 1968; *Miss Read's Country Cooking,* M. Joseph, 1969; *News from Thrush Green,* Houghton, 1970; *Tiggy,* Signet, 1971; *Tyler's Row,* Houghton, 1972; *The Christmas Mouse,* Houghton, 1973; *Farther Afield,* M. Joseph, 1974, Houghton, 1975; *Animal Boy* (juvenile), M. Joseph, 1975; *Battles at Thrush Green,* M. Joseph, 1975, Houghton, 1976. Author of school scripts for British Broadcasting Corp.

DORA JESSIE SAINT

. . . one of the Flopsy Bunnies was led on by Joseph, horribly impeded by a blanket which had slipped from his shoulder, and followed by Mary in Miss Watson's blue dressing gown which, she was sorry to see, was trailing along the wet floor, much to its detriment. ■ (From *Battles at Thrush Green* by Miss Read. Illustrated by J. S. Goodall.)

WORK IN PROGRESS: A children's book, for M. Joseph; books for infant schools, the "Red Bus" series, for Nelson.

HOBBIES AND OTHER INTERESTS: Theater, music, reading, wildlife of the countryside.

FOR MORE INFORMATION SEE: World Authors: 1950-1970, edited by John Wakeman, H. W. Wilson, 1975.

ST. JOHN, Wylly Folk 1908-
(Eleanor Fox, Eve Larson, Katherine Pierce, Mary Keith Vincent, Michael Williams)

PERSONAL: Born October 20, 1908, near Ehrhardt, S.C.; daughter of William Obed (an insurance man) and Annie Claire (Mattox) Folk; married Thomas F. St. John (advertising manager of a weekly newspaper; now retired), January 1, 1930; children: Anne Folk (Mrs. Neil D. Pratt). *Education:* University of Georgia, A.B. (journalism), 1930. *Politics:* "Vote for the man, not the party." *Religion:* "No current affiliation. Have strong religious beliefs but they are not denominational" *Home:* 198 Dogwood Ave. N.E., Social Circle, Ga. 30279. *Agent:* Lurton Blassingame, 60 East 42nd St., New York, N.Y. 10017.

CAREER: Atlanta Journal and Constitution Magazine, Atlanta, Ga., staff writer, 1941-54, 1962-75. *Member:* Authors Guild, Atlanta Press Club, Plot Club (Atlanta), Phi Beta Kappa, Theta Sigma Phi, Phi Kappa Phi, Mystery Writers of America, National Society of Literature and the Arts. *Awards, honors:* Georgia Author of the Year, 1968; Theta Sigma Phi Award for "outstanding contributions to journalism," 1970; Georgia Author of the Year in Fiction, 1973; two "Edgar" nominations from the Mystery Writers of America, 1973 and 1974.

WRITINGS: The Secrets of Hidden Creek (juvenile), Viking, 1966; *The Secrets of the Pirate Inn,* Viking, 1968;

The Christmas Tree Mystery (Junior Literary Guild selection), Viking, 1969; *The Mystery of the Gingerbread House*, Viking, 1969; *The Mystery of the Other Girl*, Viking, 1971; *The Ghost Next Door*, Harper, 1971; *Uncle Robert's Secret*, Viking, 1972; *The Secret of the Seven Crows*, Viking, 1973; *The Mystery Book Mystery*, Viking, 1976. Author of five book-length novels published in *Redbook;* contributor of stories and articles to magazines, including *Glamour, Toronto Star Weekly, Liberty, Family Circle, American,* and *American Weekly.*

WORK IN PROGRESS: The Mystery of the Gryphon Rock.

SIDELIGHTS: Wylly Folk St. John used her three grandchildren as central characters in *The Secrets of Hidden Creek* and her nieces and nephews in *The Secrets of the Pirate Inn* and subsequent juveniles. All prior stories and articles (more than a thousand) had been for adults.

HOBBIES AND OTHER INTERESTS: Reading; gardening, especially growing roses and herbs; travelling, painting.

FOR MORE INFORMATION SEE: Horn Book, April, 1972.

She pointed to it on the wall over the mantel—a water color framed in gilt, showing the white gingerbread house with trees around it and yellow roses at one end. ▪ (From *The Mystery of the Gingerbread House* by Wylly Folk St. John. Illustrated by Frank Aloise.)

WYLLY FOLK ST. JOHN

SARNOFF, Jane 1937-

PERSONAL: Born June 25, 1937, in Brooklyn, N.Y.; daughter of Murray (a jewelry executive) and Teresa (a teacher; maiden name, Rehr) Sarnoff. *Education:* Goucher College, B.A., 1959. *Religion:* Jewish.

CAREER: Sudler & Hennessey Advertising, New York, N.Y., copy supervisor, 1967-71; free-lance writer, 1971—.

WRITINGS—Books for young people all with illustrator, Reynold Ruffins: *A Great Bicycle Book*, Scribner, 1973; *The Chess Book*, Scribner, 1973; *What? A Riddle Book*, Scribner, 1974; *Annual Riddle Calendar*, Scribner, 1974; *The Monster Riddle Book*, Scribner, 1975; *A Good Aquarium Book*, Scribner, 1976.

WORK IN PROGRESS: An untitled book of superstitions, for Scribner.

HOBBIES AND OTHER INTERESTS: Travel (Japan, Hong Kong, Europe, Mexico).

Why was
the little strawberry worried?

His mom and dad
were in a jam.

What kind of nut
has some of its inside
outside?

A doughnut.

What's the best way
to catch a squirrel?

Climb a tree and act
like a nut.

Why is the highest apple on
a tree always the best one?
Because it's the tip top apple.

How far can you walk into an apple orchard?
As far as the middle — after that you are walking out.

What keeps the moon in place?
Its beams.

What is the reddest side of an apple?
The outside.

(From *What? A Riddle Book* by Jane Sarnoff. Illustrated by Reynold Ruffins.)

What does a worm do in a cornfield?
It goes in one ear and out another.

If your brother has a whole apple
and you only have a bite,
what should you do?
Scratch it.

Why can't you tell secrets on a farm?
Because the corn has ears, the potatoes have eyes, the beanstalk, and the horses carry tails.

What season is most dangerous?
Fall.

JANE SARNOFF AND REYNOLD RUFFINS

FOR MORE INFORMATION SEE: Horn Book, October, 1973, December, 1974; *New York Times Book Review,* November 3, 1974; *Saturday Review/World,* November 30, 1974; *Washington Post Book World,* December 15, 1974; *Publishers' Weekly,* December 16, 1974; *Wilson Library Bulletin,* February, 1975.

SCHELL, Orville H.   1940-

PERSONAL: Born May 20, 1940, in New York, N.Y.; son of Orville H. (a lawyer) and Marjorie Bertha Schell. *Education:* Harvard University, B.A. (magna cum laude), 1962; National Taiwan University, graduate study, 1961-64; University of California, Berkeley, M.A., 1967, doctoral candidate. *Residence:* P.O. Box 182, Bolinas, Calif.

CAREER: Correspondent in Asia for *Atlantic, Look, Harpers', New Republic, Boston Globe,* and *San Francisco Chronicle,* 1962-64; Ford Foundation, assistant in Indonesia field office, Djakarta, 1964-65.

WRITINGS: (With Herbert Franz Schurmann, editor, annotator, and author of introductions) *The China Reader,* three volumes, Volume I: *The Decline of the Last Dynasty and the Origins of Modern China,* Volume II: *Republican China: Nationalism, War, and the Rise of Communism,* and Volume III: *Communist China: Revolutionary Reconstruction and International Confrontation,* Random House, 1967; (with Frederick Crews) *Starting Over: A College Reader,* Random House, 1969; *Modern China: The Story of a Revolution,* Knopf, 1972; *Working in China,* Random House, 1976; *The Town That Fought to Save Itself,* Pantheon, 1976.

SIDELIGHTS: "Why do I write for young people? I never write *for* young people. I simply write in the belief that all books should be written clearly and simply; without jargon and pomposity. Kids seem to understand such books best. Often times they are a relief for adults as well.

"I write about China, because it is an alternative. Although not a plug-in substitute for our problems, it shows that there are indeed utterly different ways to do things. In times of collapse and despair, people search out such alternative possibilities, if not as something to adopt, then something to inspire hope that the future can be otherwise.

"*Modern China* is an attempt to sketch out and explain how the confluence of historical events in China led irrevocably to revolution. The book seeks to present China to young people, and older people unfamiliar with its history, in a simple yet accurate manner.

"*The Town That Fought to Save Itself* is the narrative of a small California town which sought to keep itself small. The narrative chronicles several years of struggle against growth; sewers, highways, houses, tourists and weather weekenders driving farmers off the land for expensive second homes."

FOR MORE INFORMATION SEE: Book Week, April 30, 1967; *Saturday Review,* May 6, 1967; *Horn Book,* June, 1972.

SCHERF, Margaret   1908-

PERSONAL: Born April 1, 1908, in Fairmont, W. Va.; daughter of Charles Henry and Miriam (Fisher) Scherf; married Perry E. Beebe, 1965. *Education:* Antioch College, student, 1925-28. *Politics:* Democrat. *Religion:* Episcopalian. *Home:* 737 First Ave. W., Kalispell, Mont. *Agent:* Lurton Blassingame, 10 East 43rd St., New York, N.Y. 10017.

CAREER: Worked as secretary, copywriter, reader, for publishers in New York, N.Y., 1928-29, 1934-39. Writer, 1940—. Member of House of Representatives, Montana State Legislature, 1965.

WRITINGS: The Corpse Grows a Beard, Putnam, 1940; *The Case of the Kippered Corpse,* Putnam, 1941; *They Came to Kill,* Putnam, 1942; *The Owl in the Cellar,* Doubleday, Doran, 1945; *Always Murder a Friend,* Doubleday, 1948; *Murder Makes Me Nervous,* Doubleday, 1948; *Gilbert's Last Toothache,* Doubleday, 1949; *The Gun in Daniel Webster's Bust,* Doubleday, 1949.

The Curious Custard Pie, Doubleday, 1950; *The Green Plaid Pants,* Doubleday, 1951; *The Elk and the Evidence,* Doubleday, 1952; *Dead: Senate Office Building,* Doubleday, 1953; *Glass on the Stairs,* Doubleday, 1954; *The Cautious Overshoes,* Doubleday, 1956; *Judicial Body,* Doubleday, 1957; *Never Turn Your Back,* Doubleday, 1959.

Wedding Train (novel), Doubleday, 1960; *The Diplomat and the Gold Piano,* Doubleday, 1963; *The Mystery of the Velvet Box,* Watts, 1963; *The Corpse in the Flannel Nightgown,* Doubleday, 1965; *The Mystery of the Shaky Staircase* (juvenile), Watts, 1965; *The Mystery of the Empty Trunk* (juvenile), Watts, 1966; *The Banker's Bones,* Doubleday, 1968.

To Cache a Millionaire, Doubleday, 1972; *If You Want a Murder Well Done,* Doubleday, 1974.

HOBBIES AND OTHER INTERESTS: Antiques and travel.

SCHULZ, Charles M(onroe) 1922-

PERSONAL: Born November 26, 1922, in Minneapolis, Minn.; son of Carl (a barber) and Dena (Halversòn) Schulz; married Joyce Halverson, April 18, 1949 (divorced, 1972); married Jean Clyde, 1973; children: Meredith, Charles Monroe, Craig, Amy, Jill. *Education:* Studied cartooning in an art school after graduation in 1940 from public high school in St. Paul, Minn. *Home:* 1 Snoopy Place, Santa Rosa, Calif. *Office:* c/o United Feature Syndicate, Daily News Building, New York, N.Y. 10017.

CAREER: Cartoonist, *St. Paul Pioneer Press* and *Saturday Evening Post,* 1948-49; creator of syndicated comic strip, "Peanuts," 1950. *Military service:* U.S. Army, served with Twentieth Armored Division in Europe, 1943-45; became staff sergeant. *Awards, honors:* Reuben award as outstanding cartoonist of the year, National Cartoonists' Society, 1955 and 1964; Yale award as outstanding humorist of the year, 1956; School Bell award, National Education Association, 1960; L.H.D., Anderson College, 1963; Peabody award and Emmy award, both 1966, for CBS cartoon special, "A Charlie Brown Christmas"; D.H.L., St. Mary's College of California, 1969.

WRITINGS—Cartoon books with captions, many collected from newspaper work: *Peanuts,* Rinehart, 1952; *More Peanuts,* Rinehart, 1954, selections from Volume 1 published as *Wonderful World of Peanuts,* Fawcett, 1963, selections from Volume 2 published as *Hey, Peanuts!,* Fawcett, 1963; *Good Grief, More Peanuts!,* Rinehart, 1956, selections from Volume 1 published as *Good Grief, Charlie Brown!,* Fawcett, 1963, selections from Volume 2 published as *For the Love of Peanuts,* Fawcett, 1963; *Good Ol' Charlie Brown,* Rinehart, 1957, selections from Volume 1 published as *Fun with Peanuts,* Fawcett, 1964,

Now he had to make his way back across no-man's land to the aerodrome. ■ (From *It's the Great Pumpkin, Charlie Brown* by Charles M. Schulz. Illustrated by the author.)

selections from Volume 2 published as *Here Comes Charlie Brown,* Fawcett, 1964; *Snoopy,* Rinehart, 1958, selections from Volume 1 published as *Here Comes Snoopy,* Fawcett, 1966, selections from Volume 2 published as *Good Ol' Snoopy,* Fawcett, 1958; *Young Pillars,* Warner Press, 1958; *But We Love You, Charlie Brown,* Rinehart, 1959, selections from Volume 1 published as *We're On Your Side, Charlie Brown,* Fawcett, 1966, selections from Volume 2 published as *You Are Too Much, Charlie Brown,* Fawcett, 1966; *Peanuts Revisited: Favorites Old and New,* Rinehart, 1959; *You're Out of Your Mind, Charlie Brown!,* Rinehart, 1959, selections from Volume 1 published as *Very Funny, Charlie Brown!,* Fawcett, 1965, selections from Volume 2 published as *What Next, Charlie Brown?,* Fawcett, 1965.

Go Fly a Kite, Charlie Brown, Holt, 1960, selections from Volume 1 published as *You're a Winner, Charlie Brown,* Fawcett, 1967, selections from Volume 2 published as *Let's Face It, Charlie Brown,* Fawcett, 1967; *Peanuts Every Sunday,* Holt, 1961, selections from Volume 1 published as *Who Do You Think You Are, Charlie Brown?,* Fawcett, 1968, selections from Volume 2 published as *You're My Hero, Charlie Brown,* Fawcett, 1968; *"Teen-ager" is Not a Disease,* Warner Press, 1961; *Happiness is a Warm Puppy,* Determined Productions, 1962; *It's a Dog's Life, Charlie Brown,* Holt, 1962, selections from Volume 1 published as *This is Your Life, Charlie Brown,* Fawcett, 1968, selections from Volume 2 published as *Slide, Charlie Brown, Slide,* Fawcett, 1968; *Snoopy, Come Home,* Holt, 1962, selections published as *We Love You, Snoopy,* Fawcett, 1970; *You Can't Win, Charlie Brown,* Holt, 1962, selections from Volume 1 published as *All This and Snoopy, Too,* Fawcett, 1969, selections from Volume 2 published as *Here's to You, Charlie Brown,* Fawcett, 1969; *Peanuts Project Book,* Determined Productions, 1963; *Security is a Thumb and a Blanket,* Determined Productions, 1963; *You Can Do It, Charlie Brown,* Holt, 1963, selections from Volume 1 published as *Nobody's Perfect, Charlie Brown,* Fawcett, 1969, selections from Volume 2 published as *You're a Brave Man, Charlie Brown,* Fawcett, 1969; *As You Like It, Charlie Brown,* Holt, 1964;

CHARLES M. SCHULZ

Christmas is Together-Time, Determined Productions, 1964; *I Need All the Friends I Can Get*, Determined Productions, 1964; *We're Right Behind You, Charlie Brown*, Holt, 1964, Volume 1 reissued as *Peanuts for Everybody*, Fawcett, 1970, selections from Volume 2 published as *You've Done It Again, Charlie Brown*, Fawcett, 1970; *What Was Bugging Ol' Pharaoh?*, Warner Press, 1964; *A Charlie Brown Christmas* (adapted from the television production), World Publishing, 1965; *Love is Walking Hand in Hand*, Determined Productions, 1965; *Sunday's Fun Day, Charlie Brown*, Holt, 1965, Volume 1 reissued as *It's for You, Snoopy*, Fawcett, 1971, Volume 2 reissued as *Have It Your Way, Charlie Brown*, Fawcett, 1971; *You Need Help, Charlie Brown*, Holt, 1965, selections from Volume 1 published as *You're Not for Real, Snoopy*, Fawcett, 1971, selections from Volume 2 published as *You're a Pal, Snoopy*, Fawcett, 1972.

Charlie Brown's All-Stars (adapted from the television production), World Publishing, 1966; *Home Is on Top of a Doghouse*, Determined Productions, 1966; *Snoopy and the Red Baron*, Holt, 1966; *The Unsinkable Charlie Brown*, Holt, 1966, selections from Volume 1 published as *What Now, Charlie Brown?*, Fawcett, 1972, selections from Volume 2 published as *You're Something Special, Snoopy!*, Fawcett, 1972; *You're Something Else, Charlie Brown*,

tions, 1970; *Peanuts Classics*, Holt, 1970; *Peanuts Date Book 1972*, Determined Productions, 1970; *Peanuts Lunch Bag Cook Book* (including recipes by June Dutton), Determined Productions, 1970; *Snoopy and "It Was a Dark and Stormy Night,"* Holt, 1970; *It's Fun to Lie Here and Listen to the Sounds of the Night*, Determined Productions, 1970; *You're Out of Sight, Charlie Brown*, Holt, 1970; *Winning May Not Be Everything, But Losing Isn't Anything!*, Determined Productions, 1970; *You're the Greatest, Charlie Brown*, Fawcett, 1971; *You've Come a Long Way, Charlie Brown*, Holt, 1971; *Play It Again, Charlie Brown* (adapted from the television production), World Publishing, 1971; *You're Elected, Charlie Brown*, World Publishing, 1972; *Ha Ha, Herman Charlie Brown*, Holt, 1972; *Snoopy's Grand Slam*, Holt, 1972; *The Snoopy, Come Home Movie Book* (adapted from the film production), Holt, 1972; *Snoopy's Secret Life*, Hallmark, 1972; *The Peanuts Philosophers*, Hallmark, 1972; *Love a la Peanuts*, Hallmark, 1972; *It's Good to Have a Friend*, Hallmark, 1972; *An Old-Fashioned Thanksgiving*, Lippincott, 1974; *The Charlie Brown Dictionary*, Random, 1973; *The Snoopy Festival*, Holt, 1974; *A Charlie Brown Thanksgiving*, Random, 1974; *There's No Time for Love, Charlie Brown*, Random, 1974; *Peanuts Jubilee*, Holt, 1975; *There's a Vulture Outside*, Holt, 1976; *It's a Long Way to Tipperary*, Holt, 1976; *What's Wrong with Being Crabby*,

(From *Peanuts Classics* by Charles M. Schulz. Illustrated by the author.)

Holt, 1966; *Happiness is a Sad Song*, Determined Productions, 1967; *It's the Great Pumpkin, Charlie Brown* (adapted from the television production), World Publishing, 1967; *Teen-Agers, Unite!*, Bantam, 1967; *You'll Flip, Charlie Brown*, Holt, 1967, selections published as *You've Got a Friend, Charlie Brown*, Fawcett, 1972; *He's Your Dog, Charlie Brown!* (adapted from the television production), World Publishing, 1968; *Peanuts Treasury* (ALA Notable Book), foreword by Johnny Hart, Holt, 1968; *Suppertime!*, Determined Productions, 1968; *You're in Love, Charlie Brown* (adapted from the television production), World Publishing, 1968; *You're You, Charlie Brown*, Holt, 1968; *A Boy Named Charlie Brown* (adapted from the film production), Holt, 1969; *Charlie Brown's Yearbook* (includes *He's Your Dog, Charlie Brown!*, *It's the Great Pumpkin, Charlie Brown*, *You're in Love, Charlie Brown*, and *Charlie Brown's All-Stars*), World Publishing, 1969; *You've Had It, Charlie Brown*, Holt, 1969; *Peanuts Cook Book*, recipes by June Dutton, Determined Productions, 1969; *Peanuts School Year Date Book, 1969-70*, Determined Productions, 1969; *Snoopy and His Sopwith Camel*, Holt, 1969.

For Five Cents, Determined Productions, 1970; *It Was a Short Summer, Charlie Brown* (adapted from the television production), World Publishing, 1970; *It Really Doesn't Take Much to Make a Dad Happy*, Determined Produc-

Holt, 1976; *Who's the Funny-Looking Kid with the Big Nose?*, Holt, 1976; *I Never Promised You an Apple Orchard*, Holt, 1976. Also author, with Kenneth F. Hall, of a child study, *Two-by-Fours: A Sort of Serious Book About Small Children*, Warner Press, 1965; (author of foreword) Morrie Turner, *Nipper*, Westminster, 1970.

Teleplays—26-minute animated cartoons, produced for CBS-TV: "A Charlie Brown Christmas," December 9, 1965; "Charlie Brown's All-Stars," June 8, 1966; "It's the Great Pumpkin, Charlie Brown," October 27, 1966; "You're in Love, Charlie Brown," June 12, 1967; "He's Your Dog, Charlie Brown!," February 14, 1968; "It Was a Short Summer, Charlie Brown," September 27, 1969; "Play It Again, Charlie Brown," March 28, 1971; "You're Elected, Charlie Brown," October 29, 1972; "It's the Easter Beagle, Charlie Brown," 1972; "There's No Time for Love, Charlie Brown," March 11, 1973; "Race for Your Life, Charlie Brown," January, 1976; "It's Arbor Day, Charlie Brown," March 16, 1976. Also writer of screenplays for "A Boy Named Charlie Brown," 1969, and "Snoopy, Come Home," 1972, both feature-length animated films produced for National General Pictures.

Illustrator: Art Linkletter, *Kids Say the Darndest Things*, Prentice-Hall, 1957; Art Linkletter, *Kids Still Say the Darndest Things*, Geis, 1961; Bill Adler, compiler, *Dear*

(From *Peanuts Classics* by Charles M. Schulz. Illustrated by the author.)

President Johnson, Morrow, 1964; Fritz Ridenour, editor, *I'm a Good Man, But . .* , Regal Books (Glendale, Calif.), 1969.

SIDELIGHTS: "Frequently in the evenings I went to the barbershop to wait for my father to finish work and then walk home with him. He loved to read the comic strips, and we discussed them together and worried about what was going to happen next to certain of the characters. On Saturday evening, I would run up to the local drugstore at nine o'clock when the Sunday papers were delivered, and buy the two Minneapolis papers. I used to wonder if I would ever see my own comics in those papers.

"My mother also encouraged me in my drawing, but, never lived to see any of my work published. She died a long lingering death from cancer when I was twenty, and it was a loss from which I sometimes believe I never recovered.

"When I was thirteen, we were given a black and white dog who turned out to be the forerunner of Snoopy. He was a mixed breed and slightly larger than the beagle Snoopy is supposed to be. He probably had a little pointer in him and some other kind of hound, but he was a wild creature; I don't believe he was ever completely tamed.

"He had a 'vocabulary' of approximately fifty words, and he loved to ride in the car. He waited every day for my dad to come home from the barbershop, and on Saturday evenings, just before nine, he always put his paws on my dad's chair to let him know it was time to get the newspapers.

"When I decided to create the dog in Peanuts, I used the general appearance of Spike, with similar markings. I had decided that the dog in the strip was to be named 'Sniffy,' until one day, just before the strip was actually to be published, I was walking past a newsstand and glanced down at the rows of comic magazines. There I saw one about a dog named Sniffy, so I had to think of another name. Fortunately, before I even got home, I recalled my mother once saying that if we ever had another dog, we should name him 'Snoopy.'

"When I was fourteen, I had a summer which I shall always remember. We had organized our own neighborhood baseball team, but we never played on a strict schedule, for we didn't know when we could find another team to play. A playground director came up with the idea that we should organize four teams and have a summer league. Our team came in first place, probably because we practiced more than the other teams, and one day I actually pitched a no-hit, no-run game. It was really a great summer.

"I still think the challenges to be faced in sports work marvelously as a caricature of the challenges that we face in the more serious aspects of our lives. Anytime I experience a crushing defeat in bowling, or have a bad night at bridge, or fail to qualify in the opening round of a golf tournament, I am able to transfer my frustrations to poor Charlie Brown.

"The summer camp ideas are a result of my having absolutely no desire as a child to be sent away to a summer camp. To me that was the equivalent of being drafted. When World War II came along, I met it with the same lack of enthusiasm.

"The three years I spent in the Army taught me all I need to know about loneliness, and my sympathy for the loneliness that all of us experience is dropped heavily upon poor Charlie Brown. I know what it is to have to spend days, evenings and weekends by myself, and I also know how uncomfortable anxiety can be. I worry about almost all there is in life to worry about, and because I worry, Charlie Brown has to worry.

"When I was just out of high school, I started to submit cartoons to most of the major magazines, as all ambitious amateurs do, but received the ordinary rejection slips and no encouragement. After World War II, however, I set about in earnest to sell my work. I visited several places in the Twin Cities to try to get some job in whatever art department might be able to use my limited talents, but I was unsuccessful. I was almost hired one day to letter tombstones, and was glad when the man did not call me back the next day for I had already begun to worry what my friends might say when I told them about my new job.

"A short while later I was hired by an art correspondence school. My job there was to correct some of the basic lessons, and it introduced me to a roomful of people, who did much to affect my later life.

"Some of the people who worked at the correspondence school with me have remained friends all of these years, and I have used the names of several in the strip. Charlie Brown was named after my good friend, Charlie Brown, whose desk was across the room. I recall perfectly the day he came over and first looked at the little cartoon face that had been named after him. 'Is that what he looks like?' he said with dismay. The characters of Linus and Frieda were also named after friends of mine who were instructors.

"During this time I continued to mail my cartoons out to major newspaper syndicates. In the spring of 1950 I accumulated a batch of some of the better cartoons I had been drawing for the St. Paul paper and mailed them off to United Feature Syndicate in New York City.

"I don't know how much time went by without my hearing from them, but I'm sure it was at least six weeks. Convinced that my drawings had been lost in the mail, I finally wrote them a letter describing the drawings I had sent and asking them if they could recall receiving anything similar. If not, I wanted to know so that I could put a tracer on the lost cartoons. Instead, I received a very nice letter from their editorial director who said they were very interested in my work and would I care to come to New York and talk about it?

"This was an exciting trip. When I arrived at the syndicate offices early in the morning, no one other than the receptionist was there. I had brought along a new comic strip I had been working on, rather than the panel cartoons which United Feature Syndicate had seen. I simply wanted to give them a better view of my work.

"I told the receptionist that I had not had breakfast yet, so I would go out and eat and then return. When I got back to the syndicate offices they had already opened up the package I had left there and in that short time had decided they would rather publish the strip than the panel. This made me very happy, for I really preferred the strip myself.

"I returned to Minneapolis filled with great hope for the future and asked a certain little girl to marry me. When she turned me down and married someone else, there was no doubt that Charlie Brown was on his way. Losers get started early.

"The initial theme of 'Peanuts' was based on the cruelty that exists among children. I recall all too vividly the struggle which takes place out on the playground. This is a struggle which adults grow away from and seem to forget about. Adults learn to protect themselves.

"In this day of organized sports for children, we forget how difficult it once was for smaller children to set up any kind of ballgame at a playground because so often there were older and bigger kids to interrupt the fun. I have always despised bullies, and even though someone once suggested that I have much psychological bullying going on in 'Peanuts,' I do consciously try to stay away from that sort of thing.

"As the strip progressed from the fall of the year 1950, the characters began to change. Charlie Brown was a flippant little guy who soon turned into the loser he is known as today.

"As Charlie Brown developed, so did characters such as Lucy, Schroeder and Linus. Snoopy was the slowest to develop, and it was his eventually walking around on two feet that turned him into a lead character. It has certainly been difficult to keep him from taking over the feature.

"There are various origins for the characters. Charlie Brown is supposed to represent what is sometimes called 'everyman.' When I was small, I believed that my face was so bland that people would not recognize me if they saw me someplace other than where they normally would. I was sincerely surprised if I happened to be in the downtown area of St. Paul, shopping with my mother, and we would bump into a fellow student at school, or a teacher, and they recognized me. I thought that my ordinary appearance was a perfect disguise. It was this weird kind of thinking that prompted Charlie Brown's round, ordinary face.

"Linus came from a drawing that I made one day of a face almost like the one he now has. I experimented with some wild hair, and I showed the sketch to a friend of mine who sat near me at the correspondence school whose name was Linus Maurer. He thought it was kind of funny, and we both agreed that it might make a good new character for the strip.

"It seemed appropriate that I should name the character Linus. It also seemed that Linus would fit very well as Lucy's younger brother. Lucy had already been in the strip from the beginning.

"We called our oldest daughter Meredith a fussbudget when she was very small, and from this I applied the term to Lucy. Schroeder was named after a young boy with whom I used to caddy at a golf course in St. Paul. I don't recall ever knowing his first name, but just Schroeder seemed right for the character in the strip even before he became the great musician he now is.

"One night, over ten years after I began drawing 'Peanuts,' I had a dream in which I created a new character whose name was a combination of Mexican and Swedish. Why in the world I had such a dream and would think of such a name as José Peterson is a mystery to me. Most of the time things that are a complete riot when you are dreaming are not the least bit funny when you wake up.

"In this case, however, it seemed like a good idea, so I developed a story about the arrival of José Peterson in the neighborhood, and he has remained ever since, usually playing on Peppermint Patty's baseball team.

"Patty has been a good addition for me, and I think could almost carry another strip by herself. A dish of candy sitting in our living room inspired her name. So in this case I

(From *Peanuts Classics* by Charles M. Schulz. Illustrated by the author.)

Something about the Author

created the character to fit the name, and Peppermint Patty came into being. Her little friend Marcie, who is always addressing her as 'sir,' has also been a good addition to the strip.

"Snoopy's appearance and personality have changed probably more than those of any of the other characters. I had observed that there were many neighborhood dogs that seemed almost smarter than the children who were their masters. The dogs seemed to tolerate the silly things the kids did; they seemed to be very wise. This was one of the initial themes of Snoopy which I have built upon in many ways. Snoopy refuses to be caught in the trap of doing ordinary things like chasing and retrieving sticks, and he refuses to take seriously his role as the devoted dog who greets his master when he returns home from school. In recent years I have played up the gag that he doesn't even remember his master's name but simply thinks of him as 'that roundheaded kid.'

"Some of my ideas for 'Peanuts' can be traced back to my own childhood. I have drawn many cartoons showing the children standing in line to buy tickets to a movie because my memories of Saturday afternoons at the Park Theater in St. Paul are still so vivid.

"I have never been a very successful kite flyer, and have used the excuse that I never lived where there were good areas to fly kites. When I was growing up, we always lived in residential areas which had too many trees and too many telephone wires. Recollections of those handicaps inspired Charlie Brown's troubles with kite flying. As I grew older and tried to fly kites for my own children, I discovered that I still had the same problems. I observed that when a kite becomes caught in a tall tree, it is irretrievable and gradually disappears over a period of several weeks. Now obviously the kite had to go someplace, so it seemed to me that the tree must be eating it. This is how the series developed about Charlie Brown's violent battles with his local 'kite-eating tree.'

"Direct ideas have been much more rare. Our youngest daughter, Jill, came up to me one day and said, 'I just discovered something. If you hold your hands upside down, you get the opposite of what you pray for.' I used this as an idea exactly as she said it.

"Another time our second daughter, Amy, provided me with an idea which I think came out as well as any that I have ever drawn. The entire family was around the dinner table and, for some reason, Amy seemed particularly noisy that evening. After putting up with this for about ten minutes, I turned to her and said, 'Amy, couldn't you be quiet for just a little while!' She said nothing, but picked up a piece of bread and began to butter it with a knife and asked, 'Am I buttering too loud for you?' This was very easily translated into a Linus and Lucy Sunday page.

"Even after twenty-five years, I still enjoy going to work each day, though friends who know me well can testify to the fact that I never actually use the term 'work.' If I have to say that I will not be free to do something on a certain day, I will always put it: 'I have to go to the studio and draw funny pictures.'

"It could be a superstition, but I guess it is really that I don't want anyone to think that what I do is that much

Happiness is sleeping in the back seat on the way home. ■
(From *Happiness is a Sad Song* by Charles M. Schulz. Illustrated by the author.)

work. It is one of the few situations in my life where I feel totally secure. When I sit behind the drawing board I feel that I am in command. I am comfortable in my studio and I am reasonably proud of many of the things that I have drawn. I think that I have done my share toward contributing to the advancement of my profession and this also makes me feel proud.

"To create something out of nothing is a wonderful experience. To take a blank piece of paper and draw characters that people love and worry about is extremely satisfying. I hope very much that I will be allowed to do it for another twenty-five years."

Schulz is the only cartoonist ever to have won the Reuben award (the cartoonist's equivalent of the "Oscar," designed by and named after Rube Goldberg) twice, in 1955 and again in 1964. In a 1969 *Saturday Review* article entitled "The Not-So-Peanuts World of Charles M. Schulz," John Tebbel wrote that "the total income from the strip, including that of its twenty-one licensed subsidiaries, has been estimated at [up to] $50,000,000 a year," and that "Peanuts" has "audiences in more than 1,600 newspapers around the world. Charlie Brown and his friends speak in twelve languages."

Schulz added an extra dimension to Charlie Brown with his introduction to television in 1965, and his associates, Lee Mendelson and Bill Melendez, plan to produce a new special every year. "Peanuts" subsidiaries manufacture everything from clothing, toys, stationery, and cosmetics to furniture, lunch boxes, and Charlie Brown baseballs, and dozens of new applications for licenses roll in every day. Reprints of "Peanuts," handled by seven different publishers at last count, have passed the 50,000,000 mark; Charlie Brown and his friends have even "emerged as modern evangelists" in Robert L. Short's two books, *The Gospel According to Peanuts,* published by John Knox in 1965, and *The Parables of Peanuts,* Harper, 1968.

(From *Reviens, Snoopy* by Charles M. Schulz. Illustrated by the author.)

The hit musical, "You're a Good Man, Charlie Brown," adapted by Clark Gesner from the comic strip, was first produced Off-Broadway at Theatre 80 St. Marks, March 7, 1967, and has since played all over the world. It was also on NBC's Hallmark Hall of Fame, February 9, 1973. The book of the same title, including music, lyrics, and adaptation by Gesner, was published by Random House in 1967, and an original cast recording of the music from the play was released by M-G-M Records the same year. The musical, "Snoopy!!!," opened at the Little Fox Theatre in San Francisco, December 8, 1975. A documentary on Schulz, produced by Mendelson and Melendez, was broadcast by CBS-TV in 1969. Schulz, Mendelson, and Warren Lockhart formed Snoopy Company in 1970 to create and develop a 300-acre Charlie Brown amusement park, probably on the Coast.

Snoopy has been adopted by NASA as a promotional device, and, "Snoopy emblems are now worn by more than 800 members of the manned space flight team as rewards for outstanding work." As everyone knows, the ubiquitous beagle made international history as the official name of the LEM (Lunar Excursion Module) of the Apollo 10 manned flight to the moon in 1969. Great Pumpkin sightings are reported almost as often as UFO's, and Schroeder and his toy piano have been immortalized in the stained glass window of the Westminster Presbyterian Church in Buffalo, New York, along with Bach, Martin Luther, Duke Ellington, and Dr. Albert Schweitzer.

HOBBIES AND OTHER INTERESTS: Outdoor sports, especially ice hockey and golf.

FOR MORE INFORMATION SEE: Saturday Evening Post, January 12, 1957, April 25, 1964; *Look,* July 22, 1958; Carmen Richards, *Minnesota Writers,* Denison, 1961; *Newsweek,* March 6, 1961; *Seventeen,* January, 1962; *Time,* April 9, 1965, January 5, 1970; *Village Voice,* March 16, 1967; *Life,* March 17, 1967; *New Yorker,* March 18, 1967; *New York Times Magazine,* April 16, 1967; *Redbook,* December, 1967; *Punch,* February 7, 1968; *Christian*

Science Monitor, November 29, 1968, November 11, 1970; *Saturday Review,* April 12, 1969; *New York Times,* May 26, 1969, June 2, 1971; *Valuator,* spring, 1969; *U.S. Catholic,* July, 1969; *Business World,* December 20, 1969; Lee Mendelson (with Schulz), *Charlie Brown and Charlie Schulz,* World Publishing, 1970; *Washington Post,* April 4, 1970; *TV Guide,* October 28, 1972; *Third Book of Junior Authors,* edited by de Montreville and Hill, H. W. Wilson, 1972; *Publishers Weekly,* August 4, 1975; *People,* September 29, 1975; *Family Circle,* October, 1975.

SCHWARTZ, Anne Powers 1913-
(Anne Powers)

PERSONAL: Born May 7, 1913, in Cloquet, Minn.; daughter of John P. and Maud (Lynch) Powers; married Harold A. Schwartz, 1938; children: Weldon, Lynn. *Education:* Attended University of Minnesota, Miss Brown's School of Business. *Religion:* Roman Catholic. *Home:* 3800 North Newhall St., Milwaukee, Wis. *Agent:* Larry Sternig Literary Agency, 742 Robertson St., Milwaukee, Wis. 53213.

CAREER: Author. Instructor at summer workshop sponsored by University of Wisconsin at Rhinelander, 1964; lecturer in college of journalism at Marquette University. *Member:* Bookfellows of Milwaukee, Allied Authors, Fictioneers. *Awards, honors:* Fiction award, National Federa-

ANNE POWERS SCHWARTZ

tion of Press Women, for *The Gallant Years*, 1946; Theta Sigma Nu award.

WRITINGS—Under name Anne Powers: *The Gallant Years*, Bobbs, 1946; *Ride East! Ride West!*, Bobbs, 1947, young people's edition (under title *Ride with Danger*), Bobbs, 1959; *No Wall So High*, Bobbs, 1949; *The Iron-master*, Bobbs, 1951; *The Only Sin*, Bobbs, 1953; *The Thousand Fires*, Bobbs, 1957; *No King But Caesar*, Doubleday, 1960; *Rachel*, Pinnacle, 1973.

WORK IN PROGRESS: Fictionalized biography of the four queens in England during the 15th-century Wars of Roses. ("told entirely through the eyes of these four women who made history yet are scarcely mentioned in texts on the period.")

SIDELIGHTS: Researched two of her books in Europe; most of them have appeared in foreign editions and in paperback.

SEARLE, Kathryn Adrienne 1942-
(Kathryn)

PERSONAL: Born July 3, 1942, in Lytham, Lancashire, England; daughter of Charles William (a bank manager) and Margaret (Baxter) Marsh; married Keith Searle (a work study officer), November 20, 1970. *Education:* Wentworth Castle Training College, graduate (with distinction in art), 1963. *Home:* 75 Sudbourne Rd., London S.W.2, England.

CAREER: Formerly a primary teacher in Oxfordshire and Cheshire, England; free-lance commercial artist. Work as an artist also includes painting, drawing, and sculpture.

WRITINGS—Self-illustrated children's books under name Kathryn: *James,* Basil Blackwell, 1966; *James and the Hat,* Basil Blackwell, 1967; *James and Lucy,* Basil Blackwell, 1968.

SIDELIGHTS: "I first came to write stories from my experiences in teaching five-to-six-year olds. We never seemed to have enough story material. I felt there was a need for more books of a suitable size to show to a small group whilst telling the story, therefore the pictures were of great importance to help hold that interest. In my own books the characters emerged pictorially first and the story wound round them."

Two stories, with pictures about James, were used on the B.B.C. TV program, "Playschool."

SERAGE, Nancy 1924-

PERSONAL: Born March 24, 1924, in Columbus, Ohio; daughter of Francis L. and Ophelia (Byers) Serage. *Education:* Ohio State University, B.F.A., 1945, M.A., 1946. *Home and office:* 3880 San Rafael Ave., Los Angeles, Calif. 90065.

CAREER: Toledo Museum of Art, Toledo, Ohio, docent, 1946-47; Cleveland Museum of Art, Cleveland, Ohio, docent, 1948-57; Self-Realization Fellowship, Los Angeles, Calif., monastic, 1958—.

Then the newborn prince spoke and said, "I am born to bring happiness to the world and to destroy all that makes sadness."
■ (From *The Prince Who Gave Up a Throne* by Nancy Serage. Illustrated by Kazue Mizumura.)

WRITINGS: The Prince Who Gave Up a Throne: A Story of the Buddha, T. Y. Crowell, 1966.

WORK IN PROGRESS: Children's biography of a great yogic master of this century.

SIDELIGHTS: "The story of the Buddha was for years an inspiration to me, also the story of St. Francis of Assisi. Both had all the world could offer but found it did not give happiness. Both had the strength to give up their material goods and way of life to seek the Giver of All Gifts. After telling the story of the Buddha to children in my work for about ten years, I found my own spiritual teacher and path and was able to take steps to turn my life Godward as I had always secretly longed to do.

"Because I suffered very deeply at one time not believing in the Divine, His love and power for good behind all life, I have always wanted to save others from similar suffering, to help them direct their thoughts, hearts and lives toward the one source of happiness."

SERVELLO, Joe 1932-

PERSONAL: Born June 19, 1932, in Altoona, Pa., son of Domenick Joseph and Mary (Spallone) Servello; married Ann Louise Breniser (a teacher), June 18, 1969; children: Maria. *Education:* The Pennsylvania State University, B.S., 1959. *Home and Office:* 1420 Surrey Lane, Overbrook Hills, Pa. 19151.

CAREER: Actor, television art director, graphic artist, muralist, teacher. Director of plays at Friends Central School in Philadelphia, Pa. Trustee of the Bridges of Understanding Foundation. *Military service:* U.S. Navy, 1950-54. *Awards, honors:* Wisconsin State Historical Society, award of merit; *Songs of the Chippewa* and *The Supreme, Superb, Exalted and Delightful, One and Only Magic Building* were both nominated for the Caldecott Award.

ILLUSTRATOR: Margaret Mitchell Preston, *Toolittle,* Viking, 1969; Elizabeth Baldwin Hazelton, *The Day the Fish Went Wild,* Scribner, 1969; William Kotzwinkle, *The Firemen,* Pantheon, 1970; William Kotzwinkle, *The Day the Gang Got Rich,* Viking, 1970; William Kotzwinkle, *Elephant Boy,* Farrar, Straus, 1970; George Panetta, *A Kitchen is Not a Tree,* Grosset, 1970; William Kotzwinkle, *Return of Crazy Horse,* Farrar, Straus, 1970; George Panetta, *The Shoeshine Boys,* Grosset, 1971; William Kotzwinkle, *The Ship That Came Down the Gutter,* Pantheon, 1971; William Kotzwinkle, *The Supreme, Superb, Exalted and Delightful, One and Only Magic Building,* Farrar,

(From *Songs of the Chippewa* by John Bierhorst. Illustrated by Joe Servello.)

Straus, 1972; William Kotzwinkle, *The Oldest Man,* Pantheon, 1973; John Bierhorst, *Songs of the Chippewa,* Farrar, Straus, 1973; William Kotzwinkle, *Up the Alley with Jack and Joe,* Macmillan, 1975; William Kotzwinkle, *The Leopards Tooth,* Seabury, 1975.

SIDELIGHTS: "I enjoy illustrating, but I also paint and do some sculpture and mural work. I became interested in children's books at an early age (I lived near a library) and still remember the great pleasure I got from picturebooks, especially the D'Aulaire's works. I try to suit the style of my illustrations to the story. I admire a great many children's book artists especially N. C. Wyeth, Lynd Ward, James Daugherty, Maurice Sendak and Ezra Jack Keats. I work hard to improve myself in my illustrations. My ambition is to *write and illustrate* my own books."

SERWER, Blanche L. 1910-

PERSONAL: Born July 13, 1910, in New York, N.Y.; daughter of Philip (a businessman) and Rebecca (Isaacson) Luria; married Zachary A. Serwer, May 15, 1938 (died May 15, 1961), married Nahum A. Bernstein (a lawyer), December 29, 1974; children: Philip, Daniel, Jeremy (all by first marriage). *Education:* Barnard College, B.A., 1931; Teachers Institute of Jewish Theological Seminary of America, B.H.L., 1931; The City College of New York, M.S., 1960; New York University, Ph.D., 1966. *Religion:* Jewish. *Home and office:* 340 East 64th St., New York, N.Y. 10021.

JOE SERVELLO

Other work includes *Comparison of Reading Approaches in First-Grade Teaching With Disadvantage Children Cooperative Research Project 2677,* The City University, 1966; *Experimental Model School Program for Children with Specific Learning Disabilities* (Title VI-A), ESEA, 1970; *Who is Who and What's What?* in *Children's Digest,* May, 1971. Articles have also appeared in *Reading Research Quarterly, Exceptional Child, Elementary English, Journal of Special Education, Journal of Perceptual Motor Skills.*

WORK IN PROGRESS: Book of Jewish folklore, with Professor DovNoy of Hebrew University in Jerusalem; research in psycho-social aspects of cleft-palate families.

SIDELIGHTS: "I had two reasons for writing *Let's Steal the Moon* for children, the first is that the tales, some of which had not been written down before had been 'simmering' in my mind since I had heard them as a child. The second is that folktales and folklore have a marvelous way of zooming into the fantasy life of a child."

SEULING, Barbara 1937-

PERSONAL: Surname pronounced Soo-ling; born July 22, 1937, in Brooklyn, N.Y.; daughter of Kaspar Joseph (a postman) and Helen (Gadie) Seuling. *Education:* Attended Hunter College, 1955-57, Columbia University, 1957-59, and New School for Social Research; also studied art and illustration privately. *Home and office:* 55 West 92nd St.,

BLANCHE L. SERWER

CAREER: The City College of New York, New York, N.Y., psychologist in counseling and testing, 1960-64; Queens College, Queens, N.Y., psychologist in speech and hearing center, 1960-64; The City University of New York, New York, N.Y., research associate, 1964-66; Harvard University, Cambridge, Mass., research associate and visiting lecturer, 1966-69; Boston University, Boston, Mass., associate professor, 1969-73, professor, 1973-75; Charles River Counseling Center, Newton, Mass., senior psychologist, 1973-75. Consultantships to SEEK at City College, Revere School Department in Massachusetts and others; board of professional affairs, professional advisory committee of Cambridge Association for Children with Learning Disorders, committee for integrated schools in New Rochelle, chairman; board of directors of child guidance clinic of New Rochelle; New Rochelle committee on problems of the aging; New Rochelle committee on character and citizenship. *Member:* Fellow of American Orthopsychiatric Association, American Psychological Association, American Association for Humanistic Psychology, Inter-American Society for Psychology, American Society for Group Psychotherapy, Psychodrama.

WRITINGS: Let's Steal the Moon, Little, Brown, 1970.

BARBARA SEULING

New York, N.Y. 10025. *Agent:* Russell & Volkening, Inc., 551 Fifth Ave., New York, N.Y. 10017.

CAREER: Has worked for an investment firm, insurance companies, a university, and at "Progressland" at the New York World's Fair; Dell Publishing Co., New York, N.Y., children's book editor, 1965-70; J. B. Lippincott (publishers), New York, N.Y., children's book editor, 1971-73; free-lance writer and illustrator, 1967—. Consultant to New York Foundling Hospital; book lecturer at local schools. *Member:* Society of Children's Book Writers, Children's Writers and Artists Collaborative.

WRITINGS—All self-illustrated: *Freaky Facts,* Xerox Education Publications, 1972; *More Freaky Facts,* Xerox Education Publications, 1973; *Monster Mix,* Xerox Education Publications, 1975; *The Last Legal Spitball and Other Little Known Facts About Sports,* Doubleday, 1975; *You Can't Eat Peanuts in Church and Other Little Known Laws,* Doubleday, 1975; *Abracadabra! Creating Your Own Magic Show from Beginning to End,* Messner, 1975; *Monster Madness,* Xerox Education Publications, 1976; *The Teeny Tiny Woman,* Viking, 1976; *The Loudest Screen Kiss and Other Little Known Movie Facts,* Doubleday, 1976; (with Winnette Glasgow) *Fun With Crafts,* Xerox Education Publications, 1976.

Illustrator: Wilma Thompson, *That Barbara!,* Delacorte, 1969; Nan Hayden Agle, *Tarr of Belway Smith,* Seabury Press, 1969; Stella Pevsner, *Break a Leg!,* Crown, 1969; Antonia Barber, *The Affair of the Rockerbye Baby,* Delacorte, 1970; Stella Pevsner, *Footsteps on the Stairs,* Crown, 1970; Moses Howard, *The Ostrich Chase,* Holt, 1974. Contributor to journals for and about children and children's books, including *Cricket.*

WORK IN PROGRESS: Several picture books; a book tentatively titled *The Self-Tipping Hat and Other Dumb Ideas,* for Doubleday; a novel.

SIDELIGHTS: "I was born and raised in Bensonhurst, Brooklyn, a short walk from Gravesend bay. We'd go there on Sundays for walks or bike rides or picnics, and watch the ships go by, on their way to sea. I remember learning to fly a box kite there.

"We played in the streets, every imaginable game plus a few we made up. My older brother made one up called 'Maze,' which became an institution on our block.... Mostly we stayed on our own block, but occasionally wandered off to a friend's. We walked a lot in those days ... 12 blocks to school, 15 to church, and went even further on our roller skates or bikes. One adventure was riding along the bay on our bikes to Fort Hamilton, then ferrying across to Staten Island and back on the same dime (a nickel for me, a nickel for my bike).

"Saturdays we spent at the library and/or the movies. For 25 cents we got to see two features (one in color usually), several cartoons, a newsreel, a serial, and sometimes a live contest with prizes on the stage. I won one of these once, for being the first one to whistle after consuming a dry saltine cracker.

"My father rented half a garage for five dollars a month which he used as a workshop. He hung up a 'Handy Andy' sign and did minor repairs on bicycles, skates, baby car-

riages and shopping carts for people in the neighborhood. I remember only occasionally his charging anything for the repairs. It was his fun. . . . The workshop was a great place for a kid ... alongside the drawers (made of cheeseboxes) marked 'nuts,' 'bolts,' 'screws,' and 'washers,' were some marked 'skate keys,' 'marbles,' 'crayons,' and so forth. There were always huge crates of games and comic books, too, and a reassembled, repainted, recycled bicycle for every member of the family. When I was nine a new brother came along to replace me as the baby of the family, and he practically grew up around that workshop.

"In junior high school I was voted wittiest in the class. Mother insists from that time on that I took after her ... she'd received a similar honor in her time ... but there's no denying that I get my peculiar, flat feet from my father. Anyway, I've been clowning around ever since.

"My pleasures outside of my work are friends, traveling, my dog Rusty, summering in Vermont, exchanging ideas about anything, planning new adventures so that life never gets dull, swimming in exotic places, banjo music, frogs, liverwurst, movies, riding a motor cycle when no one I know is watching, reading, and a sense of humor.

"One of the most valuable and interesting things I do is talking with young people about books, in schools and libraries and through correspondence."

SEXTON, Anne (Harvey)   1928-1974

PERSONAL: Born November 9, 1928, in Newton, Mass.; daughter of Ralph Churchill (a salesman) and Mary Gray (Staples) Harvey; married Alfred M. Sexton II (a salesman), August 16, 1948; children: Linda, Joyce. *Education:* Attended Rogers Hall, 1947, Garland Junior College, 1947-48; Radcliffe Institute for Independent Study, scholar, 1961-63. *Home:* 14 Black Oak Rd., Weston, Mass. 02193. *Agent:* Sterling Lord, 75 East 55th St., New York, N.Y. 10022; (lectures) Redpath Bureau, 507 Rockingham St., Rochester, N.Y.

ANNE SEXTON

Now they could only sit with the bars between them and talk. ■
(From *Joey and the Birthday Present* by Maxine Kumin and Anne Sexton. Illustrated by Evaline Ness.)

CAREER: Fashion model in Boston, Mass., 1950-51; gave poetry readings in eastern area and at colleges throughout the country. *Member:* Poetry Society of America, Royal Society of Literature (fellow), New England Poetry Club. *Awards, honors:* Robert Frost fellowship at Bread Loaf Writers Conference, 1959; *Audience* Poetry Prize, 1958-59; Levinson Prize for seven poems in *Poetry* Magazine, 1962; American Academy of Arts and Letters traveling fellowship, 1963-64; Ford Foundation grant for year's residence with professional theater, 1964-65.

WRITINGS: To Bedlam and Part Way Back, Houghton, 1960; *All My Pretty Ones,* Houghton, 1962; (with Maxine W. Kumin) *Eggs of Things* (juvenile), Putnam, 1963; *Selected Poems,* Oxford University Press, 1964; *Live or Die* (new poems), Houghton, 1966; *Love Poems,* Houghton, 1969; *Transformations* (poems), Houghton, 1971; (with Maxine Kumin) *Joey and the Birthday Present* (juvenile), McGraw, 1971; *The Book of Folly,* Houghton, 1972; *The Death Notebooks* (poems), Houghton, 1974; *The Awful Rowing Toward God* (poems), Houghton, 1975.

Poems in anthologies: *The Partisan Review Anthology; The Hudson Review Anthology,* edited by Fredrick Morgan, 1962; *Modern American Poetry,* edited by Louis Untermeyer, 1963; *The New Poets of England and America,* edited by Hall and Pack, 1963; *The Modern American Poets,* edited by John Malcolm Brinnin and Bill Read, 1963; and others. Short story in *New World Writing,* Volume XVI, 1960. Contributor of poetry to magazines, including *Harper's, New Yorker, Partisan Review, Saturday Review, Nation.*

WORK IN PROGRESS: "Tell Me Your Answer True," two-act play.

SIDELIGHTS: Anne Sexton believed that, for her, poetry is a very personal experience. She told Patricia Marx that her first poems were written during recovery from a nervous breakdown "and I got more and more serious about it, and I started out writing almost a poem a day. It was a kind of rebirth at 29." She mentioned that she had been likened to Robert Lowell and W. D. Snodgrass and, explaining the comparison, she said, "I think we all kind of got born into this about the same time, writing in a certain frank style."

Although she enjoyed the work of several contemporary poets she told Marx: "If anything influenced me it was W. D. Snodgrass' *Heart's Needle.* I had written about half of my first book when I read that poem, and it moved me to such an extent—it's about a child, and he has to give up his child, which seems to be one of my themes, and I didn't have my own daughter at the time—that I ran up to my mother-in-law's where she was living and got her back. I could only keep her at that time for a week, but the poem moved me to *action.* It so changed me, and undoubtedly it must have influenced my own poetry. At the time everyone said, 'You can't write this way. It's too personal; it's confessional; you can't write this, Anne,' and everyone was discouraging me. But then I saw Snodgrass doing what I was doing, and it kind of gave me permission."

"Mercy Street" a play by Anne Sexton was produced at the American Place Theatre, New York City, October 11, 1969 and was published by Studio Duplicating Service, New York, 1969.

She recorded some of her poetry titled "Anne Sexton Reads Her Poetry" on Phonodisc Records, 1974.

FOR MORE INFORMATION SEE: Christian Science Monitor, September 1, 1960; *Epoch,* fall, 1960; *Poetry,* February, 1961; *Atlantic,* November, 1962; *Reporter,* January 3, 1963; *Nation,* February 23, 1963; *New Yorker,* April 27, 1963; *New York Times Book Review,* April 28, 1963; *Harper's,* September, 1963; *Hudson Review,* winter, 1965-66; *Saturday Review,* December 31, 1966; *New York Times,* October 6, 1974; *Washington Post,* October 6, 1974; *Time,* October 14, 1974; *Publishers Weekly,* October 28, 1974; *AB Bookman's Weekly,* December 2, 1974; *World Authors: 1950-1970,* edited by John Wakeman, H. W. Wilson, 1975.

(Died October 4, 1974)

SEYMOUR, Alta Halverson

PERSONAL: Born in Deer Park, Wis.; daughter of Gilbert (a merchant) and Matilda (Finke) Halverson; married George Seymour (an economic consultant), June 12, 1922; children: Jean (Mrs. Robert Gardner). *Education:* University of Minnesota, B.A., 1921, M.A., 1923. *Home:* 12 Elizabeth Ct. W., Oak Park, Ill. 60302.

CAREER: Former owner and manager of public stenographic company in Pasadena and Los Angeles, Calif.; free-lance writer, mainly of juveniles. Member: Chicago Children's Reading Round Table, Nineteenth Century Club (Oak Park, Ill.; chairman of literature department, 1943-44), Phi Beta Kappa, Lambda Alpha Psi, Delta Phi Lambda. Awards, honors: Honorable mention, Midland Authors, for Toward Morning, as one of three best juveniles from Middle West in 1961.

WRITINGS: Timothy Keeps a Secret, Grosset, 1939; On the Edge of the Fjord (Junior Literary Guild selection), Westminster, 1944; Galewood Crossing, Westminster, 1945; The Tangled Skein (Junior Literary Guild selection), Westminster, 1946; A Grandma for Christmas, Westminster, 1946; At Snug Harbor Inn, Westminster, 1947; The Secret of the Hidden Room, Westminster, 1948.

The Christmas Stove: A Story of Switzerland, Follett, 1951; Arne and the Christmas Star (about Norway), Follett, 1952; The Christmas Donkey (France), Follett, 1953; Kaatje and the Christmas Compass (Holland), Follett, 1954; The Top o' Christmas Morning: A Story of Ireland, Follett, 1955; Erik Christmas Camera (Sweden), Follett, 1956; When the Dikes Broke, Follett, 1958; Toward Morning: A Story of the Hungarian Freedom Fighters, Follett, 1961; Charles Steinmetz, Follett, 1965.

Operettas with Helen Wing: "The Inn of the Golden Cheese"; "Mulligan's Magic"; "Going to the Fair"; "The Lemonade Stand." Contributor of serials, short stories, and articles to magazines for children; contributor of historical and biographical articles to Christian Science Monitor and to periodicals.

WORK IN PROGRESS: A biography of John Muir; a collection of Christmas stories.

SIDELIGHTS: Excerpts from Alta Seymour's books have been published in school readers and dramatized on radio and television, and her books have been translated into Italian, Spanish, and Dutch, and issued in Braille. She speaks German and Norwegian, reads Spanish, some Greek.

HOBBIES AND OTHER INTERESTS: Weaving, gardening, refinishing antiques, reading, making room-size braided rugs, travel.

FOR MORE INFORMATION SEE: Chicago Schools Journal, May-June, 1951; Christian Science Monitor, May 21, 1952; Oak Leaves, Oak Park, Ill., November 22, 1956.

SHANKS, Ann Zane (Kushner)

PERSONAL: Born in Brooklyn, N.Y.; daughter of Louis and Sadye (Rosenthal) Kushner; married Ira Zane (deceased); married Robert Horton Shanks (a television network vice-president), September 25, 1959; children: (first marriage) Jennifer, Anthony; (second marriage) John. Education: Attended Carnegie-Mellon University and Columbia University. Home: 201B East 82nd St., New York, N.Y.

CAREER: Photographer, film maker, writer. Columbia Broadcasting Co., New York, N.Y., script editor, 1959;

National Broadcasting Co., New York, producer of local television series, "Women on the Move," 1968; Comco Productions, New York, president, 1973-76. Producer and director of film shorts, "Central Park," Columbia Pictures, 1969, "Tivoli," 1972, and "Denmark: A Loving Embrace," Danish National Tourist Office, 1973; producer and director of syndicated television series, "American Life Style," 1972-75. Photographs have been exhibited at Museum of Modern Art, Museum of the City of New York, Metropolitan Museum of Art, Jewish Museum, Caravan Gallery, and others. Moderator of special symposia at Museum of Modern Art, Educational Alliance, and Village Camera Club, all New York.

MEMBER: American Society of Magazine Photographers (member of board of governors, 1969-71), Overseas Press Club. Awards, honors: Cine Golden Eagle Awards, 1969, 1973, 1975; Cambodia Film Festival Award, 1971, for "Central Park"; San Francisco Film Festival Award, 1971, and American Film Festival Award, 1972, both for "Tivoli"; International Film and Television Festival Gold Awards, 1972, 1973, 1974, 1975, for "American Life Style"; received four awards in Photography magazine international competitions, and three National Housing Yearbook competition awards.

WRITINGS—Self-illustrated: About Garbage and Stuff

ANN ZANE SHANKS

Their friend John, near the bottles in the back, likes to feel the moving belt while it carries the food along at the checkout counter. ■ (From *About Garbage and Stuff* by Ann Zane Shanks. Photographs by the author.)

(juvenile), Viking, 1973; *Old Is What You Get* (teenage), Viking, 1976.

Photographer: Bob Shanks, *The Name's the Game*, Chilton, 1961.

Contributor of photographs to *Adolescent Development*, by E. B. Hurlock, McGraw, 3rd edition, 1967, and to textbooks published by Behrman House, Random House, Simon & Schuster, Lippincott, and other houses. Contributor to *New Jewish Encyclopedia*, and other yearbooks and encyclopedias, and to periodicals, including *Life*, *Look*, *Time*, *Esquire*, *New York*, *Camera 35*, *Cosmopolitan*, *Redbook*, *Woman's Day*, and *New York Times*.

SHIELDS, Charles   1944-

PERSONAL: Born July 19, 1944, in Kansas; son of Charles Robert (an engineer) and Eloise (Hensen; a psy-

chologist) Shields. *Education:* Attended University of Southern California, 1962, 1965; El Camino College, A.A., 1965; Art Center College of Design, B.F.A., 1968, M.F.A., 1969. *Home and Office:* 3051 Richmond Blvd., #4, Oakland, Calif. 94611. *Agent:* Daniele Deverin, 226 East 53rd St., New York, N.Y. 10022.

CAREER: Free-lance illustrator; Colorado Mountain College, Glenwood Springs, Colorado, instructor, 1972. *Exhibitions:* Paideia Gallery, Los Angeles, Calif., 1969.

ILLUSTRATOR: John Gardner, *Dragon, Dragon and Other Tales*, Knopf, 1975.

SIDELIGHTS: "I try to approach each illustration as new and totally different than any I have done before. I start with a mood or feeling in mind that I want to convey and work up a light, detailed pencil drawing on illustration board. I then float light washes of acrylic color over areas

She pointed at them with her ivory comb, and instantly the ground opened up and swallowed them and then closed again, not leaving so much as a banner for evidence. ▪ (From *Dragon, Dragon and Other Tales* by John Gardner. Illustrated by Charles Shields.)

of the picture to establish a general color pattern and mood. After that comes many hours and layers of cross-hatching and transparent washes to build up forms, textures and intensity of colors.

"*Dragon, Dragon* is the first children's book I've worked on, though I've done several illustrations for *Sesame Street Magazine*. I enjoy the challenge of doing illustrations of all types, but find a special pleasure and satisfaction in creating visual fantasy worlds for children.

"I feel that too many of childrens' learning experiences are television oriented. Good things are being done on television, but as a dominating force in childrens' lives, it is very limited. By its nature it is an 'action' medium; the viewer is essentially 'carried along' by the flow of sounds and movements.

"Books give a totally different, and I think more valuable kind of experience. I attempt, in my illustrations, to create moods, situations and characters that the young reader can build his or her own thoughts and fantasies upon.

"Looking back, it seems like I was influenced by a different artist or illustrator every week."

FOR MORE INFORMATION SEE: New York Times Book Review, December 7, 1975.

CHARLES SHIELDS

ERIC SHIPTON

SHIPTON, Eric (Earle)   1907-

PERSONAL: Born August 12, 1907, in Ceylon; son of Cecil (a tea planter) and Alice (Earle) Shipton; married Diana Channer, December 16, 1942; children: Nicolas, John. *Home:* The Haye, Bridgnorth, Shropshire, England.

CAREER: British Consul-General at Kashgar, Sinkiang, China, 1940-42, 1946-48; Consular Liason Officer, Iran, 1943-44; Britain Military Mission, Hungary, technical advisor, 1945-46; British Consul General at Kunming, Yunnan, China, 1949-57; advisor to the Chilson Government in Boundary Dispute, 1964-66. *Military service:* Served in Indian Army, 1940. *Awards, honors:* Gold Medal of Royal Geographical Society, 1938; Gold Medal of Royal Scottish Society, 1951; Commander of British Empire (CBE), 1955.

WRITINGS: Nanda Devi, 1935, *Blank on the Map,* 1938, *Upon that Mountain,* 1943, *Mountains of Tartary,* 1951, *Mount Everest Reconnaissance Expedition,* 1951, *Everest,* Frederick Muller (London), 1955, *The North Pole,* Frederich Muller, 1956, *Land of Tempest,* 1963, *Mountain Conquest,* American Heritage, 1966, *That Untravelled World* (autobiography), 1968, *Tierra Del Fuego,* Charles Knight (London), 1972 (all published by Hodder & Stoughton, except where indicated).

WORK IN PROGRESS: Contributing further biographical work on the subject of the Bridges' family in *Tierra Del Fuego.*

SIDELIGHTS: "Most of my books are accounts of my experiences as a mountain explorer—a career which has occupied the main part of my life. I have stressed, in particular, the virtues of simple light travel. *That Untravelled World* is an autobiography. *Everest, The North Pole* and *Mountain Conquest* are historical sketches written for juvenile readers, *Tierra Del Fuego* is a selective history of that region."

SMITH, Jean Pajot   1945-

PERSONAL: Maiden name is pronounced *Pay*-zhoe; born November 14, 1945, in Saline, Mich.; daughter of Lawrence Joseph (a draftsman) and Dorothy May (Peckens) Pajot; married Pat Smith (director of Lansing's Community Design Center), August 19, 1967, divorced; children: Malcolm, Jason. *Education:* Michigan State University, B.F.A., 1968. *Politics:* Independent. *Home and office:* 1515 West Kalamazoo, Lansing, Mich. 48915.

CAREER: Michigan State University, East Lansing, medical illustrator for department of·anatomy, 1965-68; writer, 1973—. Member of National Association for the Advancement of Colored People (NAACP) Emergency Schools Assistance Act Project advisory committee, 1973-74; member of Planning Committee for the Vivian Riddle Elementary School, Lansing.

WRITINGS: Li'l Tuffy and His A.B.C.'s (juvenile), Johnson Publishing Co. (Chicago), 1973; (contributor of medical illustrations) Daris R. Swindler and Charles D. Wood, *An Atlas of Primate Gross Anatomy: Baboons, Chimpanzee, and Man,* University of Washington Press, 1973.

WORK IN PROGRESS: Li'l Tuffy and His Friends, a book for preschool-age children, for Johnson Publishing Co.

SIDELIGHTS: "There are some disadvantages to growing up. Things one loses upon becoming an adult, such as: the fresh approach to life and people, the natural curiosity, the spontaneous, honest response, qualities lost through social conditioning which so beautifully infects a child's imagination. I try to recapture some of this feeling in my work.

"One important aspect of my interest in children's literature is the 'child' within me that never outgrew comics, animated cartoons, Walt Disney, etc. And while I don't still read them for myself I do enjoy the illustrations in the books I read to my sons, Malcolm and Jason.

"Much of what I choose to draw about is generated by my boys' needs and the memories of my childhood. Once in the 1950's I was so impressed by an illustration of the poem *Wincken, Blincken and Nod,* that I faithfully copied it with crayon and presented it to my mother who preserves it in a scrapbook today.

"I've lived in three small towns in Michigan, written copious letters to friends for twenty-two years (which no doubt helped my verbalizing on paper) and invariably included pictures with the letters. Part of this small-town life was lived on a farm and I grew up appreciating the qualities given in both farm and village living.

JEAN PAJOT SMITH

"Throughout my life I've been pictorially oriented, devouring every picture magazine that came through the house, at one time idealizing myself as another illustrator of romantic novels in women's magazines. Then, I fell in love with Michelangelo and his sculpture and suddenly that was my goal, my hero. Finding a job as a medical illustrator while an undergraduate student just seemed to synthesize my adoration of Michelangelo and Da Vinci.

"It took some real sorting and exploring of various media to discover that my real love was my first love—drawing; and creating where I felt it would have the most *social* impact motivated *Li'l Tuffy and His ABC's* and *Li'l Tuffy and his Friends.* Due to my interracial marriage and my own self-educated awareness of the inequalities present throughout our various institutions, (the fact that very few books are geared toward mine and other minority children). *Li'l Tuffy* came forth from my imagination and my left hand. I've been drawing with serious intent for seventeen years and hope that, now, these lines reflect some discipline and relevance. While the vocabulary in both books is minimal, it is derived through the co-operation of my husband, the experience of living in a multi-ethnic environment and an ear for street slang. The Spanish portion of *Li'l Tuffy and His Friends* was done with the aid of a dictionary and a good friend from Chile, Angela Rojas Dedenbach.

"Getting into the children's literature field came about through a request from a friend in the minority book business and our own need to find relevant material to entertain our children. A marketplace research was established and conclusion drawn that a coloring book with a trendy ABC's would be viable and entertaining. Though the content may become dated due to the constant changes inherent in 'slang' languages, I still feel the total message of this particular coloring book will endure.

"Finally, it is marvelous, of course, to see one's work in print and selling well, but the true joy comes in the creative process, when each line comes together as planned and an exciting, childhood scene is 'reality' on my drawing board. I can't wait to start another."

HOBBIES AND OTHER INTERESTS: Sewing, crocheting, refinishing furniture, upholstering, baking bread.

SMITH, Mary Ellen (Mike Smith)

PERSONAL: Born in Melbourne, Fla.; daughter of Charles E. (a teacher) and Addie (a teacher; maiden name, Wallace) Shull; married Tom Q. Smith (a news writer); died June 6, 1954. *Education:* Attended Rollins College and Chicago Academy of Fine Arts. *Politics:* Democrat. *Religion:* Christian Scientist. *Home:* 2740 Southwest 31st Pl., Miami, Fla. 33133.

CAREER: Florida Power and Light Co., Miami, Fla., author and producer of "Builders of South Florida," a weekly radio program, 1947-70; writer of non-fiction books for children and adults, 1959—. *Member:* Women in Communications, Tropical Audubon Society, National Audubon Society, Historical Association of South Florida. *Awards, honors:* Headliner award from Miami chapter of Theta Sigma Phi, 1960.

WRITINGS—All published under name Mike Smith: *Florida: A Way of Life,* Dutton, 1959; *Florida* (juvenile), Coward, 1960; (contributor) *Beauty of the Outdoor World,* Country Beautiful, 1973; (with Virginia Matusek) *A Guide to the Everglades,* Trend, 1975; *Everglades: The Chain of Life,* Coward, 1970; *South Florida Frontiers,* Florida Power and Light Co., 1970.

Author and photographer of "Everglades: Sunlit Wilderness" (filmstrip script), Outdoor Pictures, 1975.

MARY ELLEN SMITH

Florida's sparkling waters entice the fisherman. They offer him more than 600 kinds of fish and a wide variety of ways to catch them. ■ (From *Florida* by Mike Smith. Photo from the Sarasota Chamber of Commerce.)

WORK IN PROGRESS: A children's book, *The Happy Alligator.*

SIDELIGHTS: "I have always been interested in the outdoors. . . . I am also interested in history, especially early history of Florida. I come of a long line of teachers, but early in life decided to become an artist or writer rather than a teacher. I am now interested in outdoor photography, and find this an excellent medium of communication to both children and adults."

SMITH, William A.

PERSONAL: Born April 19, 1918, in Toledo, Ohio; son of Bert Arthur (a telegrapher) and Catherine (Doan) Smith; married Mary France Nixon, September 30, 1939 (divorced, 1946); married Ferol Yvonne Stratton, October 10, 1949; children: Richard Keane, Kim, Kathlin Alexandra. *Education:* Attended Keane's Art School, Toledo, Ohio, 1932-36; University of Toledo, Toledo, Ohio, 1936-37; Grand Central Art School, New York, N.Y., 1938; Art Students League, New York, N.Y., 1946; l'Ecole des Beaux-Arts, Paris, France, 1949-50; l'Academie de la Grande Chaumiere, Paris, France, 1950-51. *Home and office:* Windy Bush Road, Pineville, Pa. 18946.

CAREER: Painter, muralist, print maker, and illustrator. Board of Directors, Welcome House (child placement agency), Doylestown, Pa., officer, 1958—. *Military service:*

U.S. Army, 1944-45. *Member:* Academician, National Academy of Design (member of council), American Watercolor Society (president, 1956-57; honorary president, 1957—), International Association of Art (president, 1973-76; honorary president for life, 1976—). *Awards, honors:* American Watercolor Society, silver medal, 1948, 1952, 1973, grand prize and gold medal, 1957, 1965; National Academy award, 1949, 1951; Obrig prize for oil painting, 1953; University of Toledo, honorary degree, 1954; Knobloch Prize for lithography, 1956; Society of Illustrators, gold medal, 1959; Freedom Foundation at Valley Forge, American Patriots Medal, 1973.

ILLUSTRATOR: Doris Shelton Still, *Sue in Tibet,* John Day, 1942; Pearl S. Buck, *The Waterbuffalo Children,* John Day, 1943; Lim Sian-Tek, *Folk Tales from China,* John Day, 1944; Lim Sian-Tek, *More Folk Tales from China,* John Day, 1948; Carl Sandburg, *Wind Song,* Harcourt, 1960; Rick K. Smith, *Exhibition Game,* G. Sack, 1973. Has contributed articles to *Harper's Bazaar* and other magazines.

SIDELIGHTS: "I work in watercolor, oil, encaustic, tempera, sculpture, and as a printmaker in lithography, intaglio, and relief. I am, also, a muralist. Have lived in many parts of Asia and maintained a Paris studio for many years. Have traveled to China, Burma, Korea, Russia, Bulgaria, Iraq, Egypt, India, Scandinavia, Turkey, Africa, Greece, Czechoslovakia, Romania, Malaya, Philippines, and all the countries of Europe.

"Welcome House is a child placement agency located in Doyestown, Pennsylvania, but operating nationally. It specializes in placing for adoption children, especially of part Asiatic and part American ancestry. The late Pearl S. Buck, the Oscar Hammersteins, the David Burpees, etc., a group of us who have been interested in the problem have worked on it through the years."

WILLIAM A. SMITH

Little girl, be careful what you say
when you make talk with words, words—
for words are made of syllables
and syllables, child, are made of air—
■ (From *Wind Song* by Carl Sandburg. Illustrated by William A.
Smith.)

SOHL, Frederic J(ohn) 1916-

PERSONAL: Surname rhymes with "pole"; born March
5, 1916, in Brooklyn, N.Y.; son of Frederick Martin (a
grocer) and Anna (Koster) Sohl; married Mildred Mantay
(now an assistant librarian), January 7, 1940; children:
Kathryn, Frederic M. *Education:* New York University,
B.S., 1951. *Politics:* Independent. *Home:* 223-08 Murdock
Ave., Queens Village, N.Y. 11429.

CAREER: Federal Bureau of Investigation, Washington,
D.C., fingerprint classifier, 1939-41; Reliable Stores Corp.,
Washington, D.C., assistant credit manager, 1941-43;
Pullman Co., New York, N.Y., and Chicago, Ill., pullman
conductor, 1943-44; Title Guarantee & Trust Co., New
York, N.Y., credit man, 1946-48; Underwriters Trust Co.,
New York, N.Y., manager of credit department, 1948-53,
assistant secretary, 1953-62, vice-president and loan officer,
1962-74. *Military service:* U.S. Army, 1944-46; served in
Burma and China; became staff sergeant; received Bronze
Star Medal.

WRITINGS: His Majesty's Wonderful Nose, Reilly &
Lee, 1967.

WORK IN PROGRESS: Additional short tales for children, with ancient China as a background.

SIDELIGHTS: Several decades passed between the
writing of *His Majesty's Wonderful Nose* and its publication; Sohl wrote the story while on Army duty in China in

FREDERIC J. SOHL

World War II, to tell his children when he returned home.
While his daughter was attending the University of Chi-
cago, she mentioned the tale to a juvenile author, Jean
Kellogg, who passed it on to a publisher.

SOULE, Jean Conder 1919-

PERSONAL: Born February 4, 1919, in Brookline, Mass.;
daughter of Ralph Edwin (an advertising manager) and
Mabel Amelia (Pierce) Conder; married George H. Soule
(administrative assistant to the Episcopal Bishop of Penn-
sylvania), June 24, 1942; children: David Conder, Douglas
Benton, Nancy Jean. *Education:* Mount Holyoke College,
A.B., 1942. *Politics:* Republican. *Religion:* Episcopal.
Home: 125 North Norwinden Dr., Springfield, Pa.

CAREER: Society editor in Springfield, Mass., one year;
editorial assistant for National Education Association,
Washington, D.C., four years; poetry workshop teacher,
conference leader, teacher of creative writing in elementary
schools in Pennsylvania. *Member:* National League of
American Pen Women (Philadelphia chapter historian,
1958-60; Delaware Valley chapter president, 1970-71,
Writers Club of Delaware County (president, 1959-61).

WRITINGS: Lenny's 20 Pennies, Parents, 1962; *Katy
Did,* Whitman, 1962; *Never Tease A Weasel,* Parents,
1964; (with N. J. Soule) *Scuttle, the Stowaway Mouse,*
Parents, 1968. Contributor of light verse to *Wall Street*

Send three frogs some sailing togs
And a yachting cap or two. ■
(From *Never Tease a Weasel* by Jean Conder Soule.
Illustrated by Denman Hampson.)

JEAN CONDER SOULE

Journal, Philadelphia Bulletin, Saturday Evening Post, Ladies' Home Journal, and *McCall's;* contributor to juvenile magazines.

SIDELIGHTS: "I was born in Southboro, Massachusetts, a town of about 2,000 inhabitants and until I graduated from high school I attended classes in a big old-fashioned frame and brick building in the center of town. I walked to school in all kinds of weather with two of my special friends and we never minded at all if the snowdrifts were deep or if we splashed through puddles in the spring. My New England background has been of good use to me in my poetry and in some of the stories I write for children. I find that I still remember with pleasure the old farmhouse where I lived from age four to eighteen. Some of the happiest times of my life were spent in that old house with its rambling attic full of trunks and boxes, its cozy fireplace, and its big old high-ceilinged rooms.

"When I went away to college I decided I wanted to be a writer but my advisor at college thought differently and suggested that I not try to earn my living with words! So it was not until I was married and living in Washington, D.C. that I began to tell stories to my son David at bedtime. Then when his brother Doug came along I told stories to him too. About that time we moved to Pennsylvania and I joined a writers club in my area. The help and counsel I got from speakers and teachers there inspired me to try my luck at sending out material to editors. No one was more surprised than I when my first poem sold to *Jack and Jill.* I wanted to frame the $10—but I spent it instead on gifts for the children.

"When our daughter Nancy was old enough to write, she used to like to help me compose stories and when we took walks with the dog, we'd write verses as we walked along. Eventually she and I collaborated on *Scuttle: The Stowaway Mouse.* That book is my favorite. I'm hoping some day to corral my daughter (now in college) long enough for us to do another story together.

"My husband is a writer, too, but the material he deals with is technical. But he's my best critic and is always interested when I have some measure of success with my work."

SPAR, Jerome   1918-

PERSONAL: Born October 7, 1918, in New York, N.Y.; son of Nathan and Celia (Meltzer) Spar; married Frances Fernbach, April 5, 1945; children: Susan Ellen, Richard Eric. *Education:* City College, New York, N.Y., B.S., 1940; New York University, M.S., 1943; Ph.D., 1950. *Home:* 18 Fieldmere Ave., Glen Rock, N.J. 07452. *Office:* Department of Earth and Planetary Sciences, City University of New York, New York, N.Y. 10031.

CAREER: New York University, New York, N.Y., instructor, 1946-50, assistant professor, 1950-53, research associate professor, 1953-56, associate professor, 1956-59, professor of meteorology, 1959-73; City University of New York, New York, N.Y., professor of meteorology, 1973—. U.S. Weather Bureau, Washington, D.C., research director, 1964-65. *Military service:* U.S. Army Air Forces, 1942-46; became major. *Member:* American Meteorological Society (fellow), American Geophysical Union, American Association for the Advancement of Science, Royal Meteorological Society, New York Academy of Sciences (fellow).

WRITINGS: The Way of the Weather (juvenile), Creative Educational, 1957, 3rd edition, 1967; *Earth, Sea, and Air,* Addison-Wesley, 1962, 2nd edition, 1965; *Willy: A Story of Water* (juvenile), Oddo, 1965.

SPENCER, Ann   1918-

PERSONAL: Born June 13, 1918, in New Hope, Pa.; daughter of Robert Carpenter (an artist) and Margaret (an architect; maiden name Fulton) Spencer; married Louis Simon (a teacher and writer), October 26, 1946. *Education:* Studied at Ecole Sevigne, Paris, 1932-33, Holmquist School, New Hope, Pa., 1934-35, and at Art Student's League, New York, 1936-38. *Politics:* Democrat. *Religion:* Protestant. *Home:* 230 Grove Acres Ave., Apt. 330, Pacific Grove, Calif. 93950. *Agent:* Diarmuid Russell, Russell & Volkening, Inc., 551 Fifth Ave., New York, N.Y. 10017.

CAREER: Artist in New York, N.Y., until 1956, and in Tucson, Ariz., 1956—. Has exhibited with Associated American Artists in New York, at Santa Barbara Art Museum, and at Rosequist Galleries, Tucson.

ANN SPENCER

WRITINGS—Self-illustrated: *The Cat Who Tasted Cinnamon Toast,* Knopf, 1969.

WORK IN PROGRESS: A story about a jet-set French poodle; other cat stories.

SIDELIGHTS: "My story about a gourmet cat was not designed for any age group and I believe is therefore referred to in the trade as adult-juvenile.

"It was really a tribute to a beloved stray who foraged off the Arizona desert for two whole years before he finally succumbed to domestication. That it ended up as a spoof of the gourmet food craze was just a natural development. . . . As an artist my subjects have always been social satire or in my light moments, humor."

SPRIGGE, Elizabeth (Miriam Squire) 1900-1974

PERSONAL: Born June 19, 1900; daughter of Sir Squire (editor of *Lancet*) and Mary Ada (Moss) Sprigge; married Mark Napier, July 23, 1921 (marriage dissolved, 1946); children: Julyan (Mrs. Cawthra Mulock), Ruth (Mrs. Timothy Lumley-Smith). *Education:* Attended Havergal College, Toronto, Ontario, Canada, and Bedford College, University of London. *Home:* 75 Ladbroke Grove, London, W11

2PD, England. *Agent:* Willis Kingsley Wing, 24 East 38th St., New York, N.Y. 10016.

CAREER: Author and translator, British Ministry of Information, London, England, Swedish specialist, 1941-44 (lived in Sweden, 1923-25). Co-founder of Watergate Theatre Club, London, England, 1949, and director, 1949-52. Lecturer and broadcaster on literature and the theater. *Member:* P.E.N.

WRITINGS—Novels: *A Shadowy Third,* Knopf, 1929; *Faint Amorist,* Knopf, 1930; *The Old Man Dies,* Macmillan, 1933; *Castle in Andalusia,* Heinemann, 1935; *The Son of the House,* Collins, 1937; *The Raven's Wing,* Macmillan, 1940.

Biographies: *The Strange Life of August Strindberg,* Macmillan, 1949, Russell, 1972; *Gertrude Stein, Her Life and Work,* Harper, 1957; (with Jean Jacques Kihm) *Jean Cocteau: The Man and the Mirror,* Coward, 1968; *Sybil Thorndike Casson,* Gollancz, 1971; *The Life of Ivy Compton-Burnett,* Braziller, 1973.

Children's books: *Children Alone,* Eyre & Spottiswoode, 1935; *Pony Tracks,* Eyre & Spottiswoode, 1936; *Two Lost on Dartmoor,* Eyre & Spottiswoode, 1940; (with Elizabeth Muntz) *The Dolphin Bottle,* Gollancz, 1965.

Plays: (With Katriona Sprigge) "Elizabeth of Austria," produced at Garrick Theatre, 1939; (translator) Bjornsterne Bjornson, "Mary Stuart in Scotland," produced at Edinburgh Festival, 1960.

Translations: *Six Plays of Strindberg,* Anchor Books, 1955; *Five Plays of Strindberg,* Anchor Books, 1960; *Twelve Plays of Strindberg,* Constable, 1962; *August Strindberg, Plays,* Aldine, 1963; Jean Cocteau, *The Difficulty of Being,* P. Owen, 1966; August Strindberg, *The Red Room,* Dutton, 1967.

(Died December 8, 1974)

SPYKMAN, E(lizabeth) C. 19?-1965

PERSONAL: Surname pronounced Speakman; born in Massachusetts; married Nicholas Spykman (Professor of International Relations at Yale); children: Angela, Patricia. *Home:* New Haven, Conn.

CAREER: Writer.

WRITINGS: A Lemon and a Star, Harcourt, 1955; *The Wild Angel,* Harcourt, 1957; *Terrible, Horrible Edie,* Harcourt, 1960; *Edie on the Warpath,* Harcourt, 1966. Articles appeared in *Atlantic Monthly.*

SIDELIGHTS: "By way partly of Salem and Cambridge and partly by way of farmers from the New England hinterland, I was born and brought up in a small town in Massachusetts. There were six of us, four boys and two girls. We spoke more English than American, had tea in the afternoons, and kept stiff upper lips like anything. My father's family lived on one side of the road in our village and my mother's on the other, and as there were very nearly ten of each kind, with land and houses to match, the children who lived among them had a kind of enormous park to use as their own.

E. C. SPYKMAN

"These people did a great many things; practised law, directed railroads, built schools, churches and stone walls, invented flavoring extracts and ran dairy farms. One joined a convent. One was a minister to Spain. But in their spare time, of which there seemed more then than now, they pursued their real vocation, which was the same for them all—to make their home acres, their meadows and pastures blossom like the rose. The tallest lilacs, the broadest syringa, the widest lawns, the brightest gardens, the best and the greatest variety of vegetables were their ambition.

"All the roads were dirt roads and there were no cars, no telephones, television, radio, or movies for quite a while. We had ponies instead. Each child had one, and my father had a furious black horse called 'The Moor.' Our stable caught fire once and no one but my father was able to get a blanket over 'The Moor's' head and lead him out. My father saved the stable, too, by making a bucket brigade of the cook, the parlor maid, our nurse, and the coachman. No one else would have been able to do that with the cook, either. But alas, we were not allowed to see it. We were sent to a maternal aunt across the road where we howled until the flames died down. There were lots of barn fires in those days and dog fights, too, which the farm hands enjoyed but which we thought tragic.

"My father was a lawyer in Boston and the relations were businessmen and farmers. Very often in the summers we went to Cape Cod. I have lived all over Cape Cod and swum all over a lot of its bay and harbors, too, but I am no sailor and never liked lying on the weather rail soaked to the skin at the command of a younger sister, though more often than not she won the race.

"In the winter we skated, coasted, and punged behind sleighs and often we sat on our sleds and longed for someone to invent a machine to pull us back uphill. Presently someone did and so there is no more punging and little coasting either, but the machine took some bad things away too. Runaway horses, dust, and not being able to get the doctor quickly when you had cut off the end of your finger in the corn chopper.

"I went to two or three schools but none of them seemed to me to be as valuable as living in the country until I was sent to a boarding school called Westover where there was a set of very remarkable women in charge. I was told there that one ought to read books and although I did not take advantage of this valuable information right away, I began to see it might be possible and perhaps worth while for the future. Also, I made a great friend and later she and I traveled all over the world. This I did for many years, by cargo boat, by bicycle, by train, on my feet, and on different kinds of steamers.

"After a trip to New Zealand in a cargo boat by way of the Canal and on through the South Seas, I wrote a piece about going to visit Robert Louis Stevenson's grave at Samoa, which was accepted by the *Atlantic Monthly*. The *Atlantic* then printed some more of my things. In 1930 I was introduced to a travelling Dutchman. We met in Farmington and were married in Honolulu. Shortly after we left for Russia by way of most of Europe. My husband started the Department and Institute of International Relations at Yale University which, since his death, has been lured to Princeton University,

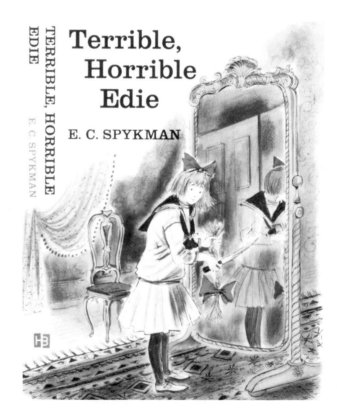

The braid came away as neat as a bunch of clover. It made her feel a little scalped as she held it in her hand with the ribbon still on the end, but she shook her head and enjoyed being so light-headed. ■ (From *Terrible, Horrible Edie* by E. C. Spykman. Jacket design by Paul Galdone.)

"I wrote my books for no other reason than that I wanted to. My husband died in 1942 and since then I have lived in Connecticut with my two daughters, growing the tallest lilacs, the broadest syringa, the widest lawn, the brightest garden and the best vegetables that can be managed in these unregenerate days when the golden bowl is broken and the Japanese beetle is abroad in the land. I have a large house and lots of land and a lot of books. I learned quite a while ago what they were for. I have a dog called Jingle, after the bad character in *Pickwick Papers* who told lies and stole things. My Jingle would tell lies if he could, especially about the things he steals off the kitchen table. But my younger daughter calls him Beautiful One. He is a Dalmatian and can run with the speed of light."

(Died August 7, 1965)

STEELE, (Henry) Max(well) 1922-

PERSONAL: Born March 30, 1922, in Greenville, S.C.; son of John M. and Minnie (Russell) Steele; married Diana Whittinghill, December 31, 1960; children: Oliver Whittinghill, Kevin Russell. *Education:* Studied at Furman University, 1939-41, University of North Carolina, 1942, Vanderbilt University, 1943; University of North Carolina, B.A., 1946; further study at Academie Julienne, Paris, France, 1951-52, and Sorbonne, University of Paris, 1952-55. *Agent:* Elizabeth McKee, Harold Matson Co., Inc., 22 East 40th St., New York, N.Y. 10016. *Office:* Department of English, University of North Carolina, Chapel Hill, N.C. 27514.

CAREER: University of North Carolina, Chapel Hill, lecturer in creative writing, 1956-58; University of California Extension, lecturer in creative writing, 1963-64; University of North Carolina, writer-in-residence, 1966—, lecturer, 1967-68, associate professor and director of creative writing program, 1968-70, professor of English, 1970—. University of California, Squaw Valley, Community of Writers, board of directors and faculty. *Military service:* U.S. Air Force, Weather Wing, 1942-46. *Awards, honors: Debby* was Harper Prize Novel of 1950, and also received Harper's Eugene F. Saxton Memorial Trust Award and the May-

flower Cup for the best book by a North Carolinian that year; National Endowment for the Arts grant, 1967.

WRITINGS: Debby, Harper, 1960, reissued as *The Goblins Must Go Barefoot,* Perennial Library, 1966; *Where She Brushed Her Hair, and Other Short Stories,* Harper, 1968; *The Cat and the Coffee Drinkers* (juvenile), Harper, 1969. Short stories have appeared in *Atlantic, Harper's, New Yorker, Collier's, Cosmopolitan, Esquire, Mademoiselle, Quarterly Review of Literature,* and other literary journals. Advisory editor, *Paris Review,* 1952—.

WORK IN PROGRESS: A children's book, for Harper; a novel.

SIDELIGHTS: "I have a son who was born in 1966 and a son who was born in 1969 and a wife who runs a nursery school. In addition, I teach at the University a course in children's literature, so that all day I am surrounded by books for and about children.

"Yet I don't seem to be able to sit down and write a book for children. I write stories for grownups and they are printed in magazines and books for adults, but gradually teachers and parents discover that children like the stories, and then editors and anthologists begin putting them into books for children. Which of course pleases me enormously because I prefer to have children liking stories. I feel then that the stories are certain to be honest if children like them.

"A short story of mine called 'Ah Love! Ah Me!' has been in more than a hundred books now so that several million young people must have read it.

"Mainly I write funny stories and I like to write about children because I had an unhappy childhood. When I write about children, I give them a happier childhood than I had. But the unhappy part is important too; or at least it was to me when I was young and read constantly and knew that I was not alone."

STEURT, Marjorie Rankin 1888-

PERSONAL: Born October 8, 1888, in Pennsylvania; daughter of a Presbyterian minister; married Roy Steurt. *Education:* Mount Holyoke College, graduate, 1911; Columbia University, M.A., 1928, Ph.D., 1929; studied engineering during World War II. *Home:* P.O. Box 72, Hemet, Calif. 92343.

CAREER: Teacher in Negro school in Alabama, 1911-12; went to China in 1912, and remained as teacher and principal of mission high school, supervisor of forty country schools, and acting head of English department at Cheloo University, during period 1912-25; caught in communist uprising in 1925 after Nanking Massacre and escaped on last train out to the coast; after further study in America returned to China in 1929 as director of experimental education at Nankai University, Tientsin, and teacher of education methods at Normal College of Tientsin; driven out again by Japanese take-over in 1932, came back to United States and worked (during depression) as dog walker and operator of gas station, among other things, then became head of psychology department of Monmouth Junior Col-

MAX STEELE AND FAMILY

MARJORIE RANKIN STEURT

lege, West Long Branch, N.J., and later, school psychologist for Hawthorne (N.J.) public schools; during World War II ran experimental engines in airplane factory; teacher of creative writing in adult education program, and public lecturer. *Member:* American Association of University Women (president, 1958-60), National League of American Penwomen (vice-president, 1962-65), Phi Beta Kappa, National Writers Club, Sierra Club.

WRITINGS: The Kingdom of Mimus, Golden Gate Junior Books, 1964; *Rocky and Sandy: The Story of Two Tortoises in the California Desert,* Ritchie, 1967; *Broken Bits of Old China,* Nelson, 1973.

SIDELIGHTS: "When I returned from twenty years teaching in China, I realized I had a fund of information no one else possessed. So I decided to get it down in stories for children. The first was *Shoeboard* from which the Chinese make the soles of their shoes. This sold immediately, so I wrote *A Name for Mother.* When Chinese women married they lost their names, were called 'the-inside-of-the-house' until the first child was born, then named that child's mother. Then came *Tiger Shoes,* about the boy who was afraid until his mother made him a pair of tiger shoes. *Music in the Air* was about the whistles people tied under the wings of pigeons.

"When I ran out of Chinese ideas I started on animal stories. My husband and I traveled all over the country by trailer, so I wrote a whole series about the birds and animals—the chipmunk that made its nest on our car engine, *The Flying Garbage Can* (the buzzards in Mexico), the difference between the walk of the robin and hop of the blue jay, etc. Each story had an interesting bit of information rather than a moral.

"Then I started writing books. My first published book, *The Kingdom of Mimus,* was about the mockingbird that lived in my yard. For five years I kept a daily record of all his activities.

"My second book, *Rocky and Sandy,* is the story of two desert tortoises. Then in 1973 Nelson published my *Broken Bits of Old China.* This contains the crazy things that happened to me on my wheelbarrow trips through the Chinese countryside. They were written in letters sent home, which my father saved. It is about the old China, but because the incidents were written on the day they happened it has an immediacy. The reader feels he is there.

"At 69 I had my first white-water trip, running the rapids of the Grand Canyon in a neoprene raft—wildly exciting. And year after year until I was 78 I had the joy of running the rapids of our wildest rivers, even up to the Nahanni, near the Arctic Circle.

"I also took many foreign trips, always out in the wilds—New Guinea, the Galapagos Islands, the Seychelles, twice to the Antarctic, Greenland, camping in New Zealand, South America and the back country of Iceland. I always kept a journal of sights, sounds, happenings and used them in my writing.

"I think my writing was due more to wanting to get down on paper the fascinating things that had happened to me and that I had seen rather than an urge to write. They were too unique to be lost.

Marjorie Steurt, researching *The Big Bend of the Columbia* in 1963 at age 75.

Something about the Author

"I've never had any children and have never taught children. My teaching has been high school, university and adults. But my teaching English for so many years to foreigners reduced my style to a simple form. It was the type of English suited for young children, which is why I've been so successful in writing for them.

"At 87, I went to Macchu Picchu in Peru and then down the Amazon. I kept a journal and reported it in my annual Christmas letter."

HOBBIES AND OTHER INTERESTS: Running river rapids, camping, desert wood arrangements, travel (has criss-crossed the United States, Mexico, and Canada in a trailer).

STINE, G(eorge) Harry 1928-
(Lee Correy)

PERSONAL: Born March 26, 1928, in Philadelphia, Pa.; son of George Haeberle (an eye surgeon) and Rhea Matilda (O'Neil) Stine; married Barbara A. Kauth, June 10, 1952; children: Constance Rhea, Eleanor Ann, George Willard. *Education:* Attended University of Colorado, 1946-50;

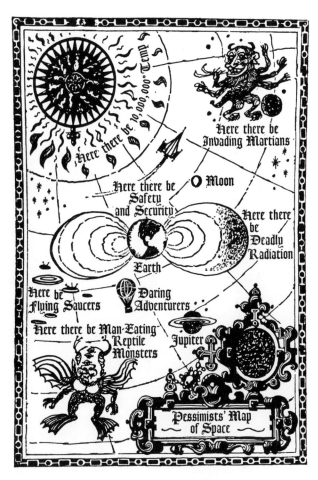

Back in the sixteenth century before men had started to sail across the Atlantic Ocean to America, many people believed that the "Western Ocean" was filled with terrifying sea monsters. Map makers filled up the unknown area of their maps with warnings, "Here there be Dragons." ■ (From *Man and the Space Frontier* by G. Harry Stine. Illustrated by Lewis Zacks.)

G. HARRY STINE

Colorado College, B.A., 1952. *Home:* 616 West Frier Dr., Phoenix, Ariz. 85021. *Agent:* Lurton Blassingame, 60 East 42nd St., New York, N.Y. 10017.

CAREER: White Sands Proving Ground, White Sands, N.M., chief of controls and instruments section in propulsion branch, 1952-55, chief of range operations division and Navy flight safety engineer, 1955-57; Martin Co., Denver, Colo., design specialist, 1957; Model Missiles, Inc., Denver, president and chief engineer, 1957-59; Stanley Aviation Corp., Denver, design engineer, 1959-60; Huyck Corp., Stamford, Conn., assistant director of research, 1960-65; consulting engineer and science writer in New Canaan, Conn., 1965-73; Flow Technology, Inc., Phoenix, Ariz., marketing manager, 1973-76; consultant and science writer, 1976—. *Member:* Federation Aeronautique Internationale (Paris), American Institute of Aeronautics and Astronautics (associate fellow), Instrument Society of America, Academy of Model Aeronautics, National Aeronautic Association, British Interplanetary Society (fellow), National Fire Protection Association, National Association of Rocketry (founder; president, 1957-67; honorary trustee), Science Fiction Writers of America, New York Academy of Sciences, Theta Xi, Explorers Club (New York City; fellow).

WRITINGS: (Under pseudonym Lee Correy) *Starship through Space,* Holt, 1954; (under pseudonym Lee Correy) *Contraband Rocket,* Ace, 1955; (under pseudonym Lee Correy) *Rocket Man,* Holt, 1956; *Rocket Power and Space Flight,* Holt, 1957; *Earth Satellites and the Race for Space Superiority,* Ace, 1957; *Man and the Space Frontier,*

Knopf, 1962; (contributor) Frederick Pohl, editor, *The Expert Dreamers*, Doubleday, 1962; *The Handbook of Model Rocketry*, Follett, 1965, 4th edition, 1975; (contributor) George W. Early, editor, *Encounters with Aliens*, Sherbourne, 1969; *The Model Rocket Manual*, Sentinel, 1969; *Model Rocket Safety*, Model Products Corp., 1970; (contributor) Ben Bova, editor, *The Analog Science Fact Reader*, Sherbourne, 1974; *The Third Industrial Revolution*, Putnam, 1975; (contributor) Ben Bova, editor, *A New View of the Solar System*, St. Martin's, 1976; *The New Model Rocketry Manual*, Arco, 1977.

Also author of six technical papers and of five filmscripts. Science fiction short stories represented in anthologies, including *Science Fiction, '58: The Year's Greatest Science Fiction and Fantasy*, edited by Judith Merrill, Gnome, 1958; *The Sixth Annual of the Year's Best Science Fiction*, edited by Judith Merrill, Simon & Schuster, 1961; *Analog Six*, edited by John W. Campbell, Doubleday, 1968.

Contributor to *Collier's Encyclopedia;* contributor of over 150 science fiction stories and science fact and model rocketry articles to magazines, including *Saturday Evening Post, Astounding, Analog, Science Digest*, and *Magazine of Fantasy and Science Fiction;* writer of monthly column, "Conquest of Space," in *Mechanix Illustrated*, 1956-57. Editor, *Missile Away*, 1953-57, *The Model Rocketeer*, 1958-64, *Flow Factor*, 1973-76.

WORK IN PROGRESS: "Too many authors talk about the stories they are going to do tomorrow. I prefer to discuss only what I have done."

SIDELIGHTS: "I had the good fortune to grow up in Colorado Springs, Colorado on one of the last physical frontiers on the North American continent, the American West. I also had the good fortune to choose a father who was an eye surgeon, who was an amateur scientist, and who surrounded me with books from as early as I can remember. In concert with my father, a number of men instilled in me a consuming curiosity about the universe around me. Once I asked one of them what I could ever do to repay him. I have been repaying him ever since because he said, 'There is no way that you can repay me directly and personally. The only thing that you can do to repay me is to do the same thing for the next generation. The obligation is always toward the future.'

"I write the sort of thing that I would like to read. I write it the way I would like to read it. I write entertainment. I am competing for the reader's time and money; if he doesn't like what I write, he will not spend his time and plunk down his hard-earned money a second time.

"The human race is going to survive. We will use the accumulated knowledge of centuries plus our rational minds to solve the problems that seem to beset us at the moment ... and they are really no worse than the problems that faced other generations in the past. The current problems seem worse because they are current and because we have not yet solved them. What is difficult to us was impossible to our parents and will be commonplace to our children. We will indeed slay the dragons of war, intolerance, and pollution. We will marry the princess of outer space. And we will live happily ever after among the stars. We now have or will soon have the capability to do anything we want to do; we must only be willing to pay for it and to live with all the consequences.

"Like it or not, we live in a technological reality. One can escape it only by regressing through centuries of human history. I have attempted to master or at least understand as much about technology as possible. I have operated or am at least aware of how to operate every possible human transportation machine—for example: I have operated railroad trains, horses, automobiles, boats, and airplanes. I am a licensed pilot, own an airplane, and fly regularly. I hope someday to fly in a rocket-powered space vehicle ... or in any sort of space vehicle. I greatly admire the fictitious man who, when asked if he could fly a helicopter, replied, 'I don't know; I've never tried.'

"The human race has a long way yet to go, and there are a lot of things left to do. According to a recent U.N. survey, nearly half the people in the world cannot read or write their native language; in the 'literate' United States of America, there are 21,000,000 people who are illiterate. Over 100,000,000 Americans have never been up in an airplane. 90% of the people on Earth have never been more than 25 miles from their birthplace, nor do they expect to travel beyond their village during their lifetimes."

STINETORF, Louise (Allender)   1900-

PERSONAL: Born February 4, 1900, in Ward Township, Ind.; daughter of Samuel Grove and Ida Elnora (Burton) Allender; married Roscoe Stinetorf, 1919 (divorced, 1937, now deceased); married Henry Loel Wilson (a pharmacist; died 1955). *Education:* Earlham College, A.B., 1925;

LOUISE STINETORF

. . . at the end of our trail, hippopotamuses were as numerous as the leaves on an old silk-cotton tree. ■ (From *White Witch Doctor* by Louise A. Stinetorf. Illustrated by Don McDonough.)

Temple University, M.A., 1941; additional study at Pendle Hill, University of Puebla, Hebrew University of Jerusalem, University of Chicago, and Bryn Mawr College. *Politics:* Republican. *Religion:* Quaker. *Home:* 2305 Harbor Point Dr., Celina, Ohio 45822.

CAREER: Former teacher, now retired. Also worked in public relations and served as missionary for two years.

WRITINGS: Children of North Africa, Lippincott, 1942; *Children of South Africa*, Lippincott, 1945; *White Witch Doctor*, Westminster, 1950; *Beyond the Hungry Country*, Lippincott, 1954; *Elephant Outlaw*, Lippincott, 1956; *Musa the Shoemaker*, Lippincott, 1959; *La China Poblana*, Bobbs, 1960; *The Shepherd of Abu Kush*, John Day, 1963; *Children of Africa*, Lippincott, 1964; *A Charm for Paco's Mother*, John Day, 1965; *Manuel and the Pearl*, John Day, 1966; *The Treasure of Tolmec*, John Day, 1967; *Tomas and the Hermit*, John Day, 1968; *The Bears of Sansur*, John Day, 1969; *The Spirit of Bireh*, John Day, 1973. Author of serials and some two hundred short stories.

WORK IN PROGRESS: An untitled manuscript for adult readers.

HOBBIES AND OTHER INTERESTS: Gardening, bird study, nature study hikes, art needle work, collecting antique pocket perfume flasks, and classical music.

STIRNWEIS, Shannon 1931-

PERSONAL: Born February 26, 1931, in Portland, Ore.; son of Theodore and Daisy (Daly) Stirnweis; married Regina Bolivar, September 6, 1958; children: Kevin, Kirk, Eric. *Education:* Attended University of Oregon, 1949; Art Center College of Design, B.P.A., 1954. *Home and Office:* 31 Fawn Pl., Wilton, Conn. 06897.

CAREER: Free-lance illustrator. Compton Advertising, New York, N.Y., sketchman, 1957-59. *Military service:* U.S. Army, illustrator, 1954-56. *Member:* Society of Illustrators (president, 1972-74; annual show chairman); Graphic Artists Guild (trustee, New York, N.Y.).

ILLUSTRATOR: John A. Wallace, *Getting to Know Po-land*, Coward, 1960; Leslie Waller, *Numbers: A Book to Begin On*, Holt, 1960; Leslie Waller, *Our Flag: A Book to Begin On*, Holt, 1960; Robert N. Webb, *Great Battles*, Whitman, 1960; Ellsworth Newcomb and Hugh Kenny, *African Adventures*, Whitman, 1961; Katharine E. Wilkie, *Zack Taylor*, Bobbs, 1962; Marjorie Fribourg, *Ports of Entry*, Little, Brown, 1962; Nardi Reeder Campion, *Kit Carson*, Garrard, 1963; Raymond F. Jones, *Great Physicians*, Whitman, 1963; H. G. Wells, *War of the Worlds*, Whitman, 1964; Tony Nesbit, *The Indian Mummy Mys-*

SHANNON STIRNWEIS

A great many cats recognize the special clink of their dishes. One cat that loved eggs would arrive in the kitchen from anyplace in the house any time its mistress cracked an egg. ■ (From *The Cat Book* by Marianne Besser. Illustrated by Shannon Stirnweis.)

tery, Whitman, 1964; Hildegard Thompson, *Getting to Know American Indians Today,* Coward, 1965; Jim Kjelgaard, *Big Red,* Garden City, 1966; Charles B. Joy, *Getting to Know Tanzania,* Coward, 1966; Marianne Besser, *The Cat Book,* Holiday, 1967; Kurt Unkelbach, *Cat & His Dogs,* Prentice, 1969; Gertrude Priester, *Who Are You, Lord?,* Knox, 1969.

Patrick Lawson, *Dogs of the World,* Western, 1971; Pauline Meek, *When Joy Came: The Story of the First Christmas,* Western, 1971; Doris M. Malone, *God's Covenant: The One Story of the Bible,* Knox, 1973; Eugene O'Neill, *Ah Wilderness,* Limited Editions Club, 1972.

STODDARD, Edward G.   1923-

PERSONAL: Born November 26, 1923, in Peking, China; son of Ross Emory (a minister) and Georgia (Luccock) Stoddard; children: Mark, Eric, Judith. *Education:* University of Chicago, Ph.B., 1947. *Politics:* Democrat. *Home:* 210 East 11th St., New York, N.Y. 10003. *Agent:* Lurton Blassingame, 10 East 43rd St., New York, N.Y. 10017. *Office:* Doubleday & Co., 673 Fifth Ave., New York, N.Y. 10022.

It's not tricks that fool an audience, but the person who does the tricks. ■ (From *The First Book of Magic* by Edward Stoddard. Illustrated by Robin King.)

CAREER: Doubleday & Co., Inc., New York, N.Y., director of advertising, book clubs division, 1964-75, president, book shop division, 1975—.

WRITINGS: The First Book of Magic (juvenile), Watts, 1953, revised, 1976; *The First Book of Television* (juve-

EDWARD G. STODDARD

164   **Something about the Author**

nile), Watts, 1955, revised, 1973; *The Story of Power* (juvenile), Garden City Books, 1956; *The Real Book of Electronics* (juvenile), Garden City Books, 1956; *Speed Mathematics Simplified* (adult), Dial, 1962.

STOLZ, Mary (Slattery) 1920-

PERSONAL: Born March 24, 1920, in Boston, Mass.; daughter of Thomas F. and Mary (Burgey) Slattery; divorced; married Thomas C. Jaleski, June, 1965; children: William. *Education:* Attended Birch Wathen School; attended Columbia University, 1936-38. *Politics:* "Liberal Northern Democrat." *Home:* 52 Prides Crossing, New Canaan, Ct. *Agent:* Roslyn Targ Literary Agency, 250 West 57th St., New York, N.Y. 10019.

CAREER: Writer of books for children and young adults. *Awards, honors:* Child Study Association Award, *Herald Tribune* Spring Book Festival Award, German Youth Festival Award; John Newbery Medal runner-up, 1963, for *Belling the Tiger,* and 1966, for *The Noonday Friends; The Edge of Next Year* was nominated for the National Book Award.

WRITINGS—All published by Harper, except as noted: *To Tell Your Love,* 1950; *The Organdy Cupcakes,* 1951; *The Sea Gulls Woke Me* (ALA Notable Book), 1951; *The Leftover Elf,* 1952; *In a Mirror,* 1953; *Ready or Not,* 1953; *Truth and Consequence,* 1953; *Pray Love, Remember,* 1954; *Two by Two,* Houghton, 1954; *Rosemary,* 1955; *Hospital Zone,* 1956; *The Day and the Way We Met,* 1956; *Good-by My Shadow,* 1957; *Because of Madeline,* 1957; *And Love Replied,* 1958; *Second Nature,* 1958; *Emmet's Pig,* 1959; *Some Merry-Go-Round Music,* 1959.

The Beautiful Friend, and Other Stories, 1960; *A Dog on Barkham Street,* 1960; *Belling the Tiger* (ALA Notable Book), 1961; *Wait for Michael,* 1961; *The Great Rebellion,* 1961; *Fredou,* 1962; *Pigeon Flight,* 1962; *Siri, the Conquistador,* 1963; *The Bully of Barkham Street,* 1963, large type edition, 1967; *Who Wants Music on Monday?,* 1963; *Mys-*

tery of the Woods, 1964; *A Love or a Season,* 1964; *The Noonday Friends,* 1965; *Maximilian's World,* 1966; *A Wonderful, Terrible Time,* 1967; *Say Something,* 1968; *The Dragons of the Queen,* 1969; *The Story of a Singular Hen and Her Peculiar Children,* 1969; *Juan,* 1970; *By the Highway Home,* 1971; *Leap Before You Look,* 1972; *Lands End,* 1973; *The Edge of Next Year* (*Horn Book* Honor List), 1974; *Cat in the Mirror,* 1975. Stories in popular magazines, including *Cosmopolitan, Seventeen, Ladies' Home Journal.*

SIDELIGHTS: "Children write to me and say, 'I'd like to be an author, what shall I do?' I have a reply I always make and fear they think I have some recipe that I'm too grudging to give them. I tell them, 'Read a lot and write a lot, read a lot, write a lot.' I don't say anything about talent, because if they have that, they are already writing and don't need my advice.

"Many people who think they want to write want, actually, to have written something. This is not the same as writing, which is very disciplined work, and there are a lot of things to be doing that are simpler and, perhaps, more fun. So—reading, reading, reading . . . writing, writing, writing. When I say this sort of thing to groups of children, I can feel them thinking, 'Then what does she *do:* She reads things, and then she goes and writes something.' I had one child tell me right out that it sounded like a funny way to go about it. I tried to explain that to me the reading, in addition to everything else it is, is a form of going to school. It's not imitating, it's learning.

MARY STOLZ

"Much of the mail I receive from children gives me the feeling that they aren't reading. They may be reading my books, at least the ones who write to me are, but what else are they reading? Stevenson, Andersen, Austen, Dickens? Sandburg? I wish I knew.

"It's important to own books. I was fortunate in growing up to have a family that gave me books. I used the public library, of course, but I also *owned* books, and that meant so much, so very very much. My Uncle Bill, who's always had a nice feeling for literature, bought me *Silver Pennies* when I was eight. *This Singing World* when I was ten, Emily Dickinson and Keats when I was twelve. Marvelous selections. I mention those, but there were many volumes, and I still own them. Most of them.

"All right then—I had that intense literary background, and the tremendous drive to write. But also involved is the matter of an editor, once you've begun writing for publication. Writers get near-sighted about their own work, jealous of their words. A good editor can gently lead you back onto the path when you've strayed, and if you're as verbose as I am, you stray a lot. A great editor can find things in you that you had no idea were there. I happen to have had, all these years, a great editor, Ursula Nordstrom, of Harper & Row. She's not the kind who says, 'Change this.' 'Do this.' 'Don't say that.' She indicates. She says, 'Would you like to think this part over?' She says, 'NGEFY.' That means, Not Good Enough For You. No one can read her NGEFY and not go back and try again. She reads a manuscript lovingly but firmly, and I trust her judgment absolutely. I've been lucky, in other words, in all my writing life.

"In writing, I want to entertain. Failing that, you might as well forget it. You must keep them turning the pages, as the writers I read must keep me turning theirs. Writers must bewitch readers. Jane Austen still bewitches me. I know how it's all going to come out, but still she delights me and I can't start one of her books without finishing it. All writers don't delight all readers, obviously. But we find each other, the one who's right for the other. The many who are right for the one. Along the line, of course, you owe your readers other things: honesty, humane feelings. I'm old-fashioned and think you also owe them proper grammar, or, more correctly, what used to be called 'the right words in the right order.'

"I went to a progressive school, Birch Wathen, in New York City, where you studied what you wanted to study. In my case, it worked out very well because all I bothered about was literature; and history. That was about it. No arithmetic or science. I never got past the multiplication tables. On the other hand, I was encouraged to read and write. I was editor of our school magazine. I worked on the school paper. I wrote and wrote and wrote . . . and the school said that was fine. I remember it fondly. Also, it was a very pretty school with a nice garden.

"As a girl I was flighty, flirtatious, impulsive, self-involved and not very thoughtful. Then I read *Pride and Prejudice* and fell in love with Elizabeth Bennett. To me, she's the loveliest female in fiction, as Rochester is the most captivating male. I use to think they should have married each other. Anyway, I tried to model myself after Elizabeth Bennett, so you can see how much the book affected me. It worked, too. Sort of. My manners improved, even my deportment changed. I think I became more considerate. And

Now he'd gone and had what their doctor called "an unusually fine growth spurt." This meant he was bigger than anyone else in his class, which was all right for knocking people down but still made him feel peculiar. ■ (From *The Bully of Barkham Street* by Mary Stolz. Illustrated by Leonard Shortall.)

Little Women . . . I don't know if anyone still reads it. I hope so. The book has such warmth and closeness—the closeness of family and friends. The death of Beth March was devastating to me. I use to go back and start over again, actually almost thinking that the next time it would turn out differently. But that book showed how a family faced a loss so great, and survived it, and went on, and even knew happiness again. Quite a lesson to learn from a book. And the marvelous animal books . . . Ernest Thompson-Seton's *Biography of a Grizzly,* for instance. I can still recall the last line, and it can still bring tears to my eyes. There was such dignity and poignancy in the bear's death. 'He lay down as softly as he had in his mother's arms, in the Gray Bull, long ago.' It saddened me, but that kind of sadness is good. *The Little Mermaid* broke my heart, but that's a good way to get your heart broken when you're young—reading a great love story. Books like that give you something to measure your own losses by.

I think that's all that teachers can do with books—read them to the children, give them to the children to read. There's another thing—there are books in which you lose yourself and there are books in which you find yourself. There's a place for both. Detective stories, for instance, are fine for getting lost in. But the great books are those in

Something about the Author

which you find yourself. And a great book needn't be a classic. It just needs to be the right book at the right time for the person who's reading it.

"I can't start a book except on a Monday. I work in my study from eight till noon, and I don't get interrupted there. Usually five days a week, maybe six. Very often, in the evening, while my husband is painting (he's a doctor professionally and an inspired amateur painter) I sit with a legal pad on a clipboard and just make notes. While I'm working on a book, I work hard. But I take time off in between books, to play, or straighten the closets. Writing is so subjective that doing something quite objective like closet-straightening is delightful."

Mary Stolz' books have been published in nearly thirty languages, some issued in Braille. Her works are represented in the Kerlan collection, University of Minnesota.

HOBBIES AND OTHER INTERESTS: "A world that contains dinner with friends, the music of Verdi, ballet, looking at cats, sitting in a garden, bird-watching, bird-*listening,* the pleasure of cooking good food, books, and—above all—people you love and want to be with—such a world has to contain joy, so I also see that when I look at what Annie Dillard calls 'our baby-blue planet the earth and all of the people, waving.'"

FOR MORE INFORMATION SEE: Wilson Library Bulletin, September, 1953; *More Junior Authors,* edited by Muriel Fuller, H. W. Wilson, 1963; *Christian Science Monitor,* November 11, 1971; *Horn Book,* October, 1971, October, 1974; *New York Times Book Review,* September 3, 1972; Lee Bennett Hopkins, *More Books by More People,* Citation, 1974; *Hartford Courant,* June 2, 1974; *Cricket,* September, 1974; *English Journal,* April, 1975, October, 1975; *Psychology Today,* July, 1975; Margery Fisher, *Who's Who in Children's Books,* Holt, 1975.

FRANK SHOWELL STYLES

STYLES, Frank Showell 1908-
(Glyn Carr, S. Howell)

PERSONAL: Born March 14, 1908, in Four Oaks, Warwickshire, England; son of Frank and Edith (Showell) Styles; married Jean Humphreys, 1954; children: Glynda Jane, Elisabeth Ann, David. *Education:* Attended Bishop Vesey's School. *Home:* Borth-y-gest, Gwynedd LL49 9TW, North Wales, United Kingdom. *Agent:* Curtis Brown Ltd., 13 King St., London W.C.2, England.

CAREER: Worked as bank clerk, 1925-35; author, 1945—. Leader, British Lyngen Expedition, 1951, North Lyngen Expedition, 1952, Baudha Himalayan Expedition, 1954. *Military service:* Royal Navy, 1939-45, became lieutenant commander. *Member:* Royal Geographical Society, Detection Club, Midland Association of Mountaineers (president, 1959-60).

WRITINGS: Traitor's Mountain, Selwyn & Blount, 1944; *Kidnap Castle,* Selwyn & Blount, 1947; *Hammer Island,* Selwyn & Blount, 1948; *Dark Hazard,* Selwyn & Blount, *Admiral's Fancy,* Faber & Faber, 1958; *Getting to Know Mountains,* Newnes, 1958; *Quinn of the "Fury,"* Faber & Faber, 1958, Vanguard, 1961; *How Underground Britain Is*

Explored, Routledge, 1958; *Shadow Buttress,* Faber & Faber, 1959; *Wolfe Commands You,* Faber & Faber, 1959; *The Lost Pothole,* Brockhampton, 1959; *The Battle of Cotton,* Constable, 1959.

Tiger Patrol Wins Through, Collins, 1960; *The Battle of Steam,* Constable, 1960; *The Flying Ensign,* Faber, 1960; *Greencoats Against Napoleon,* Vanguard, 1960; *Shop in the Mountain,* Gollancz, 1961; *Midshipman Quinn Wins Through,* Faber, 1961; *The Sea Officer,* Faber & Faber, 1961; *Gentleman Johnny,* Faber & Faber, 1962; *Byrd of the 95th,* Faber & Faber, 1962; *Look at Mountains,* Hamish Hamilton, 1962; *The Ladder of Snow,* Gollancz, 1962, Vanguard; *Greenhorn's Cruise,* Brockhampton, 1963, Van Nostrand-Reinhold, 1964; *H.M.S. Diamond Rock,* Faber, 1963; *A Necklace of Glaciers,* Gollancz, 1964; *The Camp in the Hills,* Benn, 1964; *Modern Mountaineering,* Faber, 1964; *Blue Remembered Hills,* Faber, 1965; *Quinn at Trafalgar,* Faber, 1965, Vanguard, 1968; *Red for Adventure,* Brockhampton, 1965; *Mr. Fiddle,* Hamish Hamilton, 1965; *Number Two-Ninety,* Faber & Faber, 1965; *Wolf Club Island,* Brockhampton, 1965.

If these masses of overhanging snow were the same crumbly stuff as the lower ridge, no climber in the world could scale the crest and escape death. ■ (From *First Up Everest* by Showell Styles. Illustrated by Raymond Briggs.)

1948; *The Rising of the Lark,* Selwyn & Blount, 1949; *Sir Devil,* Selwyn & Blount, 1949; *A Climber in Wales,* Cornishes, 1949.

The Mountaineers Weekend Book, Seeley Service, 1951; *Path to Glory,* Faber & Faber, 1951; *Land from the Sea,* Faber & Faber, 1952; *Mr. Nelson's Ladies,* Faber & Faber, 1953; *Mountains of the Midnight Sun,* Hurst & Blackett, 1954; *The Frigate Captain,* Faber & Faber, 1954; *Introduction to Mountaineering,* Seeley Service, 1955; *A Corpse at Camp Two,* Geoffrey Bles, 1955; *The Moated*

Mountain, Hurst & Blackett, 1955; *The Lost Glacier,* Hart-Davis, 1955, Vanguard.

His Was the Fire, Faber & Faber, 1956; *Kami the Sherpa,* Brockhampton, 1956, published by Vanguard as *Sherpa Adventure,* 1959; *Tiger Patrol,* Collins, 1956; *The Trampers and Campers Weekend Book,* Seely Service, 1957; *Midshipman Quinn,* Faber & Faber, 1957, Vanguard; *Tiger Patrol at Sea,* Collins, 1957; *How Mountains Are Climbed,* Routledge, 1957; *Introduction to Caravanning,* Seeley Service, 1958; *Tiger Patrol Presses On,* Collins, 1958; *The*

The Pass of Morning, Washburn, 1966; *The Foundations of Climbing,* S. Paul, 1966; *Mr. Fiddle's Pig,* Hamish Hamilton, 1966; *Rock and Rope,* Faber, 1967; *Indestructible Jones,* Faber, 1967, Washburn, 1968; *Confederate Raider,* Washburn, 1967; *Mallory of Everest,* Hamish Hamilton, 1967, Macmillan, 1968; *The Sea Cub,* Brockhampton, 1967; *Mr. Fiddle's Band,* Hamish Hamilton, 1967; *On Top of the World,* Hamish Hamilton, 1967; *The Climber's Bedside Book,* Faber, 1968; *Journey with a Secret,* Gollancz, 1968, Hawthorn, 1969; *Sea Road to Camperdown,* Faber, 1968; *Men and Mountaineering,* D. White, 1968; *First Up Everest,* Coward, 1969; *A Case for Mr. Fiddle,* Hamish Hamilton, 1969; *Cubs of the Castle,* Brockhampton, 1969; *Jones's Private Navy,* Faber, 1969; *The Snowdon Rangers,* Faber, 1969.

The Forbidden Frontiers, Hamish Hamilton, 1970; *First on the Summits,* Gollancz, 1970; *A Tent on Top,* Gollancz, 1971; *Vincey Joe at Quiberon,* Faber, 1971; *Cubs on the Job,* Brockhampton, 1972; *Welsh Walks and Legends,* Jones Cardiff, 1972; *Mystery of the Fleeing Girl,* Scholastic, 1972; *The Mountains of North Wales,* Gollancz, 1973; *Marty's Mountain,* Hamish Hamilton, 1973; *Admiral of England,* Faber, 1973; *Welsh Tales for Children,* Eastwood, 1974.

Under pseudonym Glyn Carr: *Death on Milestone Buttress,* 1951; *Murder on the Matterhorn,* 1952; *The Youth Hostel Murders,* 1952; *The Corpse in the Crevasse,* 1952; *Death under Snowdon,* 1954; *Murder of an Owl,* 1956; *The Ice Axe Murders,* 1958; *Swing Away Climber,* 1959; *Holiday with Murder,* 1960; *Death Finds a Foothold,* 1961; *Lewker in Norway,* 1963; *Death of a Weirdy,* 1965; *Lewker in Tirol,* 1967; *Fat Man's Agony,* 1969 (all published by Bles).

SIDELIGHTS: "If my ship hadn't been torpedoed off Tobruk during World War II, I might never have written a book. Needing something to do while enduring two weeks 'survivor's leave' in Alexandria, Egypt, I asked a fellow naval officer to name three different settings and I would try to write a book round them. He named a farmhouse in North Wales, a sinking ship, and a villa in Alexandria. I wrote the book—it was a terrible spy-thriller called *Traitor's Mountain*—and to my astonishment it was published in Britain and the United States and also translated into French. So that was the first of over a hundred books of all sorts and sizes, from books for children through accounts of mountaineering expeditions and detective novels to historical novels—and educational primers as well.

"I like to write of scenes and actions with which I'm familiar, so mountains and the sea come into most of my books. Climbing up mountains and sailing a boat are things that appeal to nearly all children, and my books for younger readers use these backgrounds, too. From where I live, on the coast of North Wales, I look out of my study window across a big sea inlet to distant mountains, and it's very satisfactory to have two lifelong friends next door, so to speak.

"In writing a book I find the most exciting—and hardest—part is starting the tale going; the most toilsome part comes when about two-thirds of it is done; and the saddest part is at the very end, when the adventure is finished, the typescript corrected and sent away, and all the imaginary friends I've been living with for months are gone."

About twenty-five of Styles' books have been published by United States publishers. Several have been published also in France, Norway, Germany, Holland, and Spain.

HOBBIES AND OTHER INTERESTS: Mountaineering and music.

TALBOT, Charlene Joy   1928-

PERSONAL: Born November 14, 1928, in Frankfort, Kan.; daughter of Charles Henry (a laborer) and Helen (Jillson) Talbot. *Education:* Kansas State College, Manhattan, Kansas, B.S. in Journalism, 1950. *Home:* 360 Greenwich St., New York, N.Y. 10013.

CAREER: After college wandered to New York, California, Mexico, and Europe, working as typist, secretary, waitress, and classified ad-taker; in 1958 found a cheap apartment in the market district of Manhattan, worked part-time as a secretary, began to write, and finally sold a children's story to a Sunday school paper. *Awards, honors:* Fellowship in juvenile literature to Bread Loaf Writers' Conference, 1966.

WRITINGS: Tomas Takes Charge (juvenile), Lothrop, 1966; *A Home with Aunt Florry* (juvenile), Atheneum, 1974. Stories have appeared in *Golden Magazine, Scholastic Newstime, Calling All Girls, Atlantic Advocate, Harvest Years,* and *American Restaurant.*

SIDELIGHTS: "Writing diaries, letters to the children's page, and school essays seemed the natural outgrowth of learning to use a pencil. The next step was the high school

CHARLENE JOY TALBOT

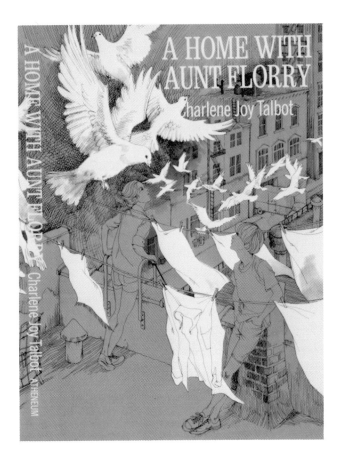

Overhead the birds were flying in a circle, wheeling as a flock, moving and turning all at the same time, like a bouquet of birds being swung round and round on a long string. ■ (From *A Home with Aunt Florry* by Charlene Joy Talbot. Illustrated by Gail Owens.)

paper, a teacher who encouraged me, a poem published in *Scholastic Magazine,* and a prize in an essay contest. After high school I lived in Los Angeles with my aunt and uncle and attended junior college at Compton for a year. At that time Southern California was still considered to be the earthly paradise by all the people left behind in the Middlewest, and I enjoyed everything about it—the palm trees, the smell of the air, the riotous geraniums. I discovered Thomas Wolfe and Dos Passos and naturally I wrote for the school paper.

"Back at Kansas State College for the next three years, I spent one of them going for walks and reading poetry instead of attending football games, and the next writing about football games for the school paper, the town paper, and the Associated Press. (Male journalism students were almost non-existent, due to World War II.) I began a novel.

"After graduation I headed east for New York and Greenwich Village, of which I had read romantic accounts, and which I'm happy to say has never disappointed me, never failed to be exciting, sometimes scary, but always interesting.

"After that, followed some years of wandering—Los Angeles, Baja, California, Topeka, Kansas City, Holland, Ibiza, England, and Wales. Eventually I came back to New York and settled into a small apartment with a part-time job, an

electric typewriter and a cat. The result has been the kind of life I wanted, numerous published articles and short stories for children and two novels. On weekends I go hiking or bird-watching to one of the wildlife areas around the city. Liking New York doesn't preclude an interest in conserving Nature, and I belong to several conservation groups.

"The wonderful thing about writing for children is that they're interested in everything. You can do all the things you wanted to do as a child, and then write about them as though you still were."

FOR MORE INFORMATION SEE: Junior Literary Guild Catalog, September, 1974.

TALLCOTT, Emogene

PERSONAL: Born in Parish, N.Y. *Education:* Oswego State Normal School (now State University of New York College at Oswego), student; Columbia University, B.S. and M.A. *Home:* 7573 West Main St., Port Leyden, N.Y. 13433.

CAREER: Teacher, principal, and supervisor at elementary schools in Garden City, N.Y., 1925-43; engaged in educational reorganization for Office of Military Government in Germany for three years; spent two years as educational technician with the International Cooperation Ad-

EMOGENE TALLCOTT

ministration in Paraguay; producer of educational television programs in Watertown, N.Y., for three years. *Member:* National League of American Pen Women, American Association of University Women, Delta Kappa Gamma.

WRITINGS: Glacier Tracks (juvenile), Lothrop, 1970.

WORK IN PROGRESS: Research for a juvenile science book, *Ice;* research on the topic of continental movement.

SIDELIGHTS: "One day when, as a high school student, I was on a hike with our science teacher, he pointed to a low, rounded hill some distance away and said, 'That is a moraine. It's a hill of gravel left by the ice sheet as it melted and retreated north.' A glacier covering these fields and our town? That was intriguing news to me.

"In college I signed up for all the geology courses available. So when I came to the Black River Valley in the northern part of New York state, where I worked as elementary supervisor, I recognized all the signs of glaciation which abound in the valley.

"When I talked with the teachers about the ice age and the tracks the ice left we discovered there were few books for children which explained in detail *how* the tracks were made. There were no books which could be used for identification of landscape features, much as you might use a bird guide to identify birds. Such a book was needed.

"As I drove from school to school in the rural area of the southern part of Lewis County I was thrilled to discover many moraines, an esker, a quarried boss, perched boulders, gravel pits, etc. As I looked at these signs I planned how I could best describe these features. When I reached home I wrote down the phrases I had composed.

"I began taking pictures, collecting material, consulting geology books until I had assembled the material which I eventually included in my book, *Glacier Tracks*. I attempted to keep the vocabulary easy, the phrases short and to explain scientific terms when first used. The book is usable in the upper. elementary and junior high school grades.

"When I was doing research for this book I became intrigued with *ice* as a topic. It is fascinating stuff, very versatile. I have the beginning of a book on this topic underway. At the same time the information which seems to prove the theory of continental movement has captured my interest and I may pursue the writing of a book on this topic before I finish the work about ice.

"I believe if one is thoroughly (in depth) knowledgeable about his own environment he is more capable of understanding other environments and has a background for understanding and interpreting the whole world, its ecology, etc. We need today this global understanding. I sincerely hope *Glacier Tracks* will aid children in gaining such an understanding."

HOBBIES AND OTHER INTERESTS: Photography, geology, oil painting, dramatics, anthropology of the Americas.

TAYLOR, Barbara J. 1927-

PERSONAL: Born June 27, 1927, in Provo, Utah; daughter of Theodore Marsden (a merchant) and Clara Mae (Orton) Taylor; married Dee Raymond Taylor (an architect), June 8, 1949; children: David Dee, Brad Lee. *Education:* Brigham Young University, B.S., 1957, M.S., 1960, Ph.D., 1971; Florida State University, graduate study, 1967-68. *Religion:* Church of Jesus Christ of Latter-Day Saints (Mormon). *Office:* Department of Child Development and Family Relationships, Brigham Young University, Provo, Utah 84602.

CAREER: Brigham Young University, Provo, Utah, instructor, 1957-68, assistant professor of child development and family relationships, 1968-74, associate professor, 1975—. *Member:* National Association for the Education of Young Children, Organisation Mondiale pour l'Education Prescolaire, British Association for Early Childhood Education, Utah Association for the Education of Young Children (past president).

WRITINGS: A Child Goes Forth, Brigham Young University Press, 1964, 2nd edition, 1975; *I Can Do* (juvenile), Brigham Young University Press, 1972; *When I Do, I Learn,* Brigham Young University Press, 1974.

WORK IN PROGRESS: A book on comparative preschool education in the United States and certain other countries; a book on administration and supervision in preschool.

BARBARA J. TAYLOR

I can care for my pet. Can you? ■ (From *I Can Do* by Barbara J. Taylor. Photos by Dee R. Taylor.)

TAYLOR, David   1900-1965

PERSONAL: Born November 11, 1900, in Aberdeen, Scotland; son of James Henry and Kate (Crabbe) Taylor; married Theodora Engstrom, 1940; children: James Henry. *Education:* Graduated from Robert Gordon's College; Aberdeen University, B.Sc., 1921. *Home:* 255 East Wendy Way, King of Prussia, Pa.

CAREER: Plantation engineer in Hawaii, 1921-25; free-lance writer and producer for radio, Los Angeles, Calif., 1926-30; American Radio Features, Hollywood, Calif., writer and production manager, 1933-38; Pacific Coast Radio, Foote, Cone and Belding, Hollywood, Calif., manager, 1941-48; Freedoms Foundation, Valley Forge, Pa., public relations executive, 1949-50, later was national historian; free-lance writer, radio producer, lecturer. Pennsylvania National Guard, 111th Infantry, historian; Philadelphia Rehabilitation Center, member of board of governors; Boy Scouts of America, merit badge counselor. *Military service:* British Army, 1914-18; became major; received Croix de Guerre. *Member:* Bucks County Writers, Bucks County Historical Society, Historic Fallsington, David Library (Washington Crossing, Pa.). *Awards, honors:* Huguenot

Cross, 1957; Freedoms Foundation Awards, George Washington Medal, 1958, 1959, Freedom Leadership Award, 1960; Athenaeum Bronze Medal for fiction for *Storm the Last Rampart*, 1960.

WRITINGS: Lights Across the Delaware, 1954, *Farewell to Valley Forge*, 1955, *Sycamore Men*, 1958, *Storm the Last Rampart*, 1960, *Mistress of the Forge*, 1964 (all published by Lippincott).

SIDELIGHTS: Wrote and produced radio show, "Meet the MacMullans," for WRCV in Philadelphia for eleven years, and presented five-minute vignettes on American history five times weekly over WIBF in Jenkintown, Pa. First two books have been printed in Arabic by the State Department. *Farewell to Valley Forge* was optioned by Walt Disney.

HOBBIES AND OTHER INTERESTS: Archaeology and music.

FOR MORE INFORMATION SEE: Jenkintown Times Chronicle, May 10, 1962.

(Died July 1, 1965)

TAYLOR, Robert Lewis   1912-

PERSONAL: Born September 24, 1912, in Carbondale, Ill.; son of Roscoe Aaron (in real estate) and Mabel (Bowyer) Taylor; married Judith Martin, February 3, 1945; children: Martin Lewis, Elizabeth Ann. *Education:*

ROBERT LEWIS TAYLOR

Southern Illinois University, student; University of Illinois, A.B., 1933. *Politics:* Republican. *Home:* Bulls Bridge Rd., South Kent, Conn.

CAREER: First job was on a weekly newspaper in Carbondale, Ill., 1934, but after a year there he sailed for Tahiti and remained in the South Seas until 1936, financing himself by serving as a correspondent for *American Boy.* Reporter for *St. Louis Post Dispatch,* St. Louis, Mo., 1936-39; *New Yorker,* New York, N.Y., profile writer, 1939—. *Military service:* U.S. Naval Reserve, 1942-46; became lieutenant commander. *Member:* Authors Guild, National Society of Literature and the Arts, Down East Yacht Club (Boothbay Harbor, Maine), Villa Monte Carlo (Chapala, Mexico). *Awards, honors:* Sigma Delta Chi runner-up award in general reporting division, 1939; Pulitzer Prize in fiction, 1959, for *The Travels of Jaimie McPheeters.*

WRITINGS: Adrift in a Boneyard (fantasy novel), 1947, *Doctor, Lawyer, Merchant, Chief* (collection), 1948, *W. C. Fields: His Follies and Fortunes,* 1949, *The Running Pianist,* 1950, *Professor Fodorski,* 1950, *Winston Churchill, An Informal Study of Greatness,* 1952, *The Bright Sands* (novel), 1954, *Center Ring, The People of the Circus,* 1956, *The Travels of Jaimie McPheeters,* 1958, *A Journey to Matecumbe,* McGraw, 1961, *Two Roads to Guadalupe,* 1964, *Vessel of Wrath: The Life and Times of Carry Nation,* New American Library, 1966 (all published by Doubleday, except where otherwise noted). Contributor to *Saturday Evening Post, Life, Collier's, Esquire, Redbook, Reader's Digest.*

SIDELIGHTS: "I was born in the Southern Mid-west, which has disgorged many other mischievous types and pretty rogues, and I'm afraid that as a child growing up I was something of a handful. After college, my family decided a healthful breather for everybody (meaning them) would be to send me around the world for two years. These I divided about equally between Tahiti and Europe, returning with some reluctance to take a job—at my father's most vigorous prompting—as a reporter for the *St. Louis Post Dispatch* in St. Louis, Joseph Pulitzer's fine old paper.

"After I'd served a term of three years there, Ross hired me to write Reporter-at-Large pieces and then Profiles for *The New Yorker* magazine. I also began to dabble with the notion of writing books. No matter how hard I tried the third person, I found myself most comfortable writing in the first person, with the perspective of approximately the kind of scamp that I apparently was some years before. As I dug more deeply and seriously into all this, I began making a conscious effort to write historical novels, with a boy telling most of the tale. I thought that might be enjoyed

■ (From "Treasure of Matecumbe" by Robert Lewis Taylor. Copyright 1976 by Walt Disney Studios.)

by both children *and* adults. To date, I've not been sorry; and it happens that, at the moment, I'm in the middle of another. My librarian friends at Yale called early this summer to tell me of some newly acquired and wondrous old diaries, journals, letters, and other material having to do with the Territory of Montana (circa 1860) in its toughest and wildest period. Thus far, I feel perfectly at home in the milieu.

"Might add that my wife and I live, for most of each year, in a walled and tiled villa that we own in southern Mexico. Everything about this—horses, bandito-filled mountains, desert growth, and · unpredictability everywhere seems agreeably rewarding. If more people move into our town of Ajijic, on Lake Chapala, we will, of course, burrow farther into the hills."

The Travels of Jaimie McPheeters was a television series; the Broadway musical, "All American," 1963, was based on *Professor Fodorski;* the musical "W.C.," 1971, was based on *W. C. Fields: His Follies and Fortunes;* the Walt Disney movie "The Treasure of Matecumbe," 1976, was based on *A Journey to Matecumbe.*

FOR MORE INFORMATION SEE: E. P. Hazard, "First Novelists of 1947," *Saturday Review,* February 14, 1948; *New York Times,* May 5, 1959; *Commonweal,* February 3, 1967; *Book Week,* February 26, 1967.

TEAL, Val(entine M.) 1903-

PERSONAL: Born February 14, 1903, in Bottineau, N.D.; daughter of August Anderson (an owner and operator of a flour mill) and Georgiana (Berntson) Moline; married Clarence William Teal (an engineering executive), September 4, 1926; children: John Moline, Peter Valentine, Thomas Augustus, Alison (daughter). *Education:* University of Minnesota, B.A., 1925. *Politics:* Independent. *Religion:* Episcopalian. *Home and office:* 5620 Western Ave., Omaha, Neb. 68132.

CAREER: Minneapolis Daily News, Minneapolis, Minn., puzzle editor, 1922-24; *Rural American,* Minneapolis, Minn., puzzle editor, 1922-24; legal secretary in Minneapolis, Minn., 1924-25; Minneapolis Council of Social Agencies, Minneapolis, Minn., secretary, 1925-27; University of Nebraska, Omaha, tutor in humanities, 1947-65; writer, 1943—. Member of board of Omaha Junior Theater; member of local family and child welfare board.

MEMBER: P.E.O. Sisterhood, American Association of University Women, Omaha Community Playhouse (historian). *Awards, honors:* Omaha Junior Theatre playwriting contest, 1954, first prize for *Grandmother's Magic Clock;* Omaha Community Playhouse Award for exceptional service, 1965 and 1975.

WRITINGS: The Little Woman Wanted Noise (juvenile), Rand McNally, 1943; *Angel Child* (juvenile), Rand McNally, 1946; *It Was Not What I Expected,* Duell, Sloan & Pearce, 1948.

Work has been anthologized in 24 books, including *Read Me More Stories,* T. Y. Crowell, 1951; Adelaid Field, *The Second Child Life Story Book,* Winston, 1953; J. Edward Lantz, *Stories to Grow By,* Associated Press, 1953;

Frances T. Humphreville, *The Years Between,* Scott, Foresman, 1953; Albert B. Tibbets, *Youth, Youth, Youth,* Watts, 1955; Eva Pumphrey and Eric W. Johnson, *Adventures for You,* Harcourt, 1968; Nicholas J. Silvaroli and William D. Sheldon, *This Cool World,* Lippincott, 1970. Contributor of short stories to popular magazines for adults and children, including *Saturday Evening Post, Ladies' Home Journal, Good Housekeeping, American, Woman's Day, Child Life, Woman's Home Companion* and *Parent's Magazine.* Contributing editor for Omaha Community Playhouse.

SIDELIGHTS: "I can't explain why I have always wanted to be a writer. Maybe there are people who simply love to tell stories. I was and am one. When I was a toddler, I'd sit in my little rocking chair and rock and sing long stories I made up. When I was five and in the first grade, we had a period of telling stories we made up and I was the most eager storyteller in the grade. My father used to say that it was silly for him to spend money to send all of the family to a show (infrequent affairs in the small towns we lived in in Minnesota and North Dakota), because all that was necessary was to send me; for I always came home and told about the whole show and made it more interesting than it had been in the original.

"When I was seven, I was delighted when a story I wrote was printed in the children's section of the *St. Paul Pioneer Press* and I was paid one whole dollar for it. I fully intended to be a writer when I grew up and what worried me was not that I might not be able to think of things to write about but that I might not be able to afford to buy enough paper. (We were taught to be frugal as children and frugality is one of my outstanding characteristics to this day.) I was encouraged by my English teachers in grade and high school and once a teacher sent a poem I had written to a magazine but nothing came of it. In high school and even in college, although I was self-supporting during college and had little time, I was continually doing extra-curricular writing, trying my hand at a novel or short stories. I had so much to say, I felt.

"One year of higher education beyond high school was all my family could give me and I went to business college, one of the smartest things I ever did, because in the jobs I held after that, which supported me while I went to the university, I learned to type rapidly. It is amazing to me that all of those writers before typewriters were invented managed to put down in *long hand* all that wealth of literature. Fortunately, I can type almost as fast as I can think.

"I got married right out of college and the actual beginning of my writing career happened because of my children. When our oldest, John, was learning to read, he would march proudly around the house reading aloud from his school reader. The stories were all about a boy named Peter, and Peter, our second child, asked John hopefully if the stories were about him. When he found they weren't, he said woefully, 'I wish I had a book about me!' So I said I would make him one and I did. I printed the story by hand, drew and colored illustrations, bound the book on the sewing machine, put hard covers on it and covered and decorated them. The finished product looked very professional, complete with end papers etc. I had so much fun making that book that I went on and made others which my children and their friends dearly loved. And, to my delight,

I sold an article about this fascinating hobby of mine to the old *Scribner's Magazine*. Finally, I made one of these books that my husband thought was pretty good—good enough, he thought that it ought to be published, so, without my knowing it, he sent it off to Rand McNally & Company. One of the biggest surprises of my life was the letter I received saying they would like to publish *The Little Woman Wanted Noise.*

"Robert Lawson had promised to do the illustrations for one book for Rand McNally that year and when he was in their office he saw my small book lying on a desk, picked it up, was delighted with it, and asked if he might do *that* one. He used my illustrations exactly—only making better drawings of them, (*much* better of course)—and, in a letter to Rand McNally he said the book was practically illustrating itself, he was, he said, 'sticking very closely to Mrs. Teal's drawings,' and added, 'If only Mrs. Teal could draw better—or worse.' And I knew exactly what he meant. My drawing is too too careful and meticulous.

"Rand McNally wrote me asking for biographical material, and, much flattered, I responded generously with the kind of material I love to read in a biography. I told about my family, about how we lived, what we did, our hobbies, lots of details and episodes. A man from Rand McNally came to town, called me, took my husband and me to dinner, and, during the course of the evening, told us how popular that letter of mine was. Everyone in their organization was reading it and people had their names on a waiting list in order to get it in their proper turns.

"After I was home, I began to think about that. If that kind of material was that good, I thought, then that was the kind of material I should write and *sell.* So I sat down and wrote a story using that familiar style and that sort of material, sent it to the *Ladies' Home Journal* and sold it immediately.

"My husband still laughs at me because the telegram making me an offer for the story was addressed to *Mister* Teal and so, I referred Western Union to his office. Later in the day I called him to tell him of the tragic thing that had happened—Peter's new bike had been stolen from the school grounds—and I asked him what the telegram was about and he said, *'Don't you know?'* They had never called me back. Anyway, my husband claims that I was much more interested in the loss of Peter's bike (at a time when we could not get another because the war was on and no metal was being put into bicycles) than I was in having sold my first story to one of America's leading magazines. I *was* interested, of course, and impressed; and I telegraphed the *Ladies' Home Journal* accepting their fabulous offer and wishing the editor, all *Ladies' Home Journal* employees, *and,* to their amusement, Western Union a Merry Christmas.

"At once I acquired an agent, Elsie McKeogh, who, until her death, was of infinite help to me, and I began to sell stories regularly. (I had already been selling children's stories and continued to handle that part of my writing for myself.)

"I spent every morning writing—and sometimes continued into the afternoon and evening. But, only after I had spent a half day at writing did I consider that I had earned the

VAL TEAL

privilege of doing the laundry, baking, cooking, cleaning, etc. The war was now on and my days of full-time maids were a thing of the past. My family always came first, however, and I never did any writing at the neglect of them and their affairs, big or small.

"My husband and I have been active in the Omaha Community Playhouse since 1929 and still are. He was on the board of trustees for thirty-four years, president for three years, treasurer for twenty-eight years, and our whole family worked backstage and out front, acted in many plays, and have done everything it is possible to do in connection with a theatre, including raising funds for one of the outstanding little theatre buildings in the country. The Playhouse recently honored us by dedicating two seats in the auditorium to us, the highest honor they bestow, and which had been awarded to only four people previously, one of them being Henry Fonda who got his start there.

"My husband is an ardent and award-winning photographer and I enter into this hobby also. For a while I dabbled in oil painting—portraits—and have had two of my paintings hung in the Joslyn Museum's six-state show. My husband is on the library board, another activity I share with him, and we have worked in other civic capacities.

"I am a zealous conservationist and environmentalist. I wash dishes by hand, wash clothes with a wringer-type washer to conserve water. I hang them out to dry to conserve energy. I even make my own laundry soap and my clothes are cleaner and whiter than those washed with detergents which are polluting our streams. I have no garbage disposal. I have always baked our bread. I make braided rugs—one room-size one and have even made braided carpeting for the front hall, stairs, and long upstairs hall. I am interested in early American antiques. Our early American house is completely furnished with them, many of them family heirlooms, all refinished by us. I suppose we are among the few couples in the country who had a house built for themselves back in 1933 and have lived in it ever since. I also make quilts—right now crazy quilts of silk or velvet pieces and rich with embroidery. We have traveled almost all over the world.

"We are proud of our children. John is an oceanographer (in marine biology) and co-author, with his wife, of several books, one of which won the Phi Beta Kappa Science Award. They live on a nine-acre place on Cape Cod and have orchards, vegetable and flower gardens, strawberries and raspberries, many animals from chickens and geese up to goats and horses. Peter is an orthopedic surgeon, living in Billings, Montana. Thomas ('Topper') is a translator of books and on the *New Yorker* staff. Alison is assistant director of the New York State Council for the Humanities. John's degrees were all from Harvard. Peter went to Dartmouth, then to Harvard Medical School. Topper went to Harvard and to graduate school at Berkeley plus one year on a Fulbright fellowship at the University of Helsinki. Alison has a B.A. from Smith. The boys all won topnotch honorary scholarships and graduated with honors. We have seven grandchildren."

TEE-VAN, Helen Damrosch 1893-
(Helen Therese Damrosch)

PERSONAL: Born May 26, 1893, in New York, N.Y.; daughter of Frank (a musician) and Hetty (Mosenthal) Damrosch; married John Tee-Van (an ichthyologist and zoological park director), July 17, 1923 (died, 1967). *Education:* Attended New York School of Display and Veltin School, New York, N.Y.; studied art under George de Forest Brush and Jonas Lie; also studied anatomy at Columbia University Medical School. *Home:* 120 East 75th

HELEN DAMROSCH TEE-VAN

The Raccoon will eat almost anything. It is extremely clever with its handlike forepaws. It can open garbage cans, turn doorknobs, or sort small edible food from pebbles. ■ (From *Small Mammals Are Where You Find Them* by Helen Damrosch Tee-Van. Illustrated by the author.)

St., New York, N.Y. 10021; and Route 1, Box 275, Sherman, Conn. 06784 (summer).

CAREER: Artist and illustrator; writer. New York Zoological Society, New York, N.Y., scientific artist participating in expeditions to South America and the Caribbean, at various times, 1922-63, designer of New York World's Fair exhibits, 1939-40, designer of zoo aquarium murals, 1941, and of murals for Children's Zoo, 1949. Work is in permanent collections at Berkshire Museum, Pittsfield, Mass., where commissioned, 1938-39, and at Bronx Zoo. Landscape and undersea paintings, and silk designs have been exhibited in numerous galleries and museums, including National Academy of Design and American Museum of Natural History (both New York, N.Y.), Buffalo Museum of Science, Pennsylvania Academy of Fine Arts, and Los Angeles Museum of Art. Occupational therapist, U.S. Army, 1918-19. *Member:* Society of Animal Artists, Society of Woman Geographers (vice-president and chairman of New York chapter, 1945-48), New York Zoological Society (life member), China Institute of America, Cosmopolitan Club.

WRITINGS—Juveniles, except as noted; all self-illustrated: *Red Howling Monkey,* Macmillan, 1926; (adapter) *The Trees Around Us* (adult), Dial, 1960; *Insects Are Where You Find Them,* Knopf, 1963; *Small Mammals Are Where You Find Them,* Knopf, 1966.

Illustrator: Emily Niles Huyck and Frank Damrosch (under name Helen Therese Damrosch) *A Birthday Greeting and Other Songs,* G. Schirmer, 1918; Satis Coleman, *Creative Music in the Home,* Lewis E. Myers & Co., 1927; Elswyth Thane, *Reluctant Farmer* (adult), Duell,

Something about the Author

Sloan & Pearce, 1950; Roger Burlingame, *Mosquitoes in the Big Ditch: The Story of the Panama Canal*, Winston, 1952; Clifford Pope, *Reptiles Round the World*, Knopf, 1957; William Knowlton, *Sea Monsters*, Knopf, 1959; Alfred Milotte, *The Story of the Platypus*, Knopf, 1959; Naomi Talley, *Imported Insects* (adult), Dial, 1961; Alfred Milotte, *The Story of the Hippopotamus*, Knopf, 1964; Alfred Milotte and Elma Milotte, *The Story of an Alaskan Grizzly Bear*, Knopf, 1969.

Contributor of illustrations to *Encyclopaèdia Britannica*, *Collier's Encyclopedia*, New York Zoological Society publications, and to scientific journals and popular periodicals.

SIDELIGHTS: "I use oils, watercolors, ink and black and colored pencil on dino base. I have been interested in drawing from age seven. I did childrens portraits and illustrations in watercolor. In 1922 I was invited by William Beebe to British Guiana, and that was how I became a scientific artist. My personal philosophy is to enjoy your work and do it as best you can. I was influenced by Jonas Lie.

"I have traveled through most of the United States, Europe, Canada from the Atlantic to the Pacific, British Guiana, Venezuela, Panama, Trinidad, Puerto Rico, Haiti, Australia, New Zealand, Hongkong, Taiwan, Figi, Hawaii, but never got to Africa.

"I speak French, German, Norwegian (but have forgotten most of it), studied Chinese for three years but still have no competence."

Helen Tee-Van's work is collected at the research library, University of Oregon, Eugene, Oregon.

HOBBIES AND OTHER INTERESTS: Ecology, particularly conservation of land resources and animal preservation; color photography.

THOMPSON, Harlan H. 1894-
(Stephen Holt)

PERSONAL: Born December 25, 1894, in Brewster, Kan.; son of William Lewis (a rancher) and Clara Cornelia (Shultz) Thompson; married Gail Gertrude Friend, May 31, 1960; children: (former marriage) Charlotte, James Van De Water (deceased), Harlan Trenholm, Barbara (Mrs. Charles F. Wheeler). *Education:* University of Southern California, student, 1917-19. *Politics:* Republican. *Religion:* Methodist. *Home and office:* 1160 Oakwood Dr., San Marino, Calif. 91108. *Agent:* William Morris Agency, Beverly Hills, Calif.

CAREER: Writer. Owner TX Ranch, Alberta, Canada. *Member:* P.E.N. (international president, 1958-59), California Writers Guild, Westerners (Los Angeles Corral), Commonwealth Club (San Francisco). *Awards, honors:* Boys' Clubs of America gold medal, 1948, for *Prairie Colt;* Commonwealth Club juvenile silver medal, 1957, for *Spook, the Mustang.*

WRITINGS—Under pseudonym Stephen Holt: *Wild Palomino*, Longmans, Green, 1946; *Prairie Colt*, Longmans, Green, 1947; *Phantom Roan* (Junior Literary Guild selection), Longmans, Green, 1949; *Whistling Stallion*, Long-

mans, Green, 1951; *Stormy*, Longmans, Green, 1955; *We Were There with the California Forty Niners*, Grosset, 1956; *We Were There with the California Rancheros*, Grosset, 1960; *Ranch Beyond the Mountains*, Longmans, Green, 1961.

Under name Harlan Thompson: *Star Roan*, Doubleday, 1952; *Spook, the Mustang* (Junior Literary Guild selection), Doubleday, 1956; *Outcast Stallion of Hawaii*, Doubleday, 1957. Contributor of short stories to national periodicals.

WORK IN PROGRESS: Lasso Land—Six Famous Ranchers of the World, for McKay; *Ride a Red Horse*, for McGraw; *Hawaiian Fire Ranch;* and a novel, *Reach for Heaven.*

TIMMINS, William F(rederick)

PERSONAL: Born in Chicago, Ill.; son of Harry L. (an illustrator; painter) and Pauline (Beckford) Timmins; married Marjorie Vail; children: Gary William, Dana (Mrs. Stephen P. Leane). *Education:* Attended Grand Central Art School, New York, N.Y., 1933-34; Art Students League, New York, N.Y., 1933-34. *Home and office:* P.O. Box 5685, Carmel, Calif. 93921.

CAREER: Free-lance illustrator; painter. Airadio, Incorporated, Stamford, Conn., art director, 1942-45. *Exhibitions:* Darien, Connecticut Art Show, 1963-64; Cochrane Gallery, one-man show, Darien, Conn., 1963; New Canaan Art Festival, 1963; Society of Illustrators, New York, N.Y., 1955; Perry House Gallery, Monterey, Calif., 1965-75; Carmel Valley Gallery, Carmel Valley, Calif., 1965-75; Phippen-Obrien Gallery, Scottsdale, Arizona, 1974-76;

WILLIAM TIMMINS

House of Bronze Gallery, Prescott, Ariz., 1975-76; Village Artistry, Carmel, Calif., 1975-76; Makai Art Village, Lihue, Hawaii, 1975; A Huney Gallery, San Diego, Calif., 1976. *Member:* Society of Western Artists. *Awards, honors:* Society of Illustrators, New York, N.Y., first prize, 1955; Cohama Fabrics Design, 1955; Darien Art Show, First Award Oil, 1963, Second Award Watercolor, 1964.

ILLUSTRATOR: Ethel Stone, *Wild Bill Hickok,* Rand McNally, 1955; Bruce Grant, *Davey Crockett,* Rand McNally, 1955; *Super Circus,* Rand McNally, 1955; Bruce Grant, adapter, *Robin Hood,* Rand McNally, 1956; Helen Wing, *Emmet Kelley: Willie the Clown,* Rand McNally, 1957; *Cowboys,* Rand McNally, 1958; *Boy Scout Handbook,* Boy Scouts of America, 1959-70; *Boy Scout Troop Activities,* Boy Scouts of America, 1962; Mabel Watts, *Cub Scout,* Rand McNally, 1964; Marjorie Barrows, *Look! A Parade,* Rand McNally, 1965; *Lassie,* Western, 1966; A. A. Milne, *Winnie the Pooh,* Western, 1967. Also illustrated various publications for Providence Lithograph Company, 1960-75; various publications for McGraw, 1970-76.

SIDELIGHTS: "With a long career as a versatile illustrator, I have developed an interest in painting a variety of subjects: marines, landscapes, old buildings, barns, people and animals. The medium I use mostly is watercolor, some oil, some acrylic, some pen and ink. Naturally I was influenced by my father, artist Harry L. Timmins. I was strongly influenced in drawing by Karl Godwin of Westport, Connecticut.

"I have travelled throughout the United States, Canada, France, Spain, Italy and Belgium."

TODD, Barbara K(eith)   1917-

PERSONAL: Born September 11, 1917, in Durango,

"My, my" said Tia Delfina.
"I wonder if you are big enough
to help me make tortillas.
Come in the kitchen and we will see.
■ (From *Juan Patricio* by Barbara K. Todd. Illustrated by Gloria Kamen.)

BARBARA K. TODD

Colo.; daughter of Keith Sunderland (a banker) and Doris (a secretary; maiden name, Dyer) Rucker; married John Edwin Todd (a station attendant), July 11, 1945; children: John Anthony, Stanley Keith, Richard Dwight. *Education:* Arizona State University, B.A., 1939. *Politics:* Republican. *Religion:* Episcopal. *Home:* 368 West 23rd St., Durango, Colo. 81301. *Office:* Florida Mesa Elementary School, Durango, Colo. 81301.

CAREER: Third-grade teacher, Prescott, Ariz., 1939-43; hospital student nurse, 1943-44; Florida Mesa Elementary School, Durango, Colo., first-grade teacher, 1959—. *Member:* American Association of University Women (vice-president of programming, 1973-75), National League of American Pen Women, Delta Kappa Gamma. *Awards, honors:* First place in National League of American Pen Women Biennial Contest, 1974, for *Juan Patricio,* second place for unpublished fiction, 1975, for *Where Have All the Colors Gone?*

WRITINGS: Juan Patricio (juvenile), Putnam, 1972.

WORK IN PROGRESS: Salamanders; How They Celebrated Admission.

TONER, Raymond John   1908-

PERSONAL: Born June 8, 1908, in Chicago, Ill.; son of James Ambrose and Virginia (Casey) Toner; married Eve Martha Zink, June 13, 1936; children: David Lawrence Shannon, Rosemond Eve, Virginia Anne. *Education:* Attended U.S. Naval Academy Preparatory School; Northwestern University, B.S., 1949, M.A., 1950, certificate from Institute of Management, 1961; Armed Forces Staff College, graduate. *Religion:* Episcopalian. *Home:* 2158 N.W. 5th Ave., Gainesville, Fla. 32603.

CAREER: U.S. Navy officer, 1933—, captain, 1954-65, retired, 1965; University of Florida, Gainesville, assistant director of Center for Latin American Studies, 1965-75. Sea

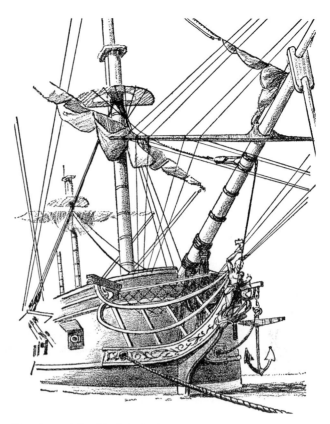

In a moment the frigate's rigging was black with topmen laying aloft to loose topsails. The fiddler struck up the tune "The Girl I Left Behind Me." Willing hands grasped the capstan bars. Soon the anchor broke clear of its holding ground. ■ (From *Gamble of the Marines* by Capt. Raymond J. Toner, U.S.N. Illustrated by Jack Merryweather and the author.)

duty during World War II included command of ships and a division of destroyer escorts in Atlantic and Pacific, at forward area until Japanese surrender. Also, has served as commander of various service schools, naval training centers, and reserve units; held command of flagship "Destroyer Squadron 6" assigned to Korean waters; served as naval advisor to Minister of Defense of Ecuador; served in Office of the Chief of Naval Operations as head of Foreign Naval Training Branch; assumed command of flagship (Service Force, "Sixth" Fleet), during crisis in Lebanon, commander, U.S. Naval Station, San Juan, Puerto Rico, 1962-65. *Member:* U.S. Naval Institute, Phi Delta Kappa.

WRITINGS: *Midshipman Davy Jones* (Junior Literary Guild selection), Whitman, 1938; *Meeheevee* (American Library Association selection), Whitman, 1940; *Gamble of the Marines,* Whitman, 1963. Contributes articles, principally on Latin American affairs, to professional journals. Writes professional studies and proposals concerning naval training.

WORK IN PROGRESS: *Cruise of the Frigate "Essex 32";* *The Wild Geese: Irish Exiles; O'Higgins: Viceroy of Spain;* research on the Latin American military.

HOBBIES AND OTHER INTERESTS: Shakespearian literature, marine painting, model railroading, history of Latin America, and history of the United States, particularly the War of 1812 and the Civil War.

RAYMOND JOHN TONER

TREVOR, (Lucy) Meriol 1919-

PERSONAL: Born April 15, 1919, in London, England; daughter of Arthur Prescott and Lucy (Dimmock) Trevor. *Education:* St. Hugh's College, University of Oxford, B.A., 1942. *Religion:* Roman Catholic. *Home:* 70 Pulteney St., Bath BA2 4DL, England. *Agent:* Harold Ober Associates, Inc., 40 East 49th St., New York, N.Y. 10017.

CAREER: United Nations Relief and Rehabilitation Administration, Italy, relief worker, 1946-47; professional writer.

WRITINGS—Novels: The Last of Britain, Macmillan (London), 1956; *The New People,* Macmillan (London), 1957; *A Narrow Place,* Macmillan (London), 1958; *Shadows and Images,* Macmillan (London), 1960, McKay, 1962; *The City and the World,* Dent, 1970; *The Holy Images,* Dent, 1971; *The Two Kingdoms,* Constable, 1973; *The Fugitives,* Hodder & Stoughton, 1973; *The Marked Man,* Hodder & Stoughton, 1974; *The Enemy at Home,* Hodder & Stoughton, 1975; *The Forgotten Country,* Hodder & Stoughton, 1975; *The Fortunate Marriage,* Dutton, 1976.

Biography: *Newman: The Pillar of the Cloud,* Doubleday, 1962; *Newman: Light in Winter,* Macmillan (London), 1962, Doubleday, 1963; *Apostle of Rome,* Macmillan (London), 1966; *Pope John in His Time,* Doubleday, 1967; *Prophets and Guardians,* Doubleday, 1969; *The Arnolds,* Scribner, 1973.

Poems: *Midsummer, Midwinter,* Hand and Flower Press, 1957.

Juveniles: *Forest and the Kingdom,* Faber, 1949; *Hunt the King, Hide the Fox,* Faber, 1950; *Fires and the Stars,* British Book Service, 1951; *Sun Faster, Sun Slower,* Collins, 1955; *The Other Side of the Moon,* Collins, 1956; *Merlin's Ring,* Collins, 1957; *The Treasure Hunt,* Hamish Hamilton, 1957; *Four Odd Ones,* Collins, 1958; *The Sparrow Child,* Collins, 1958; *The Caravan War,* Hamish Hamilton, 1963; *The Rose Round,* Hamish Hamilton, 1963, Dutton, 1964; *William's Wild Day Out,* Hamish Hamilton, 1963; *Lights in a Dark Town,* Macmillan (London), 1964; *The Midsummer Maze,* Macmillan (London), 1964; *The King of the Castle,* Macmillan (London), 1966.

HOBBIES AND OTHER INTERESTS: Looking at buildings, old and new, at pictures, old and new, and listening to music.

TROTTER, Grace V(iolet) 1900- (Nancy Paschal)

PERSONAL: Born November 23, 1900, in Dallas, Tex.; daughter of William Daniel and Nancy (Paschal) Trotter. *Education:* Attended public and private schools in Dallas. *Religion:* Christian Church. *Home:* 2028 Whitedove Dr., Dallas, Tex. 75224.

CAREER: Writer; speaker on creative writing. *Member:* Dallas Story League.

*WRITINGS—*All junior novels, all under name Nancy Paschal: *Clover Creek* (Junior Literary Guild selection),

GRACE V. TROTTER

Nelson, 1946; *Magnolia Heights* (Junior Literary Guild selection), Nelson, 1947; *Sylvan City,* Viking, 1950; *Spring in the Air,* Viking, 1953; *Promise of June* (Junior Literary Guild selection), Nelson, 1955; *Someone to Care,* Westminster, 1957; *Portrait by Sheryl,* Westminster, 1958; *Name the Day,* Westminster, 1959; *Prescription for Two,* Westminster, 1960; *Song of the Heart,* Westminster, 1961; *No More Good-Bys,* Westminster, 1962; *Make Way for Lauren,* Westminster, 1963; *Hillview House,* Westminster, 1963; *Emeralds on Her Hand,* Farrar, Straus, 1965.

WORK IN PROGRESS: Short stories for young children and "a book about my life."

SIDELIGHTS: "My real name is Grace Trotter, under which I have written short stories for adults. Under the name of Nancy Paschal, my mother's maiden name, I have written fourteen junior novels. Looking back to my great-greats, it is a wonder that I was ever born, for my father's family in Missouri and my mother's family in Texas showed slight chance of ever getting together.

"I am the proud possessor of a flute that my Grandpa James Trotter carried throughout the Civil War while fighting for the North. Besides the chore of fighting, he played flute in the band.

"My mother's father, Tom Paschal (John Thomas Franklin

Paschal) fought for the South in Hood's Brigade, as did her maternal grandfather, Joab McManus. All three emerged from the war unscathed. Tom Paschal was saved from a bullet through the heart by a copy of the New Testament which he carried in his pocket. When I consider their safety, I remember my favorite verse from the ninety-first Psalm: 'He shall give his angels charge over thee, to keep thee in all thy ways.'

"The two young husbands came home from the war, not only with life but with a mutual problem. They had learned to like alcohol. In the wretched weather, often with inadequate clothing and unpredictable meals, through dysentery and pneumonia and chills and fevers, they depended on whiskey to keep them above ground. Oddly enough, at the end of the conflict, James Trotter received his honorable discharge in Texas.

"With my blood-mixture of North and South, I have often referred to myself as the Civil War in person. The returning soldier Trotter and the returning soldier Paschal set joyfully to work to restore their farms and bring order out of chaos. Before the war, James Trotter's young wife, the former Sarah Riem, had borne him a daughter and a son. Tom Paschal's young wife, the former Mary Elizabeth McManus, had borne him twins, which died in infancy, then a healthy son, followed by a daughter whom he did not see until after war's end.

"James Trotter and Sarah were destined to have six children in all, the one daughter and five sons, the youngest being my father, William Daniel Trotter, who, to his great disgust, was called Willie throughout his childhood. Later, he graduated to being called Dick, after a favorite uncle.

"Tom Paschal and Mary Elizabeth were destined to have eight children, four of whom died young. Two sons and two daughters survived, the youngest being my mother, Nancy Paschal, who always deplored the name Nancy because her country neighbors invariably pronounced it 'Neency.'

"In her teens Nancy Paschal moved from Athens, Texas, to be with friends who had established themselves in Dallas. My mother-to-be earned her living by doing fine sewing for the high-fashion dressmaker, Miss Carrie Waller. Shortly afterward, Dick Trotter, my father-to-be, moved with his family from St. Joseph, Missouri, to Dallas. The two young people met at a summer ice-cream social, held in a friend's garden, and ate ice cream from the same dish with the same spoon. On March 5, 1899, they married.

"I was born on November 23, 1900. My parents were every book salesman's prayer-come-true. I grew up in a white cottage well stocked with everything from Grimms' and Andersen's fairy tales to sets of Kipling, Robert Louis Stevenson, Richard Harding Davis, O. Henry, George Eliot, Balzac, and on and on. I was reading and understanding most of such books at a surprisingly early age. My childhood was ideal. In grade-school days I was writing serials, reading each installment to certain of my classmates at recess. Neither my parents nor I thought there was anything unusual about that. They saw to it that I had lessons in piano, dancing, dramatic art, and later in voice—overlooking the obvious fact that my life was to be wedded to pencil, paper, and typewriter.

"My first short stories, for adults, began selling in my twenties and were published under the name Grace Trotter. Many years later a literary agent suggested that I could write novels, particularly novels for girls. The short stories continued to sell, the agent passed away, and it was almost ten years before I put her suggestion into effect and wrote *Clover Creek,* my first novel for girls. To my surprise it sold to the first publisher to whom I submitted it. To my further surprise, it was selected by the Junior Literary Guild and it ran serially in the *American Girl.* That did it. *Magnolia Heights* soon followed and the Junior Literary Guild also selected it. Then came *Sylvan City,* followed by *Spring in the Air.* Obviously, it was up to me to keep on turning out books for girls, which I proceeded to do. I am grateful to my Maker for giving me the ability to write."

HOBBIES AND OTHER INTERESTS: Has made a study of the flowers of her native state, and is a garden enthusiast. Interested in pets, bird lore, poetry, painting—but most of all in the study of personality.

FOR MORE INFORMATION SEE: Texas Week Newsmagazine, January 18, 1947; *Dallas Times Herald,* October 5, 1947, September 24, 1950; Hans Holzer, *The Phantoms of Dixie,* Bobbs, 1972.

TURNER, Alice K. 1940-

PERSONAL: Born May 29, 1940, in China; daughter of William T. (a diplomatic officer) and Florence B. (Green) Turner. *Education:* Bryn Mawr College, B.A., 1962. *Home:* 184 West Tenth St., New York, N.Y. 10014. *Office:* Ballantine Books, 201 East 50th St., New York, N.Y. 10022.

ALICE K. TURNER

CAREER: Has been employed as editorial assistant for *New York Post*, features editor for *Charlie* magazine, and contributing editor for *Eye* magazine; David Frost Show (television), New York, N.Y., associate producer, 1969; *Holiday*, New York, N.Y., senior editor, 1969-70; *Publishers Weekly*, New York, N.Y., paperback editor, 1971-74; Ballantine Books, New York, N.Y., senior editor, 1974—.

WRITINGS: *Yoga for Beginners*, Watts, 1973.

SIDELIGHTS: "I am employed as a book editor now, and in the past I have worked on several magazines, also as an editor. I have always written, however, mainly for magazines, and I continue to do so whenever I find the time, averaging about six published pieces a year."

UDALL, Jan Beaney 1938-
(Jan Beaney)

PERSONAL: Born July 31, 1938, in Worcester Park, England; daughter of Jack and Audrey (Hames) Beaney; married John D. Hurman, July 31, 1961 (divorced, 1967); married Stephen James Nicholas Udall (a general manager), July 14, 1967; children—second marriage: Nicholas Jason James, Victoria Emma. *Education:* Attended College of Art, Southampton, 1954-55; College of Art, West Sussex, N.D.D., 1958; Hornsey College of Art, London, A.T.C., 1959. *Home:* 51 North Town Rd., Maidenhead, Berkshire 5L6 7JQ, England.

CAREER: Artist. Teacher of art and hand embroidery as an assistant mistress in grammar school in Middlesex, England, 1959-64; Whitelands College of Education, London, England, lecturer on creative embroidery, 1964-68; teacher of modern embroidery and design for Inner London Education Authority (evening courses), 1966-69. Has exhibited work in shows in Great Britain and Australia, including in Victoria and Albert Museum and Commonwealth Institute, both London, and Museum of Wales, Cardiff. *Member:* Embroiderer's Guild (chairman of 62 Group, 1969-71).

WRITINGS—Published under name Jan Beaney: *The Young Embroiderer*, Nicholas Kaye, 1966, published as *The Young Embroiderer: A How-It-Is-Done Book of Embroidery*, Warne, 1970, revised edition published as *Fun with Embroidery*, Kaye & Ward, 1975; *Adventures with Collage*, Warne, 1970 (published in England as *Fun with Collage*, Kaye & Ward, 1970); *Landscape in Picture, Collage, and Design*, Pelham Books, 1976; *Buildings in Picture, Collage, and Design*, Pelham Books, 1976; *Textures and Surface Patterns in Design*, Pelham Books, in press. Contributor of articles to *Embroidery*.

WORK IN PROGRESS: A book about *starting creative embroidery for adults*, completion expected in 1976.

SIDELIGHTS: "I have written the books because I feel very strongly that if children are helped to look at things about them *properly* and then how to select, expand, emphasize certain aspects, their creative talents can be really stretched. I believe that everyone can achieve quite a high standard of work with real enjoyment. I remember with horror the number of parents at school open evenings who had already conditioned their children to think that they could not draw and that only a few have any talent!!

JAN BEANEY UDALL

"As much as I enjoy teaching art and modern embroidery, working with children and adults and working on books, my first priority is my own creative embroidery in the form of wall panels. Although trained as a painter, I feel I can express my ideas more satisfactorily in fabrics and yarns. My sources of design for the last few years have been derived from all aspects of landscape. As I live in the Thames Valley, I am able to look at and draw on a variety of landscapes."

UNDERHILL, Alice Mertie (Waterman)
1900-1971

PERSONAL: Born September 14, 1900, in Watertown, S.D.; daughter of Nathan Tupper and May (Hull) Waterman; married John Fredrick Underhill, June 1, 1923; children: Charles Melwood, Norene (Mrs. Milo Struble), Delores (Mrs. Charles Vose), Ruth (Mrs. Donald Peterson). *Education:* Attended schools in South Dakota. *Residence:* Paris, Tex.

CAREER: South Dakota, rural school teacher, 1921-23; nursing homes for elderly people in Lincoln, Neb., and Denver, Colo., nurse, 1947-57; elementary school teacher, Newbury Park, Calif., 1957-65; teaching in Paris, Tex., 1965-71.

WRITINGS: *Adventures of Kado*, 1953, *Little Flower and the Princess*, 1955, *Sharna of Rocky Bay*, 1957, *Sharna and Poggy*, 1958, *Dookie, Sookie and Big Mo*, 1961 (all published by Pacific Press). Stories and poems in *Our Little Friend, Primary Treasure, Junior Guide, The Young Soldier, More Fun*, and in teaching and religious journals; songwriter (words and music of more than 150 songs).

WORK IN PROGRESS: A sequel to the "Sharna" books.

(Died September 6, 1971)

VARLEY, Dimitry V.   1906-

PERSONAL: Born February 10, 1906, in Russia; son of Vladimir and Maria Varley; married Bessie Schoenberg (a college director of dance). *Education:* Columbia University, B.S., 1928, M.A., 1930. *Home:* 9 McIntyre St., Bronxville, N.Y. 10708.

CAREER: With New York State Department of Labor, 1932-33, New York State Unemployment Insurance, 1934-37; research director, advisory council, 1937-42; with United Nations Relief and Rehabilitation Administration (UNRRA), 1944-46. Ceramist, 1952-66—has exhibited in Connecticut, New York, Kansas, Virginia. *Military service:* U.S. Army, 1942-44.

WRITINGS: Whirly Bird (juvenile), Knopf, 1961.

WORK IN PROGRESS: Queenie, The Singing Seal.

HOBBIES AND OTHER INTERESTS: Philately, gardening.

The cat was flat on his belly on a tree stump, his eyes fixed on the robin, his soft short paws bent, his tale swishing slowly in wide half circles. ■ (From *The Whirly Bird* by Dimitry Varley. Illustrated by Feodor Rojankovsky.)

JANET VIERTEL

VIERTEL, Janet   1915-

PERSONAL: Surname is pronounced *Veer*-tell; born August 4, 1915, in Newark, N.J.; daughter of Albert Eugene (a physician) and Hilda (a real estate broker; maiden name, Isaacs) Man; married Joseph Maurice Viertel (in real estate and a novelist), September 13, 1939; children: Thomas, Alice Viertel Krieger, John. *Education:* Attended New York University, 1932-37. *Home address:* Box 3081, Christiansted, St. Croix, Virgin Islands 00820. *Alternate address:* 275 Dogwood Lane, Stamford, Conn. 06903.

CAREER: R. H. Macy, New York, N.Y., saleswoman and model, 1937-38; Limited Editions Book Club, New York, general office work, 1938-39; photographer and writer. *Member:* American Society of Photographers in Communication, Connecticut League of Women Voters (director), Stamford League of Women Voters (president).

WRITINGS: Undersea Garden of the Virgin Islands, Dukane Press, 1969; (photographer) *Blue Planet,* with text by Alice Beaton Thompson (for junior high school students), Grosset, 1973.

WORK IN PROGRESS: Underwater Holidays (tentative title) for Grosset.

SIDELIGHTS: "I have always been very fond of children and admire their open minds and willingness to be inter-

The grunts are no parade-ground winners, though. They are a bit disorganized as they swim first one way, and then, for no apparent reason, reverse direction. ■ (From *Blue Planet: Man's Hopes for Life in the Sea* by Alice Thompson Beaton and Janet Viertel. Photos by Janet Viertel.)

ested in everything. It made me sad to see so many young people discouraged with their lack of career opportunities and with the almost hopeless problems of the world and I wanted to show them the beautiful underwater world where life exists as it is created without any influence of Man. I also wanted to tell young people of the exciting careers in oceanography and its related sciences and simultaneously to show that our understanding of the oceans could be beneficial to humans as well.

"My new book—tentatively called *Underwater Holidays* is not primarily addressed to young children—but as they grow into adolescence, it will be a guide to learning how to snorkel and where to learn to dive and tell them all of the places in the Americas where they can see the underwater world—from wrecks to reefs—and exactly what they will see when they get there."

HOBBIES AND OTHER INTERESTS: Travel (Africa, Europe, including Russia, the Caribbean).

VILLIERS, Alan (John) 1903-

PERSONAL: Born September 23, 1903, in Melbourne, Australia; son of Leon Joseph (a poet) and Anastasia

(Hayes) Villiers; married Daphne Kay Harris, 1924, divorced, 1936; married Nancie Wills, December 24, 1940; children: (second marriage) Christopher Alan, Katherine Lisbeth, Peter John. *Education:* Attended state schools and Essendon High School, Melbourne, Australia. *Home:* 1A Lucerne Rd., Oxford OX2 7QB, England. *Agent:* Armitage Watkins, 77 Park Ave., New York, N.Y. 10017; Curtis Brown, 1 Craven Hill, London W2 3EW, England.

CAREER: Sailor, writer, photographer, adventurer. Went to sea in 1919: on Antarctic whaling ships, 1923-24, in command of ship *Joseph Conrad,* 1934-36, on Arab dhows, 1938-39, on Portuguese dory-fishing schooner, 1950, captain of *Mayflower II,* 1957, on nuclear ship *Savannah,* 1962. Newspaper reporter in Tasmania, 1925-27; freelance writer and photographer, 1925—. British National Maritime Museum, trustee. *Military service:* Royal Navy, World War II; became commander, R.N.V.R.; awarded Distinguished Service Cross. *Member:* Royal Geographic Society (fellow), Cosmos Club (Washington, D.C.), Circumnavigators Club (New York). *Awards, honors:* Camoes Prize, Portugal, for *Quest of the Schooner Argus;* Commendator, Order of St. James, Portugal.

WRITINGS: Whaling in the Frozen South, Bobbs, 1925; *Falmouth for Orders,* Scribner, 1929; *By Way of Cape Horn,* Scribner, 1930; *Vanished Fleets,* Holt, 1930; *The Sea in Ships* (pictures), Morrow, 1932; *Grain Race,* Scribner, 1934; *Cruise of the Conrad,* Scribner, 1934; *Last of the Wind Ships* (pictures), Morrow, 1934; *Making of a Sailor* (pictures), Morrow, 1938; *Sons of Sinbad,* Scribner, 1940; *The Set of the Sails* (autobiography), Scribner, 1949; *The Coral Sea,* McGraw, 1950; *Quest of the Schooner Argus,* Scribner, 1951; *Monsoon Seas,* McGraw, 1952; *The Way of a Ship,* Scribner, 1954; *Posted Missing,* Scribner, 1956; *Sailing Eagle* (pictures), Scribner, 1956; *Wild Ocean,* McGraw, 1957; *Give Me a Ship to Sail,* Scribner, 1958; (main author and editor) *Men, Ships and the Sea,* National Geographic Society, 1962.

Juvenile books: *Whalers of the Midnight Sun,* Scribner, 1934; *Joey Goes to Sea,* McGraw, 1952; *And Not to Yield,* Scribner, 1953; *Pilot Pete,* Museum Press, 1953; *Stormalong,* Routledge & Kegan Paul, 1958; *The New Mayflower,* Scribner, 1959; (compiler) *Of Ships and Men: A Personal Anthology,* Newnes, 1962; *The Ocean: Man's Conquest of the Sea,* Dutton, 1963 (published in England as *Oceans of the World: Man's Conquest of the Sea,* Museum Press, 1963); *Battle of Trafalgar,* Macmillan, 1965. Contributor to *National Geographic.*

SIDELIGHTS: "I suppose the fundamental reason why I went to sea in big sailing-ships was because the ships were there, in the Melbourne (Australia) of my childhood. I could see them. They seemed beautiful, challenging, adventurous—so different from the humdrum life of day-after-day school going. I found the sea books and I read—Conrad, Marryat (rather out of date then), Captain Bone, Captain Hendry—always the real thing and no nonsense. I knew that these men were sailing-ship seamen themselves, for the ships they wrote about were there in the Melbourne docks for me to see.

"But for years I was stuck with school, for this was the law. All that earnest and well-meaning but uninspiring stuff about becoming 'qualified' at something and 'getting on'

had me caught. Then my poet-father died when I was fifteen. We were six children of whom I was second oldest. I could leave school then and begin (I hoped) a man's life. I got a berth in the half-deck—boy's quarters—of an old Scots barque, and I was off! Off for good, for those ships don't bring you back. At first it was rough, tough, and hungry, and sea-sickness was hell. But I'd made the choice. I knew what I wanted to do. It was to sail and learn until I might qualify as Master of one of those great ships. It wasn't to write: I had no idea of writing anything except letters home.

"But as the years passed and it became harder and harder to get a berth in anything like a real ship, I slowly realised that *all* these great ocean-going sailing-ships were on their way out from a heedless world which seemed content to forget all that it had learned about them, their handling and efficient sailing without use of any power save the ocean winds. I realised very slowly that these ships were indeed a splendidly useful and beautiful creation for Man under God, for the Lord had provided the Ocean Winds in pattern for Man's use, when understood. There were zones of useful and more or less permanent winds—the Westerlies, the Trade Winds, the so-called counter-Trades. Only slowly had man acquired knowledge and ability to use these areas of useful winds: he was indeed still learning when all was given up—for the delusion that now Power was thoroughly understood and its sources and abilities were with him for ever. Were they?

"Well, I was doubtful. I'd seen coal-fields worked out, oilwells dry up. Might not these fates await them all? So I stayed with sailing-ships wherever I could find them—in the

ALAN VILLIERS

East, around the world, from my own Australia first, then Britain, Finland, Portugal, Germany, Arabia. I learned all I could of the techniques of using the ocean winds—not much, but a useful little; and I did what I could to preserve that knowledge. I bought a full-rigged ship and sailed her round the world to keep at least something *real* sailing with the wind alone; for I knew that the introduction of auxiliary power was ruinous. There can never be enough. For a few years, I was able to keep my ship, *Joseph Conrad*, sailing, taking on both Cape Horn and the westwards beat of the North Atlantic in the depths of winter. I did my best, for such ships were a great achievement and beautiful. It seemed clear to me that it was mad to throw away the know-how of sailing them on long and useful voyages, doing their share of the world's work without benefit of power. Some day this could very easily be needed again."

In 1934-36, Villiers sailed the ship *Joseph Conrad* round the world. The ship is now at Mystic, Conn. Ship's Museum. In 1957, Villiers sailed the *Mayflower II*, a replica of the 1620 sailing vessel over the same course taken by the original *Mayflower*. The voyage took 54 days. In 1962, Villiers wrote in the preface to *Oceans of the World*, he was invited to sail in the Nuclear Ship *Savannah* "when she made history by being the first cargo and passenger merchantman to go to sea under nuclear power." He wrote *Oceans of the World* while aboard the *S.S. Helenus*, on passage from Australia via Suez to France and England, "among seamen of today." He often handles sea-going sailing-ships for movie producers—Huston's "Moby Dick," Ustinov's "Billy Budd," and other films.

FOR MORE INFORMATION SEE: Newsweek, January 10, 1949; *U.S. News and World Report,* June 21, 1957; *Scholastic,* April 12, 1957; *Oceans of the World: Man's Conquest of the Sea,* by Alan Villiers, Museum Press, 1963.

VISSER, W(illem) F(rederik) H(endrik) 1900-1968

PERSONAL: Born January 15, 1900, in Zwaqgwesteinde, Netherlands; son of Anne and Aaltje (Lemstra) Visser; married Bieuwkje Kerkhof, September 18, 1928; children: Wim, Peter. *Education:* Educated at a teacher training college in Leeuwarden, Netherlands, 1914-18. *Home:* Akker flat c30, de Bilt, Netherlands.

AWARDS, HONORS: Niku, de koerier received the 1964 award of the Dutch Association for the Promotion of Books as the best book of the year for young people.

WRITINGS: Onder de laars van Napolean (title means "Under the Boot of Napoleon"), Van Goor Zonen, 1960; *De tijdbaan* (readers; title means "The Course of Time"), two books, Van Goor Zonen, 1960; *William van Oranje* (title means "William of Orange"), Van Goor Zonen, 1960; *Sikke en ik* (title means "Sikke and I"), Arbeiderspers, 1961; *Het gezin Algera* (novel; title means "The Family Algera"), Strenholt, 1961; *Het spook van de burcht* (title means "The Ghost of the Castle"), Van Goor Zonen, 1961; *Schippersjongens* (title means "Bargeman's Boys"), Kruseman, 1961; *Op de vleugels van de tijd* (history of Holland in stories; title means "On the Wings of Time"), Van Goor Zonen, 1962; *Robie en de tovenaar* (title means

"Robin and the Sorcerer"), Van Goor Zonen, 1963; *Niku, de zigeunerjongen* (title means "Niku, the Gypsy Boy"), Van Goor Zonen, 1964; *Niku, de koerier,* Van Goor Zonen, 1964, translation by Marian Powell published in England as *Niku, the Messenger,* Oliver & Boyd, 1966, and in the United States as *Gypsy Courier,* Follett, 1969; *Niku, de zwerver* (title means "Niku, the Wanderer"), Van Goor Zonen, 1964; *Hans van de Polle,* De Fontbin, 1970; *Storm Over de Polle,* De Fontbin, 1970.

Author with M. Bijpost of a language series, "Taal voor allemaal," twelve books, all but two of the volumes published by Van Goor Zonen. Contributor to *Kinders van de werelt* (title means "Children of the World"), published by Albertin (Capetown, South Africa).

SIDELIGHTS: Among the papers left by the Dutch teacher his widow found the following biographical memo (intended for his young readers): "I was born in Zwaqgwesteinde, a little Frisian village, in the year 1900 (Friesland is one of the eleven provinces of Holland). So you can easily calculate how 'young' I am. Probably I was in my youth as good and as naughty as you are now. I was already a form master being eighteen years old. After that I had the function of head-teacher at Oranjewoud (also in Friesland) and at The Hague. At first I had my trouble at school, of course, but one thing came very easy to me: telling a story! Doing that the most troublesome pupils were singing small. From telling stories till writing them is not a long step. I began with short stories. For writing larger books I hardly had time before my retirement. That's all of it! Read pleasantly?"

FOR MORE INFORMATION SEE: Library Journal, May 15, 1969.

(Died December 13, 1968)

WADDELL, Evelyn Margaret 1918- (Lyn Cook)

PERSONAL: Born May 4, 1918, in Weston, Ontario, Canada; daughter of Edward Frank and Emma (Crawford) Cook; married Robb John Waddell, September 19, 1949; children: Christopher Robb, Deborah Lyn. *Education:* University of Toronto, B.A. (honors), 1940, B.L.S., 1941. *Home:* 72 Cedarbrae Blvd., Scarborough, Ontario M1J 2K5, Canada. *Agent:* Scargall of Markham, 1 Talisman Cres., Markham, Ontario L3P 2C8, Canada.

CAREER: Librarian in public libraries in Toronto, Ontario, 1941-42; Sudbury Public Library, Sudbury, Ontario, children's librarian, 1946-47; Canadian Broadcasting Corp. (CBC), Toronto, Ontario, script writer, director, and narrator of children's show "A Door Way in Fairyland," 1947-52. Teacher of creative drama to children for New Play Society Theatre School, 1956-65. Conducts storytelling and creative drama group for pre-school children in a branch of Scarborough Public Libraries. *Military service:* Royal Canadian Air Force, Women's Division, meteorological observer, 1942-46; received Canada Service Medal.

*WRITINGS—*Books for nine-to-twelve-year-old children, all under name Lyn Cook: *The Bells on Finland Street,* Macmillan, 1950; *The Little Magic Fiddler,* Macmillan, 1951; *Rebel on the Trail,* Macmillan, 1953; *Jady and the

EVELYN MARGARET WADDELL

General, Macmillan (Toronto), 1955, St. Martin's, 1956; *Pegeen and the Pilgrim,* St. Martin's, 1957; *The Road to Kip's Cove,* Macmillan (Toronto), 1961, St. Martin's, 1962; *Samantha's Secret Room,* Macmillan (Toronto), 1963, St. Martin's, 1964; *The Brownie Handbook for Canada,* Girl Guide Association of Canada, 1965; *The Secret of Willow Castle,* Macmillan, 1966; *The Magical Miss Mittens,* Macmillan, 1970.

Picture-story books; under name Lyn Cook: *Toys from the Sky,* Clarke, Irwin, 1972; *Jolly Jean-Pierre,* Burns & MacEachern, 1973; *If I Were All These,* Burns & MacEachern, 1974. Writer for "Sounds Fun," a radio series for Canadian Broadcasting Corp., and "The Mystery Makers," a television series for Canadian Broadcasting Corp., 1967.

WORK IN PROGRESS: Two novels for ten- to twelve-year-old readers, one set in the French River area of Ontario, and the other set in the Ottawa Valley; several picture-story books.

SIDELIGHTS: "I have always wanted to be a story-teller. Even as a child, attending a two-room country school, I was given opportunities to share with my class the stories I had read in the precious books received at birthdays and other festive times. I could not resist the urge to embellish these stories with frills from my own imagination for the sake of dramatic effect, as drama was another consuming interest. The desire to create with words, mood, character and situation developed side by side with the joy in performing what others had written. Beginning with the musical drill of the Christmas concert and the recitation at the Fall Fair, I found myself on many stages through secondary school and a university career and was actually given the chance, by the 'grande dame' of Canadian theatre, Dora Mavor Moore, of joining a repertory theatre company but regretfully declined in the interests of a more secure bread-and-butter 'role' with books in the children's library.

"My first serious attempts at writing began on the long, lonely 'graveyard' shifts from twelve to eight a.m. in the control tower of the Canadian Flying Training Station at Centralia, Ontario, during World War II. Alone here, as a meteorological observer, with a blizzard howling outside and the teletype sending me the code for the latest weather map, I wrote poetry of the war, the surrounding landscape and of personal relationships and had the results of my nightly efforts published in the Exeter town paper and bound in three little booklets for my friends. At this time I began, too, a series of personality sketches of interesting station personnel, and these, too, appeared in the local paper.

"It was not until I went, after the war, to Sudbury, the nickel supplier of the world, as that centre's first girls' and boys' librarian, that my longing to create a book was fulfilled. Here, with the bleak and rugged Northern Ontario landscape on every side, I met, in this vigourous and friendly city, those who had come from many varied European lands to work in the mines, and especially I met and worked with their warm, intelligent and delightful children. When I attended my first skating carnival there and saw, in a starring role, a ten-year-old skater of Finnish parentage, my book, *The Bells on Finland Street,* was conceived and a writing career born.

"Each book begins in a small way with a fascination for a name, a place, a conversation overheard or an experience remembered. To this small beginning are added other remembrances of people, places, events in times past and present. Since my stories are regional tales of Canada, my research in the specific area brings many plot ideas. My husband is a great help on 'field trips' with his interest in local history and his amazing memory for detail. The name, Samantha, for example, occurred in a family history used in *The Road to Kip's Cove.* My heroine came to life at once as a contemporary twelve-year-old living on a farm, and that farm my husband's cousin's property overlooking Penetang Bay. *The Road to Kip's Cove* began when friends took up residence in a schoolhouse over one-hundred-years old, and with a very real admiration for the Bay of Quinte

I HATE EATING LUNCH IN SCHOOL. The lunchroom smells like fish or frankfurters. ■ (From *The Terrible Thing that Happened at Our House* by Marge Blaine. Illustrated by John C. Wallner.)

area. *The Secret of Willow Castle* was born on a spring walk with a dear friend, as she told me of her childhood adventures in a big old willow tree on the St. Lawrence River.

"As for the total plot, it is to me as if it had all actually happened in some other time and I am remembering it, piece by piece, but not in sequence. When it is all 'remembered,' the pieces fall naturally into place in plot order. At this time I call in a housekeeper, Doris Hooper, who runs house and family while I write, and has done so for all but two of my books. I need her here because when I write I want to live the reality of the book completely as I do for two weeks, writing eight or nine hours a day. This usually sees the first draft of the book completed. There may be changes, a tightening of plot, more incisive descriptions,

some work on characterization, but generally the first draft is substantially the form in which the book is published.

"There is for me great joy in writing and in knowing, by the letters that come to me, that others have shared the realities that I have created. The most wonderful compliment that I have ever received was the question of an eleven-year-old boy in a school assembly I was addressing, 'How do you know so well what we're thinking?'

"Perhaps the reason for immersing myself in the writing experience with such real pleasure can be found in a statement by the well-known English story-teller, J. B. Priestly, in his book, *Margin Released: Reminiscences and Reflections,* 'Our experience has been enlarged and enriched by the inventions of our trade. Nobody looking at us could

guess all that we have seen and known. We have lived more lives than one.'

"I feel strongly that novels have a great role to play in a child's development, helping him to adventure freely in the realm of emotions, and exercising and strengthening the imaginative faculty with which he was endowed and which can, as the years go by, illumine every area of his life."

All of Evelyn Waddell's books were published in Canada before they were published elsewhere. *The Bells on Finland Street* has also been published in a German edition in Switzerland.

FOR MORE INFORMATION SEE: In Review, spring, 1967; *Quill and Quire,* October 24, 1969; *Index,* May, 1970; Irma McDonough, editor, *Profiles,* Canadian Library Association, 1971, 1975; *Writer's Directory,* St. James' Press, 1973; Virginia Davis, editor, *Connections, Writers and the*

Land, Manitoba School Library Audio-Visual Association (Winnipeg), 1974.

WALLNER, John C. 1945-

PERSONAL: Born February 3, 1945, in St. Louis, Mo.; son of John C. (an insurance agent) and Rita (Ziegler; a beautician) Wallner; married Alexandra Czesnykowski (an illustrator/writer), July 16, 1971. *Education:* Washington University, St. Louis, Mo., B.F.A., 1968; Pratt Institute, Brooklyn, N.Y., M.F.A., 1970. *Agent:* Kirchoff/Wohlberg, 331 East 50th Street, New York, N.Y. 10022.

CAREER: Free-lance illustrator. *Exhibitions:* Holmes

JOHN C. WALLNER

Lounge Graphic Exhibition, 1967, 1968; Steinberg Library Recognition Show, 1968; Maryhurst College Invitational for Graphics, 1969; Corcoran School of Art, Washington, D.C., 1970; Albany Small Print Show, 1970; Pratt Traveling Miniature Print Show, 1971-73; Audubon Society, twenty-ninth annual, New York, 1971, thirtieth annual, 1972; Society of Graphic Artists Annual, 1972; Society of Illustrators Annual Exhibit, 13, 14, 16, 17. *Awards, honors:* Society of Illustrators, certificate of merit, 1972-75.

ILLUSTRATOR: James & Ruth McCrea, *Marvelous Machines,* Holt, 1971; Georgess McHargue, *Mummies,* Lippincott, 1972; *Encyclopedia of Economics,* Doskin, 1972; Jay Bennett, *The Killing Tree* (jacket), Watts, 1972; Simone Beck, *Simca's Cuisine,* Knopf, 1972; Eriche Goode, *Drugs in American Society* (jacket), Knopf, 1972; Cecil Vye & Elizabeth Canar, editors, *Different Drummers,* Random, 1972; *Scenes from American Life,* Random, 1972; Norma Fox Mazer, *A Figure of Speech* (jacket), Dell, 1972; *American Language Today,* McGraw, 1973; Sharyla Gold, *Amelia Quackenbush* (jacket and frontpiece), Seabury, 1973; Marge Blaine, *The Terrible Thing That Happened at Our House,* Parents' 1975; Hila Coleman, *Ethan's Favorite Teacher* (Junior Literary Guild selection), Crown, 1975; Jan Wahl, *Follow Me Cried Bee,* Crown, 1975. Text book illustrations for Harper & Row, Ginn & Company and American Book Company. A cartoon story "Rolls and Jellylord" appeared in *Yo Yo Maga-*

zine in 1972. Illustrations have appeared in *Children's Digest, Hi Fi and Stereo* and *Good Housekeeping.*

SIDELIGHTS: "I attempt to find the physical characteristics of a character in the stories I illustrate and emphasize those. I believe in the drawing and structure of a picture. With these I try to create a world for the child to believe in. If my pictures give the written story a new dimension and excite a child's imagination, then I'll feel I have done my job.

"I enjoy looking at and studying the artists of the Northern Renaissance German school. The basic mediums I use are watercolor and colored pencil, pencil and pen and ink."

HOBBIES AND OTHER INTERESTS: Collecting antiques, crafts and collecting and reading books.

WARREN, Mary Phraner 1929-

PERSONAL: Born March 27, 1929, in New York; daughter of Wilson W. (a warehouse executive) and Mary (Arthur) Phraner; married Lindsay Dune Warren (a freelance calligrapher), May 5, 1956; children: Rose Ann, Bernadine, Roy, Mike, Fred, Mary Belle, Linda Marie. *Education:* Attended Mount Holyoke College, 1948-49; University of Colorado, B.A., 1951; Union Theological Seminary, New York, N.Y., M.A., 1954. *Religion:* Epis-

MARY PHRANER WARREN

"Well, I can't stay around to feed cuddles if you're going to act like a jerk," said Corky hotly. "I've got an emergency—" ■ (From *River School Detectives* by Mary Phraner Warren. Illustrated by Joe and Beth Krush.)

copalian. *Home:* 2607 Northeast 14th Ave., Portland, Ore. 97212. *Agent:* Lenniger Literary Agency, Inc., 437 Fifth Ave., New York, N.Y. 10016.

CAREER: St. Luke's Hospital, New York, N.Y., play director in pediatrics, 1955-56; free-lance writer, 1956—. Teacher of weekly writing workshop sponsored by Portland Community College.

WRITINGS—Juvenile: *Walk In My Moccasins,* Westminster, 1966; *Shadow on the Valley,* Westminster, 1967; *Eight Bells for Wendy,* Westminster, 1968; *A Snake Named Sam,* Westminster, 1969; *Ghost town for Sale,* Westminster, 1973; (with Don Kirkendall) *Bottom High to the Crowd,* Walker & Co., 1973; *The River School Detectives,* Westminster, 1974; *The Haunted Kitchen,* Westminster, 1976.

SIDELIGHTS: "When I began first grade, I thought I could not learn to read. How could anyone ever decipher those funny little marks running across a page? But by second grade I not only became a book-gobbler, I became a book-maker! I had discovered that the stories inside my own head were more interesting than those printed in my school reader. Where could I put them for safe-keeping? Experimenting, I folded two sheets of drawing paper in half

and pinned them with straight pins. I ruled lines on each page. I had a book!

"Later when my stories overflowed the confines of these four-page books, I spent my allowance at a little stationery store and purchased a 'blank book'—the kind so popular then, black-and-white pebbled covers and snow-white pages ruled with pale blue ink.

"To this day, the sight of a brand new notebook waiting to be filled sends a delightful shiver up and down my backbone.

"When I grew up I never let go the dream of writing books one day. But first I did other things. I studied at Mt. Holyoke in Massachusetts, and I studied some more at the University of Colorado. In fact I went out to the Rocky Mountains one summer because of a very famous writers conference held at the University in Boulder each year. I liked Colorado so much that I decided to stay a while.

"Later, in New York, I became recreation director of the children's wing of St. Luke's Hospital. They called me The Play Lady. While there I saw many things to write about but still I put it off. I got married and moved to Montana and we began to raise our family of six children which many years later became a family of seven.

"Our children are all adopted. When they were little I read books and articles about adopted families but they were for adults. I found very few stories about adopted families written for the enjoyment of children. And that is how I came to write *Walk in My Moccasins,* my first book. It is fiction but based on many true experiences our family had together.

"When we moved to Oregon and our children had the opportunity to attend a public school with a new kind of a program, I began the Corky Downs series. *A Snake Named Sam* is about a true snake and his name was really Sam. He lived in my son Roy's room for four years. So you see, like most writers, I get my ideas from my family and from the children around me. Often when I speak in schools children say 'Write a book about kids like us.' And so I do.

"I teach writing too, in various workshops and courses. Many well-known authors, including Florence Crannell Means and Solveig Paulson Russell and, yes, Walt Morey of *Gentle Ben* fame, helped me to learn how to improve my writing. It is exciting now for me to encourage others who want to write stories.

"One of the best parts of having your books in print is that you receive letters from all over the United States and from different countries too. I answer these letters carefully for a special reason. The reason is this: When I was a little girl I wrote to Laura Ingalls Wilder. And from her home in Missouri she wrote me not one but *two* letters in her own handwriting. I thought she was wonderful to take the time to do that when she was so busy writing books. At the time I promised myself . . . if my stories ever got printed I would answer every letter I received, just like Laura did.

"There is another nice thing about writing. You are never bored. At dull meetings or while you wait in a dental office you can always observe your surroundings and find new characters and backgrounds for books. You can look at people's eyes and cheekbones. You can listen to the sound of their voices and notice how they walk. You can observe the details of buildings and streets, trees, flowers, birds. You can discern how different the sky looks from one day to the next.

"And all of this can go into your writing."

WASHBURNE, Heluiz Chandler   1892-

PERSONAL: Born January 25, 1892, in Cincinnati, Ohio; daughter of Charles Colby (a civil engineer) and Julia (Davis) Chandler; married Carleton W. Washburne (a professor and writer), September 15, 1912; children: Margaret Joan (Mrs. D. K. Marshall), Beatrice (Mrs. John E. Visher), Chandler. *Education:* Attended School of Industrial Arts and Women's School of Design, both Philadelphia, Pa. *Politics:* Democrat. *Religion:* Quaker. *Home and office:* 2248 Kent St., Okemos, Mich. 48864.

CAREER: Carson, Pirie, Scott & Co. (department store), Chicago, Ill., home fashion adviser, 1928-30; *Chicago Daily News,* Chicago, Ill., travel columnist, 1940-42; freelance writer. *Member:* League of Women Voters, Women's International League.

WRITINGS: Letters to Channy: A Trip Around the World (Junior Literary Guild selection), Rand McNally, 1932; (with husband, Carleton W. Washburne, and Frederick Reed) *Stories of the Earth and Sky* (Junior Literary Guild selection), Appleton, 1933; *Little Elephant Catches Cold,* Whitman, 1937; *Little Elephant's Christmas,* Whitman, 1938; *Little Elephant's Picnic,* Whitman, 1939; *Fridl, a Mountain Boy,* Winston, 1939; *Rhamon, A Boy of Kashmir,* Whitman, 1939; (with Anauta Blackmore) *Land of the Good Shadows: The Life Story of Anauta, an Eskimo Woman,* John Day, 1940; *Little Elephant Visits the Farm,* Whitman, 1941; (with Blackmore) *Children of the Blizzard* (Junior Literary Guild selection), John Day, 1952; *Tomas Goes Trading,* John Day, 1959. Contributor of articles to *Britannica Junior Encyclopaedia.*

SIDELIGHTS: Heluiz Washburne has lived in Italy, Mexico, and Cambodia, and traveled in Europe frequently, and in China, Japan, Korea, India, Russia, the Near East, Africa, South America, and Australia. *Letters to Channy* has been published in England and Poland, and *Children of the Blizzard* in Denmark, Germany, Sweden, Japan, and England.

WATSON, James   1936-

PERSONAL: Born November 8, 1936, in Darwen, Lancashire, England; son of James (a wages clerk) and Miriam (a clerk; maiden name, Arnold) Watson; married Catherine Rose Downey (a nurse), July 6, 1963; children: Rosalind, Miranda, Francesca. *Education:* University of Nottingham, B.A. (honors), 1958. *Home:* Vale Towers, Flat B, 58 London Rd., Tunbridge Wells, Kent, England. *Agent:* A. D. Peters & Co., 10 Buckingham St., London W.C.2, England. *Office:* West Kent College, Tunbridge Wells, Kent, England.

JAMES WATSON

CAREER: British Council, Milan, Italy, teacher of English, 1960-61; *North East Evening Gazette,* Middlesbrough, Yorkshire, England, journalist and art critic, 1961-63; Dunlop Co., London, England, education officer and editor of educational literature, 1963-65; West Kent College, Tunbridge Wells, Kent, England, lecturer in English and liberal studies, 1965—. Founder of local arts cooperative; member of Tunbridge Wells No-Censorship Committee. *Military service:* British Army, Royal Army Educational Corps, National Service Officer, 1958-60. *Member:* Association for Liberal Education, Tunbridge Wells and West Kent College Film Society (treasurer); Teesside Film Club (founder-secretary), Purcell Recorder Consort (amateur recorder and early music enthusiasts).

WRITINGS: Sign of the Swallow (juvenile), Thomas Nelson, 1967; *The Bull Leapers* (juvenile), Coward, 1970; *Legion of the White Tiger* (juvenile), Gollancz, 1973; *Liberal Studies in Further Education,* National Foundation for Educational Research, 1973; *The Freedom Tree* (juvenile), Gollancz, 1976. Author of "Gilbert Makepeace Lives!," a radio play for British Broadcasting Corp., 1972. Contributor to *London Times, Guardian, Studio,* and *Arts Review.*

WORK IN PROGRESS: Miscellaneous works of fiction, including radio drama for children.

SIDELIGHTS: "As a child, in addition to wandering the Lancashire moors, playing football in the street and gathering wood for Guy Fawkes' Night, I was chiefly interested in puppets and magazines. I made my own hand puppets and eventually my own string puppets and marionette theatre. I started magazines of one sort or another and told people I wanted to be a jet pilot or a journalist.

"I ended up a word-pilot, taking flights of fancy on the printed page. There have been some long and perilous journeys, both in time and space. I'd no ambitions to write for children until, one day during military service, I read how Georges Simenon could write a novel in fourteen days. I was stationed in Anglesey, a bare, sea-swept isle swilled by the wild Irish Sea, and there was little call on my services as an education officer. I was looking back, rather forlornly, on three years at university reading history. I'd obtained a degree but ceased to enjoy history. Three years of intensive academic study had rubbed off every dewdrop of curiosity or romance: it seemed such a waste.

"So in fourteen days I wrote my first historical novel for children—the first draft, that is. I relished the experience and the challenge; yet it was a year at least before I really got the story right. Since then, though I may have become more technically adept at writing for the young reader, the books have taken me longer and longer to research and complete.

"I'd like to mention a coincidence concerning my second book, *The Bull Leapers,* which I've grown to cherish. A life-long fascination for things Greek had set me writing an imaginary historical reconstruction of the tale of Theseus and the Minotaur. I'd been to Crete with my wife and returned enchanted by the ruins of the palace of Knossos.

"An aunt then revealed to me that my grandfather had been similarly interested in Greek archeology and that he had visited Knossos in 1900 when the discoverer of the palace, Arthur Evans, was excavating there. My aunt gave me some fragments of Minoan pottery which my grandfather had brought back with him—and a book on Crete.

"Inside the cover of the book I found a pencil-written note describing how my grandfather had been present at the unearthing of the beautiful painting now famous as 'The Boy with the Drinking Cup.' The great archeologist had shown him round the excavations and then given him tea. The hidden dimensions of history were never more alive in me as I read those neatly written notes.

"From that point on, writing fiction set in history restored for me the infinite variety and richness of the past; and attempting to give history the 'livingness' of fiction helped to highlight the ongoing validity of man's experience, whether he existed in 500 B.C. or 2000 A.D., at the same time reflecting one's own preoccupations concerning the meaning and purpose of life.

"If history has a continuing relevance, then sooner or later the author chooses a period which has a particular relevance to his own attitudes. *The Freedom Tree,* set in the Hungry Thirties in Britain, and the Spanish Civil War, amounts to a declaration of faith, of taking sides. The fictitious villains of the earlier books are replaced by the true villainy of Fascist Spain; another perilous journey, of course, but one I felt impelled to make."

HOBBIES AND OTHER INTERESTS: The arts, archeology, exploring old castles and churches, soccer, cricket, and camping.

WESTERVELT, Virginia (Veeder)   1914-

PERSONAL: Born September 19, 1914, in Schenectady, N.Y.; daughter of Eugene W. (a pharmacist) and Millicent (a writer and teacher; maiden name, Winton) Veeder; married Ralph V. Westervelt (a school superintendent), September 1, 1936; children: Dirck Eugene, Deidre Virginia (Mrs. David Hunt). *Education:* Attended Pomona College, 1931-33; Wellesley College, A.B., 1935; graduate study, summers, Central School of Speech and Drama, London, England, 1935, New York University, 1940, Columbia University, 1954; Syracuse University, M.A., 1960. *Religion:* Protestant. *Home:* 1050 Bermuda Dr., Redlands, Calif. 92373. *Agent:* McIntosh & Otis, 475 Fifth Ave., New York, N.Y. 10027.

CAREER: Jordan Marsh Co., Boston, Mass., executive trainee, 1935-36; high school teacher of English at public and private schools in Schenectady, N.Y., 1938-40, 1948-57, and in New Hartford, N.Y., 1958-66; University of Redlands, Redlands, Calif., instructor in English, 1969-73; Crafton Hills College, Yucaipa, Calif., instructor in En-

VIRGINIA WESTERVELT

glish, 1973-74. Teacher of extension courses, Ithaca College, 1960-66; visiting professor, Hong Kong Baptist College, 1975; consultant to leadership conferences. *Member:* P.E.N. International, American Association of University Professors, American Association of University Women, National League of American Pen Women, Lutheran Church Women (president, 1971), California Writers' Guild, Chapparral Poets, Sierra Club, Friends of Smiley Library, Foothill Wellesley Club. *Awards, honors:* American Newspaper Publishers Association grant, 1960; Achievement Award, 1970, and state poetry, article and short story prizes, 1969, 1970, 1972, and 1975, from National League of American Pen Women.

WRITINGS: Getting Along in the Teen-Age World, Putnam, 1957; *Choosing a Career in a Changing World,* Putnam, 1959; *The World Was His Laboratory,* Messner, 1964; *Incredible Man of Science: Irving Langmuir,* Messner, 1968. Writer of church school curriculum materials and pamphlets for Muhlenberg Press. Contributor of articles, reviews and stories to *The New York Times, American Girl, Christian Science Monitor, The Lutheran, Modern Maturity, Nature Magazine, Wilderness Camping,* and other periodicals.

WORK IN PROGRESS: A fictional account of the Battle of Saratoga for young people in collaboration with mother, Millicent Winton Veeder, tentatively titled *Guns on the Heights;* a biography of Pearl Buck for young people entitled *Pure Gem.*

SIDELIGHTS: "I have been writing ever since, as a twelve year old, I started to keep a journal. Now the day seems lost unless it has been recorded, or at least the essence of it after 'the skin of the day has been cast into the hedge,' which Virginia Woolf calls reality. Jo, in *Little Women* and *Emily of New Moon* also kept journals and no doubt influenced my urge to capture emotion as well as activity.

"My mother encouraged me in this, as she did in everything else all her life, so that self doubts were gradually replaced by her confidence that 'of course I could' do it.

"There is no way of knowing whether determination, attitude or luck should be credited with one's success and happiness, but I am sure encouragement was an important factor in my decision to major in English composition at Wellesley. In my senior year I wrote a play and a novel and also did a weekly column for the *New Haven Register* and frequent college news stories for the *Boston Herald* and the *Christian Science Monitor.*

"I had inflated ideas about being a newspaper woman or an editor in a publishing house, but this was 1935, newspapers had few women on their staffs, and there was a scarcity of jobs anywhere. I considered myself most fortunate to be selected for the Executive Training Course at Jordan Marsh Department Store in Boston at $18.00 a week. The only writing I had time for that year of learning the merchandising business was a weekly letter to the man I married the following September.

"I taught part time in a private school all sorts of subjects I knew little about, like Latin, which I had loathed in high school, biology and geography. But it counted for practice teaching, and after taking a few education courses in the summer, I tucked away teaching certificates for English and distributive education. When our two children were both in school, I began to substitute and also to have time to try short stories, long, twenty-page things that never sold.

"The first article I wrote, however, did sell (for ten dollars), and the same magazine took four more within the year. After that, when people asked what I did, I no longer felt apologetic about saying 'I write.' Some articles I wrote upon request, but without pay, developed into my first book for teen-agers, which critics said was written 'informally, gaily, sympathetically,' and was a 'practical reassuring handbook to help teenagers get through those perplexing years happily and satisfactorily.'

"More than my name on the cover, however, I treasure my teen-age son's comments scribbled throughout the book, from 'Too long; you've made your point,' to 'Good. Wish I'd read this two years ago.'

"The next book was about choosing a career, to be followed by biographies of two scientists, Dr. Willis Whitney, founder of the General Electric Research Laboratory in Schenectady, and Dr. Irving Langmuir who won the Nobel Prize for chemistry in 1932. The latter book was translated into Burmese. By the time the biographies were published, I was teaching high school English full time and so could only work weekends and summers on the books. Both children finished college, went to graduate school, married and made us grandparents, and we moved to California.

"Whatever I write reflects my interest at the moment, and so I have done articles on travel, camping, interesting personalities, faith, historical events, conservation, social service, etc. At the same time I've taught courses in creative writing and literature in a junior college, a university, a private college in New York State and one in Hong Kong. Every experience has been recorded in some way, and each bit of writing has led to new experiences. Who could ask for a better way of life?''

WESTWOOD, Jennifer 1940-

PERSONAL: Born May 1, 1940, in England; daughter of Wilfrid James (a builder) and Beatrice (a teacher) Fulcher; married Trevor Frank Westwood, in 1958 (divorced, 1966), married Brian Herbert Chandler (a management consultant), in 1968; children: Jonathan James (son by first marriage). *Education:* St. Anne's College, Oxford University, England, B.A., 1963, M.A., 1970; New Hall, Cambridge University, England, B.A., 1965, M.A., 1972, M.Litt., 1973. *Religion:* Church of England. *Home:* 133 Shepherdess Walk, London N.1, England. *Agent:* Laura Cecil, Flat 10, Exeter Mansions, 106 Shaftesbury Ave., London, England.

CAREER: University of Cambridge, England, university classes and tutorials in Old Norse and Anglo-Saxon, 1965-68. Free-lance editor and publishing adviser, 1969—. *Member:* Viking Society for Northern Research, Children's Book History Society (British Branch of Osborne Society), Folk-lore Society, National Book League.

WRITINGS: Medieval Tales, Rupert Hart-Davis (England), 1967, Coward, 1968; *Gilgamesh and Other Babylonian Tales,* Bodley Head (England), 1968, Coward, 1970;

JENNIFER WESTWOOD

The Isle of Gramarye, Rupert Hart-Davis, 1970; *Tales and Legends,* Coward, 1971; *Stories of Charlemagne,* Bodley Head, 1972; *Alfred the Great,* Wayland (England), 1976.

SIDELIGHTS: "Read Old and Middle English course at Oxford, Anglo-Saxon Tripos at Cambridge. Became aware of fund of stories unavailable to children, or available only in Victorian retellings long out of print. Tried to retell in intelligible modern English whilst keeping flavour of style of originals—particularly *Gilgamesh* where semi-liturgical style aimed at.

"I speak French, some Danish and Icelandic. Read dead languages: Latin, Old Norse, Anglo-Saxon (Old English), and Old French. Have travelled extensively in Europe, and stayed for some time in Sweden, Denmark and Iceland for work purposes."

HOBBIES AND OTHER INTERESTS: Fairy tales and folklore, mythology and legend; early children's books.

WHITCOMB, Jon   1906-

PERSONAL: Born June 9, 1906, in Weatherford, Okla.; son of Lemley Preston and Melissa (Hull) Whitcomb. *Education:* Ohio Wesleyan University, student, 1923-27; Ohio State University, B.A., 1928. *Home:* 211 East 70th St., New York, N.Y. 10021.

CAREER: Radio-Keith-Orpheum theatres, poster artist in Chicago, Ill., 1928-29; advertising artist in Cleveland, Ohio, 1930-34; Charles E. Cooper, Inc. (advertising art), New York, N.Y., vice-president, 1935—. Artist and illustrator.

JON WHITCOMB

Cover artist for *Cosmopolitan;* illustrator for *Ladies' Home Journal, McCalls,* and other magazines. *Military service:* U.S. Navy, 1942-45; became lieutenant junior grade. *Member:* Society of Illustrators, New York Athletic Club. *Awards, honors:* Elected to Society of Illustrators Hall of Fame, 1973.

WRITINGS—All self-illustrated: *Pom-Pom's Christmas,* Holt, 1959; *All About Girls,* Prentice-Hall, 1962; *Coco, the Far-Out Poodle,* Random House, 1963. Contributor of regular column and articles to *Cosmopolitan,* 1947-52.

WHITE, Dori   1919-

PERSONAL: Born July 13, 1919, in Portland, Ore.; daughter of Charles Elmer (an educator) and Jessie (Hyde) Cleveland; married first husband, 1940; married second husband, Irle E. White (a teacher), September 16, 1957; children: (first marriage) Elizabeth (Mrs. Dean Douglas), Ronald. *Education:* Whitman College, student, 1938-40; University of Iowa, B.A., 1940; University of Oregon, M.A., 1956. *Home:* 1700 West Hillsdale Blvd., San Mateo, Calif. 94402. *Agent:* Elizabeth Otis, McIntosh & Otis, Inc., 475 Fifth Ave., New York, N.Y. 10017.

CAREER: Virginia City Players, Virginia City, Mont., actress, director, public relations, 1948-53; Marylhurst College, Oswego, Ore., drama teacher, 1956-57; Kresge Eye

DORI WHITE

Institute, Detroit, Mich., research assistant, 1957-60. *Member:* California Writers Association (honorary member), Burlingame Writers Association (president, 1966).

WRITINGS: Sarah and Katie (juvenile), Harper, 1972. Contributor of short fiction to national magazines, including *McCalls', Redbook,* and *Good Housekeeping.*

WORK IN PROGRESS: An adult novel.

SIDELIGHTS: During 1971 and 1972 Dori White cruised to Mexico and Hawaii with her husband on their schooner, "Miranda."

FOR MORE INFORMATION SEE: Horn Book, June, 1972.

WHITE, Laurence B(arton), Jr.   1935-

PERSONAL: Born September 21, 1935, in Norwood, Mass.; son of Laurence B. (an engineer) and Anna (a teacher; maiden name, Dewhurst) White; married Doris E. Pickard (a teacher aide), September 10, 1960; children: William Oliver, David Laurence. *Education:* University of New Hampshire, B.A., 1958. *Home:* 12 Rockland St., Stoughton, Mass. 02072. *Office:* Needham Public Schools, Needham, Mass. 02192.

CAREER: Museum of Science, Boston, Mass., supervisor of programs and courses, 1958-65, acting director of Theatre of Electricity, 1960-65; Needham Public Schools, Needham, Mass., assistant director of Needham Science Center, 1965—. *Military service:* U.S. Army, Signal Corps, combat photographer, 1958-59. *Member:* Society of American Magicians, Mycological Society, Beekeepers Association. *Awards, honors: So You Want to Be a Magician* was chosen one of the children's books of the year, 1972, by Child Study Association of America.

WRITINGS—For children; all published by Addison-Wesley, except as indicated: *Life in the Shifting Dunes,* Boston Museum of Science, 1960; *Investigating Science with Coins,* 1969; *Investigating Science with Rubber Bands,* 1969; *Investigating Science with Nails,* 1970; *Investigating Science with Paper,* 1970; *So You Want to Be a Magician?,* 1972; *Science Games,* 1975; *Science Puzzles,* 1975; *Science Toys,* 1975; *Science Tricks,* 1975; *The Great Mysto: That's You,* 1975. Author of material for Eduquip-Macallaster Co. Contributor to children's magazines.

WORK IN PROGRESS: A magic book for first readers; a book on the human body, written in a "believe it or not" format, for elementary school and junior high school students.

They talked until it was almost time to set the table, and with every word, Sarah felt lighter and happier. Her mother had such a comforting way of putting things. ■ (From *Sarah and Katie* by Dori White. Illustrated by Trina Schart Hyman.)

Is Your Cat Right or Left Pawed?
Put some food in a tall jar.
Put it near your cat.
Which paw does he use to get it out.
Try Again.
■ (From *Science Games* by Laurence B.
White, Jr. Drawings by Marc Tolon Brown.)

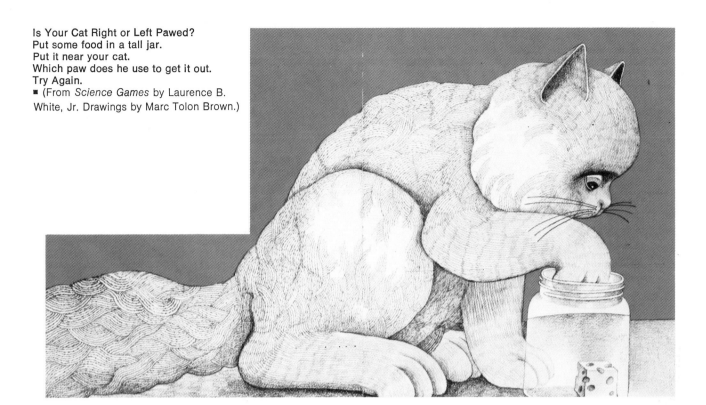

SIDELIGHTS: "My entire life has revolved around the education of young children. I believe they are the salvation of our world. They must be taught to enjoy their curiosity and find delight and pleasure in new discoveries. The books that I have written have simply shared with my readers some of the magic tricks I have had fun with and the science I have enjoyed learning in hopes they will discover the same pleasure in life that I have!"

FOR MORE INFORMATION SEE: New York Times Book Review, August 20, 1972.

WIDERBERG, Siv   1931-

PERSONAL: Born June 12, 1931, in Bromma, Sweden; daughter of Nils (an art critic) and Gertrud (a midwife) Palmgren; married Bertil Widerberg (an editor); children: Gertrud. *Education:* Educated in Sweden. *Politics:* Communist. *Religion:* None. *Home:* Hagagatan 16, 113 48 Stockholm, Sweden.

CAREER: Teacher in Sweden, 1951-55; journalist, 1955—, and full-time writer, 1966—. Member of board of directors of Swedish Authors Fund, 1972-74. *Member:* Society of the Swedish Union of Authors (member of board of directors, 1971-72), Writers' Centre.

WRITINGS—Children's books: *Gertrud paa daghem* (title means "Gertrud in kindergarten"), Raben & Sjoegren, 1966; *Snart sjutton* (title means "Soon Sixteen"), Raben & Sjoegren, 1966; *Apropaa mej* (title means "About Me"), Raben & Sjoegren, 1967; *Aakes trafikskola* (title means "Aakes Traffic School"), Raben & Sjoegren, 1967; *Mamma pappa barn,* Zindermans, 1967, translation by Irene D. Morris published as *The Kid's Own XYZ of Love and Sex,* Stein & Day, 1972; *Alldeles vanliga Hjalmar och Hedvig* (title means "Not Unusual Hjalmar and Hedvig"), Raben & Sjoegren, 1968; *Se upp moln* (title means "Look! The Sky"), Gebers, 1968; *Min baesta vaen,* Raben & Sjoe-

LAURENCE B. WHITE, JR.

gren, 1969, translated and published as *My Best Friend,* Putnam, 1970; *Agneta och Bjoern* (title means "Agneta and Bjoern"), Raben & Sjoegren, 1969; *En syl i vaedret* (title means "Please Talk"), Gebers, 1969; *Ett enda stort ljug* (title means "A Big Lie"), Raben & Sjoegren, 1970; (with Goeran Palm) *Graeddvargen* (play; title means "The Cream Wolf"), Foerfattarfoerlaget, 1970; *Jag heter Siv* (title means "My Name Is Siv."), Foerfattarfoerlaget, 1971; *Nya byxor och gamla* (title means "New and Old Trousers"), Gebers, 1972; *Ingrid och Soeren* (title means "Ingrid and Soeren"), Raben & Sjoegren, 1973; *I'm Like Me,* translated from the Swedish by Verne Moberg, Feminist Press, 1973; *Sitt inte paa mej* (title means "Don't Sit on Me"), Gebers, 1973; *Vi aer maanga* (title means "We Are Many"), Gebers, 1974; *Folhets kraft ar stor,* Gidlunds, 1975.

SIDELIGHTS: "Nobody ever told me that I emerged from my mother's womb, pen in hand. But as long as I can remember I have written poems, books and little papers. My first journalistic deed was called *Mosquito Daily;* the news page described a massacre on 10,000 innocent mosquitoes.

"It took a long time, though, before I dared to take the leap to become a writer. Like many women I kept putting off what I really wanted to do, for I didn't dare to take the time nor believe in my capacity.

SIV WIDERBERG

"As a journalist, however, I worked also as a reviewer of books for children and young people. Most of the books bored me, for they didn't take children seriously. They stuck to fantasy as a protection against the real world; they didn't deal with children's ordinary everyday life.

"In a kind of response I finally dared to write myself. My starting point was that I wanted my books to be a dialogue with the readers on what you experience in our world.

"Sex, problems, tears, joy, politics—all these things are included in a children's world. Consequently, I wanted to reflect and talk about sex, problems, tears, joy and politics.

"I feel that my latest book is the one I always wanted to write. I wrote it after a journey to China. I describe to children feudalism, imperialism, communism, the struggle, power and victory of the people, the importance of serving the people. My book doesn't paint China as Paradise, for Paradise, free from all troubles, doesn't exist anywhere, and never will. Longing for and hoping for Paradise, instead of struggling for the best possible life, is wasting your power, in vain."

FOR MORE INFORMATION SEE: Horn Book, June, 1971.

WINTERBOTHAM, R(ussell) R(obert) 1904-1971 (Ted Addy, J. Harvey Bond, Franklin Hadley, R. R. Winter)

PERSONAL: Born August 1, 1904, in Salina, Kan.; son of Jonathan (doctor) and Gertrude (Bond) Winterbotham; married Nadine Schick, November 25, 1932; children: H. Ann Winterbotham Jones. *Education:* University of Kansas, B.A., 1927. *Home:* 30314 Westlawn Dr., Bay Village, Ohio. *Office:* Newspaper Enterprise Association, 1200 West Third St., Cleveland, Ohio.

CAREER: Wrote for numerous newspapers in Kansas, Missouri, Illinois, Oklahoma, New Mexico, and South Dakota; Little Blue Book Co., Girard, Kan., editorial assistant, 1928-31; *Pittsburgh* (Kan.) *Sun,* police reporter, 1931-42; *Daily Republic,* Mitchell, S.D., news editor, 1942-43; Newspaper Enterprise Association, Cleveland, Ohio, 1943-71, started as staff writer, became assistant to the comic arts director. Member, Civil Defense Ground Observer Corps, 1952. *Member:* Western Writers of America.

WRITINGS—Novels: (Under pseudonym J. Harvey Bond) *Bye-Bye Baby,* Ace, 1958; *The Space Egg,* Avalon, 1958; (under pseudonym J. Harvey Bond) *Murder Isn't Funny,* Ace, 1958; *Man From the High Plains,* Arcadia, 1958; (under pseudonym J. Harvey Bond) *Kill Me With Kindness,* Ace, 1959; *Wind of a Bullet,* Arcadia, 1960; (under pseudonym J. Harvey Bond) *If Wishes Were Hearses,* Ace, 1961; (under pseudonym Ted Addy) *The Dutch Schultz Story,* Monarch, 1962; *The Red Planet,* Monarch, 1962; *The Men From Arcturus,* Avalon, 1963; (under pseudonym J. Harvey Bond) *The Other World,* Avalon, 1963; *Puppet Planet,* Avalon, 1964; (under pseudonym Franklin Hadley) *Planet Big Zero,* Monarch, 1964.

Contributor: *Omnibus of Science Fiction,* Crown, 1952.

Juveniles: *Tom Beatty, Ace Detective, Scores Again*, Whitman, 1937; *Lee Lanthrop, G-Man*, Whitman, 1938; *Len Robins and the Phantom Dirigible*, Whitman; (under pseudonym R. R. Winter) *Hal Hardy and the Lost Land of Giants*, Whitman, 1938; (under pseudonym R. R. Winter) *Tom Mix Avenging the Range King*, Dell, 1939; *Maximo, the Amazing Superman*, Whitman, 1940; *Gene Autry, Cowboy Detective*, Whitman, 1940; *Superman Maximo and the Super-Machine*, Whitman, 1941; *Superman Maximo and the Crystals of Doom*, Whitman, 1941; *Allen Pike, Parachute Trooper*, Whitman, 1941; *Mole, The Small Man*, Whitman, 1941; *The Ghost Avenger*, Whitman, 1941; (with cartoonist, Fred Harman) *Red Ryder and the Whispering Walls*, Whitman, 1941; *Joyce of the Secret Squadron*, Whitman, 1941; (with Zack Mosley) *Smilin' Jack and the Daredevil Girl Pilot*, Whitman, 1942; *Ray Land of the Tank Corps U.S.A.*, Whitman, 1942; *Bob Trent and the Flying Wing*, Whitman, 1942; *Tank Destroyers*, Whitman, 1942; *Keep 'Em Flying*, Whitman, 1942.

Little Blue Books (published by E. Haldeman-Julius): *Lindberg, Hero of the Air*, 1928; *Curious and Unusual Deaths*, 1929; *Curious and Unusual Love Affairs*, 1929; *How Comic Strips Are Made*, 1946; *How to Get Ideas for Stories*, 1947. Author of 200 comic strip continuities for newspapers including "Captain Midnight," 1941-42, "Captain Easy," 1943-50, "Red Ryder," 1943-49, "Chris Welkin," 1951-65, "Vic Flint," 1962, "The Good Guys," 1964; some scripts for others. Contributor of 200 short stories to pulp magazines; contributor to comic books. Revised books for Whitman from 1937-42, converting six British detective stories to American idiom and "modernizing" six juvenile science fiction stories originally published from 1908-13.

HOBBIES AND OTHER INTERESTS: Duplicate bridge.

(Died June 9, 1971)

WIRTENBERG, Patricia Z(arrella) 1932-

PERSONAL: Born May 21, 1932, in Arlington, Mass.; daughter of Joseph S. and Lillian M. (Lepore) Zarrella; married Leon Wirtenberg (a writer), August 26, 1965. *Education:* Attended Mt. Holyoke College, 1949-50, and Jackson Von Ladau School of Design, 1950-54. *Home:* 111 Perkins St., Jamaica Plain, Mass. 02130. *Office:* Folio Communications Service, 581 Boylston St., Boston, Mass. 02116.

CAREER: Artist and sculptress, 1949—; has exhibited work at institutions and associations, including Columbus Museum, Georgia, Mint Museum, N.C., Children's Art Centre, Boston, Cambridge Art Association, and in Positano, Italy; work in many private and public collections, including Columbus Museum, Huntington Hartford Collection, and Stone Library, Boston. Children's Art Centre, Boston, Mass., assistant director, 1956-65; Folio Communications Service, Boston, vice-president, 1965—. Special writer for *Boston Globe Magazine*, 1965-66. *Awards, honors:* Copley Society annual prize, 1958; Huntington Hartford Foundation fellowships, 1960 and 1961.

WRITINGS: The All-Around-the-House Art and Craft Book, Houghton, 1968.

PATRICIA Z. WIRTENBERG

WORK IN PROGRESS: "My second book—if I can get the time to write it!"

SIDELIGHTS: Patricia Wirtenberg is the originator of the unique medium of vegetarian mosaics. She has appeared and shown her work on the national television shows, "Today," "To Tell the Truth," and "Mike Douglas."

WOLFF, Robert Jay 1905-

PERSONAL: Born July 27, 1905, in Chicago, Ill.; son of Aaron Russell (a businessman) and Martha (Marks) Wolff; married Alice Wolbach, September 3, 1929; married second wife, Elizabeth Bogert, November 8, 1941; married third wife, Elizabeth Leighton Arango, August 3, 1949; children: (first marraige) Wendy (Mrs. Stephen Blumberg); (third marriage) Guy; stepchildren: Peter Leighton Arango-Wolff. *Education:* Yale University, student, 1923-26; independent study in New York, N.Y., and England, 1926-29; Ecole des Beaux Arts, Paris, France, student, 1929-30. *Politics:* Democrat (independent). *Home and studio:* Garland Rd., New Preston, Conn. 06777.

CAREER: Artist. Federal Art Project, supervisor of easel painting for state of Illinois, 1937-38; School of Design (now Institute of Design, Illinois Institute of Technology),

ROBERT JAY WOLFF

Chicago, Ill., dean and head of painting and sculpture, 1938-42; Knoll Associates, New York, N.Y., publications designer, 1945-46; Brooklyn College, Brooklyn, N.Y., professor of art, 1946-71, chairman of department, 1947-64, professor of art emeritus, 1971—. University of Wisconsin, visiting artist, 1955; Massachusetts Institute of Technology, visiting Bemus Professor of Design, 1961. Paintings in permanent collections of Brooklyn Museum, Rhode Island Museum, Guggenheim Museum, Art Institute of Chicago, Tate Gallery, Baushaus Arkiv Museum (West Berlin), Wadsworth Ateneum (Hartford, Conn.); had one-man shows at Art Institute of Chicago, 1935, and Guggenheim Museum, 1953, along with other one-man shows in Chicago galleries, 1937-38, 1939-40, and New York galleries, 1938, 1946-47, 1954-55, and 1957-58; work included in group exhibitions at Whitney Museum, Corcoran Gallery, San Francisco Museum, Art Institute of Chicago, and elsewhere in United States, France, Italy, West Germany, Belgium, and Switzerland. Consultant to General Electric Co., 1945-46, and Boris Kroll Fabrics, 1946-71. *Military service:* U.S. Army and U.S. Air Forces, 1942-43; became sergeant. U.S. Navy, 1943-45; became lieutenant senior grade. *Member:* College Art Association, American Abstract Artists (former member).

WRITINGS: (Contributor) *Vision and Value,* Volume I, *Education of Vision,* edited by Gyorgy Kepes, Braziller, 1965; *Seeing Red* (juvenile), Scribner, 1968; *Feeling Blue* (juvenile), Scribner, 1968; *Hello Yellow* (juvenile), Scribner, 1968; *On Art and Learning,* Grossman-Viking, 1971. Author-designer of teaching portfolio, "Elements of Design," Museum of Modern Art, 1946. Contributor to *Kenyon Review* and art journals.

WOODSON, John Waddie Jr.
(Jack Woodson)

PERSONAL: Born January 23, 1913, in Richmond, Va.; son of John Waddie (a salesman) and Grace (Fitzgerald) Woodson; married Iris Snead, June 25, 1943; children: Pamela (Mrs. Robert G. Folger). *Religion:* Baptist. *Home and office:* 18 Ralston Road, Richmond, Va. 23229.

CAREER: Artist. *Member:* Company of Military Historians, Torch Club.

ILLUSTRATOR: Manhart, *Plain Folk,* Williams, 1955; *Adventure Bound* (cover), Houghton, 1961; *Journeys Into America* (cover), Houghton, 1961; Gilbert, *Henry Ford,* Houghton, 1962; Watkins, *Co. Aytch* (cover), Houghton, 1962; *This is America's Story* (cover), Houghton, 1963; Ross, *Illustration Today,* International Textbooks, 1963; Lattimore, *Lee,* National Park Service, 1964; Rutledge, *Ballard of the Howling Hound* (cover), Rutledge, 1965; Horner, *Shipwrecks, Skin Divers and Sunken Gold,* Dodd, 1965; Manhart, *The Verdies,* Hill, 1966; Donald E. Cooke, *For Conspicuous Gallantry,* Hammond, 1966; Donald W. Cox, *Explorers of the Deep,* Hammond, 1968; Schwartz, *Mammouth Cave,* National Park Service, 1968; Hathaway, *Hallelujah Chariot* (cover), Knox, 1969; Henry T. Wall-

JOHN WADDIE WOODSON JR.

One Marine pilot, Lieutenant Christian F. Schilt, brought his plane into the battle-torn town through a hail of hostile bullets. He landed and took off ten times under the hazardous conditions succeeding in saving many lives and in delivering desperately needed supplies. He was awarded the Medal of Honor. ■ (From *For Conspicuous Gallantry* by Donald E. Cooke. Illustrated by Jack Woodson.)

hauser, *Pioneers of Flight*, Hammond, 1969; Icenhower, *American Sea Heroes*, Hammond, 1970; Happel, *Jackson*, National Park Service, 1971; Fouts, *Moose and a Goose and a Mouse Named Bruce*, Carmine, 1975.

WORK IN PROGRESS: Several books pertaining to the sea.

SIDELIGHTS: "My interests in illustration lie mostly in nautical and historical themes, mechanical illustrations of airplanes in action, locomotives, ships, interesting architecture, historical sites, costume, character studies, extreme realism in all mediums.

"I work entirely from models and original costumes and equipment, if possible. Realism plays an important part in my illustrations and a great deal of time is devoted to research before beginning the art. I try to suit the style, technique and medium to the mood of the copy as well as suitably for reproduction.

"More formal paintings are in museums such as the Mariner's Museum, also, in private collections, these including portraits and landscapes."

WOODWARD, (Landon) Cleveland   1900-

PERSONAL: Born June 25, 1900, in Glendale, Ohio; son of Harry L. (a doctor) and Eloise (Cleveland) Woodward; married Emily Proctor Crosby, December 20, 1919; children: Cleveland C., Eloise C. (Mrs. Frank Gardner), Ralph C. *Education:* Attended Cincinnati Art Academy, 1923-26; Charles Hawthorne's Cape Cod School of Art,

summer, 1924; British Art Academy, Rome, 1928-29. *Home:* 354 Boone Lane, Fairhope, Alabama 36532.

CAREER: Biblical illustrator for fifty years, also marine

CLEVELAND WOODWARD

portraits and landscape. Cape Cod Art Association, co-founder and member, first board of directors, 1948-49; Eastern Shore Art Association, board of directors, 1966-69, 1971-74; Eastern Shore Academy of Fine Arts, Fairhope, Ala., advisor, instructor in oil painting, 1972-73. Lecturer in Biblical art at schools, colleges and museums.

EXHIBITIONS: Cincinnati Art Museum Spring Exhibition, 1925; Traxel Art Gallery (one-man show), Cincinnati, 1929; The Fine Arts Museum of the South (one-man show), 1968, 1971; Percy B. Whiting Museum (one-man show), Fairhope, Ala., 1969, 1971; Arctic Museum, Brunswick, Maine; Boardman Press, Nashville, Tenn.; United Lutheran Publishing House, Philadelphia, Pa., Christian Board of Publications, St. Louis, Mo., Orleans Art Gallery, Cape Cod, Mass.

ILLUSTRATOR: By an Unknown Disciple, Harper, 1919; Henry Van Dyke, *The Other Wise Man,* Harper; Miriam MacMillan, *Kudla and His Polar Bear,* Dodd, 1953; *Painting Christ Head,* Abingdon; *World Bible* (revised standard version), World Publishing.

FOR MORE INFORMATION SEE: American Artist Magazine, May, 1973.

WRIGHT, Esmond   1915-

PERSONAL: Born November 5, 1915, in Newcastle-on-Tyne, England; son of Esmond and Isabella (Gray) Wright; married Olive Adamson, 1945. *Education:* University of Durham, England, B.A., 1937, M.A., 1948; University of Virginia, M.A., 1940. *Home:* 31 Tavistock Sq., London W.C.1, England. *Agent:* Curtis Brown, King St., Covent Garden, London W.C.2, England. *Office:* University of London.

CAREER: University of Glasgow, Glasgow, Scotland, lecturer, 1946-51; senior lecturer, 1951-57, professor of modern history, 1957-67; member of Parliament, 1967-70; University of London, professor of American history, 1971—, director of institute of United States studies, 1971—. Visiting lecturer in United States, 1948, 1952, 1961, 1963, 1968, 1973, 1975, 1976. *Military service:* British Army, Intelligence, 1941-46, became colonel; served in Middle East. *Awards, honors:* Commonwealth (Harkness) Fellow, 1938-40, 1952; Rockefeller Fellow, Yale University, 1961.

WRITINGS: Short History of Our Own Times, 1919-1950, Watts, 1951; *Washington and the American Revolution,* English Universities Press, 1957; *Fabric of Freedom: 1763-1800,* Hill and Wang, 1961; *The World Today,* McGraw, 1961; (editor with Kenneth Stampp) *Illustrated World History,* McGraw, 1964; *Benjamin Franklin and American Independence,* English Universities Press, 1966; *The Causes and Consequences of the American Revolution,* Quadrangle Books, 1966; *A Time for Courage,* Dutton, 1971; (editor) *A Tug of Loyalties,* Athlone Press, 1975; (editor) *Red, White and True Blue,* A.M.S. Press, 1977. Contributor to professional journals.

WORK IN PROGRESS: Benjamin Franklin.

SIDELIGHTS: Appears regularly on British Broadcasting Corporation radio and television programs.

FRANCES FITZPATRICK WRIGHT

WRIGHT, Frances Fitzpatrick   1897-

PERSONAL: Born June 26, 1897; daughter of Robert Harrison and Roberta (Johnson) Fitzpatrick; married George W. Wright, December 8, 1918 (died April 8, 1956); children: Ann Puryear Bagley, Roberta Wright Martin, George Francis. *Education:* Attended public schools in Phoenix, Ariz., and Gallatin, Tenn. *Politics:* Independent but currently Democrat. *Religion:* Catholic convert. *Home:* Faraway Hills, Gallatin, Tenn. 37066.

CAREER: Free-lance writer. Formerly lesson writer for Baptist Sunday School Board, Nashville, Tenn., for twenty years. Gallatin Library Board member. *Member:* Women's National Book Association, Association for Preservation of Tennessee Antiquities, Hermitage Association, Review Club (past president). *Awards, honors:* Voted most popular *American Girl* author.

WRITINGS—All juvenile books: *Lucy Ellen,* Farrar & Rinehart, 1940; *Lucy Ellen's College Days,* Farrar & Rinehart, 1943; *Lucy Ellen's Heydey,* Farrar & Rinehart, 1945; *Secret of the Old Sampey Place,* Abingdon, 1946; *Your Loving Sister, Pat Downing,* Holt, 1948; *Number Eleven Poplar Street,* Abingdon, 1948; *Surprise at Sampey Place,* Abingdon, 1950; *Poplar Street Park,* Abingdon, 1952; *Sam Houston* (biography), Abingdon, 1953; *Daybreak at Sampey Place,* Abingdon, 1954; *Andrew Jackson* (biography), Abingdon, 1958; *American Girl Book of Pat Downing Stories,* Random House, 1963; *Bless Your Bones, Sammy,* Abingdon, 1968.

A strong odor of skunk was everywhere but Sammy didn't think it would cling to him. . . . But when he entered the schoolroom, which was well warmed by the big stove, Tub Thompson grabbed his nose, and some of the girls began to giggle. ■ (From *Bless Your Bones, Sammy* by Frances Fitzpatrick Wright. Illustrated by Steele Savage.)

Contributor of articles and short stories to religious and farm periodicals, and of several articles to *Spur* and *Saturday Evening Post*.

SIDELIGHTS: Some of Frances Wright's stories have been put in Braille, several reprinted in textbooks. Her early writings for the Baptist Sunday School Board have been translated into Chinese and Portuguese.

WRONKER, Lili Cassel 1924-
(Lili Cassel, Lili Wronker)

PERSONAL: Born May 5, 1924, in Berlin, Germany; daughter of Joseph (a medical doctor) and Edith Cassel; married Erich Wronker (a printer), September 25, 1952; children: Eytan, Rona. *Education:* Attended Art Students League, New York, N.Y., 1944. *Religion:* Jewish. *Home:* 144-44 Village Road, Jamaica, N.Y. 11435.

CAREER: Time, Incorporated, New York, N.Y., art department, 1945-47; World Publishing Company, New York, N.Y., designing book jackets, 1947-48; United Nations International School, New York, N.Y., taught calligraphy, 1968-72; The Calligraphy Workshop, Queens College, Flushing, N.Y., taught calligraphy, 1974-75. *Member:* Graphic Artists Guild, Society of Scribes, Society of Scribes and Illuminators, Society for Italic Handwriting, American Printing Historical Society, Goudy Chappel of Private Presses. *Awards, honors:* Book award for best bookjacket, 1955; *Mother Goose in Alga,* American Institute of Graphic Arts fifty best books, 1948.

LILI CASSEL WRONKER

"Leave that be. You get a little bump when you hit the rail and Doctor poultice it, but he say it don't amount to much. He say you mostly exhausted in head and body." ■ (From *Boy Wanted* by Ruth Fenisong. Illustrated by Lili Cassel-Wronker.)

ILLUSTRATOR: May Lamberton Becker, editor, *Rainbow Mother Goose,* World, 1948; Virginia Sorensen, *The House Next Door,* Scribners, 1954; Carl Withers, Sula Benet, *Riddles of Many Lands,* Abelard, 1956; Sadie R. Weilerstein, *Jewish Heroes* (volumes 1 & 2), United Synagogue Book, 1956; Alvan Rubin, *Picture Dictionary of Jewish Life,* Behrman, 1956; Eileen Bigland, *Madame Curie,* Phillips, 1957; Dale Fife, *Weddings in the Family,* Farrar, Straus, 1957; Dale Fife, *The Unmarried Sisters,* Farrar, Straus, 1958; Diana Pullein-Thompson, *Boy and the Donkey,* Phillips, 1958; Grace Rasp-Nuri, *Yusuf, Boy of Cyprus,* Phillips, 1958; Ruth Fenison, *Boy Wanted,* Harper, 1964; Hal Borland, *Sundial of the Seasons,* Lippincott, 1964; Joan Bel Geddes, *Calling All Children,* UNICEF, 1965; Lois J. Johnson, *Happy New Year Round the World,* Rand, 1966; Eileen Bigland, *Helen Keller,* Phillips, 1967; Lois J. Johnson, *What We Eat: The Origins and Travels of Foods Round the World,* Rand, 1969.

WORK IN PROGRESS: Ideas for own private printing press.

SIDELIGHTS: "I write and speak German fluently. Am taking silk screen courses and plan to learn how to put letter forms on batik. I try to develop interesting calligraphy courses with cultural backgrounds of music, art, literature, history, and architecture of the period. My husband

and I collaborate on publishing books on our own hand press."

FOR MORE INFORMATION SEE: *American Artist Magazine,* February, 1958; *Illustrators of Children's Books: 1957-1966,* Horn Book, 1968; *Italix,* summer, 1975.

WYSS, Thelma Hatch   1934-

PERSONAL: Born November 17, 1934, in Bancroft, Idaho; daughter of A. Wilder (a rancher) and Agatha Pratt (Van Orden) Hatch; married Lawrence Frederick Wyss (an interior designer), December 18, 1964; children: David Lawrence. *Education:* Brigham Young University, B.S., 1957. *Religion:* Church of Jesus Christ of Latter-Day Saints (Mormons). *Home:* 1119 Stansbury Way, Salt Lake City, Utah 84108.

CAREER: Glamour (magazine), New York, N.Y., assistant production manager, 1958-59; high school teacher of English in Salt Lake City, Utah, 1959-66. *Member:* Utah State Historical Society, Utah Heritage Foundation Guild, Utah Symphony Orchestra Guild.

WRITINGS: Star Girl (youth book), Viking, 1967.

Star Girl's favorite time was summer when the tribe wandered along the Snake River, a great water god lying on his back. ■ (From *Star Girl* by Thelma Hatch Wyss. Illustrated by John Pimlott.)

SIDELIGHTS: "When I was a young girl living a rather isolated life on a ranch in Idaho, I planned when I grew older to write books about glamorous city life.

"Later on I learned that an author draws extensively from his own experiences and background. So my first book, *Star Girl,* was written about what I knew best as a child—wild flowers, meadow larks, and Indians."

FOR MORE INFORMATION SEE: *Book World,* March 3, 1968.

YOUNG, Ed   1931-

PERSONAL: Born November 28, 1931, in Tientsin, China; son of Qua-Ling (an engineer) and Yuen Teng Young; married, 1962 (divorced, 1969); married Natasha Gorky, June 1, 1971. *Education:* Attended City College of San Francisco, 1952, and University of Illinois, 1952-54; Art Center College of Design, Los Angeles, B.P.A., 1957; graduate study at Pratt Institute, 1958-59. *Residence:* Hastings-on-Hudson, N.Y. 10706. *Office:* Shr Jung School, 87 Bowery, New York, N.Y. 10003.

CAREER: Mel Richman Studio, New York, N.Y., illustrator and designer, 1957-62; Pratt Institute, Brooklyn, N.Y., instructor in visual communications, 1960-66; Shr Jung Tai Chi Chuan School, New York, N.Y., secretary and instructor, 1964-73; director, 1973; free-lance illustrator, 1962—; Sarah Lawrence College, Bronxville, N.Y., instructor in Tai Chi Chuan (a Chinese exercise), 1975—. *Awards, honors:* Caldecott runner-up award, 1968, for *The Emperor and the Kite;* Horn Book Honor List, and Child

THELMA HATCH WYSS

Study Association Book Award, 1969, for *Chinese Mother Goose Rhymes; The Girl Who Loved the Wind* was named a Children's Book Showcase Title, 1973.

ILLUSTRATOR: Janice M. Udry, *The Mean Mouse and Other Mean Stories,* Harper, 1962; Leland B. Jacobs and Sally Nohelty, compilers, *Poetry for Young Scientists,* Holt, 1964; Margaret Hillert, *The Yellow Boat,* Follett, 1966; Jane Yolen, editor, *The Emperor and the Kite,* World Publishing, 1968; Robert Wyndam, editor, *Chinese Mother Goose Rhymes,* World Publishing, 1968; Kermit Krueger, *The Golden Swans: A Picture Story from Thailand,* World Publishing, 1969; Mel Evans, *The Tiniest Sound,* Doubleday, 1969; Jane Yolen, *The Seventh Mandarin,* Seabury, 1970; Renee K. Weiss, *The Bird from the Sea,* Crowell, 1970; Diane Wolkstein, *8,000 Stones,* Doubleday, 1972; Jane Yolen, *The Girl Who Loved the Wind,* Crowell, 1972; L. C. Hunt, editor, *The Horse From Nowhere,* Holt, 1973; Donnarae MacCann and Olga Richard, *The Child's First Books,* 1973; Elizabeth F. Lewis, *Young Fu of the Upper Yangtze,* new edition, Holt, 1973.

WORK IN PROGRESS: Researching American Indian folktales; *The Prince and the Lion,* a Persian tale; *Cricket Boy,* a Chinese tale.

SIDELIGHTS: "I learned Tai Chi Chuan from an old Chinese master. It can be described as a form of moving meditation which is beneficial to mind and body; the whole of the person. I started to teach Tai Chi Chuan in 1967 and have become a director of the Shr Jung Tai Chi Chuan School in New York City's Chinatown. This exercise has had profound influence upon my way of thinking and on the things that I do."

FOR MORE INFORMATION SEE: Publisher's Weekly,

ED YOUNG

"Dragon's Breath from the hills" . . .

■ (From *Young Fu of the Upper Yangtze* by Elizabeth Foreman Lewis. Illustrated by Ed Young.)

September 2, 1968; *Third Book of Junior Authors,* edited by de Montreville and Hill, H. W. Wilson, 1972.

ZAPPLER, Lisbeth 1930-

PERSONAL: Born September 30, 1930, in Geneva, N.Y.; daughter of Maxmillian (a physician) and Anne (Bolton) Moses; married Peter Cohen, November 22, 1953; married Georg Zappler (a zoo director), January 15, 1961; children: (first marriage) Daniel, Joshua; (second marriage) Leopold, Amanda, Konrad. *Education:* University of Miami, Coral Gables, Fla., B.A., 1952. *Home:* 7 Laurel Ave., Kingston, N.J. 08528.

CAREER: Singer, journalist.

WRITINGS—Children's books: *The World after the Dinosaurs: The Evolution of Mammals,* Natural History Press, 1970; *The Natural History of the Tail,* Doubleday, 1972; *Amphibians as Pets,* Doubleday, 1973; *Science in Summer and Fall,* Doubleday, 1974; *Science in Winter and Spring,* Doubleday, 1974.

WORK IN PROGRESS: Mammals in the Suburbs; The Natural History of the Nose.

ZIEMIENSKI, Dennis (Theodore) 1947-

PERSONAL: Surname pronounced "Zee-men-ski"; born May 6, 1947, in San Francisco, Calif.; son of Francis W. (a maritime engineer) and Angela M. (an artist) Ziemienski. *Education:* California College of Arts and Crafts, Oakland, Calif., B.F.A. (cum laude), 1972. *Home and office:* 244 Emerson St., Palo Alto, Calif. 94301. *Agent:* Jessica Bradley, 2714 Pacific Ave., San Francisco, Calif. 94115.

DENNIS ZIEMIENSKI

CAREER: Steven Jacobs Design, Inc., Palo Alto, Calif., designer/illustrator, 1972-74. Freelance illustrator in Palo Alto since 1974. *Exhibitions:* Western Art Directors Club, Palo Alto, Calif., 1973, 1974, 1975; San Francisco Society of Communicating Arts, 1973, 1974; Los Angeles Society of Illustrators, 1974, New York Society of Illustrators, 1974, 1975, 1976; San Francisco Society of Illustrators, 1975, 1976. *Military service:* U.S. Navy Submarine Force, Pearl Harbor & Pacific, 1968-70. *Community activities:* San Francisco Polish Community Center. *Member:* San Francisco Society of Illustrators.

AWARDS, HONORS: Western Art Directors Club, six merits, 1973, four merits (1 distinctive merit), 1974, two merits, 1975; San Francisco Society of Communicating Arts, 1973, 1974; Los Angeles Society of Illustrators, Award of Merit, 1974; New York Society of Illustrators, Award of Merit, 1974, 1975, 1976; Illustrator's Annuals of American Illustration 16, 17 and 18.

ILLUSTRATOR: Thomas O. Ryder, *Learning Magazine,* Education Today, 1974, 1975; *The Electric Co. Textbooks,* Addison, 1974, 1975; Marc Siegler, *Educational Filmstrips,* Harcourt, 1975; Susan Warton, *Children's Crafts,* Sunset, 1976.

SIDELIGHTS: "Art has always been great fun. My favorite toy has grown up with me to become my career. I'm continually experimenting with new techniques, visiting the libraries, galleries and museums and travelling when I can. Although my work is very time consuming and sometimes arduous, one can barely apply the old maxim that 'all work and no play makes Dennis a dull boy.'"

ZIMMERMAN, Naoma 1914-

PERSONAL: Born August 2, 1914, in St. Louis, Mo.; married Alvin Zimmerman, 1939; children: Ann, Frank. *Education:* Attended Washington University (St. Louis), 1932-34; University of Chicago, B.A., 1935, M.A., in Social Service, 1940. *Home:* 465 Drexel Avenue, Glencoe, Ill. 60022.

CAREER: Psychiatric social worker, family therapist, lecturer, consultant. University of Chicago, Chicago, Ill., on faculty of summer institute on family therapy. *Member:* National Association of Social Workers, Academy of Certified Social Workers, American Orthopsychiatric Association.

WRITINGS: Sleepy Forest, Ziff-Davis, 1944; *Party Dress,* Ziff-Davis, 1944; *Timothy-Tick-Tock,* Ziff-Davis, 1944; *Sleepy Village,* Ziff-Davis, 1945; *The New Comer,* Ziff-Davis, 1945; *Baby Animals,* Rand McNally, 1955; *Little Deer,* Rand McNally, 1956; (with Ruby Schuyler) *Corky Meets a Space Man,* Reilly & Lee, 1961; (with Ruby Schuyler) *Corky in Orbit,* Reilly & Lee, 1962; *Farm Animals,* Rand McNally, 1966.

SIDELIGHTS: "The Ziff-Davis series was an outgrowth of my experience in child-guidance work and my belief that books for the pre-school child could play a significant role in shaping the personalities of the citizens of tomorrow. Since the storybook enjoys an easy access into the home, it had far-reaching possibilities as a medium for offering constructive values to the child during his impressionable formative years.

"Drawing upon my background, I planned a series of sto-

NAOMA ZIMMERMAN

At that moment, two minds had but a single thought! Without saying a word, each boy grabbed a straw. Both stuck it into the floating ball of pop. ■ (From *Corky in Orbit* by Naoma Zimmerman.)

ries which I thought would be helpful to both the parent and the child in dealing with some of those everyday situations which so often give rise to friction.

"My aim in this series was threefold: (1) to make more *meaningful* and attractive to the child, some of those realistic demands with which he is daily confronted; (2) to indicate *to the parent,* a sound approach; (3) to offer stories and illustrations that would also appeal to the interest and imagination of children who are beginning to read for themselves.

"*The Party Dress* was written to forestall the error of overstressing cleanliness. We do want the child to learn that 'certain clothes merit special care' but this idea can be put across in a way that will not inhibit the child's entire freedom of expression and play.

"*Timothy-Tick-Tock* is an attempt to make the entire concept of TIME more understandable to the child. Since all children resent the restrictions imposed by the clock. TIME itself must be explained to the child before we can expect him to overcome his basic resistance to the clock, and to be receptive to routines and schedules, or to be at all interested in learning to tell time.

"*The Sleepy Forest* and *The Sleepy Village* offer a mood and atmosphere which is conducive to relaxation and sleep. Parents are apt to forget that children sometimes need a little help in making the transition from the excitement of the previous hours to the quiescent state necessary for sleep. Not all stories which are read to children at bedtime have a quieting effect. These books were specifically designed for this purpose, and much thought and care went into the planning of the text and illustrations.

"*The New Comer: Jealousy* is a very human feeling—whether we feel it about a new baby, a friend, or a schoolmate. We cannot help having a bad *feeling*. This does not make us 'bad.' What we can control is our *actions* (what we *do* about the jealous or angry feelings). This story tells us about Ophelia the elephant who was jealous of the new puppy who came to live with him, and how he finally came to realize that each person is 'special' in his own way.

"Space stories: *Corky Meets a Space Man* and *Corky in Orbit* were specifically planned for children who enjoyed the new experience of reading for themselves, but wanted lively stories about the Space Age, rather than 'Dick and Jane' books. *Corky in Orbit* has some *fun* ideas about weightlessness."

SOMETHING ABOUT THE AUTHOR

CUMULATIVE INDEXES, VOLUMES 1-10
Illustrations and Authors

ILLUSTRATIONS INDEX

(In the following index, the number of the volume in which an illustrator's work appears is given *before* the colon, and the page on which it appears is given *after* the colon. For example, a drawing by Adams, Adrienne appears in Volume 2 on page 6, another drawing by her appears in Volume 3 on page 80, and another drawing in Volume 8 on page 1.)

AUTHORS INDEX

(In the following index, the number of the volume in which an author's sketch appears is given *before* the colon, and the page on which it appears is given *after* the colon. For example, the sketch of Aardema, Verna, appears in Volume 4 on page 1).